A HISTORY
OF AMERICAN
ENTERPRISE

A HISTORY
OF AMERICAN
ENTERPRISE

John M. Dobson
Iowa State University

Prentice Hall
Englewood Cliffs, New Jersey 07632

Library of Congress Cataloging-in-Publication Data

Dobson, John M.
    A history of American enterprise.

    Includes bibliographies and index.
    1. United States—Commerce—History.   2. United States—
Industries—History.   3. Business enterprises—United
States—History.   I. Title.
HF3021.D6   1988   338.0973   87-18679
ISBN   0-13-389081-3

Editorial/production supervision: Linda B. Pawelchak
Manufacturing buyer: Ray Keating/Ed O'Dougherty
Photo research: Kay Dellosa
Cover design: George Cornell
Cover photos: (top) Courtesy of
    McDonnell Douglas Corp.
    (middle) Sante Fe Railway
    (bottom left) Courtesy of Ford Motor Co.
    (bottom right) Courtesy of Citibank

 © 1988 by Prentice-Hall, Inc.
A Division of Simon & Schuster
Englewood Cliffs, New Jersey 07632

Printed in the United States of America
10   9   8   7   6   5   4   3   2   1

ISBN   0-13-389081-3   01

Prentice-Hall International (UK) Limited, *London*
Prentice-Hall of Australia Pty. Limited, *Sydney*
Prentice-Hall Canada Inc., *Toronto*
Prentice-Hall Hispanoamericana, S.A., *Mexico*
Prentice-Hall of India Private Limited, *New Delhi*
Prentice-Hall of Japan, Inc., *Tokyo*
Simon & Schuster Asia Pte. Ltd., *Singapore*
Editora Prentice-Hall do Brazil, Ltda., *Rio de Janeiro*

To my sons David and Daniel —who so graciously let me use "our" computer whenever I asked

CONTENTS

PREFACE

I have interpreted very broadly the word *enterprise* that appears in this book's title. The frontier trapper bartering a bundle of beaver pelts for flour and sugar, the pioneer farmer trading produce for supplies, the urban householder shopping for groceries, the financial mogul bidding for control of a multi-billion-dollar conglomerate—all these people were engaging in business enterprises. This history, then, tells the story of how Americans provided for their own needs, developed surpluses to trade with others, and accumulated or lost wealth in large or small amounts.

These topics are incorporated into a larger description of the land and the nation. Early European settlers viewed this continent as an underpopulated land of many opportunities begging to be exploited. Imperial neglect allowed British colonists wide scope for their endeavors; a devotion to laissez-faire principles and competition continued to assure nineteenth-century Americans free rein to seek their fortunes. More recently, a balance between advocates of government regulation and proponents of a free-market economy has kept the United States busy exploring and exploiting various types of enterprise.

The evolution and expansion of business activities and organizations from the colonial period to the present provide a central framework for this book. The enterprises it examines range from basic ones like subsistence farming to corporations employing tens of thousands of workers and conducting business worldwide.

Business developments, industrialization, and technological change have obviously profoundly altered American society.

At the same time, people's attitudes, ambitions, and desires shaped business decisions, access to capital, consumer products, and countless other aspects of a competitive market system. Consequently, this book also analyzes the interrelationships between people and business institutions. Sometimes the people appear as members of groups like farmers or factory workers but many individuals are introduced as well. Several occupy a whole section of a chapter either because they represent a class like southern planters or northern bankers, or because their drive and inventiveness marked them for memorable achievements in their chosen fields of enterprise. Shorter sketches profile other notable people, and some are quoted at length.

One pleasure of studying or writing history is the license it grants to use any convenient tool. Ranging across disciplinary boundaries, I have incorporated information collected or theories developed by economists, sociologists, financial experts, political scientists, and authorities in many other fields. The work of these specialists has helped me analyze the factors that affected American enterprise over time such as monetary policies, inflation, depression, consumer behavior, technological change, international trade, and government regulation.

I have adhered to one practice common among my fellow historians: the story is organized along chronological lines. Many writers on business and economic affairs follow quite a different approach, dividing their material into topical chapters. That strategy allows for smooth generalizations about the progress and development of, say, banking or retailing over a century or more, but it also forces readers repeatedly to adjust their historical sensitivity. I feel more comfortable projecting myself into a given period, orienting my perspective to it, and then examining what was occurring more or less simultaneously. That is, after all, how we live in the real world, and most business decisions strongly reflect the current state of affairs. An automaker, for example, is far more likely to decide what sort of car to produce on the basis of contemporary consumer preferences, foreign and domestic competition, gasoline prices, and current government regulations than because of conditions his industry faced fifty or even a dozen years earlier. Each chapter therefore constitutes a tour through a particular time period.

The chief drawback of chronological division is that, quite obviously, developments in many sectors continue over a much longer time span than any single chapter encompasses. Banking and monetary issues and problems crop up periodically, for example, and so must be dealt with in every chapter. Similarly farm practices, profitability, and opportunities change over the centuries, so the current agricultural situation is noted in most of the chapters as well. Industries producing items like aircraft and electronic devices make their first appearances at particular points and then continue to demand attention in subsequent chapters. I have tried to leave few loose ends so that the reader will come away from the book fully informed about the historical development of a number of business sectors.

Written primarily for college-level courses on the history of American business, the material in this book was read and, in many cases, severely criticized by students in my own courses. I hope I have succeeded in eliminating the confusing or incorrect passages they discovered. Several academic reviewers have also helped identify weaknesses. Among them are my colleagues in the history department at Iowa State University who read several of the chapters and provided many suggestions for improvement, as well as James H. Broussard, Lebanon Valley College; and A. O. Edmonds, Ball State University. The university also granted me a faculty improvement leave to facilitate the research and writing of the manuscript.

I also wish to acknowledge the encouragement that Katie M. Vignery gave me in the early stages of the project. Stephen Dalphin at Prentice Hall then enthusiastically picked it up and has been most helpful in encouraging me to refine and shape the manuscript. Linda Pawelchak handled the editing and production with remarkable efficiency. And, as always, my wife Cindy has been most supportive throughout this project as well as supplying me with useful references to a variety of materials she encountered in her own work.

A HISTORY
OF AMERICAN
ENTERPRISE

Chapter 1

THE ORIGINS
OF
AMERICAN
ENTERPRISE

Business affects all Americans in countless ways. They buy goods that businesses have manufactured, transported, and distributed. Literally thousands of advertising messages bombard potential consumers every day, encouraging them to switch, improve, renew, or expand their buying patterns. Television and newspapers keep people informed about stock prices, mergers, bankruptcies, and hundreds of other business stories. Private enterprise employs the vast majority of American workers, providing them with opportunities ranging from menial jobs to top executive positions. Government officials consult business leaders; special interest groups contribute to political campaigns, lobby for favorable legislation, and profit from government contracts.

All of these characteristics of modern American business have deep historical roots. The use of investment capital, the formation of partnerships and companies, the development of an influential merchant class, speculation in land and industrial endeavors—all of these were occurring in the colonies long before the United States won its independence. In the early nineteenth century, corporations blossomed as useful devices for building canals and railroads. Buying and selling shares through stock exchanges soon became a popular pastime. Plenty of mergers and consolidations took place before the turn of the twentieth century, but the rise of heavily-capitalized corporate and conglomerate giants is a fairly recent development.

Some of these aspects of modern American business can be traced directly to individual initiative and brilliance. Eli Whitney popularized the use of interchangeable parts in manufacturing. David MacCallum drafted a model organizational plan for running a railroad in the 1850s. Samuel C. T. Dodd did the same for conducting interstate business with the trust he created in the 1880s. Henry Ford combined a number of concepts in developing his moving assembly line that sped production of his popular Model T cars in the early 1900s. Ray Kroc, in turn, adapted similar techniques to the restaurant business in the 1950s for his chain of McDonald's hamburger stands, the foundations for today's booming fast-food industry.

The ambitions and activities of innovators make for fascinating reading, but they should not overshadow less obvious or dramatic human contributions to American enterprise. The labor of millions of workers was essential in creating the most advanced, wealthiest nation in the history of the world. Whether they were the free or enslaved agricultural laborers of the colonial and early national periods; the miners, factory laborers, or sweatshop workers who toiled for minimal wages around the turn of the century; or the organized, self-conscious blue and white collar employees of today, business enterprises could never have succeeded without them.

The people worked within a changing institutional and structural environment that added its own color and variation to American enterprise. Land was the predominant means of production in the early days, so speculators risked all in bidding to control it. Expansion affected the nation as a whole, causing Louisiana, Oregon, California, and everything in between to be added to its resource base. To facilitate commercial exchanges throughout this vast land mass, a railroad network was completed in the 1800s and a comprehensive highway and airport system built in the 1900s. The insolvency and uncertainty of the money supply in the colonial period slowly responded to the federal government's often awkward attempts to develop a financial system adequate to U.S. needs. It succeeded so well that today the American dollar serves as the whole world's leading medium of exchange.

Because the people and institutions of each era made unique contributions and succeeding generations exploited and built upon the earlier foundations, this book has been organized chronologically. The early chapters describe the largely rural and agrarian enterprises of the colonial and early nation years. Industrialization plays the dominant role in the central portion of the book. Many modern businesses are concerned with providing goods and services for a mass consumption society, so these activities predominate in the later chapters.

In each period Americans discovered particular opportunities to exploit. In the beginning, the land bonanza in the New World offered the most obvious means of production and profit. Later, industrial and transportation enterprises would attract the enthusiasm of ambitious entrepreneurs. In the twentieth century technological developments like the automobile, the airplane, motion pictures and television, plastics, electronics, and the like would push aside railroads and factories as the most attractive business ventures.

As the nature of business opportunities changed and expanded, those eager to exploit them had to develop appropriate mechanisms. In the agrarian age, that meant experimenting with planting, cultivating, harvesting, and marketing techniques. The rise of industry required mechanical inventiveness as well as the accumulation and investment of capital on a large scale. To meet the financial needs of industrial entrepreneurs, banks and stock exchanges had to become far more sophisticated and efficient. Similarly, advertising developed into a highly refined speciality—some even insist on calling it an art—to manipulate buyers in the twentieth century's mass consumption society.

A third characteristic of each period of the history of enterprise is that various constraints hindered or obstructed business activity. Some of these obstacles were natural in origin. The wilderness, for example, severely limited transportation and movement in Colonial America. In the 1960s, after luxuriating for over three centuries in abundance, Americans suddenly became aware of scarcities of fundamental resources and concerned over the impact of their activities on the natural environment. Economic forces also affected business activity fundamentally. Inflation and deflation, depression and prosperity, these often seemed far beyond the control of the human beings who suffered or thrived as a result of their impacts. The people had at least some direct control over the government regulations and taxes that influenced business behavior. But international political forces often discouraged or encouraged particular types of enterprises. Wars have been particularly uneven in their impacts, inflicting very high costs on some individuals while simultaneously rewarding others with extraordinary profits.

Over the years, many opportunities have been ignored or misused, many mechanisms have failed to achieve their objectives, many obstacles have stubbornly resisted any attempt to dislodge them. Fortunes have been made and lost for thousands of reasons. Even so, the United States has always prided itself on being dedicated to progress, to moving forward and improving lives and lifestyles. The progress discussed in this book developed from a business system, based on capitalism, that has managed to provide more than two hundred million Americans with a higher standard of living and material welfare than the wealthiest monarchs enjoyed at other times and in other places.

EUROPEAN ROOTS

The United States developed out of a group of relatively poor British colonies clinging to the Atlantic coastline. The colonists there relied on the Mother Country to provide a continuing stream of settlers, supplies, and money. They also naturally exhibited British cultural values. In addition to importing the English language, religions, family structure, and many political beliefs, those who ventured across the ocean carried in their cultural baggage economic and entrepreneurial concepts that still influence American business practices.

Many of these concepts, in turn, can be traced back into medieval times. The expansionist drive that led to the planting of the American colonies had become feasible only because the emerging nation states of Europe were shedding many vestiges of the feudal system that had prevailed during the Middle Ages. The key actors in the older system were land-owning nobility and gentry who lived off the products of the labor of impoverished peasants or serfs. A depressed standard of living was quite characteristic of this largely static society. Progress was painfully slow where it could be said to occur at all.

The crusades that swept thousands of Europeans eastward toward the Holy Land disturbed many of the traditional relationships. Even as they were dislocating the props of feudalism, these religious forays were introducing new, exciting products to Europe. The most desirable of these were spices like pepper and cinnamon that Europeans of all classes used to invigorate their bland, boring diets. Ample profits were available to anyone who had access to these products. Soon regular caravans were hauling spices to the Western Mediterranean where Italian merchants shipped them to Venice and Genoa for distribution to the rest of Europe.

These Italians began to grow very wealthy by exploiting capitalism, the process of using money for productive investments. To keep track of their activities, they had to develop rather sophisticated accounting procedures including double-entry bookkeeping. And, because their wealth soon exceeded the amount of gold and silver in circulation, they had to write receipts or bills of exchange to facilitate buying and selling. These substitutes for coinage were the forerunners of the paper currency now in universal use.

Other Europeans envied the Italians' profits but the more conservative among them considered their activities as violations of God's laws. Catholic doctrine prohibited usury—the charging of interest for loans—and insisted that both buyers and sellers use what it vaguely defined as a "just price" for all transactions. As long as they lacked the inducement of a return on an investment or a profit on a sale, individuals were little inclined to conduct business at all. Gradually, however, society began to agree that interest and profits were just rewards for the services that lenders and merchants performed.

Beginning in 1517 the Protestant Reformation further eroded the authority of the Catholic church. The early protestants tended to be sober, dedicated, and self-reliant. Deliberately rejecting the comfort and stability the church provided, these dissenters placed a high value on individual virtue. They considered any material success that resulted from their endeavors as proof of their worthiness and godliness. This attitude lay at the heart of what came to be called the "Protestant Ethic." The Puritans who colonized New England firmly believed in demonstrating their virtue through hard work and dedication. Ever since colonial times, Americans generally have prided themselves on their willingness to be productive in a material sense, whether or not they subscribe to the religious beliefs that underlay the Protestant Ethic.

Another development crucial for encouraging individual enterprise of all sorts was recognition of private property rights. Royal grants of estates to the nobility as well as the tradition of primogeniture in which the eldest son inherited all of his father's possessions weakened the proprietary claims of even the most absolute of monarchs. Some peasants and the emerging group of merchants also obtained recognition of their ownership claims. English common law came to reflect these changes so that property rights were well established by the time of the founding of the American colonies.

Assurance of a fair return on trade and of an individual's right to do what he wished with his property encouraged a broadening of economic activity in Europe. Individuals began to specialize in producing items that were difficult or expensive for the average person to make. Having become recognized as craftsmen, they hired apprentices and established shops. Other individuals became roving merchants, traveling from one location to another with a backpack, a cart, or a caravan full of goods. As villages grew into towns, both craftsmen and merchants settled there, participating in the community's permanent market structure.

As the demand for commercial services grew, it stimulated the formation of larger enterprises. To finance these, merchants and other interested parties had to pool their resources. An individual might well spread the risk and the prospect of return by dividing investments among a number of enterprises. Some of these would be formal or informal partnerships. Others, often requiring royal permission or legal sanction, were organized generally along the lines of a corporation with shares sold to anyone with the funds to buy them. The colonists brought to America a working knowledge of individual entrepreneurship, partnerships, and joint-stock companies and quickly adapted these structures to their own needs.

The line separating private enterprises from governmental or royal ventures was often indistinct in Medieval and Renaissance Europe. For their own protection, investors or partners were wise to obtain government consent in the form of a royal charter or grant before undertaking a major business venture. Public officials inevitably involved themselves directly in many such endeavors, and interested parties became accustomed to petitioning the monarch directly, a royal council, or a parliament for particular benefits or protections. Despite the distance, lack of reliable or speedy communication, and laxity of legal enforcement, the colonists in North America remained subject to the British government's policies.

Beyond the specific relationships the government entered into with its citizens, evolving political institutions altered and affected the overall environment within which business was conducted. The emergence of centralized authority in nation states like Portugal, France, Spain, and more particularly in England itself, calmed or discouraged regional quarrels that interfered with the expansion of trade and access to broader markets. A national government provided a degree of stability and predictability that encouraged commercial activities. Centralized control also assisted the imposition of standardized weights, measures, exchange values, and other factors vital to business enterprises. The American colonists benefited a great deal from the stability the British imperial system provided. After breaking loose from English authority in the Revolution, they created a constitutional framework of their own to provide the constancy they missed.

The colonists who left England for an uncertain existence in the New World thus brought with them many concepts fundamental to business. They understood the importance of private property rights and placed a high value on private initiative. Their economic philosophy was capitalistic in the sense that they recognized the potential profits that could accrue to those willing to invest and to engage in trade. Accounting procedures, the use of bills of exchange, and other mechanisms commonly employed by merchants were imported and widely used. The benefits of partnerships and joint stock companies were recognized. Finally, the settlers acknowledged the value of a stable government which either actively encouraged or passively permitted individual enterprise at all levels.

The colonies as such might never have existed at all, in fact, had national governments been disinterested in founding and supporting them. The Spanish monarchy paid for the explorations of Columbus because it feared neighboring Portugal would find a lucrative all-water trade route around Africa to the Far East. The wealth that Spain subsequently extracted from her extensive possessions in the New World convinced other nation states to follow her lead. Colonizing America could be viewed as essentially a massive business speculation in which some nations earned far higher returns on their investments of capital, supplies, and lives than did others.

Totaling up all the returns was a difficult task, however, because many of them were intangible. In addition to producing gold and silver, colonial empires performed a variety of other useful economic functions. England found, for example, that America provided an ideal location to disperse some of its cramped, impoverished urban residents. Colonial supplies of raw materials like furs, food, and minerals contributed to an empire's resource base, though hardly as obviously as gold. The existence of a growing colonial population offered merchants and traders expanding trade opportunities. Indeed, by the 1700s, English merchants had become very dependent upon the profits they could earn from marketing their processed goods in the American colonies.

Few individuals were farsighted enough to recognize all the potential tangible and intangible benefits of colonization. The early investors and adventurers in North America hoped for more immediate, bankable profits. But establishing a plantation, as the early colonies were called, was a costly and complex business. A few Englishmen had at least some relevant experience. Several trading companies had come into being in the late 1500s with the active personal encouragement of Queen Elizabeth I. The East India Company was typical. Formed in 1600, its goal was to assert British control over the tea trade in India. The company was still preeminent in that region more than two centuries later, relying on the British army for protection of its commercial activities. The early business ventures with close ties to the crown established precedents for the companies that sought royal permission to plant colonies in North America after 1600.

THE COLONIZATION BUSINESS

The Englishmen who decided to send settlers to North America approached colonization as they would any other business venture. They were willing to invest some capital and take some risks in return for future dividends. Perhaps the most common characteristic all the early colonizers' shared, though, was a great deal of unjustified optimism. Harvesting riches from the wilderness was a monumental task; all too often impatient adventurers and investors became discouraged, unwilling to see it through.

The start-up costs for a major enterprise like a colony were substantial. Sir Walter Raliegh claimed he had spent £40,000 on his futile attempt to establish one on Roanoke Island in the 1580s. A group effort might have a better chance of success. Several potential investors were close personal friends of King James I who ascended the British throne in 1603. A royal connection was a valuable asset because the king automatically owned all newly discovered lands. He therefore had to grant both his royal permission and the land itself to those wishing to plant colonies. The government proved quite willing to condone the efforts of anyone foolish enough to risk a life or a fortune in an attempt to transform a worthless, untamed area into a productive part of the king's domain.

The first group to succeed in its colonizing project was the "Treasurer and Company of Adventurers of the City of London for the First Colony in Virginia." Several of the Virginia Company of London's directors were wealthy investors who put up capital for the enterprise expecting it to bring a reasonable return. While the company was establishing the first permanent British foothold in North

Sir Walter Raliegh. (New York Public Library)

America at Jamestown, it was also proving itself quite inept at handling both its own and its colony's business affairs. Consequently, a new royal charter was is-sued in 1609 to turn the company into a joint-stock enterprise that sold its shares to more than seven hundred investors. With a par value of £12/10, they added about £50,000 to the company's operating funds.

A SHARE OF STOCK IN THE VIRGINIA COMPANY OF LONDON

With its specific reference to gold and silver, the following share shows the optimism of those who invested in the company in its early days.

Whereas the Mayor Juratts and Cominaltye of the Towne and Porte of Dover have payde in readye monye to Sir Thomas Smyth Knight Treasurer of Virginia, the some of Twentye fyve pounds for three adventures towards the sayd voyadge. It is agreed that for the same, they the sayd Mayor, Juratts and Cominaltye, and there successors, shall have notablye accordinge to there adventures, these full part of all suche lands—Tenementes, and heredita-mentes, as shall from tyme to tyme be there recovered, planted and inhabited, And of suche Mynes, and Minnerales of Golde, silver, and other Metall or Treasure Pearles, precious stones, or anye kinde of was or marchandizes, comodeties, or profitts whatsoever which shalbe obteyned, or gotten in the sayd voyage, accordinge to the portion of monye by them ymployed to that use, in an ample manner as anye other adventurer therein shall reteyne for the like sume. Written this 23th of Maye Domini 1610.

(Reprinted in Warren M. Billings, *The Old Dominion in the Seventeenth Century, A Documentary History of Virginia, 1606-1689* [Chapel Hill: University of North Carolina Press, 1975], pp. 27-28.)

The Jamestown colony clinging to the shore of the Chesapeake Bay just barely survived; it certainly was in no position to turn a profit. The company's funds disappeared as quickly as the supplies it sent over to the starving settlers. In 1612 the company won royal permission to conduct lotteries to raise additional money, but it all drained away. The company's primary asset was the land—nearly two million square miles of it—that the king's generous charter had granted. The company held on to this resource until 1616 when it finally made some of it avail-able for private ownership. Yet another company reorganization in 1618 led to a system of bribes in the form of small land grants to encourage people either to set-tle in the colony or pay the transportation costs of other settlers. The granting of "headrights" of fifty acres per person was so popular that other colonies used them to stimulate migration to the New World. The land distribution policy did not save the Virginia Company, though. The crown canceled the lotteries in 1623 and, a year later, the company lapsed into receivership, forcing the royal government to assume full responsibility. The Virginia Company had obviously failed as a business venture, but it had barely succeeded as a colonizing tool.

Other groups planning to settle in North America therefore used company structures. Some dissenters who desired to separate themselves completely from the Church of England formed such an organization to assist their pilgrimage to the New World. Like its Virginia counterpart, the company the Pilgrims left behind in England was unprofitable, but the settlers managed to save enough to buy title to their land in the late 1620s. A much larger, more prosperous group of Puritans obtained their own royal charter in 1629 to form the Massachusetts Bay Colony Company. The document authorized the investors to settle in New England and permitted them to take the charter and therefore the company along with them. This arrangement gave the so-called theocracy in Boston direct control over the colony's business affairs as well as its political and religious activities. Like Virginia, Massachusetts and its offshoots of Connecticut and Rhode Island developed without any grand imperial design.

The royal government paid closer attention to subsequent colonial ventures, particularly those involving proprietors. The first of these was George Calvert, an intelligent statesman who had served in the king's cabinet before converting to Catholicism. King James's successor, Charles, decided to reward the old retainer with a royal grant to establish a Catholic refuge in America. Calvert died before his colony of Maryland could be founded north of the Potomac River, so his sons inherited the proprietorship. The Calverts hoped to profit from their venture by retaining the best lands for themselves and collecting quitrents on the tracts they gave away or sold to others. Although the colony remained in the family's possession at the time of the American Revolution, it had never been the money-maker the Calverts had expected.

After a pause, the colonization business revived when Charles II was restored to the throne in 1660. His friends included energetic, worldly men involved in business activities around the globe. The king was only too happy to assign them proprietary grants to the unsettled parts of the North American coast. Like the Calverts, the eight proprietors of the Carolina region hoped to augment their fortunes by collecting land rents. Charles granted his brother, James, Duke of York, the British claim to the Dutch colony laying between the Delaware River and New England. After he had arranged for it to be captured, James left the existing Dutch land grants intact because one of his major objectives was to people New York with individuals capable of paying quitrents.

William Penn may have founded his colony as a refuge for persecuted Quakers, but it was hardly accidental that it developed into the most commercially oriented and prosperous proprietary colony. Penn designed an attractive governing scheme to attract settlers to the bountiful lands around Philadelphia. He mounted advertising campaigns to attract immigrants from Germany and Scotland. Rents and taxes in Pennsylvania remained low as yet another inducement to enterprising settlers. The population grew and thrived but, even so, the colony was a financial disappointment. When the Penn family lost its colony to the American Revolution, it also lost something of a financial liability.

The lack of profits from colonization could hardly be blamed on the government. The king demanded remarkably little from the proprietors in return for his generous grants. Although he retained some mineral rights like one-fifth of all the gold and silver that might be found, the royal dues were mere tokens. The Calverts had to send the king two Indian arrowheads a year; Penn's obligation was two beaver pelts. The proprietors' costs were high because of the colonists' insatiable need for supplies and the substantial costs of transporting them and more settlers across the ocean. Many people willing to relocate in the New World could not finance their voyages, so the proprietors often paid these costs to insure that at least some of their land would be developed.

Despite the elaborate planning, optimistic projections, and costly developmental activities, the colonies were disappointing business ventures. The companies and proprietors seldom managed to break even, and many suffered bankruptcy or drains on their fortunes. The potential wealth of the New World therefore failed to rise to the top to be skimmed by colonial promoters. Instead, it was yielded up grudgingly to those individuals who actually lived and worked in America.

READING SUGGESTIONS

Those seeking a general survey of the development of American business might begin with Thomas C. Cochran's *Basic History of American Business* (1968). It focuses more attention on commercial activities than does *Two Hundred Years of American Business* (1977), which examines the broader social and political influence of business activities in the United States. A similar approach appears in Arthur H. Cole, *Business Enterprise in Its Social Setting* (1959). Peter D'A. Jones, *The Consumer Society: History of American Capitalism* (1965) provides a scholarly interpretation. Alex Groner, *The History of American Business and Industry* (1972) is a lavishly illustrated volume designed to appeal to a general audience.

Readers interested in specific business leaders have several choices. John Chamberlain's *Enterprising Americans: Business History* (1963) touches on hundreds of individuals. Authors who focus their attention on relatively few entrepreneurs are Fritz L. Redlich, *History of American Business Leaders* (2 vols., 1940, 1951); Ben Seligman, *The Potentates: Business and Business Men in American History* (1971); Stewart H. Holbrook, *The Age of the Moguls* (1953); and John Brooks, *Business Adventures* (1968).

In *The Economic Transformation of America: 1600 to the Present*, Robert L. Heilbroner and Aaron Singer spend a good deal of time studying European origins. Other sources on this topic are Miriam Beard, *A History of the Business Man* (1938) and F. L. Nussbaum, *History of Economic Institutions of Modern Europe* (1933). English entrepreneurs are examined in W. E. Lugelbach, *Merchant Ad-*

venturers of England (1902), George N. Clark, *The Wealth of England, 1496-1760* (1946), and Theodore K. Rabb, *Enterprise and Empire: Merchant and Gentry Investment in Expansion of England, 1575-1630* (1967).

Chapter 2

TRANSFORMING A WILDERNESS INTO A NATION 1607-1783

From the earliest days of the Age of Discovery, Europeans had looked upon America as a land of many opportunities. Individuals came to settle in the New World to escape religious persecution, indebtedness, family responsibilities, or a lack of employment. A goodly number saw the New World as a new start in life, and they could count themselves successful if they improved their standard of living even marginally. Surviving in the wilderness on a rude homestead capable of supporting one's family was a signal accomplishment.

All the immigrants were infected with the same disease—hunger for land—and America had plenty to offer. Millions upon millions of tillable, bountiful acres lay unclaimed, unencumbered and, in European eyes, underused. A temperate climate, forests teeming with wildlife, and intricate inland waterways giving access to the Atlantic coastline contributed to the attractiveness of American land. Property on such a scale, available to so many thousands of individuals was a remarkable bonanza indeed. European property owners could lord it over the peasants because their estates represented the major means of production in an agrarian age. In America that means of production lay readily available to all.

Exploitation of the land, the forests, and the seas therefore predominated in the early decades of British settlement in North America. The first profits came directly from the natural environment, and some individuals were far more successful than others in utilizing its resources. The great planters of the tidewater South, owning in excess of 100,000 acres, lived worlds apart from the frontiersmen in Appalachian valleys, hacking meager livings out of a few, scrappy acres. By the mid-eighteenth century, America had a highly diversified economy, with new opportunities cropping up alongside the prevailing agrarian pursuits. The dispersion of settlers up and down the coast allowed traders to earn profits carrying goods from one outpost to another. The increasing importance of the colonies as elements in the British Empire stimulated trade east and west. The diversification of economic activities provided work for merchants, craftsmen, miners, lumberjacks, millers, and laborers of all sorts.

By the 1760s, however, many American colonists were becoming disenchanted with their subordinate positions within the empire. What began as a protest against relatively minor taxes escalated into an all-out conflict over whether the king and his Parliament or the colonists themselves had the right to rule. The shots that rang out at Lexington and Concord in the spring of 1775 signaled the outbreak of the bloody military struggle the Americans called the Revolution. The patriots' behavior during that war—their economic opportunism, their failure to cope with monetary troubles, their ability to do without imported goods—clearly reflected their colonial upbringing. Yet their earlier experiences had created the conditions which led to the defeat of the world's leading mercantile nation at the hands of an undisciplined rebel force consisting primarily of farmers.

COLONIAL AGRICULTURE

Profits alone were seldom the primary concern of the earliest colonial settlers. A struggle for basic survival often overwhelmed all other considerations. Both the Jamestown colony and the Pilgrim settlement at Plymouth originated as communal societies in which the company owned everything and provided a common store house for supplies, food, and tools. Neither collective experiment was successful or popular so, after a few years, land—the chief means of production—was turned over to individuals to seek their own fortunes. Culling more than a bare subsistence from the land required considerable effort as well as luck in finding a market for any surplus produced.

The Atlantic coastline presented a spectrum of colonial agricultural enterprise. To the South were the West Indies. There relatively few, often absentee plantation owners profited enormously from the insatiable worldwide demand for sugar. Staple crop production also predominated in the Carolinas, Virginia, and Maryland, but trade was increasingly important in the middle colonies. Farming became less profitable further up the coast, with southern New England marking the limit of the area in which a family could reasonably expect to prosper off the produce of its land. In the Maritime Provinces still further north, farming was an avocation, definitely subordinate to other endeavors.

The New England farmers were reluctant to admit that nature had failed to endow their property with the same agricultural potential it had lavished on other parts of the American continent. The hilly, rock-infested country-side and relatively short growing season were discouraging enough, but the original political structure imposed additional barriers to profitable production. The basic unit within the Massachusetts Bay Colony was a ten-square-mile township assigned to a particular congregation. Woodlots and pastures were held in common for the use of all inhabitants. As they cleared the land, the members of the congregation received small units. A family could end up owning a patchwork of tiny, inefficient tracts. Many a villager drifted southwest in search of better, more concentrated lands or east to the shore where trade and industry offered more chance for advancement.

In the middle colonies between New England and the tidewater South, climate and geography made farming much more attractive. Puritans from New England had migrated south to Long Island and the Hudson River Valley even before the Dutch lost it to the British in 1664. Settlers who heeded William Penn's invitation to his proprietary colony discovered it to contain inviting, bountiful farmland. New Jersey was ideal for growing vegetables and fruits. Such a variety of food and livestock could be produced in the middle colonies that they quickly achieved regional agricultural self-sufficiency. The abundance of the area then enabled colonists to export cereal products. Wheat was the chief cash crop through the Revolution.

A considerably longer growing season, reasonably good soil, and broad navigable rivers stretching into the interior were typical of the southern colonies. This region naturally developed into the most successful producer of agricultural surpluses. Looking for a staple export, John Rolfe had begun experimenting with tobacco cultivation as early as 1612. The ease of growing tobacco and a rapidly expanding market for it caused tidewater Virginia and Maryland to specialize in its production.

Although the slave-owning planter emerged as the role model for most southerners, successful tobacco cultivation did not require a plantation structure. Any farmer residing in the appropriate latitudes could plant an acre or two of tobacco to sell as a cash crop. After curing, tobacco leaves were rolled and packed into wooden barrels or hogsheads, some large enough to hold 1500 pounds. The barrels were then rolled to the banks of the nearest river to be loaded on ships for transport to England.

Tobacco production grew rapidly. The first major shipment from Virginia in 1617 consisted of about 20,000 pounds. Ten years later the colony was exporting a half million pounds annually. By 1670 the figure had risen to fifteen million pounds a year, and an average of over sixty-six million pounds was leaving the Chesapeake Bay each year for European sale just prior to the Revolution. Prices fluctuated over time. It sold very well at first to Englishmen who welcomed Virginia leaf as a substitute for more expensive tobacco imported from Holland. But production was so easy to undertake that output quickly exceeded demand, forcing the price down below a penny a pound. In a brief burst of prosperity in the late 1600s, the price crested at more than 2.3 pence a pound before declining to a little over a penny a pound through the the the next century.

Despite the disappointing price level, output continued to rise, especially after a major secondary market for tobacco developed in the mid-1700s. English law did not prohibit the reexport of colonial produce from Great Britain, and the Euro-

Alternative methods for "conveyance of tobacco to market." (Rare Book Division, The New York Public Library, Astor, Lenox and Tilden Foundations)

pean demand for American tobacco rose at a rate nearly five times as great as did the domestic demand in England. The vast majority of the colonial crop was therefore routinely reexported to European customers, bringing profits to British merchants, shippers, and exporters as well as to those planters able to grow tobacco at low costs. Tobacco consistently ranked as the chief export from the North American continent, accounting for almost half of the total value of colonial commodity exports in 1750. Just as cotton was to dominate the agricultural export market in the next century, tobacco was king in the earlier period.

In the 1700s, the center of tobacco cultivation migrated westward as pioneers settled the Piedmont Plateau and the valleys beyond. Overcropping had leached the tidewater lands of their fertility, so the business naturally moved to more productive regions. Several Scottish merchant houses facilitated this transfer by establishing trading centers and stores in the interior. They served as middlemen, supplying the tobacco to the European market, providing credit for land-hungry farmers, and furnishing them with tools and other commodities.

Other staples also provided healthy returns. In the Carolinas, Charleston had first prospered as a center of the lucrative southern fur trade. Once it declined, the local entrepreneurs turned to the production of rice. Conditions were so oppressive in this region that many landowners maintained their homes in Charleston and hired overseers for the slaves imported to toil in the unhealthy paddies along the coast. Rice found ready markets in southern Europe and the Caribbean. By the mid-1700s Carolina and adjacent Georgia plantations were shipping an average of thirty million pounds a year, a figure that more than doubled in the next quarter century.

The average price hovered at just over a penny per pound throughout this period, making rice as profitable as tobacco on a bulk basis. Not surprisingly, the Charleston rice planters considered themselves the social and financial equals of the Virginia tobacco barons. They all shared concerns about markets, slave prices, and land. A look at the business activities of one of the most prominent of the Virginia gentry will illustrate the life style of the successful southern colonial planter.

VIRGINIA PLANTERS: THE BYRD FAMILY

The number of tobacco growers who qualified for the designation of planter was limited, but, as a class, they definitely wielded political and social authority in the southern colonies. Because of the generally depressed price for tobacco, an individual had to work hard at reducing his production costs to emerge as one of the planter elite. The basic requirement was ownership of or access to plenty of land since tobacco exhausted the soil's natural nutrients in seven years or less. No matter how well off they seemed to be, the great planters constantly engaged in real estate transactions to augment or improve their holdings.

William Byrd was prominent among the Virginia tobacco growers who had amassed sizable estates by 1700. But Byrd had never specialized exclusively in agriculture. Many of his commercial activities related only tangentially to farming. He was a consummate trader, exchanging goods with the Indians on the western frontier as well as importing a great variety of items from abroad to sell to others. In addition to goods, he brought workers of all sorts to the Chesapeake Bay. At one point, he owned a slaver engaged in the profitable business of supplying laborers for his fellow tobacco planters. Byrd also took an active part in politics, sitting in the Virginia House of Burgesses and serving as the royal tax collector for the colony.

This cosmopolitan gentleman naturally insisted upon nothing but the best for his son. In the colonial period, that meant a British education. Consequently, seven-year-old William Byrd II was bundled off to England to attend school. He left the classroom at sixteen for a commercial apprenticeship in Holland where he

William Byrd II. (Library of Congress)

learned firsthand the workings of business and international trade. Then he returned to England to study law. He visited his American home only briefly before
returning to London designated as an agent of the colony of Virginia, a role at
which he was rather unsuccessful.

When his father died in 1704, William Byrd II inherited an estate of 26,000
acres. The youthful heir hastened back across the Atlantic to assert his claim to
these lands as well as to make sure that his father's political offices would be
passed on as well. Skillful maneuvering won the younger Byrd a seat on the influential governor's council which he held until his death in 1744. He also succeeded
his father as the crown's receiver general in charge of tax collecting. He maintained these colonial positions despite the fact that he spent a major portion of the
next twenty years in England. Shortly after he married, his wife inherited valuable
lands but also a substantial number of debts. Even after his wife had died several
years later, Byrd worked to keep his father-in-law's property within his own family's control.

In the mid-1720s, Byrd returned to Virginia to cut his living expenses, repay
his debts, and spend the rest of his life as a gentleman planter. Although this

lifestyle was imitative of the landed gentry in England, Virginia planters tended to be much more actively involved in the day-to-day management of their estates. Byrd toured his property personally, checking on his overseers, servants, and slaves almost daily. In addition to organizing the planting, harvesting, and marketing of his crops, the wise planter saw to the adequate housing and feeding of his work force, often serving as a doctor as well. In addition to tobacco, Byrd's workers grew corn, wheat, oats, and hay and cultivated orchards and gardens to supply fruits and vegetables for the master's table. Livestock roamed uncultivated areas. Housing materials and fuel came from woodlots. A colonial Virginia tobacco plantation required little outside support. From one year to the next a planter like Byrd had almost no need for circulating currency as such.

His chief external expenditures went toward the expansion of his holdings. Byrd and his fellow tidewater planters were incessantly engaged in surveying and purchasing new acreage. When the colonial government opened the Piedmont area to private ownership in the 1720s, members of the governor's council used their influence to line up the best parcels for themselves. Byrd also toured the interior as a commissioner for Virginia and, in 1728, he purchased a tract of 20,000 acres in the back country of North Carolina which he called the "Land of Eden." Seven years later he obtained a grant to a huge tract of 105,000 acres, tax free for two years if he could find one family to live on each thousand acres. The sturdy Swiss seemed reliable, but a shipwreck carried away his boatload of Swiss immigrants. Byrd paid his taxes and distributed parcels of land to the Scotch-Irish frontiersmen making their way south through the mountains from Pennsylvania. Although he maintained a beautiful mansion and associated estate at Westover, the cost-conscious planter sold off tobacco-exhausted lands to farmers planning to raise corn and live

Buckingham Hall: An example of the southern plantation ideal. (Courtesy of the New-York Historical Society, New York City)

stock. Such rapid turnovers of land investments would probably have unnerved the staid English gentry, but Virginians of all classes were avid land speculators.

Byrd himself would have been hard put to determine his exact financial position at any given moment. So many of his business dealings involved barter or credit that a strictly monetary accounting could never be done with any accuracy. Because he often steered close to bankruptcy, he continually sought colonial offices which carried either salaries or fees in order to obtain a monetary income. These, in turn, brought intangible rewards as, for example, his seat on the council which gave him insider access to the choicest bits of land. He played the game well. When he died in 1744, he had discharged all of his own and his father-in-law's extensive debts, leaving 179,000 acres free and clear to his heirs. Although Byrd was hardly the wealthiest landowner in the colony, his influence was extensive. He is representative, therefore, of the group who were most successful in generating wealth directly from the land. The Virginia tobacco planters were truly the agrarian elite of colonial America.

All the same, the world William Byrd II inhabited remained comparatively conservative. The established planter dynasties continued to buy land, traffic in slaves, and export tobacco. As direct shippers of the region's major commercial commodity, the tidewater gentry felt no need to center their activities in ports or inland market towns. A visitor to restored Williamsburg today discovers it to be a pleasant little village. One can scarcely believe that colonial Williamsburg was the political nerve center for the largest British colony in America both in geographic extent and population.

Business in this cozy setting was conducted in a leisurely, informal fashion. Most farmers and planters only rarely had contact with the world outside. Although they often envied the profits of the outsiders who bought their produce and arranged for the importation of goods and workers to their isolated holdings, these middlemen provided necessary services that few living in the sprawling agrarian colony wished to perform. British merchants and sea captains predominated at first; then Scottish mercantile houses grew in importance in the decades just prior to the Revolution. These agents, in turn, faced competition from ambitious merchants hailing from Philadelphia and New York, as well as from the New England commercial centers of Newport and Boston.

NORTHERN TRADE AND INDUSTRY

Colonial mercantile pursuits in the Northeast established the foundations for that region's dominance of business, commerce, and industry in the years following the Revolution. The percentage of time devoted to non-agricultural activities was directly related to the growing conditions in a particular area. Considerably more trade and industry occurred in New England, for example, because the region never developed a staple crop for export. Colonists there quickly began to diversify in order to achieve more comfortable standards of living.

WILLIAM BYRD II—from "History of the Dividing Line"

In 1728, Governor Spotswood commissioned Byrd and two other Virginians to run the long disputed line between Virginia and North Carolina. The following excerpt from his published journal of the trip bursts with his enthusiasm at the prospects for the virgin lands, but it proved far more difficult to farm profitably than Byrd's optimistic predictions would have suggested.

All the Land we Travell'd over this day, and the day before, that is to say from the river Irvin to Sable Creek, is exceedingly rich, both on the Virginia Side of the Line, and that of Carolina. Besides whole Forests of Canes, that adorn the Banks of the River and Creeks thereabouts, the fertility of the Soil throws out such a Quantity of Winter Grass, that Horses and Cattle might keep themselves in Heart all the cold Season without the help of any Fodder. . .

I question not but there are 30,000 Acres at least, lying Altogether, as fertile as the Lands were said to be about Babylon, which yielded, if Herodotus tells us right, an Increase of no less that 2 or 300 for one. But this hath the Advantage of being a higher, and consequently a much healthier, Situation than that. So that a Colony of 1000 famalies might, with the help of Moderate Industry, pass their time very happily there.

Besides grazing and Tillage, which would abundantly compensate their Labour, they might plant Vineyards upon the Hills, in which Situation the richest Wines are always produc'd. . .

They might too produce Hemp, Flax and Cotton, in what quantity they pleas'd, not only for their own use, but likewise for Sale. Then they might raise very plentiful Orchards, of both Peaches and Apples, which contribute as much as any Fruit to the Luxury of Life. There is no Soil or Climate will yield better Rice than this, which is a Grain of prodigious Increase, and of very wholesome Nourishment. In short every thing will grow plentifully here to supply either the Wants or Wantonness of Man.

(John Spencer Bassett, ed., *The Writings of Colonel William Byrd,* 1901, [rep. ed. New York: B. Franklin, 1970], pp. 207-8.)

The first British settlers in the Massachusetts Bay area relied on the perennial classic of frontier livelihoods: the fur trade. The Pilgrims established communities up and down the coast to assure access to the furs of the hinterland. They had trapped out the immediate vicinity by 1635, but New Englanders located further inland continued trapping and trading for another forty years. Some intrepid souls pushed well into the interior, searching for a vast legendary lake which would contain a mother lode of beaver pelts. Skins captured or bartered from the Indians were of little value to the colonists themselves; the market lay in England and on the Continent. Fine furs were dressed to be worn as clothing, but inferior pelts were scraped and the resulting hair was pressed into felt for the hats that were fashionable in those days. Furs also generated income for those in remoter regions of the middle and southern colonies, and the trade remained a rudimentary method for exploiting the wilderness well into the nineteenth century.

Fishing was another alternative to farming. Seafarers from the West Country of England controlled the waters along the American continental shelf in the early seventeenth century, discouraging American colonists from taking to the sea. Political disturbances swept England in the 1640s, though, allowing New England fishermen to replace those caught up in the turmoil in the home country. They initially used established English factors to market their catches, but the abundance of their output soon drove them to seek additional markets in the Catholic countries of southern Europe. Fishing was a constant if only modestly profitable way of developing foreign exchange through the Revolution.

The political strife in England also distracted many of the British intermediaries engaged in colonial trade. New Englanders wasted no time in taking responsibility for distributing American goods as well as locating needed supplies and arranging for their shipment to the New World. Boston served as the hub of a worldwide trade network. At first this trade followed predictable lines, replacing or supplementing the shipping services of British merchants. New England traders later took advantage of the opportunities that arose in, for example, the West Indies. British planters in the Caribbean specialized even more than their tobacco-raising counterparts in tidewater Virginia. Food, labor, and supplies were essential to maintain a sugar plantation, and New England merchants were happy to provide these necessities.

Colonial merchants further expanded their range of activities when the British began a trade war with the aggressive Dutch in the 1660s. Naval stores were vital in a conflict fought largely at sea. At the height of the conflict, a New England mast fetched as much as £135, a handsome return indeed for cutting down and trimming a tree. The unsettled times also provided new openings for American traders. New Englanders extended their services to the southern colonies, and direct links with Ireland and Scotland developed as well. The more adventuresome even dealt directly with France and her Caribbean Islands. While the British government never sanctioned this trade, a French passport was easy to obtain and it opened access to rich sources of sugar and other tropical products.

A NEW ENGLAND MERCHANT: THOMAS HANCOCK

In the 1690s the government in London imposed its authority on New England, effectively replacing the Puritan Theocracy that had ruled since 1630. That change allowed the growing mercantile class to rise far above the local clergy in social and economic status. Typical of the poorly paid ministers who struggled to make ends meet was Harvard-educated John Hancock, the son of a shoemaker. Although he was a popular and respected head of a congregation in Lexington, Reverend Hancock could only afford to send his oldest son to Harvard. A second son, Thomas, born in 1703, was sent to Boston at the age of fourteen as an apprentice to a bookseller. Young Thomas Hancock spent seven years learning the bookseller's trade which included many associated crafts like that of book binding. From these humble beginnings, he rose to become one of the leading merchants in Massachusetts. Hancock thus exemplifies the industrious and ambitious individuals who boldly took advantage of the broad range of opportunities colonial commerce offered.

Naturally enough, young Thomas opened his own bookstore when he had completed his apprenticeship. Because he imported most of the books he stocked from England, he had to find an American export to pay for his purchases. As noted above, Massachusetts failed to develop surplus agricultural products, so Hancock turned to the produce of the sea. The Nantucket and New Bedford whaling fleets provided just what he needed. Whale oil, bone, and fins found ready markets in England, and Thomas served as a major factor in this trade into the late 1730s.

But no colonial merchant could afford to specialize. Hancock's bookshop grew to resemble a general store, stocking all sorts of imported and domestic items. Hancock accumulated many of the local products almost inadvertently as both urban and rural customers brought whatever surplus goods they had to his shop to exchange for other items. Sometimes Thomas held goods on consignment, crediting the profit from their sale to the accounts of their owners. More often, the merchant himself was left to dispose of the strange assortment of goods he had accepted in payment for his stock. In the mid-1750s nearly two-thirds of the articles displayed in Hancock's store were clothing items, including yard goods, buttons, and the like. Even so, he dealt in virtually anything and everything including food, weapons, ships' equipment, coal, paper, salt, and leather. The variety of goods he handled was quite typical of all merchants confronted with the necessity of accepting and then attempting to resell whatever their customers had to trade.

From the beginning, Thomas Hancock maintained extensive contacts in England. One man in particular, Francis Wilks, served as his major agent at the other end, providing him with credit as well as goods and services. Wilks disposed of the whale oil and fins Hancock dispatched to pay for his purchases, and the Englishman rounded up and shipped the items the Bostonian had ordered. Communication was slow and chancy at best, so trust had to exist on both sides for any business arrangement to work. After Wilks died, Christopher Kilby handled Hancock's London affairs for the most part, and he proved particularly helpful in arranging government contracts for his American correspondent. In addition to these long-standing relationships, Hancock entered into literally hundreds of other arrangements with individuals on both sides of the Atlantic, many as single-venture enterprises, others on a regular basis.

Partnerships were quite common in the buying of ships. Hancock's activities obviously required vessels to transport goods between Boston and his markets and

---

THOMAS HANCOCK – LETTER TO S. CHASE OF PROVIDENCE

This letter dated September 16, 1754, conveys more than a hint of annoyance with Mr. Chase.

Sir,

Herewith I send you the Account of Sales for the 45 bb. Flower which proved very Indifferent & 9 of them quite bad, but you were so Lucky as to have it here when there was no Good flour in Town so I pushed it off for Good at 6.10/–Except the 9 bb. was very Glad to Sell them for Brown Bread at 5.5/–p bb.–I Charge you no Commission, and beg you to Remitt me the Remander as Soon as possible its' Long Due, & you must pay me the Interest after one years Credit I assure you I pay Interest for the very money I want this to Discharge.

I am
Your huml Servt

(Reprinted in W. T. Baxter, *The House of Hancock: Business in Boston, 1724-1771,* [Cambridge, MA: Harvard University Press, 1945], p. 218.)

---

sources. Furthermore, ships themselves were a major export commodity from the New England colonies and could be sold profitably in England to help balance the books. Hancock's ownership of a particular vessel was usually short-term, a year or so at most. He ordinarily bought only a share of a ship to spread the risk of his investments. Insurance for sailing vessels and their cargos was never certain because the brokers were concentrated in England. Premiums sometimes arrived in London after the ship and cargo they covered had docked and been sold. Despite the inherent risks and uncertainties, personal involvement in shipowning gave a merchant better control over his trading ventures. Fixed shipping schedules were rare in the age of sail, so markets and prices could seldom be predicted with accuracy. Diversity and flexibility were essential.

Hancock's ships ranged the Atlantic in search of cargo. He shipped fish to Portugal, bought wine in Madeira, loaded sugar and molasses in the West Indies, and purchased tea in Holland. Tea became his major concern in the 1750s, and Hancock frequently smuggled it past British tax collectors. The 20 percent tariff on tea imported from non-British sources made smuggling very profitable. At the same time, the ambitious merchant engaged in legal trade whenever it could be made financially rewarding. In the 1760s, for example, the House of Hancock shipped tons of potash to England. British authorities encouraged the import of this colonial product which served as a basic ingredient in the manufacture of glass, soap, drugs, and explosives.

Government contract work provided some of Hancock's greatest profits. Such contracts were common during the periods of war which punctuated the eighteenth century. In addition to acting as a commission agent supplying British forces with food and equipment while they campaigned in America, Hancock found other ways to profit from wars. For example, he might serve as a banker for British officials located in the New World, exploiting his many overseas contacts to expedite financial transfers. When war broke out in 1739 between Spain and England, Hancock and his associates sent out privateers to prey on Spanish merchant vessels in the Caribbean. Trade with the French West Indies and Holland proved particularly profitable during the early stages of this conflict, but when France herself entered the fray on the side of Spain in 1744, it became extremely hazardous. Always the opportunist, Hancock rounded up supplies for Massachusetts Governor Shirley's successful campaign to capture the French fort at Louisbourg on an island at the mouth of the St. Lawrence River. After England returned Louisbourg to France at the 1748 Treaty of Aix-la-Chapelle, Hancock continued as a major supplier for the British construction of a military outpost at Halifax, Nova Scotia.

Having suffered through a generally depressed period in the early 1750s, Hancock once again benefited from the outbreak of the French and Indian War. With the return of peace in 1763, British taxation schemes began to intrude on the activities of merchants, particularly those operating out of Boston. Thomas Hancock died in 1764, leaving his nephew and heir, John Hancock, to face these new difficulties. An intelligent and well-trained businessman, John Hancock owed much of his prominence and wealth to the activities of his energetic uncle.

Although Thomas Hancock appears to have been a remarkably successful merchant, his story is by no means unique. Many other colonists rose from humble origins to positions of wealth and influence. To cite a more famous example, Benjamin Franklin, like Hancock, had started out as a poor apprentice in Boston. One does not usually consider Franklin a merchant, but he engaged in many commercial activities. In conjunction with his printshop in Philadelphia, he ran a stationery store and profited from government printing contracts. He also bought shares in ships and even served as a military provisioner during the French and Indian War. As Franklin's example shows, merchants were not confined to Boston but played increasingly important roles in the commercial lives of all of the major cities and settlements in the colonies. Indeed, all sorts of colonists pursued trade beginning with the humble farmer exchanging his produce for necessities. Diversity of activities and nonspecialization characterized colonial businessmen at all levels.

LABOR

Many roads to wealth stretched ahead of enterprising American colonists in the seventeenth and eighteenth centuries, but economic and institutional constraints delayed or slowed progress. The most important of these limitations was the inadequacy of the labor supply. The colonial world was almost exclusively natural or handmade. Rough-hewn cabins, deerskin clothing, plank tables, water-carrying gourds, and many other items of frontier life were crudely carved from the wilderness. Although the colonial lifestyle became more refined as settlements matured, Americans continued to be surrounded by handcrafted items like homespun clothing, utilitarian furniture, clapboard and brick houses, and cast-iron or pewter cookware and utensils. No factories as such existed in colonial America; indeed, factories for mass producing goods were extremely rare anywhere in the world at that time.

Hand labor could only produce so much. A colonial farmer could barely cultivate a dozen acres on his own. A skilled joiner required weeks to complete a single article of furniture. If a farm wife spent all of her "spare" time spinning, she might at the end of a year produce enough yarn to weave into a single change of linens and clothing for her family. Where human labor added so much to the value of finished products, a scarcity of workers was bound to limit overall productivity. Never enough hands were available to shape all the furniture, clothing, and utensils desired; never enough backs, shoulders, and legs could be marshaled to work all the land crying out for cultivation.

A chronic labor shortage would hinder American development well into the nineteenth century despite unparalleled population growth in the British colonies and, later, in the United States as well. In absolute terms, the population increased tenfold between 1700 and 1775, rising from about a quarter of a million inhabitants to two and a half million on the eve of the Revolution. Only about one-fourth of the change came from immigration; the high fecundity of the American population and its relatively moderate mortality rates produced the rest. The ample supply of land allowed most American-born whites to become independent farmers. In the towns and cities of the Northeast where apprenticeships were more common, the trainees planned to establish their own shops. Neither farmer nor craftsman was willing to work for others.

Planters and city dwellers wealthy enough to hire workers therefore had to rely largely on the services of recent immigrants or slaves. About half of the whites who came to America carried with them a burden of debt. In the 1600s most immigrants came from England where the indenture system was well established. Apprentices signed legal contracts called indentures in which they agreed to work for a master for a set period of time. To pay for the costs of their transportation to the New World, individuals with no prospect of employment in England signed indentures obligating them to work, on the average, for four years. The ship captain or agent who paid for the worker's passage would then sell the labor contract to an American employer. Costs varied according to the skills a worker might have. Some leading colonial families traced their roots to indentured servants who had completed their contracts and then energetically gone to work for themselves.

Immigrants from other parts of Europe took up some of the slack when the number of indentured servants coming from England declined after 1700. A hun-

INDENTURES

The first item is the legal record of a 1688 indenture agreement. In the second, dated 1680, an already indentured servant agrees to remain in service for an additional year in return for certain benefits. Both servants wished to avoid farm work, which many found demeaning.

Roger Jones Servant to Mr. William Churchill Comes and adknowledges that hee is freely Willing to Serve his Master Seaven yeares from his Arival, The said Churchill promising that hee will imploy his said Servant in the Stoar and other his occasions and not imploy him in Common workeing in the Ground.

John Talbert Servant to mr. Richard Willis Comes in Court and Acknowledges to Serve the Said Willis one Compleate Yeare more then by his Indenture Expressed, in Consideration the Said Willis doth promis to keep the Said Talbert Constantly at the Shoomakers Trade and not to worke in the ground and also to give the Said Talbert a New Searge Suite Shooes Stock and hatt more then the Law Enjoynes att the time of his Freedome.

(Reprinted in Warren M. Billings, *The Old Dominion in the Seventeenth Century, A Documentary History of Virginia, 1601-1689*, [Chapel Hill: University of North Carolina Press, 1975], pp. 27-28.)

dred thousand Germans from the Rhineland and an even larger number of Scotch-Irish came to America seeking religious toleration or economic opportunity. Some signed indentures before they left, others took passage on credit, hoping to find a sponsor when they arrived in the New World. Many of these impoverished immigrants discharged their debts by signing contracts much like indentures and then working to "redeem" their freedom. Called redemptioners, they served their masters in the same status as did indentured servants.

The terminal nature of the indentures meant that they were, at best, a short-term solution to the labor needs. Slavery provided a more permanent alternative. The first shipload of workers from Africa dropped anchor at Jamestown in 1619, and thousands more arrived over the next century and a half. Their position in colonial society lacked clear definition for some time, but, by the late seventeenth century, most blacks had become legally defined as the chattel property of their masters. The slaves were thus trapped in what amounted to lifetime labor contracts.

The earliest arrivals were so different culturally from the whites that they were difficult to train. Over time and particularly among slaves born in the colonies, these problems faded. Because living conditions were better in North America than in other colonies, natural increase among the slaves eventually supplied most of the new members of the labor force. The growth rate of the slave population kept pace with and even exceeded that of the whites in certain locations.

The distribution of slaves from south to north paralleled the agricultural spectrum. Slaves constituted a majority of the population in South Carolina in the mid-1700s, while just under half of the inhabitants of Virginia were black. Only a third of Maryland's population worked in bondage, and further north the percentage of slaves to whites declined rapidly, averaging around 5 percent. The extensive use of slave labor in the southern colonies suggests that blacks were essential to the production of export crops like rice, indigo, and tobacco. The plantation economy remained in an immature stage before 1800, however, its full development to come later when cotton became king. That system will be examined more closely in a subsequent chapter.

MONEY

No matter how poor or wealthy they were, all American colonists suffered from the inadequacies of the monetary system. At first glance, one might be inclined to blame an unfavorable balance of trade for the perennial shortage of money in the colonies. They were, after all, economically dependent regions, and the Parliament in London passed laws specifically designed to keep them that way. Once the initial settlements had been established in North America, however, their drain on British capital resources moderated. The extensive trading activities of American merchants and ship captains guaranteed that a good deal of American produce entered either Caribbean or European markets, helping to pay for the continuing flow of imports into the colonies.

The manner in which both international and imperial trade occurred, however, certainly contributed to the monetary crises. The colonists found it particularly difficult to obtain or retain the hard currency so highly prized in this era. The British government's mercantile philosophy dictated that the realm's specie should be kept at home. Indeed, the colonies were expected to add to the Mother Country's store of bullion. Because sterling was most valuable for making purchases from England, British coins flowed back to London virtually as soon as they arrived in America. Colonists kept their accounts in pounds, shillings, and pence but they saw precious few of them throughout the whole colonial period.

The pinetree shilling briefly served as an alternative to British hard currency. First minted in Boston in 1652, this coin was issued sporadically until the royal government specifically prohibited it in 1684. The colonists found another substitute in the great variety of foreign coins they collected from their trading ventures beyond the limits of the British Empire. Spanish dollars or pieces of eight (consisting of eight reals or "bits") had become widely distributed by the time of the Revolution. All too often, of course, foreign gold and silver coins chased their British cousins across the sea to be exchanged for goods in England.

Because the Massachusetts government that mounted an invasion of French Quebec in 1690 had no cash to pay for its military supplies, it issued £7000 in paper currency. These bills were essentially promissory notes, I.O.U.s to be redeemed from future tax revenues. Issuing paper notes became common throughout the colonies, particularly in times of military crises. Most colonial currency quickly deflated in value, especially when irresponsible governments insisted on printing very large amounts of currency. Debtors favored this deflation, though, and they often delayed paying their obligations until they could obtain cheaper monetary instruments in the future. Colonial attitudes about their paper currency were mixed, and many Americans were quite annoyed when the British government refused to certify it as legal tender in New England in 1751. A similar prohibition extended to all of the colonies thirteen years later.

No such legal obstacle blocked the use of personal promissory notes. An individual lacking paper money or specie to pay his debts might write out a note or bill of exchange promising to make good on it in the future. If he had a good credit rating, his note might pass through the hands of several people, each of whom could endorse it, just as one currently endorses a check. Such notes might circulate for extended periods of time before being presented for payment. Instead of money, some private bills of exchange referred to specific quantities of a commodity and thus substituted for the actual transfer of goods from one person to another.

The exchange of commodities, either physically or on paper, was another widespread substitute for cash. Commodity money often won full governmental sanction. Tobacco served as money in Maryland and Virginia, lumber in New Hampshire, and grain and meat in the Middle Colonies. Salaries, contracts, and wages were frequently quoted in commodity terms, but commodity prices fluctuated widely, causing the value of one's contract or pay to vary accordingly.

The bartering of goods and services was undoubtedly the most important way in which exchanges took place in colonial America. One tends to think of barter agreements as a rural phenomenon, but city-based merchants engaged in them as well. A shopkeeper like Thomas Hancock received all sorts of goods in exchange for his wares. He then transferred these goods to others for services or more useful commodities. His dealings with the Mother Country also involved commodity exchanges. The American merchant would send a shipload of goods to England and request his agent there to trade that cargo for the items he wished to import.

Direct, value-for-value commodity exchanges were seldom possible, so merchants and shopkeepers used accounting systems to keep track of each individual's debts and credits. Book credit, as it was called, offered a means for carrying out exchanges without constantly balancing all accounts. A merchant who dealt with several customers and agents could periodically square accounts by transferring credits and obligations from one individual's column to another within his own books. The colonial businessmen who performed this service were essentially acting as bankers for their customers, although the debts and credits they shifted about might never have taken the form of specie or currency. Because their accounts might involve customers, other merchants, and agents both in the colonies and in foreign ports, book credit facilitated worldwide exchanges.

The absence of a reliable money supply obviously did not force the colonists to wallow in poverty. Instead, its importance lay in the barriers it posed to the free and profitable exchange of goods and services. Monetary shortages and instability would continue to hamper American businessmen, workers, and farmers right through the Revolution, an event that generated a financial catastrophe greater than any the Americans had yet experienced.

TRANSPORTATION

Getting to America was always easier than getting through America. Primitive transportation technology combined with the wilderness environment imposed serious limitations on land transportation. The only way to go most places overland was on foot or horseback, and these means were obviously inadequate to move many goods. Wagons of various types existed, but the roads were crude and ill-maintained even within cities and towns. Pioneers who settled along the frontier or in the valleys of the Appalachian Mountain chain risked being completely cut off from outside commerce and communication.

Waterways therefore served as the major colonial avenues of commerce. The population clung to the eastern coast of North America, penetrating into the interior primarily along navigable rivers that allowed contact with seaborne transportation. The British settlements in the New World maintained a vital shipping umbilical cord to England. This 3000-mile life line carried people, food, animals, housewares, and building materials to the colonies. The transplanted Englishmen there gathered, dug up, caught, or produced goods to ship back home.

The amount of trans-Atlantic trade is striking given the difficulties it involved. Items destined for shipment to England had to be collected at coastal loading points. The broad, meandering tidewater rivers along the Chesapeake Bay were quite useful in facilitating the export of bulk agricultural products. No one could have afforded to ship a relatively inexpensive commodity like tobacco to England if it not been grown close to the water's edge. Once potential exports had been collected on shore, they had to be loaded and then spend many weeks or months at sea. At the other end, they were unloaded, taxed, sorted, warehoused, and redistributed—each step adding to the costs of American products. Colonial planters therefore routinely received much lower prices for tobacco bought at their plantation wharfs than it brought in London after the shipping charges were paid. In a recent historical analysis, Gary Walton and James Shepherd maintain that shipping costs declined substantially, perhaps as much as one-half between 1675 and 1775. So dramatic was the decline, these historians maintain, that it was the most significant factor contributing to the rising level of productivity apparent in the colonial period.

Fortunately for the colonists, the amount of trade within the empire rose year after year, and its character changed as well. In 1700 the American settlements absorbed only about 13 percent of all British exports; by 1770 they imported fully one-third of all British goods shipped overseas. In monetary terms, colonial imports from England rose from an annual average of £509,000 in the decade of the 1720s to £1,704,000 in the 1750s. The importance of the American colonies as markets for manufacturers and merchants in the Mother Country was obviously growing both in absolute and relative terms in the years prior to the Revolution. Export figures show a corresponding rise in the importance of America as a raw materials supplier. In 1700 the British gathered from America just under one-fifth of all the overseas goods they imported. Seventy years later American exports were nearly twice as significant, with the home islands relying upon the New World for 37.4 percent of their imports.

As shipping became more reasonable and reliable, though never really inexpensive, it encouraged regional specialization. Differing geographic and climatic conditions in the colonies also contributed to specialization as did technological, capital, and population differences between them and the Mother Country. It was not always efficient. Beaver pelts traded in New York for a few pennies might return to the colonies manufactured into hats priced at ten times the cost of their American raw materials. The high distribution costs an inefficient and primitive transportation system levied on all colonial trade thus undermined some of the benefits of relying on colonies to be markets for manufactured goods in England. The existence of millions of potential customers living in a geographically contiguous area would be a major inducement to industrialization within the United States in the future, but that vast market potential remained underutilized before 1800. Americans were far more likely to consider England their ideal trading partner and supplier than they were an adjacent colony much closer at hand. But this belief was not necessarily irrational given the high costs of intercolonial transportation when compared to those of trans-Atlantic shipping.

LIFE IN THE EMPIRE

Each colony had a unique origin. The royal government served as the source of charters and land grants, but it initially provided very little supervision or regulation. King Charles II's restoration to the throne in 1660 coincided with and was itself a major cause for the developing of a British imperial policy that later became known as mercantilism. Adam Smith first used the term in describing the British empire in his book *The Wealth of Nations* (1776). The founder of classical economy theory, Smith disapproved of the "mercantile system" in which the central government attempted to determine the patterns for all economic activity within its realm. Imperial planners hoped to develop protected, preferably British-owned colonial sources of exotic goods so they could be obtained without exporting specie. Mercantilists measured the wealth of a nation according to the stock of bullion—gold and silver—it had accumulated. Specie flowed into the British empire whenever it engineered a favorable balance of international trade. That was more likely to occur if most essential goods could be obtained from within the empire and valuable exports could be delivered outside at high profits. The theoretical mercantile empire Adam Smith described would be carefully regulated, with each individual and sector performing its assigned functions that added to the nation's store of precious metals. The British system as it existed in fact strayed far from this ideal.

Parliament's first major legislation with a colony-wide impact was the Navigation Act of 1651. At that point, Dutch traders handled an inordinate share of the whole world's commerce and, in the process, siphoned off considerable British wealth. The act would prevent Dutch profiteering by specifying that all trade within the empire must be conducted on British-owned and British-manned vessels. New England shipowners and seamen qualified as British in this definition, though, so they benefited from this attempt at trade monopolization.

A second navigation act passed in 1660 reaffirmed the British character of shipping within the empire and added another key mercantile concept. It enumerated or listed certain colonial goods which were to be shipped directly to England, Ireland, or another British outpost. West Indian sugar, tobacco, cotton, indigo, ginger, and certain natural dyestuffs were the commodities to be strictly reserved for the British market. An immediate effect of the Enumeration Act was a glut of tobacco in the empire since the British economy simply could not absorb the high annual yields from Virginia and Maryland. Tobacco prices therefore remained depressed for years, severely limiting planters' income. British merchants meanwhile collected tidy profits by selling the popular American staple in Holland and other European countries. Not incidentally, these foreign sales helped add specie to the nation's vaults.

ELIZA PINCKNEY

The Navigation Act of 1660 enumerated indigo as a valued colonial product, but it was not successfully grown on the continent until Elizabeth Lucas Pinckney singlehandely introduced it in the 1740s. Her father was an army officer who moved from post to post, so Eliza Lucas spent her early years in London and the West Indies even though the Lucases had owned land in South Carolina for decades. In 1738, her family settled at Wappoo Plantation, a 600-acre tract near Charleston with a workforce of twenty slaves. In the very next year a conflict called the War for Jenkins' Ear broke out between England and Spain. Army orders sent Eliza's father back to the Caribbean, so he had to leave his sixteen-year-old daughter to run both Wappoo Plantation and to supervise the overseers who managed his other properties.

While Eliza participated fully in Charleston society and continued to pursue her academic studies, she worked to develop a new export product.

The trade war in the Caribbean, which would continue for nine years, had closed off the normal market for Carolina rice. Using seeds her father sent from the West Indies, Eliza experimented with indigo. Earlier attempts to grow the plant on the mainland had failed, but the determined young woman patiently tried one type of seed after another in a variety of growing conditions. She also hired a dye maker to build vats and process the crop. Her efforts produced a meager twenty pounds of dye cakes in 1741, but three more years of experimentation enabled her to determine the proper cultivation techniques to set the industry on its feet. She graciously shared her seed and expertise with neighboring planters, and the colony exported 135,000 pounds of high quality dye stuff in 1747 and more than a million pounds in several subsequent years.

The agricultural innovator had become Mrs. George Pinckney in 1744 when she married a prominent local attorney. The couple's two sons, Thomas and Charles Coatesworth Pinckney both became famous as diplomats and vice-presidential candidates after the Revolution. Eliza traveled a good deal herself but returned periodically to manage the plantations she and her husband owned. She also passed her spirit and skill on to her daughter, Harriot, who lived most of her life in South Carolina as a prominent landowner and plantation manager.

Parliament struck again at Dutch traders in a third navigation act, often referred to as the Staple Act of 1663. The colonists imported goods from many sources, so the royal government decided both to regulate and profit from this trade. The Staple Act ordered that all items destined for the New World were to be collected in England first, then dispatched to the colonies on British ships. Once again, American shippers stood to prosper from the exclusion of foreign competition. Imports now sometimes cost more than before, however, particularly those that first had to be brought to England, unloaded, assessed port duties, and then reshipped. But lax enforcement of this and later navigation acts kept their impact on the Americans within reasonable bounds.

A new conception of the colonies' function developed in the early 1700s. They were to be much more than simply sources of exotic goods and raw materials. The rapidly growing overseas population represented potential consumers for British industries. Politicians and business leaders favored the creation of home manufactures in England, Ireland, and Scotland to produce goods for export not only to foreign countries but also to the colonies.

The abundance of agricultural opportunities in America already distracted colonists from doing their own manufacturing, but the British government wanted to discourage it even more. The chief British commercial weapons in international trade wars were the quantities and quality of the woolen goods it exported. To maintain control of this trade, Parliament passed the Woolens Act of 1699 that prohibited the establishment of commercial wool-processing operations in the American colonies. Raw wool could be exported to England where the weaving and finishing of the cloth would take place. Parliament similarly outlawed commercial hatmaking in the colonies in 1732, and the Iron Act of 1750 discouraged the fashioning of items out of iron. Mines and ore-reduction operations stretched from New England to the Carolinas by the mid-eighteenth century. Although a substantial amount of pig iron was exported each year, the Iron Act decreed that rolling, slitting, and forging mills should remain strictly British ventures.

None of the navigation or manufacturing acts particularly disturbed most of the colonists, so the British imperial yoke rested easily on America. In many ways, the colonial environment fostered free enterprise in a most fundamental sense. The absence of ingrained or traditional social, landholding, and political structures left the settlers very much on their own. Natural rather than institutional factors had the greatest impact on the behavior of the colonists. The labor shortage, the inadequate monetary situation, and the cumbersome and costly transportation system influenced colonial economic and business developments much more than did mercantilism.

Colonial America thus provided something of a test case of how a free enterprise system would affect the people. One obvious result was that individuals could move rather easily from one class or caste level to another. New World freedom allowed an apprenticed bookseller in Boston to become one of America's leading businessmen and an apprenticed printer in Philadelphia to achieve international fame as a scientist, philosopher, and statesman. Heredity and formal education counted for little in taming the wilderness; individual initiative and drive determined who would succeed or fail.

Not everyone became wealthy. An individual's ambition might be limited to carving out a self-sufficient farmstead for a family. Recent historical studies suggest that very quickly a considerable variance in the distribution of wealth came to characterize the colonial population. Alice Hanson Jones based her figures on probate records from the 1770s, but similar patterns were well established much earlier. As is the case in present-day America, she found that a small number of wealthy individuals controlled a disproportionate share of the property and capital in the colonies. In New England, for example, the richest 10 percent of the population possessed about 40 percent of the region's wealth, while the richest 10 percent in the Middle Colonies controlled nearly one-third of the resources. An even more substantial concentration of wealth may have rested in the hands of the richest group of southerners.

The colonial test case suggests that equality of opportunity certainly does not assure uniformity of success. Wealth was the key to social status in the colonies. And, because wealth usually stemmed from successful entrepreneurial activity or agricultural endeavors, social class was closely related to business acumen. Profitable trading, expansion of land holdings, development of new enterprises, clever speculation—all of these marked the successful colonist.

The free enterprise system in which the colonists operated made them quite susceptible to the liberal political doctrines of the age. Americans who had left behind rigid, aristocratic societies in Europe already enjoyed much greater freedom than their relatives across the Atlantic. When, after 1760, the British government suddenly seemed intent on altering the colonists' relationship to the empire, the Americans reacted with increasing emotion to real or perceived infringements on their freedom. In one sense, then, the subsequent "revolution" was less directed at change than it was an attempt to protect the lifestyle under which the colonists had prospered in the late colonial period.

THE PARTING OF THE WAYS

The treaty that ended the French and Indian War in 1763 added vast new territories to British North America. France surrendered its claims to all of Canada north of the Great Lakes as well as to the central part of the continent east of the Mississippi River. Debts stemming from the conflict and the expenses of military occupation of this expanse made the colonies a major drain on the royal treasury. British administrators thought it only reasonable that the colonists should be taxed to pay their own expenses. But growing resentment greeted each succeeding revenue measure: the Sugar Act, the Stamp Act, the Townshend Acts, and the Tea Act.

The resulting revolutionary zeal was in no way confined to radicals or propertyless malcontents. The Tea Act of 1773, for example, created an imperial monopoly for the British East India Co., an arrangement that excluded American shipowners, merchants, importers, and distributors from the business. John Hancock had maintained the profitable tea importing business his uncle Thomas had begun, so it was quite logical for him to paint his face and put on a feather headdress to participate in the Boston Tea Party. Much more was at stake, of course, than the tea merchants' livelihoods. Parliament apparently felt it could arbitrarily determine the whole context of business in North America—and to the benefit not of American but of British and East Indian entrepreneurs.

As the center of the protests over the tea monopoly, Massachusetts received quick retribution. Parliament passed a series of Coercive Acts in 1774 that closed the port of Boston and imposed martial law on the whole colony. American radicals proclaimed these punitive laws "Intolerable Acts" and urged all the colonists to join in protesting against them. The military confrontations at Lexington and Concord soon followed.

Were British imperial policies so oppressive as to cause a revolution? Despite the American rhetoric, the financial drain on the colonists was negligible. The war was less a result of actual economic harm than it was a response to the British failure to understand or accept the colonists' point of view. In their eyes the advantages of imperial membership—and there were still a great many in 1775—had become less important than the principle of self government. The most compelling patriot arguments often related less to what the British had actually done than to what they might do. American development had been so unrestricted up to that point that even minor regulations seemed intolerable.

Beyond the stated grievances lay other factors that made independence a viable concept. The continental population was approaching the three-million mark, and it included a number of leaders fully able to govern without outside supervision. Ironically, the British government decided to strengthen its authority in America just when the colonists had become capable of making it on their own. Unfortunately it took six years of conflict and two more of diplomacy to convince the British of that fact.

The Revolutionary War had a characteristically American hand-crafted look to it. Flexibility and adaptability were crucial. Yesterday's farm wagon served as today's supply transport. In the hands of a skilled frontier hunter, a long-barreled muzzle-loader could be more deadly than any weapon issued to a British regular. Mounting a couple of light cannons converted a cargo sloop into a commerce-destroying privateer. George Washington's Continental Army resembled an irregular force, maintaining a weak perimeter around a much more powerful British occupying army. The United States' victory was concocted out of tenacity rather than brilliance, evasiveness rather than confrontation, and spirit rather than materiel.

Fortunately, the fighting was by no means continuous. Conventional military strategy placed such an emphasis on maneuver that combat occurred on only a handful of days. The geographic extent of the war was equally misleading. Most areas of the country rarely saw soldiers, and even then they might only be scattered groups of militiamen going to or coming from some distant skirmish or battlefield. Farmers planted their crops fully confident they would be around to harvest them. Few buildings were destroyed. Indeed, the Continental Congress specifically ordered General Washington not to put the torch to any area he could not defend.

The war thus had a remarkably minor impact on the day-to-day lives of most Americans. At the same time, the conflict offered numerous opportunities for those enterprising Americans willing to tackle them. They employed a variety of techniques for exploiting the conflict and adapted quickly to changing conditions. The wartime economy enabled a good many businesses and entrepreneurs to prosper far beyond their expectations.

TRADE AND THE SEALANES

When the Revolutionary War began, both the Continental Congress and the British Parliament suspended economic relations and thereby closed the traditional trade channels. But America could not so easily overcome its economic dependency; its prosperity had always been closely associated with a brisk foreign trade. Fortunately, American products retained their overseas appeal. Chesapeake Bay tobacco, for example, set the standard of quality for the world. If American merchants could take over the lucrative tobacco trade, they could profit handsomely.

But losses seemed unavoidable at the war's outbreak, particularly in the Northeast. Both fishing and transoceanic trade collapsed. Unemployment loomed

for both vessels and crews until the Continental Congress and the state governments came to the rescue with privateering commissions. Investors provided all
the financing for privateers who hunted for booty along the sea lanes. Any British
vessel they captured could be sailed to a friendly port where its cargo and the ship
itself were sold and the proceeds divided among the privateer's owners and crew.
Those who funded a voyage usually collected half or two-thirds of the profits while
the crew split the remainder. Several states established prize courts to give the enterprise a legal facade, and the Continental Congress established a court of appeal.

Privateering became a booming business, inflicting some $18 million worth
of losses on the British merchant fleet. Massachusetts alone commissioned nearly
a thousand ships, and the Continental government issued nearly 1700 authorizations during the course of the war. Nor was privateering a short-lived phenomenon; dozens of American corsairs were still on the prowl in 1782. This legally
sanctioned piracy thrived in part because the entry of France and Spain into the
conflict after 1778 spread the Royal Navy's forces very thin. The English fleet
simply could not defend the Caribbean outposts and the home islands and simultaneously provide effective convoy service for merchantmen. British authorities
dealt very harshly with the many offenders they captured, but the financial returns
for a successful privateering mission were so great that businessmen continued to
invest eagerly. At the same time, this early form of profit-sharing encouraged
thousands of American seamen to risk their lives or long imprisonment in maritime
guerrilla warfare.

Shipping: The key element in colonial commerce. (Library of Congress)

GEORGE CABOT

Joseph Cabot of Beverly, Massachusetts, founded a modestly successful distilling, trading, and fishing business. Well before the Revolution, he relinquished control to two of his sons, John and Andrew, while a third, younger son, George, attended Harvard. The boy dropped out of school, however, and went to sea as a cabin boy on one of the family's ships. He quickly mastered the seafaring art and, at the age of nineteen in 1770, he conducted a typical colonial trading voyage as captain of one of the family's schooners. He carried Massachusetts rum and cider to Virginia to trade for wheat. Then he headed for Bilbao, Spain, where he exchanged the grain for silk handkerchiefs he could market in New England.

His visit to Spain was hardly accidental since the Cabots had been trading there for years. These Spanish connections proved very valuable during the Revolution. The family's fleet of privateers obtained good prices for the British prizes they sold to trusted agents in Bilbao. The Cabots also armed their merchant vessels so they could run the British blockade and defend themselves on the high seas. The scarcity of American products in Europe and the widespread demand for just about any imported goods in the United States guaranteed high profits on both legs of a voyage.

The Cabots emerged from the war as one of the leading merchant families in the Northeast. George Cabot pooled his resources with one of his brothers in a partnership so profitable that he retired from it in 1785. His social and political status rose in conjunction with his business prominence, so the local Federalists chose him to represent the state in the U.S. Senate in the 1790s. After returning home, he served as the president of both a bank and an insurance company. George Cabot and his family thus exemplify those ambitious Americans who took full advantage of the opportunities the Revolutionary War created.

The distinction between a privateer and a regular cargo ship became rather blurred. Prudent shipowners and captains armed their vessels before weighing anchor for a trading voyage to the West Indies or beyond. British efforts to blockade the long, intricate American coastline were perfunctory in the first years of the war, so blockade runners enjoyed a high rate of success. Astute traders who reached friendly ports recognized the advantages of bringing back less bulky luxury goods that were in great demand. Linens, tableware, lead, sailcloth, and similar items might be irrelevant to the war effort, but they commanded premium prices.

The French connection proved extraordinarily helpful. Even before the Continental Congress officially declared independence, it sent agents abroad to seek assistance from England's archenemy. While conducting his own affairs in London, Virginia businessman Arthur Lee made the first informal contacts with Pierre de Beaumarchais. This opportunistic French courtier obtained supplies from French military arsenals and created a dummy company to transport them to the West Indies. American blockade runners then ferried the war goods from the Caribbean to the beleaguered states. France is estimated to have supplied 90 percent of the gunpowder the rebels used in the first two years of the war. The enterprising Beaumarchais tried to bill the United States for goods he had obtained free from his own government, but, like many a more legitimate claimant, he received no compensation from the Continental Congress.

French aid mushroomed after Benjamin Franklin convinced Louis XIV's government to sign a formal treaty of alliance in February 1778. Simultaneously, the wily American diplomat negotiated a Treaty of Amity and Commerce. It offered a partial answer to the nagging question of whether the United States could function commercially as an independent entity. The treaty included a most-favored-nation clause, granting the United States the same trading rights other countries enjoyed with France.

Neutral Holland proved friendly as well. Tons of military and civilian goods arrived at the tiny Caribbean island of St. Eustatius, and American merchants took full advantage of the booming trade with this conveniently located supply point. By 1780 the British government's patience with the Dutch was exhausted, so it declared war on Holland. The Royal Navy then raided the island warehouse and closed it down. By that time, though, American ships were calling at a much wider assortment of ports than they ever had under British rule. Even Spain opened her West Indian possessions to direct commerce with the United States. Overall, American trade recovered much of its prewar vigor from 1778 to 1782.

This appearance of health proved to be fleeting as Great Britain methodically reestablished her dominance as a seapower. The blockade along the American coastline became increasingly effective, throttling both privateering and commercial shipping. The fishing and whaling fleets, idled for so many years, would be slow to recover. The depression that settled over the maritime interests of the United States lingered long after the peace treaty had been signed.

THE HOME FRONT

The changing external trading patterns inevitably affected domestic commerce as well. The predominantly hand-labor economy of the colonies lacked the flexibility to adapt quickly to new demands, so the American people had to do without many manufactured and processed goods. Some items they had formerly imported could be produced locally, but seldom as efficiently or cheaply. The war lasted so long, though, that the continuing shortages encouraged a transfer of energies to lines of endeavor that otherwise might not have developed in the United States until much later.

Americans devoted considerable political and philosophical attention to the problem of stimulating "home manufactures." Both the Continental Congress and the state legislatures hoped their respective constituencies would strive for economic self-sufficiency. Because so many manufactured and processed products had come to be considered necessities, the governments' interest lay in expanding American enterprise beyond its basic extractive and agrarian emphases.

In the eighteenth century, the term "manufacturing" did not connote large-scale, capital-intensive, integrated factories. Instead it might involve several stages of handwork on a single product at different locations. Raw materials might initially go to a mill or processing plant. Logs, for example, would typically be shaped into planks and timbers at a local lumber mill. After this initial processing step, skilled or semi-skilled workers had to do the bulk of the finishing work with hand tools. Colonial manufacturing operated on a small scale in a number of isolated, independent shops or homes. This highly differentiated structure persisted through the Revolution, although the number of workers and work places increased in response to the premium prices being offered for scarce manufactured goods.

The United States ended up producing a surprising diversity of goods during the Revolution. Woolens had always been Great Britain's chief export commodity, and the North American colonies had been a prime market. But after 1776 the value of the finished wool Americans imported dropped to less than 2 percent of its prewar total. Fortunately, the raw material was readily at hand, allowing American families to spin, weave, dye, and tailor their own wool textiles. They sometimes combined locally grown wool and flax into a rough, durable fabric known as linsey-woolsey. Textile manufacturing took place in urban as well as rural locations. In Philadelphia alone, 4000 women were fashioning yarn, cloth, and clothing in their own homes. American textile processing remained very primitive, though, in comparison to the much more efficient technologies already in use in England.

The domestic iron industry was more advanced. On the eve of the Revolution, the thirteen colonies together were producing one-seventh of the whole world's output of crude iron. Pockets of ore strewn throughout the colonies allowed iron mongering to continue during the conflict in a number of locations. Most villages supported a forge and blacksmith, a versatile craftsman who could create all sorts of useful products. Cast iron pots, pans, tools, and utensils supplied the domestic demand for metalware. New techniques that Americans developed for manufacturing nails and card teeth were so successful that the states were able to supply all of their own needs by the end of the war. Military contracts encouraged some investors to establish major foundries in Massachusetts and elsewhere, and the quality of their products matched those of the goods imported from abroad. Americans also rapidly developed domestic supplies of gunpowder.

The United States had also become virtually self-sufficient in two basic consumer commodities by 1783. Paper mills sprang up in a variety of locations and leather goods of all sorts were produced in quantity. Americans were less successful in their efforts to avoid importing glass, silverware, high-grade textiles, brass, clocks, and machinery. An individual craftsmen like Paul Revere might be able to match the work of any English silversmith, but the level of artistic quality in America generally remained inferior to that coming out of England's apprentice, journeyman, and master system. Only a handful of American craftsmen had joined guilds by end of the Revolution, testifying to the scarcity of highly-skilled artisans.

Despite successes in a few isolated areas, the United States made only modest progress in its drive to achieve economic independence during the Revolution. Worse yet, wartime shortages and price inflation exerted an unhealthy, hothouse influence on American manufacturing. Once these artificial stimulants disappeared, as they did in the postwar Confederation years, interest in manufacturing quickly declined as well. A full-scale industrial revolution would be delayed on this side of the Atlantic for some time.

Manufacturing therefore offered ambitious American only limited opportunities for financial gain during the Revolutionary War. Merchants continued to be the most effective exploiters of commercial opportunities. An experienced colonial businessman with a diversity of interests, partners, and contacts was ideally equipped to profit from the conflict. As would be the case in later wars, those who supplied the military forces were in very good positions to prosper.

The Continental Congress was the largest, but by no means the only organization making military expenditures. At first, it used a commission rather than a contract system to obtain supplies for the Continental Army. The individual or firm which provided the requested materials collected a commission of between $2^1/_2$ and 5 percent of the price paid for them. This procedure might have worked effectively in calmer times or if accurate records could be kept, but it was a clumsy, unreliable method of obtaining goods. Unscrupulous or careless merchants could easily doctor their books to inflate their commissions or otherwise overcharge the government. Worse yet, the rapidly inflating currency Congress used to pay most of its bills could leave an honest merchant with unrecoverable losses. Congress replaced the commission system with contracts in 1781. Under that arrangement, merchants signed contracts at set prices for specific items, their profits, if any, deriving from their skill as purchasing agents.

The new system was designed to eliminate some of the earlier abuses, but war profiteering definitely occurred. Merchants lacking integrity or short on patriotism felt no qualms about supplying both sides in the conflict. The royal government deliberately paid its soldiers and contractors in hard currency, a shrewd policy at a time when specie alone maintained universal acceptance as a medium of exchange. Many ambitious merchants therefore avidly bid for commissions to supply the occupying forces. Other Americans were equally eager to obtain British specie. Soldiers usually purchased food locally so farmers could sell their produce directly to British quartermasters. Frequently, of course, the farmers reappeared later as militiamen taking potshots at the very customers who had recently lined their pockets.

While individual farmers could escape detection, many of the businessmen who traded with the enemy had to leave the country as the war drew to a close. Their departure significantly altered the business and commercial structure of the newly independent country. Influential individuals often lost substantial amounts of property. Sir William Pepperall, for example, abandoned nearly thirty miles of the Maine coastline as well as substantial lumbering and shipbuilding operations. The Massachusetts state government confiscated most of his property to sell to those who had demonstrated their patriotism to the new order. At the same time, the contracting business, privateering, and other war-related activities had augmented older fortunes or created new ones. The owners of these fortunes would lead the nation's enterprises in its uncertain future.

REVOLUTIONARY FINANCIER: ROBERT MORRIS

Although he earned the nickname "Financier of the Revolution," Robert Morris lined his own pockets while conducting the infant nation's business. A personally engaging, astute entrepreneur, he had been born in Liverpool, the son of a tobacco agent with American connections. The Morris family came to Maryland in 1747 when Robert was thirteen. He later moved to Philadelphia to become an apprentice in Charles Willing's commercial firm. The young man's intelligence, energy, and charm earned him, at the remarkably early age of twenty-three, an invitation to form a partnership with Charles Willing's son and heir, Thomas. During the next several years, the firm of Willing and Morris expanded its interests and influence world wide. Robert Morris achieved such prominence that he won election to a seat in the Pennsylvania Assembly in 1775. That body then sent him as one of its delegates to the Continental Congress.

Morris made no secret of his intention to pursue his personal business activities during the war, and his seat on the Secret Committee of Commerce placed him in an ideal position to keep informed about changing opportunities. After all, the commerce committee's major responsibility was to locate, purchase, and deliver materials to the Continental Army. Not surprisingly, the partnership of Willing and Morris handled orders for around $850,000 of the slightly more than $2 million Congress spent from 1775 to 1777. The mix of public and private business Morris and other merchants conducted, often on the same trading vessels and under complex partnership arrangements, generated some concern about conflicts of interest. Political rivals eventually charged that Robert Morris had illegally sought compensation from Congress for goods actually lost along with one of his ships engaged in private business. He successfully defended himself in this instance, and his scrupulous accounting practices kept his record clean.

The activities of American diplomatic agents illustrate the complexities of business in this period. An ambitious New Yorker named Silas Deane left his seat in Congress in 1775 to go to France armed with a diplomatic commission to obtain financial and material support for the American Revolution.   Simultaneously, Deane intended to establish his own mercantile firm as well as to serve as an overseas agent for Willing and Morris. Robert Morris kept Thomas Bingham on his payroll after Congress sent him to the French Caribbean island of Martinique as its

Robert Morris. (The Pennsylvania Academy of Fine Arts)

diplomatic representative. These and other overseas connections proved vital in locating goods for the army, so Congress and the public were quite tolerant of them.

Morris left Congress in 1778, at the same time his firm disbanded, to devote full attention to his private affairs, but Congress pleaded for him to return three years later to help resolve its intractable monetary problems. During the war, the familiar colonial expedients of promissory notes, personal bills of exchange, and bartering were employed. Symbolic of its break with the British Empire, the Continental Congress abandoned the pound sterling and adopted the dollar as its basic monetary unit. It was defined as having an intrinsic weight of 88 hundredths of an ounce of silver and an exchange value equal to four shillings sixpence. But silver and gold were so scarce during the war that most cash transactions involved paper money of some sort.

Some currency was quite literally worth less than the paper it was printed on. Both the state governments and the Continental Congress mounted military campaigns and, to supply and pay their troops, issued bushels of paper notes, ostensibly redeemable out of future tax revenues. Because the Continental government had no reliable source of income, its promissory notes were even less sound than those of some of the states. The Continental currency fiasco began in 1775 when

Congress printed notes amounting to $6 million. The states were expected either to redeem these notes directly or collect them to donate in lieu of taxes to the central government. Few did either. The unredeemed, unwanted notes remained in circulation.

The mass of unbacked notes caused severe price inflation. One consequence of that development was that Congress had to make each succeeding issue larger than the last just to buy the same quantity of supplies. In 1779 alone, Congress cranked out just under $125 million in new notes, and the grand total for the five-year period stood at $226,200,000. As early as 1777 traders were discounting Continentals by a factor of 3:1 in comparison to specie. The discount rate steadily rose, hitting 7:1 in 1778, 42:1 in 1779, 100:1 in 1780, and an appalling 146:1 in 1781 when they ceased to have any market value whatsoever.

Morris was summoned to deal with this morass after the Articles of Confederation had been ratified in 1781. The articles did little to expand the authority of Congress but did lead to a more structured bureaucracy. Morris assumed the key administrative post of Superintendent of Finance. Fortunately, some much-needed foreign financial assistance arrived just when he took up his new duties. France, Spain, and Holland ultimately gave or loaned the United States several million dollars worth of sound money. Rather than waste it trying to retire the existing mass of inflated Continental currency, Morris used it to back new notes he signed personally. Some of these were payable immediately, others were warrants which

A Continental note, issued in 1779. (Library of Congress)

specified a future date for redemption. He adroitly managed to redeem these so-called Morris Notes at full value, preventing them from depreciating like the earlier Continental notes had.

From his first days in office, the Superintendent of Finance urged Congress to create a central bank to help the nation establish a sound national monetary system. His bank should also encourage wealthy Americans to participate in the central government's financial activities and, consequently, build public confidence in the Confederation. To attract investors, he was more than willing for the institution to handle their private banking needs. Here is another example of the easy alliance between public and private business so characteristic of Robert Morris.

Congress readily accepted the proposal, issuing a preliminary permit in May 1781 and a formal charter on December 31, 1781. The Bank of North America opened its doors in Philadelphia, the Confederation's capital, under the presidency of Thomas Willing, Robert Morris's long-time business partner. An initial stock subscription of $400,000 was solicited, to be paid only in specie. Because each share in the bank had a $400 price tag, only wealthier Americans could invest. Stockholders were to elect directors and receive dividends on their shares based on the bank's overall profits. The enterprise seemed headed for failure, however, when private citizens bought only $70,000 worth of stock. Morris came to the rescue by investing $254,000 of the specie France had just loaned to the Confederation government. It was a wise move. In addition to stimulating the national economy, the bank paid a 14 percent dividend to its shareholders, including the federal government, in 1783.

The first major banking institution in America, Morris's bank performed a number of functions. It made short-term loans to businessmen and collected interest on them. It accepted private and public deposits, but, instead of establishing checking accounts, the bank handed out its own engraved banknotes in exchange for deposited funds. These bank notes circulated throughout the United States, being used to buy goods and settle accounts, thus serving the same purpose as the private bills respected merchants had issued. The institution's sound reputation made its notes universally acceptable at face value. In addition to being its largest stockholder, the Confederation government was the bank's most substantial client. Based on its deposits, Congress could use banknotes to pay its soldiers and their suppliers. The bank's respectability coupled with the notes Morris personally endorsed as Superintendent of Finance finally put the Confederation's public credit on a sound basis.

The bank's popularity waned as the wartime crises eased. The peace treaty in 1783 halted the supply of specie from abroad, and foreign loans had been crucial to the maintenance of the bank's reserves. As its resource base shrank, the bank had to reduce the scope of its operations and become very cautious. Only citizens with impeccable credit standing could obtain loans. Correctly perceived as a rich man's institution, the bank did serve its favored customers well. Merchants from Massachusetts and New York therefore studied its operations and convinced their respective state legislatures to charter similar institutions in New York City and

Boston. These three banks constituted the cornerstones for the sprawling banking industry that serves American and international customers today.

The troubles Morris's bank encountered after the war were symptomatic of the nation's general financial malaise. Fighting and sacrifice had won political independence from the British Empire, definitively ending the colonial phase of American history. But to ensure an independent, prosperous future for themselves, the American people had to create a viable political framework. The Constitution that emerged out of the controversy and turmoil of the 1780s would provide such a framework and allow for much greater growth and prosperity than even the most optimistic patriots had anticipated.

READING SUGGESTIONS

An older, exhaustive general history of the colonies is Charles M. Andrews's *The Colonial Period of American History* (4 vols., 1934-1938). Daniel J. Boorstin's *The Americans: The Colonial Experience* (1958) focuses upon the people who settled in the New World. Comprehensive textbooks include Curtis P. Nettles, *The Roots of American Civilization* (2nd ed., 1963); John C. Miller, *The Rise of the American Colonies* (1977); and Clarence Ver Steeg, *The Formative Years, 1607-1763* (1964). Shorter surveys of the same era are Bradley Chapin, *Early America* (1968); Benjamin W. Labaree, *America's Nation-Time 1607-1789* (1972); and Darrett B. Rutman, *The Morning of America 1603-1789* (1971). Stuart Bruchey's *The Roots of American Economic Growth, 1607-1861* (1968) provides good coverage of colonial enterprise. Two recent works that draw on newer scholarship are Edwin J. Perkins, *The Economy of Colonial America* (1980) and Gary Walton and James Shepherd, *The Economic Rise of Early America* (1979).

Focusing on particular aspects of colonial enterprise are two classical reference works: Lewis Gray, *History of Agriculture in the Southern United States to 1860* (2 vols., 1933) and Percy Bidwell and John Falconer, *History of Agriculture in the Northern United States, 1620-1860* (1941). Carl Bridenbaugh's *Cities in the Wilderness* (1938) is equally helpful for urban developments. The impact that reduced shipping costs had on colonial productivity is described in *Shipping, Maritime Trade, and the Economic Development of Colonial North America* (1972) by James Shephard and Gary Walton. The rise of the mercantile class is the focus of Bernard Bailyn's *The New England Merchants in the Seventeenth Century* (1955). Michael Kammen dissects the complex relationships in England that affected American trade in *Empire and Interest: American Colonies and the Politics of Mercantilism* (1970).

The colonists themselves have received a great deal of attention. James Henretta's *The Evolution of American Society, 1700-1815* (1973) is a thought-provoking multi-disciplinary study of the period. In *The House of Hancock: Business in Boston, 1724-1771* (1945), W. T. Baxter not only describes his subject's life but how he handled his diverse business affairs. Two good biographies of Byrd are R. C. Beatty, *William Byrd of Westover* (1932) and Pierre Marambaud, *William Byrd of Westover, 1674-1744* (1971). Another major colonial dynasty is the subject of Byron Fairchild's *Messrs. William Pepperrell: Merchants at Piscataqua* (1954). Elise Pinckney has edited *The Letter Book of Eliza Lucas Pinckney, 1739-1762* (1972).

The early steps toward revolution are the subject of Bernhard Knollenberg's *Origin of the American Revolution 1759-1766* (1960) and of Arthur M. Schlesinger, Sr.'s *The Colonial Merchants and the American Revolution* (1918). In *Agents and Merchants* (1965), Jack M. Sosin discusses the relationship between colonial agents' activities and the development of British policies between 1763 and 1775. Oliver M. Dickerson, in *The Navigation Acts and the American Revolution* (1963), rationally assesses the effect these laws had on the colonies as do Robert W. Tucker and David C. Hendrickson in *The Fall of the First British Empire* (1982).

Two useful works on the Revolutionary War itself are Esmond Wright's *Fabric of Freedom* (1961) and John R. Alden's *The American Revolution* (1954) which focuses on the actual conflict. One of the most respected American historians is Richard B. Morris whose book *The American Revolution Reconsidered* (1967) does just that. John C. Miller's older works examine the underlying economic and social developments in two volumes: *Origins of the American Revolution* (1943) and *Triumph of Freedom* (1948).

Reginald A. East, in *Business Enterprise in the American Revolutionary Era* (1938), examines particular individuals and regional developments. Clarence Ver Steeg's *Robert Morris, Revolutionary Financier* (1954) provides thorough coverage of that figure's public and private activities. Curtis P. Nettles' broad-ranging work *The Emergence of a National Economy* (1962) is a good source for basic economic information. Drawing on her many studies of the colonial and Revolutionary periods, Alice Hanson Jones published *Wealth of a Nation to Be: The American Colonies on the Eve of the Revolution* (1980).

Chapter 3

PROGRESS IN THE NEW REPUBLIC 1783-1819

The American people won their political independence in the Revolutionary War, but whether the United States would be capable of full economic independence remained to be seen. A number of factors threatened to hamper that objective. Some, like the chaotic monetary system, were internal in nature. Others were external, many of them associated with a worldwide conflict that began in 1793 and persisted for a quarter century. After avoiding involvement for many years, the United States finally lost its patience and declared war on Great Britain in 1812. In many ways this second war was a replay of the first Anglo-American conflict, but it did help the United States end its overly dependent relationship on Europe.

In the new nation's early years, technological and societal changes came about rather slowly, allowing Americans to pursue familiar lines of endeavor in rather traditional ways. Agricultural exploitation of the land continued to stimulate settlement and speculation; merchants continued to profit from the carrying trade. As long as the land and the sea offered plenty of opportunities, few were inclined to innovate.

When international conflicts began disturbing trade patterns, though, they also encouraged new types of enterprise. Elements essential for such endeavors stood ready to be used in innovative ways. Capital resources, developing technologies, expanding markets, improving transportation, changing labor patterns, and versatile business and management structures enabled energetic entrepreneurs to prosper. Although Americans approached industrialization cautiously at first, its ability to increase productivity soon led it to supplant traditional manufacturing methods. Patriotic optimism swept the nation through its second war with England and into a period of exhilarating postwar prosperity. The Panic of 1819 then dampened the nation's spirits, but it could not erase the progress already made.

POSTWAR GROWING PAINS

The political compromises that led to the ratification of the Constitution in 1788 put down firm foundations for expansion. The delegates who allocated economic and jurisdictional power in the Constitution did so on the basis of their common experiences under the Confederation. Many Americans had considered the early 1780s to be an era of excesses: too free enterprise, too little restraint, too weak a government.

When the Revolutionary War ended, the United States experienced first a boom, then a disheartening depression. After this brief rollercoaster ride, the economy moved ahead at a more deliberate pace. A similar pattern of instability would follow future conflicts. Peace removes the lid of wartime constrictions and introduces a period of overheated activity. Once the pent-up pressures evaporate, an abrupt decline occurs. At that point, the economy moves toward a natural peacetime equilibrium. The post-Revolutionary War boom dissipated by the late summer of 1784. Depressed conditions set in for a year or so, but many sectors of the economy had recovered by 1786.

British merchants anxious to reestablish their former dominance of American foreign trade fueled the early boom. English manufacturers had run up large stockpiles of items they usually supplied to the American market, but the fighting had prevented regular shipments. British exporters were eager not only to reduce their inventories but to nail down favored positions for future trade. Hundreds of merchant ships battled their way across the Atlantic. Very low prices and attractive credit arrangements encouraged American merchants and importers to buy far more than they should have. Warehouses in eastern ports were soon bulging and exerting further downward pressures on prices. For a few months Americans could buy all sorts of items, sometimes at prices well below production costs. The war meanwhile had restricted American output so that goods for shipment to England were comparatively scarce. These scarcities gave domestic exporters higher prices than usual for whatever they could find to sell.

All too soon, the good times ended. American merchants scrambled to reduce their heavy indebtedness to British agents. Within a few months of the peace treaty, most of the specie in North America had gone to settle accounts in England, and the continuing scarcity of potential exports exaggerated the trade imbalance. The English merchants who had enthusiastically extended credit to Americans found themselves in serious straits. Several British trading firms collapsed when they could not collect what was due from their trans-Atlantic customers.

The persistence of low prices soon hurt Americans more than it helped them. By late 1784 few potential customers had money to buy anything no matter how attractive the price. New England was particularly hard hit because of its heavy reliance on the carrying trade. Falling prices also injured farmers by reducing the value of their crops and livestock. Despondency replaced the exuberance of the previous months. The finger of blame was pointed in many directions: the state governments, the Confederation government, creditors, debtors, merchants—even women with extravagant tastes were accused of causing the depression. But the most popular scapegoats by far were the British merchants and traders who had ignited the brief period of postwar prosperity and then seemed bent on dowsing it again.

Fortunately, the people could survive the worst of any depression since 90 percent of them were engaged in agricultural pursuits in this period. Most farms could be operated on a subsistence basis. Soon glimmerings of recovery appeared, especially in the South where tobacco and rice continued to be in demand overseas. Some healthy changes accompanied the growth of southern farm production after the war. Many planters streamlined their operations, hoping to avoid the indebtedness that had burdened them in the colonial period. Some farmers diversified, planting corn and other grains to export in addition to the traditional staples.

The primitive American manufacturing system had been particularly sensitive to the postwar instability. Most American textile producers could not meet the price reductions that the British dumping imposed, so only the most efficient survived. Ironically, the disappearance of foreign exchange after 1784 relieved much of the pressure. American manufacturers could sell their output as long as they did not insist on the hard currency British sellers demanded. The depression therefore nudged the United States toward manufacturing self-sufficiency. Paper and glass manufacturers held their own, and craftsmen lobbied sympathetic state legislators, urging them to erect protective tariffs.

Shippers and merchants took advantage of their freedom from British navigation rules. The New England fishing, whaling, and shipbuilding trades gradually revived. France, Spain, and Holland had all profited from their wartime trade with the United States, and each country wanted to maintain high levels of exports and imports. The French were especially interested in continuing the direct purchase of tobacco and other American products they had earlier obtained only through British reexporters. Tobacco accounted for 70 percent of the American exports to France in 1781, and large quantities of this high quality product also flowed directly to Holland.

Closer to home, United States trade with the French and Dutch West Indies flourished. Americans exported far more food and other commodities to these than they imported sugar, creating a very favorable balance of trade. While direct commerce with Spain remained legal after the war, the Madrid government closed down United States access to its Caribbean possessions. The British West Indies also officially remained off limits. Many unscrupulous traders ignored these restrictions. Americans continued to smuggle goods in and out of other empires just as they had before and during the Revolution.

Seeking new market opportunities, a group of businessmen including Robert Morris dispatched a ship, aptly named the *Empress of China*, around Cape Horn in 1784. The vessel completed the long voyage to Hong Kong in good time, sold its cargo of ginseng root at a fat profit, and sailed home loaded with attractive and exotic articles. Many other ships followed this pioneering enterprise as part of a continuing trading connection with the Far East. Some New Englanders established permanent warehouses and offices in Hong Kong, where they rubbed shoulders with other seafaring traders from all corners of the globe.

On the whole, then, the American people found independence a mixed blessing. Some made money, others lost it; some enterprises thrived, others failed. Whatever an individual's occupation or status, each felt something could be done to improve it, although there was no overall agreement on what remedy should be applied. Merchants wanted beneficial navigation laws, craftsmen felt higher tariffs would protect their jobs and wage levels, and farmers wanted a reliable, expanding money supply. Nor could they agree about who should provide these benefits. Some favored the state governments which, being closer to the people, might be more responsive to persuasion. Others insisted that prosperity could only come with the establishment of a strong central government serving the diversity of individuals and interests in the United States. One area of consensus did exist: most Americans felt that government at all levels was responsible for encouraging economic development and enterprise.

THE GOVERNMENTAL DIMENSION

Political ideology infused many aspects of Revolutionary America. Opposition to external controls had led the Continental Congress to issue its Declaration of Independence in 1776. While that document disposed of one government, it did not specify what should replace it. The states quickly proclaimed themselves sovereign and viewed with suspicion attempts at a broader, national government. After literally years of debate and delay, they ratified the Articles of Confederation that assigned a few limited functions to the Continental Congress. As George Washington complained, the Confederation was a "rope of sand."

Many Americans wanted to leave it that way, but a younger generation of revolutionaries led by Alexander Hamilton and James Madison were eager to strengthen the central government. They hoped that it could, for example, resolve the nation's debilitating financial problems. Conflicting state monetary policies were obviously disrupting and discouraging commerce. Assigning taxation authority to the central government along with tools to manage the money supply became a major goal of those known as Federalists in the 1780s. They also favored centralized control over western lands to clear the way for full development of wilderness regions.

Federalists also deplored interstate rivalries that led to discriminatory taxation. Shippers naturally preferred to unload their cargos in New Jersey, Connecticut, or Delaware which levied no duties on foreign imports. New York and Pennsylvania depended upon tariffs to generate revenue and to protect home manufactures. Logic dictated, therefore, that they collect customs duties on any goods "imported" from neighboring, tariff-free states. New York went a step further in 1787 when it began taxing New Jersey and Connecticut farm products that New Yorkers claimed were draining currency out of Manhattan. New Jersey retaliated with a heavy tax on the Sandy Hook lighthouse that guided ships safely into New York harbor. Making the central government responsible for tariffs and the regulation of interstate commerce would presumably benefit all parties and eliminate these destructive domestic trade rivalries.

An attempt to end bickering over interstate river navigation started the process of finding a comprehensive solution to all these problems. Because Virginia's boundaries extended across the southern entrance of the Chesapeake Bay, she could collect transit fees from Marylanders shipping goods down the Potomac River to the open sea. George Washington generously invited representatives of the two states to his mansion at Mount Vernon for discussions in 1785. Because other states with river borders had similar concerns, the Mount Vernon group issued invitations for a river navigation conference at Annapolis the following year. Five states sent delegates who agreed with Hamilton and Madison that a thorough review of the Confederation's powers was in order.

The Confederation Congress therefore notified all of the states that a convention would meet in Philadelphia in the summer of 1787 to consider additions or alterations to the Articles of Confederation. The assembled Federalists decided that a completely new frame of government should replace the document drafted in the stress of wartime. They closed the doors and began the secret discussions that ultimately produced a new constitution for the United States.

Long before historian Charles Beard published his famous economic interpretation of the Constitution in 1913, other historians examined the question of what motives and prejudices activated the members of the Philadelphia convention. Beard's answer was that, being property owners and businessmen, the delegates were primarily concerned with creating a government that would protect their interests. More recently, Forrest MacDonald has argued that the delegates really represented the prevailing agrarian interests in the new nation. Other historians rate economic determinism far lower than other factors in determining the nature of the Constitution. Yet one of Beard's fundamental points remains quite persuasive: self interest definitely played a central role in shaping the document and in assigning within it the responsibilities and powers to the executive, judicial, and legislative branches of the government.

Several parts of the Constitution have fundamentally influenced business and commerce over the years. The document addressed the Confederation's financial problems by granting Congress authority to collect taxes to pay off its debts and to fund "the common defense and general welfare" of the United States. The federal government was given exclusive authority to coin money and regulate its value. Additional techniques for defining the character of money in the United States and for regulating its supply would develop soon after the new government was inaugurated.

The recent history of interstate strife convinced the delegates in Philadelphia that the central government must have exclusive judicial authority to handle claims of one state against another and of private parties against the states. Furthermore, Congress was assigned the task of regulating both domestic and foreign commerce. States no longer could discriminate against one another or attract foreign shipping with low or nonexistent tariffs. The commerce clause drafted to prevent such abuses has become one of the most versatile government tools for manipulating business and economic affairs.

The Constitution also specified items essential to a well-managed and efficient nation. By ordering the government to maintain a postal service and post roads throughout the country, it recognized the importance of nationwide communication. The delegates also sought to encourage "the progress of science and useful arts" through patent and copyright protection. To cover eventualities not mentioned elsewhere, Congress could make "all laws which shall be necessary and proper for carrying into execution the foregoing powers." Controversy over the use and abuse of the necessary and proper clause would continue for decades.

Perhaps the most remarkable aspects of the Constitution were its brevity and its ambiguity. Even after hundreds of hours of debate, negotiation, and compromise, the document's architects admitted they could not resolve some issues. They produced a sketch rather than a detailed blueprint for government. That left the Constitution flexible enough to adapt to changing conditions.

The impassioned discussions over ratification and the transition from confederation to constitutional government overshadowed some of the document's most important consequences. The new arrangement, for example, established a large, unified national marketplace. Petty jealousies at the state level would be less likely to hinder economic development in the future. The gulf between the North and the South that would tear the nation apart in the 1860s was as yet only a minor rift. Businessmen could now operate in a stable, predictable national rather than a local arena. After years of uncertainty, the fundamental extent and nature of the nation's central political framework had been resolved.

MONEY MATTERS: ALEXANDER HAMILTON

One of the first and most pressing items on the new government's agenda was to deal with the monetary mess. As the economy sunk into its postwar depression, neither private bankers, state governments, nor the Confederation government seemed capable of easing the suffering. Specie was extraordinarily scarce but depreciated Continental and state bills continued to flood the country. To the financially unsophisticated, issuing still more paper currency seemed a good idea. If more money were in circulation, it should generate price inflation which would ease the burden of debtors. Fearing just that outcome, creditors and most businessmen opposed any attempt to increase the money supply artificially.

Each state developed its own strategy for coping with the national financial crises. Rhode Island won the dubious distinction of generating the largest blizzard of paper notes. Pennsylvania issued a limited amount of paper currency to pay interest on its debts and to loan to real estate buyers, but this move caused a fateful collision with the Bank of North America. The bank's officers refused to redeem the newly issued bills at face value, arguing quite reasonably that they simply were not equal in value to the bank's specie-backed notes. The legislature retaliated by temporarily annulling the bank's charter in 1785. It had to limp along until 1791 on an alternative authorization from the state of Delaware. A Massachusetts decision to insist on a strictly hard money system stimulated an even more disturbing crisis. A Revolutionary War captain named Daniel Shays gained notoriety as the supposed leader of the farmers who rioted in favor of paper money. The legislature stubbornly refused to retreat, and it authorized the governor to use military force to put down Shays' Rebellion in 1786.

The sea of unpaid Revolutionary War debts seemed likely to drown any rescue attempts that President Washington might mount after he took office in 1789. But the Constitution had given the central government several tools for dealing with money matters. All that was needed was a plan of attack. The exceptional young man the president chose to head his Treasury Department was never short of ideas. Alexander Hamilton had already distinguished himself as an army officer, a lawyer, and a politician. Now his skill as a financial statesman would be tested.

His first objective was to establish public faith in the United States government's credit both at home and abroad. He then hoped to use this sound credit rating as the foundation for expanding the money supply. Ultimately, he wanted to use government capital to encourage the diversification of the American economy so that it would become largely self-sufficient. He outlined his plans in a series of reports he delivered to Congress.

The first was the *Report on the Public Credit* he prepared in December 1789 when the public credit could hardly be said to exist at all. The United States owed more than $10 million to the foreign governments which had provided loans during the Revolutionary War. Approximately $40 million more remained outstanding in the form of Continental bills, warrants, and bonds. Hamilton also favored the federal government's assuming responsibility for the $25 million that certain states had borrowed to fight the war. Rather than pay off all these debts, the treasury secretary suggested that revenue from the tariff system be placed in a fund to make interest payments on the outstanding obligations. If bondholders received the interest, he argued, they would consider their investments sound and the market value of government notes should rise to match their face value.

Alexander Hamilton. (The Old Print Shop)

Many opposed this package of proposals. Some objected to Hamilton's re-fusal to arrange immediate payment of the debts. On the other hand, speculators who had bought land on contract in anticipation of paying with depreciated Continental notes disliked the Treasury plan because it would bring these notes up to par. States that had already paid their war debts objected to a federal bail-out of those that had not. Perhaps the most telling criticism was that Hamilton's scheme would reward currency speculators who had purchased devalued Continental and state notes at a fraction of their cost. James Madison was particularly concerned that the original recipients of the notes should be fully compensated.

Despite these objections, Congress approved Hamilton's plan. The federal government assumed responsibility for state war debts, Hamilton established a fund to pay interest on all government obligations, and tariffs were raised to provide the necessary funding. To clean up the bookkeeping and reduce interest rates, the Treasury exchanged new federal bonds for the old Continental and state paper. The interest burden was so large that Hamilton later asked that an excise tax be levied on domestically produced liquor and tobacco. Resentment over the liquor tax later fomented the Whiskey Rebellion of 1794, but a combination of import and excise taxes financed most of the federal government's operations for over a century.

To handle the government's financial affairs and create sound paper money, Hamilton urged Congress to charter a national bank. Although the Constitution made no mention of banks, enough congressmen accepted Hamilton's loose con-structionism in 1791 to charter the Bank of the United States for twenty years.

Like its predecessor, the Bank of North America, the new institution was located in Philadelphia and was privately owned and managed. The government did buy one-fifth of its stock, though, and therefore had a good deal to say about its operations. The initial capitalization of the bank was supposed to be $10 million, one-fourth in specie and the remainder federal bonds. The bank never held more than $6.2 million worth of federal bonds, but it did collect about half of the specie in the country.

Like other banks, the institution could issue notes based on its current deposits. These circulated at par because anyone could exchange them for specie or the bonds on deposit in the bank. Hamilton's use of the public debt as backing for currency converted what most would consider a liability into a genuine asset.

Stephen Girard. (Library of Congress)

The bank was so cautious in issuing notes that the total in circulation never exceeded its current capitalization. Branches located throughout the country enabled the bank to transfer funds from one place to another and provide a clearing house for transactions of all kinds.

STEPHEN GIRARD

Stephen Girard rose from humble origins in Bordeaux, France, to a position as one of the leading bankers in the United States. At the age of fourteen in 1764, he ran away to sea as a cabin boy. Although blind in one eye, he qualified as a licensed sea captain in his early twenties. While he worked for other ship owners, he traded for himself on the side. He seemed to have a Midas touch in many enterprises. One story has it that two wealthy French families living in Haiti loaded all of their possessions on his ship just before being massacred by rebelling slaves. Girard later sold these goods for $50,000. When the British blockade closed the port of Philadelphia, he invested his savings in a grocery and cider-bottling business in New Jersey. Later he reentered the wartime shipping business, and his astuteness as a trader enabled him to accumulate a huge fortune by the end of the war.

As a prominent merchant in Philadelphia, he was just the sort of wealthy businessman Alexander Hamilton's financial programs were intended to attract. Girard responded by becoming one of the federal government's staunchest supporters. He was furious when Congress failed to renew the charter for the Bank of the United States in 1811, and he determined to keep it operating anyway. He bought its building and assets for $1.2 million and ran it as a private firm called, simply, The Bank of Stephen Girard. When Treasury Secretary Albert Gallatin despaired of selling bonds to finance the War of 1812, Girard purchased most of a multimillion-dollar issue himself. He did, of course, get them at a steep discount that guaranteed him a huge profit when the government made good on the bonds after the war. Girard stepped in again in 1816 to buy $3 million worth of the slow-selling stock of the Second Bank of the United States. His support was crucial in setting that institution on its feet.

In the 1820s, Girard retired to a farm in South Philadelphia. A crusty, individualistic man with few close friends, many considered him to be the epitome of a miser. In doing so, they were overlooking the fact that he had almost alone run a free hospital for cholera victims in the 1790s and had financed many other charitable projects. When he died in 1731, he willed $6 million, the bulk of his estate, to build a school and home for orphaned boys. Stephen Girard thus set a pattern for the ambitious industrialists and financiers of the future who would devote their vast fortunes to philanthropic purposes.

Despite its generally benevolent influence, the bank was unpopular in many quarters. Its stabilizing influence thwarted those who had hoped to benefit by using depreciated money. Hamilton's political foes criticized it even when it was working well. After 1800 the government managed to pay off so much of the public debt that the bank's capital base eroded. Treasury Secretary Albert Gallatin, who served under Presidents Jefferson and Madison, recognized the bank's usefulness and lobbied for a renewal of its authorization. But the rechartering legislation lost by a single vote in 1811, forcing the United States to enter its second major war in the next year without the services of a central bank.

WILD LANDS

Some of the most outspoken opponents of the bank's sound money influence were to be found among the nation's horde of land speculators. Buying and selling land had, of course, been a primary preoccupation of all Americans since the earliest colonial days. Indeed, one of the pre-Revolution period's most strident grievances had been the Proclamation Act of 1763, in which Parliament had prohibited white settlement beyond an arbitrary line drawn along the western slopes of the Appalachian Mountains. Administrators in London working with inaccurate maps actually had little impact on American behavior. The western boundaries of many colonies had never been accurately defined anyway so settlement along the western frontier had always had extralegal aspects. The region was simply too attractive to be left undisturbed.

White penetration of this wilderness began with traders and hunters. These hardy souls coexisted with the Indian population in the interior. They brought the Native Americans goods they could not otherwise obtain and benefited in turn from the Indians' prowess at hunting and trapping game. Soon prospective farmers were heading west as well. Several hundred families illegally moved into the area in the five years after the Proclamation Act's passage. Frontier families typically included enough children, uncles, aunts, and cousins to defend themselves while they brought the land under cultivation.

The formation of larger groups of pioneers reduced some of the risks of settlement. Land companies like the one that Judge Richard Henderson and his associates created in 1775 promoted group migration. Appropriately named the Transylvania Company, Henderson's organization convinced the Cherokees to surrender title to a large block of land in present-day Kentucky. The company then rounded up settlers to move into the region, planning to sell them land on which to establish farms. Among many other agents, the company engaged the services of a famous hunter named Daniel Boone. He had previously tried to move his family into Kentucky but had turned back when an Indian attack killed some members of his party. Now he built a fortified village at Boonesboro, and the Transylvania Company established other towns surrounded by palisades to ward off attack.

The Revolutionary War dampened enthusiasm for western migration. A few pioneers filtered across the mountains, but a host of legal and political questions remained unresolved. By 1781, however, all colonial claims to the Northwest Territory laying north of the Ohio River had been surrendered to the Continental Congress. That body hoped to pay some of its Revolutionary War debts by selling this land. Before any sales could actually take place, though, the land had to be surveyed. Congress therefore approved an ordinance in 1785 that created a rectangular survey system based on meridians and baselines that was subsequently extended across the continent.

Government surveyors immediately began locating and marking various parcels of land for sale. Congress established a base price of one dollar per acre but hoped that public auctions would generate higher returns. The government also stipulated that the minimum purchase at an auction must be one section or 640 acres. Few pioneers heading west had $640 in cash to make the minimum purchase, so the government's rules actually encouraged farmers to settle in the wilderness without paying anything at all. Preemption, or squatting as it was called, had occurred in the past and would continue to be a major means of frontier settlement even after the passage of the Homestead Act in 1862.

Squatters, of course, did nothing to solve the government's financial woes, so Congress looked favorably on any group that promised to do so. During the war many soldiers had been paid either in land bounties or with depreciated Continental bills they were told could be cashed in for government land. Groups of veterans gathered, intent on redeeming their paper promises. At the same time, speculators formed companies that would attempt to resell any real estate they obtained from the government at much higher prices than they had paid.

Land company lobbying persuaded Congress to pass the Northwest Ordinance of 1787. This legislation created a territorial government for the wilderness. It also prohibited the introduction of slavery and proclaimed that no less than three nor more than five states could be carved out of it. In addition to abiding by these rules, prospective settlers in the Ohio Valley were keenly aware of the danger from the unpredictable Indians.

Despite the risks, many Americans were eager to settle in the fertile Ohio Valley. Of the many groups organized to exploit the region after the war, the most famous were the Ohio and the Scioto Companies. The Ohio Company Associates solicited a capitalization of $1 million on the basis of which they convinced Congress to sell them a huge tract of 1.5 million acres at well below the established price of a dollar an acre. The Reverend Manasseh Cutler was the company's most valuable asset, personally maneuvering Congress into approving the sale to his company and getting the Northwest Ordinance passed to protect its interests. In the spring of 1788 General Rufus Putnam led a band of forty-eight settlers to the mouth of the Muskingum River where they established a community later named Marietta. Like the early colonial settlements in the seventeenth century, this little outpost suffered hardships and mismanagement, but it survived and grew.

The Scioto Company was far less successful. Many Ohio Company investors also bought shares in the highly speculative Scioto Company. William Duer headed this venture which obtained a congressional pledge of five million acres. To raise money to pay for even a small fraction of this vast tract, the company advertised abroad. The company's highly deceitful publicity campaign convinced 500 French citizens to take passage to America. Whey they arrived they discovered that the Scioto Company actually had no land to give them. The Ohio Company provided a temporary refuge, but Congress finally had to pass a special act appropriating 25,000 acres to insure that these hoodwinked settlers got the land they thought they had bought. Duer and his mismanaged company collapsed in 1792, helping to set off a general business panic.

THE LURE OF THE OHIO COUNTRY

To attract European settlers, William Playfair wrote this description for the Scioto Company. Englishman Playfair had never been to America, so his description is even more extravagant than William Byrd's comments quoted in the previous chapter.

. . . a lovely plain between the Muskingum and the Scioto Rivers, where would be found a salubrious climate in which frost, even in winter, was almost unknown. The great river skirting it, destined in a few years to become the leading channel of territorial commerce, was called "The Beautiful," and was so crowded by large and delicately edible fish that they struggled in piscine rivalry first to swallow the baited hook or achieve entanglement in the fatal meshes of the net. The native trees produced spontaneously great quantities of delicately flavored sugar, a peculiar plant yielded ready-made candels, coal, iron, lead, silver and gold were jutting out of every stony ledge, and a single boar and sow in the course of three years would produce three hundred pigs without the least care being taken of them.

(From *Prospectus pour l'etablissement sur les revieres d'Ohio et de Scioto en Amerique* [Paris: De l'Imprimerie de Prautt, 1789-90].)

Robert Morris had frequent business dealings with Duer, and the famous financier exhibited many other symptoms of a virulent case of land speculation fever. After attending the Constitutional Convention, Morris became a U.S. Senator representing New York. That position gave him insider knowledge about upcoming land deals. After some informal cooperation, he pooled his considerable resources with those of John Nicholson and James Greenleaf in the North American Land Company, the largest of its kind yet formed. The company eventually amassed claims to six million acres in several states and territories. The company's worldwide network of agents peddled its scrip that could be redeemed for acreage anywhere in the company's vast holdings. By the late 1790s, however, the tax burdens on unsold property and the shortage of potential settlers had become acute. Both Morris and Nicholson landed in a debtor's prison where Nicholson died in 1800, leaving behind $12 million in unpaid obligations.

Other prominent politicians and businessmen also engaged in risky speculation involving both federal and state lands. Georgia created one of the most convoluted legal tangles. In 1790 the state legislature granted 25 million acres of land to four companies for a pledge of $200,000 in state obligations. The hitch was that these lands lay in the "Yazoo Territory" along the east bank of the Mississippi River in what are now the states of Alabama and Mississippi. Georgia could scarcely claim clear title to this region, especially since the Spanish government insisted that it was still part of its Florida colony. The claim problems made no immediate difference since all four of the companies failed to fulfill their contracts to the satisfaction of state officials.

In 1794 a group of northerners including Albert Gallatin, the future secretary of the treasury, promised to pay in specie for a renewal of the Yazoo contract. After considerable lobbying and outright bribery, the Georgia legislature agreed to offer thirty million acres in return for half a million dollars. Morris's North American Land Company was one of the many groups that rushed to obtain a portion of this vast territory. The price was so low, about a penny and a half an acre, that astute speculators made huge profits overnight by reselling their shares to those who had missed out on the first round. The deal roused a political storm in Georgia, though, and a year later the chastened legislature voted unanimously that the contract had been unconstitutional and was therefore void.

The speculators refused to accept defeat, so litigation over the Yazoo lands continued for years. In 1810, the United States Supreme Court finally ruled in the case of *Fletcher* vs. *Peck* that the federal Constitution prohibited a state government from interfering with a contract—even if that contract had resulted from the bribery of state officials. By that time, the territories of Mississippi and Alabama had long since passed out of Georgia's control. Because the federal government now owned the disputed lands, the U.S. Congress had to liquidate the Yazoo claims with federal land scrip valued at over $4 million. Most of the claimants at that point were speculators who had bought the old shares at reduced prices from the original purchasers.

As the eighteenth century gave way to the nineteenth, land speculation continued, but often on a more rational scale. Perceptive investors recognized the dubious value of wild lands, hundreds of miles beyond the settlement line. Furthermore, alterations in federal land-sale policies favored individual buyers rather than speculators. The size of a minimum purchase at federal land auctions declined over the years to just forty acres in 1832. The minimum bid of $1.25 enabled a prospective settler to buy a farmstead for as little as $50. To stay in business, land companies had to offer lenient mortgage terms with low down payments.

JOHN CLEVES SYMMES

While others formed companies to promote settlement along the Ohio River, John Cleves Symmes behaved like one of the colonial proprietors. A sense of command came naturally to a man with a distinguished military record in the Revolutionary War. He volunteered for service with the New Jersey militia, quickly rose to the rank of colonel, and fought bravely in several battles. Like many other soldiers, he had been paid with Continental bills and land warrants. He hoped to convince a number of his fellow veterans to cash their own warrants in on land in a frontier settlement he would manage.

Another attribute Symmes brought to the project was his political prominence. After serving in several state positions, he became one of New Jersey's delegates to the Confederation Congress in 1785, just in time to participate in the drafting of its famous land ordinance. Congress later named him a territorial judge under the provisions of the Northwest Ordinance of 1787. In that same year, Symmes toured the Ohio River as far west as Louisville and returned brimming with enthusiasm. He asked Congress for a grant of two million acres between the Miami and Little Miami Rivers, but long before it had been approved, he was earmarking parcels of land for anyone willing to give him Continental paper or warrants. He used these to begin making payments for the grant, reduced to one million acres and formalized as the Miami Purchase in 1788.

Symmes had already gone to the frontier, leaving behind agents and advertisements to attract others to join him. Like most colonizing ventures, delays, shortages, injuries, and Indian problems abounded. Symmes personality caused additional problems. Because he insisted on running the venture singlehandedly, he could never pay enough attention to all of the details. He was so eager to entice settlers that he promised attractive parcels to more than one applicant. He also failed to conduct or respect accurate surveys, and conflicting claims and lawsuits piled up as a result of his sloppy management.

Symmes failed to make his payments on time and therefore saw his grant whittled down to a little over 300,000 acres in 1794. He lost virtually all of his own property to creditors and claimants and so had little to leave his heirs upon his death in 1814. Although he certainly fell short of being a great businessman, his drive and enthusiasm for his project were effective in founding Cincinnati, which quickly developed into a thriving commercial enclave in the wilderness.

Another way for speculators to make money was to anticipate where new towns would be located. They would buy likely tracts, carve them into town-sized lots, and offer these lots for sale at much higher prices than the surrounding farm land. Rival groups competed with one another in attempting to attract buyers or to have the government select their undeveloped communities to be county seats. Some towns actually developed as expected, but many other prospective townsites were eventually plowed under.

Land speculation was popular with merchants, bankers, and politicians in the East who enjoyed gambling at high stakes, but it did little to make the land itself productive. The bankruptcies that speculators suffered were a natural consequence of their attempts to squeeze profits out of the land bonanza long before it had ripened. Without the crucial addition of labor, land alone simply could not fulfill the speculators' exaggerated expectations.

TAMING THE LAND

The tools and techniques for turning forests into farmlands changed very little in this period. A pioneer homestead in western Ohio or Tennessee closely resembled the frontier settlements of colonial New York or Virginia. Burning and clearing trees, planting corn among the stumps, cultivating small vegetable patches, and hunting wild game continued well into the nineteenth century. The time needed to transform the wilderness into a commercial farm varied depending upon latitude, climate, and population density, but a typical family could anticipate at least a decade of backbreaking labor. A generation might pass before a farm reached full production.

Inevitably some areas were better suited to agriculture than others. Rural New Hampshire and Vermont had absorbed virtually all the inhabitants they could support by 1810. At that point, the prospect of employment in the region's industrializing towns and cities began to drain population from the comparatively poor agricultural lands. Other New Englanders migrated westward through the Berkshires into upper New York State. There they discovered that much of the prime land along the rivers lay in the hands of speculators or the heirs to its original Dutch owners. Consequently, many new arrivals leased farmland from absentee owners until they had saved enough to buy their own. The superb growing conditions for field and orchard crops there made such an investment well worthwhile.

The Pennsylvania countryside filled in after the Revolution as well, though the mountains running through the middle of the state acted as a trade barrier. Pittsburgh's location on the Ohio River turned it into a thriving market center for farmers west of the Alleghenies. Goods were collected there for shipment down to the Mississippi and beyond. The city also became something of a manufacturing center, as artisans and craftsmen produced household goods and tools to sell to neighboring farmers.

To the south in western Virginia and eastern Kentucky, farming took on a southern aspect with its emphasis on corn and hogs. The pork was often smoked and sold down the river. Those who nestled in the mountain valleys never prospered like the pioneers who ventured into the bluegrass region around Lexington. This was prime cattle and horse country, but individuals wealthy enough to own slaves could also prosper by growing staples like tobacco and hemp. Kentucky entered the Union in 1792 and, four years later, Tennessee broke off from North Carolina to become a separate state. Corn and hog production predominated in the eastern mountainous part of the state, while the west supported a more varied agrarian economy.

Spanish control of the mouth of the Mississippi River restricted the commercial possibilities of the west until the Jefferson administration completed the Louisiana Purchase in 1803. Hoping for a smooth take-over, the United States government recognized all pre-existing legal and real estate arrangements. The Spanish and French Creoles who had lived in Louisiana for generations were therefore able to maintain their social influence and economic power. The growing volume of river and ocean traffic that flowed through the port of New Orleans enabled many an enterprising businessman to become a prosperous merchant. Sugar cane flourished along the humid bayous, and slave labor made many planters wealthy. The fertile silt the great river had deposited throughout its extensive delta produced bumper crops of cotton, a staple destined to dominate agriculture throughout the Lower South.

Limited quantities of cotton had been grown in the region in the colonial era. The sea-island variety was the most popular, with its long, fine fibers and small, smooth seeds. It grew best on the islands laying off the coast of South Carolina and Georgia. Hardier green-seed cotton could thrive almost anywhere in the Deep South. Its relatively short fibers were firmly attached to large seeds, however, and even the most industrious worker could separate little more than one pound of lint from the seeds in a day. In the early 1790s, some growers increased their cotton planting in anticipation of the invention of a more efficient method of removing the seeds. Eli Whitney gained the historical credit for doing so.

ELI WHITNEY

The cotton gin was a simple machine that transformed the American South from a depressed agrarian backwater to a bustling, booming region so cocky it declared itself an independent nation in 1860. The machine also permanently altered clothing styles around the world. But it did not make its inventor rich.

Eli Whitney spent much of his life trying to rise above poverty. As a child he had grown to hate agricultural labor on his father's farm in Connecticut. He much preferred to work in the workshop and, during the Revolutionary War, established a forge there to produce scarce products like nails and pins. But young Eli was too envious of wealth and social prestige to remain a country blacksmith. He took a job as a school teacher and studied hard to gain the academic background and polish he needed to enter Yale. When he graduated at the age of 28 in 1792, he had not only absorbed a good deal of classical knowledge, but he had developed friendships and contacts that would open doors for him throughout his life.

His very first job, in fact, depended on an acquaintance with another Yale graduate, Phineas Miller, who had become a plantation manager in South Carolina. The property belonged to Catherine Greene, the widow of General Nathaneal Greene who had commanded the southern arm of the Continental army during the Revolution. Although Whitney had been hired as a tutor, he observed the operations of the plantation and recognized the need for an efficient way of separating cotton fibers from seeds.

He claimed to have gotten the idea from a cat that reached through a fence for a chicken but came away with a bunch of feathers. On his machine he inserted wire teeth onto a drum that spun around and pulled lint from seeds restrained by wooden slats. It was Mrs. Greene who handed him her hearth brush and suggested that he attach it to the rig to collect the fiber from the rotating teeth. She was so delighted with the invention that she invited her friends over to observe it in operation.

Whitney and Miller were excited, too, and they formed a partnership to exploit the invention. Miller's plan was to locate gins throughout the South to process customers' cotton for a share of the output, just as flour millers did. Whitney headed north, filed for a patent in Philadelphia, and set up a shop in New Haven. Unable to locate enough skilled artisans, he built specialized tools and machines to make component parts. In 1794 he completed his patent application and rushed back to South Carolina with six gins.

It was too late. Catherine Greene's friends had taken the concept away with them and built more or less sophisticated copies of their own. Whitney and Miller immediately entered into an escalating round of lawsuits based on their patent. But southern juries were reluctant to agree that these northern partners should monopolize a concept so crucial to the development of their region. Although Whitney eventually began to collect some royalties, they were never enough to offset the legal costs his partnership had incurred. If nothing else, Whitney learned one lesson: rather than rely on patents to dominate a market, a manufacturer should instead produce as many items as quickly and efficiently as possible. He would apply that lesson in his later manufacturing endeavors.

Once the ginning bottleneck had been broken, cotton cultivation expanded explosively. Prices remained high through the 1790s, averaging thirty-two cents per pound. Even when they declined by a third after 1800, planters could make ample profits. The United States output rose from around 3 million pounds in 1793 to 80 million by 1810, three-fourths of it grown in South Carolina and Georgia.

An Early Cotton Gin

Most of the crop was shipped directly to Europe where both England and France maintained mechanized spinning and weaving facilities. But a substantial amount of the southern cotton found its way north where it served as the primary raw material in the opening stages of the industrialization of the United States.

THE INDUSTRIAL EVOLUTION

The industrialization of the United States seems to have been predestined, but many Americans in the late eighteenth century neither favored it nor saw it as inevitable. The agrarian influence was naturally powerful in a nation where 90 percent of the workforce engaged in some form of farming. As a result the industrialization of the United States came about through a process of gradual evolution. New methods for increasing productivity were truly revolutionary, capable of altering the character first of individual communities, then of states, and finally of whole regions. But the industrialism spread slowly enough in the United States to allow the resilient American people to adjust to it with a minimum of strain.

Household manufacturing was, of course, already widespread. Pioneers built or made all sorts of items by hand. As their settlements matured, though, a few individuals began to specialize. Able to create better quality products at affordable prices, many craftsmen moved from one farmstead or cluster of cabins to the next to find customers for their services. Itinerent spinners, weavers, cobblers, tailors, and other artisans brought the benefits of their skills to those living in isolated areas.

When the population became denser, artisans could find enough work to keep them busy year round in a fixed location. The techniques they employed might differ very little from those of the pioneers, but constant practice and the accumulation of specialized tools increased their productivity. Even a small village might support a shoemaker, a tanner, a blacksmith, and a carpenter. A progressive southern plantation might gain similar efficiencies by assigning particular slaves to perform specialized tasks. Along streams or rivers, water-powered lumber and flour mills processed their raw materials far more economically than an individual household or farmstead could.

A putting-out system characterized many enterprises. Textile producers in the early national period hired women wishing to earn a little income to card and spin yarn in their own homes. Weaving was generally considered a man's work, but many weavers also worked alone on looms in their houses. As the workers in a community became adept, they could produce more cloth than they needed for themselves. Textile manufacturing in private homes became widespread in the Northeast and enabled the region as a whole to export finished goods to other parts of the country.

The manufacturing of more complex products encouraged the establishment of shops where several workers cooperated in finishing a job. Specialization might take place in larger shops where each worker could be assigned tasks at which he was particularly skilled. Even a rudimentary division of labor along the lines Adam Smith described in *The Wealth of Nations* could substantially increase a shop's productivity. The more successful shops were likely to be located in cities where enough customers lived to absorb their output. Paper, glass, candles, hats, stockings, furniture, and other goods of all sorts were produced in artisans' shops.

The putting-out system and shops performed most of the manufacturing in the United States in the first two decades of the nineteenth century. When diplomatic troubles cut off imports, these inadequate systems strained to supply the growing nation's needs. During the long interruption in normal international trade beginning in 1807 and climaxing with the War of 1812, household and shop manufacturing increased in extent if not in overall efficiency. Wartime demand inflated prices so much that profits could be made off operations whose techniques, management, and labor skills were inferior to those of already established manufacturers. These less-efficient enterprises naturally went under when peace returned and threw large quantities of cheap imports back on the market.

In many cases, though, the wartime stringencies encouraged those in the forefront of an industry to improve their performance to meet increased demand. Innovative changes in techniques and management did occur but only in isolated instances and in particular sectors of the economy. These pioneering industrial efforts drew together a number of threads. Fundamental to most factories, for instance, was an application of machinery and power to processes formerly done by hand. The development of a marketing and business structure that would encourage large-scale production was also crucial. The bigger the operation, the more capital and innovative management it required. Fortunately, the United States was capable of providing these necessities by 1810. All that was required were forward-looking industrialists to exploit them.

THE TINKERERS

The United States has always been blessed with a talented population capable of solving practical problems. In contrast to Europe, where entrenched guilds and class distinctions impeded change, the freer society on this side of the Atlantic encouraged experimentation and inventiveness. Although armed with inadequate tools and training, American artisans successfully coped with the complexities that the frontier and, later, the industrializing economy posed. A few examples from the nation's army of practical and impractical mechanics will illustrate how they replaced human and animal labor with machinery.

Oliver Evans of Delaware contributed two major innovations even before the adoption of the Constitution. First he developed a mechanized system for uniformly inserting pins into leather blocks. His technique quickly became standard for manufacturing the cards used to comb wool and cotton fibers prior to spinning. Later, Evans participated in a partnership engaged in flour milling, a process which had already been partially automated. Wind- or water-driven mills dotted the American landscape wherever grain stocks warranted, but these processing plants required considerable hand labor. Men hauled heavy loads of grain to the top of a mill and then had to spread the milled flour by hand for drying. Applying fundamental scientific and mechanical principles, Evans eliminated one human step after another until, in 1787, he patented a plan for a fully automated flour mill. A single man could supervise the whole enterprise. A bucket and belt contraption carried the grain aloft to be dropped between the mill stones. A second conveyor transported the flour to the drying area where it was automatically spread and stirred. Gravity fed the dried flour into barrels for shipment. Like Eli Whitney's cotton gin, Evans's concepts altered milling practices all over the country but brought their inventor virtually no financial rewards.

Instead of brooding, Oliver Evans pursued his fascination with steam power. Newcomen and Watt in England had already put the basic concepts to practical use in low-pressure engines. After years of experimentation, Evans produced a powerful high-pressure steam engine whose water pipes ran through the firebox—a technique which would become widely adopted in the future. He mounted his engine on a vehicle capable of propelling itself on land or water with a belt and paddle apparatus. Although it failed to catch on as a transport, this queer amphibious vessel and its successors served as dredges in coastal rivers for many years. Oliver Evans, then, deserves recognition as an inveterate fiddler, whose work sometimes fell short of full practicality but who helped refine the union between power and machinery.

As in many other instances, the United States imported some of its mechanical genius. The British textile industry was far ahead of all others in the use of water-powered carding and spinning machinery. Fully aware of the value of this technological superiority, Parliament passed laws prohibiting the export of plans or models of British textile machinery or the emigration of workers who had knowledge of them. Samuel Slater had spent several years as an apprentice at a textile mill in northern England and had literally memorized every aspect of the spinning process. Disguising himself as a farm laborer to avoid the emigration restrictions, he took passage to the United States in 1789.

SAMUEL SLATER'S FIRST CONTACT WITH MOSES BROWN

Slater had just arrived in the United States and was working in a small spinning mill in New York when he wrote this enquiry letter to Brown. The "perpetual card and spinning" statement refers to the Arkwright patented system which no one in the United States had yet copied successfully.

New York, December 2d, 1789.

Sir,–A few days ago I was informed that you wanted a manager of *cotton spinning, &c.* in which business I flatter myself that I can give the greatest satisfaction, in making machinery, making good yarn, either for *stockings* or *twist*, as any that is made in England; as I have had opportunity, and an oversight, of Sir Richard Arkwright's works, and in Mr. Strutt's mill upwards of eight years. If you are not provided for, should be glad to serve you; though I am in the New York manufactory, and have been for three weeks since I arrived from England. But we have but *one card, two machines*, two spinning jennies, which I think are not worth using. My encouragement is pretty good, but should much rather have the care of the perpetual carding and spinning. *My intention* is to erect a *perpetual card and spinning*. If you please to drop a line respecting the amount of encouragement you wish to give, by favour of Captain Bown, you will much oblige, sir, your most obedient humble servant,

Samuel Slater

(Reprinted in Gary Kulik, Roger Parks, and Theodore Z. Penn, eds., *The New England Mill Village, 1790-1860* [Cambridge, MA: MIT Press, 1984], p. 58)

There he contacted Moses Brown who, with his son-in-law William Almy, were wealthy merchants of Providence, Rhode Island, keenly interested in spinning machinery. Brown promised to reward Slater generously if he could reproduce the English system. After some initial problems, Slater built what no other American had: a water-powered spinning machine. Although he then became a full partner of Almy and Brown, the young mechanic managed the firm's mill and the nine workers it employed, all of them children between the ages of four and ten. Visitors were always welcome at the mill on the Pawtucket River, and many copied the technology on display there for installation throughout the Northeast. These mills broke the spinning bottleneck. American weavers no longer had to purchase imported yarn to keep their looms in operation. Meanwhile, the Rhode Island firm expanded and made large profits on the basis of Slater's technical skills and the American partners' salesmanship and business acumen.

Eli Whitney's timely invention of the cotton gin soon insured an expanding supply of raw material for Slater's mill, but the Connecticut inventor had fallen deeply in debt by 1798. He hoped a federal contract would reverse his fortunes. An undeclared war with France had just begun, and the United States government was eager to support any enterprises that promised to make the nation more self-sufficient. Whitney's contract called for him to deliver 10,000 muskets in twenty-eight months, but his shop near New Haven managed to assemble just 500 weapons in that period. To reassure his sponsors, the entrepreneur demonstrated his innovative manufacturing technique in the nation's capital. Before a skeptical audience, he dismantled ten musket firing mechanisms and mixed up their component parts. Then, claiming he had developed methods for fashioning interchangeable parts, he reassembled them into ten working mechanisms again. Like many later defense contractors, Whitney was not being completely honest here. The craftsmen in his shop had painstakingly filed and fitted these supposedly machine-made parts so they would all work with each other. His factory was still wrestling with production and quality control problems when he died in the 1820s.

Eli Whitney's chief contribution, then, was not his personal success so much as the publicity he generated about his manufacturing methods. He had designed "jigs" to guide his cutting and shaping tools to produce identical pieces. Constantly engaged in refining his machines and jigs, Whitney exhibited his factory, ike Slater's mill, as a model for others to emulate. Whitney became the most prominent exponent of what came to be known as the "American System" of manufacturing. The methods he pioneered ultimately transformed machine and small appliance manufacturing, especially in his home state.

Like Whitney, Robert Fulton received more historical adulation than he deserved. The steamboat he demonstrated in 1807 was neither the first nor the most efficient application of steam power to water transportation. John Fitch of Philadelphia had built successful vessels more than two decades earlier. His early models used clumsy, mechanical oars, but by 1790 his stern-wheeler was carrying passengers up and down the Delaware River. Because Fitch could never get his low-pressure steam engine to move the boat against the current faster than competing forms of land transportation, he became discouraged and eventually committed suicide.

ROBERT FULTON DESCRIBES HIS FIRST STEAMBOAT TRIP

Fulton wrote this enthusiastic letter to a friend shortly after his trip to Albany aboard the boat whose full name was the "North River Steamboat of Clermont." The letter shows Fulton's recognition of the great potential his achievement had not only personally but for the United States as a whole.

My steamboat voyage to Albany and back has turned out rather more favorable than I had calculated. The distance from New York to Albany is one hundred and fifty miles: I ran it up in thirty-two hours, and down in thirty. I had a light breeze against me the whole way, both going and coming, and the voyage has been performed wholly by the power of the steam engine. I overtook many sloops and schooners beating to windward, and parted with them as if they had been at anchor.

The power of propelling boats by steam is now fully proved. The morning I left New York there were not perhaps thirty persons in the city who believed that the boat would even move one mile per hour, or be of the least utility; and while we were putting off from the wharf, which was crowded with spectators, I heard a number of sarcastic remarks. This is the way ignorant men compliment what they call philosophers and projectors.

Having employed much time, money and zeal in accomplishing this work, it gives me, as it will give you, great pleasure to see it fully answer my expectations: it will give a quick and cheap conveyance to the merchandise on the Mississippi, Missouri, and other great rivers, which are now laying open their treasures to the enterprise of our countrymen; and, although the prospect of personal emolument has been some inducement to me, yet I feel infinitely more pleasure in reflecting on the immense advantage my country will derive from the invention.

(Reprinted in John H. Morrison, *History of Steam Navigation* [New York: W. F. Sametz, 1903], pp. 23-24.)

Colonel John Stevens, a member of one of New Jersey's leading commercial families, was more successful. He ordered a high-pressure engine constructed and, drawing upon his mathematical skills, designed screw propellers for a relatively small but quite efficient vessel he exhibited in 1804. He then abandoned screw propulsion for side-mounted paddle wheels. To his consternation, he discovered he could not operate this boat in New York State. Robert R. Livingston, Stevens's former partner and a relative by marriage, had obtained an exclusive charter for the operation of steamboats. When the New Jersey colonel's little vessel left Hoboken, therefore, it had to head south to Philadelphia on the world's first steam-powered ocean voyage.

Meanwhile, Livingston's new partner, an accomplished painter and skilled draftsman named Robert Fulton, had been designing a boat of his own. He purchased the engine in England but had great difficulty getting an export license from a British government reluctant to share its technology. The engine was finally installed on the *Clermont*, constructed and demonstrated on the Hudson River. Considerably larger than anything Fitch or Stevens had built, the side-wheeler profitably carried passengers and cargo up and down the river. While some conventional ferryboat operators tried to sabotoge the *Clermont*, others who wanted to build steam vessels of their own protested the partnership's monopoly. Fulton and Livingston eventually issued licenses to some of their more insistent critics.

In Pittsburgh in 1811 one of John Stevens's associates named Nicholas Roosevelt constructed a steamboat that inaugurated two-way traffic on the Ohio-Mississippi River system. Fulton protested this extension of "his" concept to western waterways, but, like so many other innovators, he could not control the spread of such a useful technology. Monopoly grants and patents offered scant protection. Although it sometimes hurt individual inventors, the openness of the American society was a definite spur to the spread of industrialization. Several other societal characteristics also encouraged it.

THE SOCIAL CONTEXT

Many scholars have studied the question of what characteristics are vital to the industrialization of a traditional agrarian economy. Practical motives lay behind this inquiry because economists, historians, and sociologists hoped to develop models useful in stimulating the "modernization" of impoverished nations. Attempts to implement such programs have generally been disappointing partly because the models emphasize economic and financial factors at the expense of social and cultural conditions. The comparative ease with which the United States adapted to industrialization owed a great deal to its people's intrinsic character and attitudes.

The openness of American society has often received high praise. Relatively few legal and social barriers hindered the expansion and growing sophistication of United States enterprise. No monarchy jealously guarded its authority; no entrenched hierarchy monopolized capital and initiative; no rigid class structure prevented talented individuals from realizing their ambitions. When the Constitution abolished internal trade restrictions, entrepreneurs in any part of the country could buy and sell everywhere. The limited scope of all government in the early days—whether local, state, or federal—created an economic environment as close to a truly free enterprise system as the world had yet seen.

The character of the American society encouraged full utilization of this freedom. The prevailing religious beliefs emphasized the benefits of hard work and individual responsibility. The frontier experience many Americans shared directly or through immediate ancestors placed a premium on self-reliance and individualism. To improve the living and working conditions in the wilderness, individuals had to become accustomed to doing a number of different jobs. The resulting workforce therefore possessed a flexibility that would allow it to exploit new technologies. By 1800 the population concentration along the Atlantic coastline from Boston to Baltimore constituted a substantial market that justified the division of the labor force into specialized functions. And this specialization, in turn, increased worker productivity and improved product quality.

While the Royal Navy was hampering coastal trade during the Revolutionary War, it was encouraging the improvement of land communication among the eastern seaboard cities. Well-traveled routes linked Baltimore, Philadelphia, New York, New Haven, Providence, and Boston. After the war hundreds of corporations attempted to improve these routes by constructing toll roads, bridges, and short canals. The revived merchant marine engaging in coastal trade was even more important than the internal improvements. The vast majority of the population continued to live close to ocean and river ports. While coastal voyages might lack the drama of trans-Atlantic, Caribbean, or Far Eastern trade, their quick turnarounds and reliable agents insured profitability. As the costs of moving goods from one location to another became more reasonable, regional specialization of processing and manufacturing made sense.

A flexible institutional structure complemented the social and environmental setting. The American legal system remained in a formative stage with each jurisdiction experimenting with the absence of imperial restraints. Legislatures and courts generally avoided intruding into private affairs. Indeed, virtually no cases involving business issues arose in the 1790s. Even after the turn of the century, a business practice or controversy had to be particularly outrageous to call forth a legal or legislative response. Judges tempered by the unsophisticated colonial and revolutionary years often relied on common sense and pragmatism to adjudicate the few cases that did end up in court.

The virtual absence of institutional restraints allowed entrepreneurs to experiment with all sorts of strategies. The business practices that developed in this open society resembled the machinery American tinkerers produced. Experiments led to both success and failure, but the free exchange of information and the resiliency of the entrepreneurial class helped shape and improve the nation's business structure.

THE CORPORATION IN EARLY AMERICA

The widespread use of corporations clearly differentiated early American business practice from its European counterpart. Whereas a monarchical government tended to be reluctant to grant corporate charters, they were easy to obtain on this side of the Atlantic. The states had declared themselves sovereign during the Confederation period, and they refused to surrender their authority in many areas after the ratification of the federal Constitution. Each state legislature felt responsible for encouraging enterprise within its borders, and granting a corporate charter was an easy way to promote business activity.

Entrepreneurs quickly came to appreciate the advantages incorporation had over other organizational arrangements. Except for a few, very circumscribed corporations and unincorporated companies, individuals or partnerships had conducted colonial businesses. Thomas Hancock and Robert Morris employed both modes of operation. Hancock's store in Boston was an individual enterprise, but many of his shipping ventures involved one or more partners. Morris, too, did a lot of personal speculating, but he slipped in and out of partnerships when it suited his purposes. Some early firms resembled formal corporate structures in that they issued stock and elected boards of directors, but these unincorporated companies shared many drawbacks of both individual and partnership operations.

An individual entrepreneur faced all sorts of dangers. If the venture was a large one, considerable amounts of personal capital would be at risk. If the enterprise failed, its operator not only suffered a lost investment but might be held personally responsible for damages and debts to others. Harsh laws against indebtedness sent many unsuccessful entrepreneurs to prison even though they might only be guilty of a lack of business acumen. Another drawback was that the death of a proprietor could throw a family's affairs into a chaos of uncompleted projects and financial complications.

Partnerships reduced some but not all of these dangers. Partners could often pool enough capital to fund enterprises no single person could swing, but they all shared any losses. Partnerships reduced their members' individual responsibility but, under the prevailing laws, not their personal liability. Because each partner could be held liable for all of a firm's affairs, one impecunious participant could drag down the rest. Similarly, plaintiffs could sue any or all of the partners for actions their firm had taken. And the death of a partner often created as much or more trouble for the surviving members of the firm as it did for the deceased's heirs.

A chartered corporation, by contrast, offered a number of advantages, among them the protection of limited liability. Although many of the earliest corporation charters did not mention this concept, it soon became an accepted, expected feature of incorporation. It meant that an investor who bought shares in a corporation was liable only up to the value of the stock purchased. A shareholder could not be sued personally for the corporation's failings nor risk imprisonment if it went into debt. Instead, the corporation itself could sue and be sued, declare bankruptcy, and, in some cases, continue operating under receivers after becoming insolvent. The death of a stockholder need have no effect on the operations of the business; the corporation existed independent of any individual.

Corporations offered a method for conducting enterprises well beyond an individual's personal worth. Corporate shares could be sold on the open market and were usually issued in relatively small denominations to encourage even those with modest savings to buy. Shares could continue to exchange hands long after a corporation's original financiers had died or moved on to other enterprises. In addition to selling stock, many charters allowed corporations to borrow money by selling bonds. The financial community in Philadelphia organized a primitive exchange in the 1790s where speculators could buy and sell stocks and bonds. In New York in 1792, brokers agreed to meet at specified times under a buttonwood tree on Wall Street for the same purpose. They moved indoors two years later. The amount of trading began to rise significantly around the time of the War of 1812, stimulating the development of more formal structures like the New York Stock Exchange, founded in 1817.

The management of a corporation could differ from that of other business structures as well. A common stock represented a share of the corporation itself, so owners of stocks had the right to participate in running the company. In practice most buyers considered their stocks as financial investments and were perfectly willing to allow those truly interested in managing the corporation to do so even if they owned or controlled only a limited amount of stock. This enabled some ambitious entrepreneurs to finance their projects with other people's money. At the same time, the corporate form was flexible enough to permit a group of individuals to retain all of the stock and cooperate as they would in a partnership while enjoying the benefits of limited liability and long-term stability.

In the early years corporations conducted only a small fraction of the nation's business. The huge majority of people engaged in agriculture rarely entered into partnerships and never incorporated. Individual ownership or partnerships adequately served the purposes of most merchants, craftsmen, manufacturers, and shippers. Even so, the corporations were often the most exciting and energetic businesses in operation. Their ability to deploy large amounts of capital as well as their usually close connections with leading politicians and businesses made them far more influential than most other enterprises.

The troubled times of the Revolution and the Confederation period temporarily discouraged the use of this remarkably adaptable device. Few people were willing to experiment with the corporate form until the distribution of governmental responsibilities and authority had been clarified. After the Constitution accomplished that task, incorporation became quite routine. Groups interested in highway and transportation projects accounted for about two-thirds of the 300 corporations chartered before 1800, while another 11 percent promised to provide other types of local public service. New England led the nation, granting approximately 60 percent of these charters, while the mid-Atlantic and southern states issued about 20 percent each.

A typical early charter specified the basic character of the corporation to be formed and outlined any special or exclusive rights and privileges it could exercise. The document usually included information on the company's anticipated capitalization and how that money would be raised. Stock issues were the most common, but some charters granted public service projects the right to hold lotteries. Most of these early corporations were small: those planning highway projects averaged around $50,000 in anticipated capitalization. Only prospective banks and insurance companies sought funding on the order of half a million dollars or more.

Once the steps in the chartering process had become standardized, charters became even easier to obtain. Legislators interested in encouraging local industrial and construction projects needed very little coercion to vote for acts of incorporation. Transportation and highway projects continued to be the most popular after 1800. Local boosters provided not only the incentive but also much of the capital for projects important to their own districts. Many of these projects were never realized, of course, and many that did reach completion failed to generate substantial dividends for their stockholders. Their encouragement to community growth was often far more important than their financial return.

Between 1800 and 1815, Maryland chartered 61 corporations, of which 21 were for banks and 25 for highway and bridge projects. Of the total of 81 corporations formed in New Jersey in this period, 45 performed public service projects, while only 13 engaged in banking. Not surprisingly, New York led the nation in issuing charters, approving 481 in the same 15-year period. Of these, a scant 17 were for banks, 246 for bridge and highway companies, and 168 for manufacturing establishments. To encourage this latter activity, the New York legislature passed one of the United States's earliest general incorporation laws in 1811. This act permitted a group of businessmen to establish a manufacturing corporation without obtaining a separate charter. At least five investors and a maximum capitalization of $50,000 were the major restrictions on the use of this general incorporation procedure. In its first five years, 112 groups took advantage of this streamlined incorporation process. Wartime shortages of imported manufactured goods obviously played a large part in encouraging New Yorkers to invest in such activities. In the four years following the war, when shiploads of British goods were dumped on the American market, only twenty firms incorporated under the law.

COLLECTING CAPITAL

Whether developmental, speculative, industrial, or agricultural, enterprises of all types required capital. The United States continued the colonial pattern of being chronically short of specie. As the nation grew, however, it developed new substitutes for scarce hard money. These substitutes often served both as investment funds and as methods for distributing capital. Banks and insurance companies were especially useful in providing funds for a variety of projects.

The Bank of the United States provided some impetus toward investment. Indeed, Alexander Hamilton had considered that one of the institution's key functions. He outlined his views in the *Report on Manufactures* he sent to Congress in December 1791. The United States must industrialize, the treasury secretary argued, and therefore the government should encourage it first with protective tariffs and then with bounties or subsidies for those willing to establish factories. Meanwhile, the Bank of the United States would provide investment capital. Hamilton's proposals had a mercantilist ring in urging the central government to guide the nation's economic development. Despite his earlier success in moving Congress, Hamilton was disappointed in this instance. The representatives of agrarian interests did not accept the inevitably of industrialization nor were they convinced that the federal government should actively support private enterprise.

Capital from private sources was becoming available anyway. Just three banks had been operating in the United States in 1789, but 26 more had opened by 1800. The growing demand for financial services increased the number to 90 in 1811 and to 246 five years later. The services offered changed as well. Conservative management catering to a limited clientele prevailed through the 1790s. Most institutions established in that decade were designed to assist merchants in the larger cities. They would deposit their funds in a bank directly or purchase its stock. The institution's directors would accept loan applications only from established local figures. Insider loans were common. By keeping a careful rein on their stock and note issues, these banks could assure relatively high dividends to their shareholders. At the same time, this elitist behavior alienated those outside the charmed circle and encouraged the formation of other banks to serve a broader spectrum of the population.

Banking became a political issue because members of the Federalist party controlled most financial institutions and deliberately snubbed the members of the opposition Republican party. Aaron Burr, New York's cleverest Republican party organizer, executed an end run around the Federalists by obtaining a charter from the state legislature for a corporation to supply pure water to Manhattan. Burr tucked away in the charter a provision authorizing his Manhattan Company to issue notes and accept deposits. The bank the corporation established quickly became far more important than its water utility. Other interest groups like mechanics and farmers adopted similar tactics to establish their own financial institutions.

Some sympathetic state governments responded to citizen lobbies and organized public banks. South Carolina's state-owned bank proved highly successful and popular. The Vermont Bank, though, collapsed in 1812 after only six years of operation. The state legislature had to make good on some $200,000 in deposits.

Most banks followed similar operating procedures. Each began by amassing capital. Stock sales financed incorporated banks, legislative appropriations funded state banks, and individual fortunes underwrote the few privately owned banking houses like the one Stephen Girard ran in Philadelphia. Ideally the capital should have been in the form of specie, but it was so scarce that alternatives had to be used. Trusted investors took advantage of time payment arrangements or wrote out personal promissory notes to purchase their shares. Consequently, a bank's specie holdings could be well below its authorized level at any given moment.

Banks accepted all kinds of collateral for their loans. Land, warehouse inventories, anticipated profits, or personal reputation might serve as surety. Commercial banks in the Northeast specialized in loans to merchants, shippers, and local developers. Terms of thirty to sixty days were standard, although favored customers could renew their notes as they fell due. The less conservative banks in other regions supported many different individual and corporate enterprises. Those that required long-term financing often took out loans in the form of mortgages.

Banknotes were a popular mechanism for extending credit. A bank might pass them out as receipts for deposits or issue them to borrowers. In either case, the notes entered general circulation where, as alternatives to specie and United States banknotes, they increased the nation's money supply. Because both the population and economic activity were growing rapidly in these years, the banknotes caused very little inflation. Issuing banks were supposed to redeem their notes with specie, but many institutions distributed far more currency than they could retire. As long as the number of notes presented for redemption in any given period remained low, however, the system benefited everyone. The ratio of notes issued to specie reserves varied from bank to bank, with the national average estimated at about five or six to one in 1815.

American banks of all types posted a remarkable safety record in this period. No failure occurred until 1809, when a small institution in Rhode Island folded after a virulent case of mismanagement. To ensure stability several states had included restrictive clauses in the charters they granted, and such provisions became more common when the nation entered troubled economic times. Most of these restraints seem eminently reasonable: some required a bank to issue regular reports of its financial condition, others that it refrain from issuing more notes than a prescribed multiple of its specie holdings.

Larger, more respectable institutions often monitored general banking behavior by acting as clearing houses for other banks' notes. With several branches around the country, the Bank of the United States was well equipped to perform this service. Fear that a major bank might present a large bundle of notes for conversion to specie kept many smaller banks honest. The Northeast developed the soundest banking system. Not only were that region's bankers more scrupulous, but they tended to collect surplus capital from all of the nation's business activities.

Northeasterners also had access to investment funds from local insurance companies. British underwriters, informal partnerships, or risk-sharing arrangements insured colonial enterprises. The continuing need for marine insurance encouraged the creation of domestic companies after the Revolution. Philadelphia was the obvious location for the founding of the Insurance Company of North America in 1792. The company offered 60,000 shares for sale at $10 a share, hoping to capitalize at more than half a million dollars. The company's primary function was to insure ships and their cargos, but its charter allowed it to write fire and life policies as well. The company's directors managed its affairs so prudently that it paid shareholders dividends approaching 30 percent in good years. Only twice in its first three decades of operation did it dip into its capital to pay claims.

Philadelphia also provided the setting for the birth of the American fire insurance business. As early as the 1730s, private companies were organized not only to fight fires but also to compensate those who suffered losses. Two Philadelphia companies so dominated the local market that the Insurance Company of North

America had to seek clients elsewhere when it began offering fire insurance in 1794. Spreading the risk geographically made good sense anyway, since flames often engulfed whole blocks or districts. As the insurance concept caught on, other companies were formed. To extend their operations, they opened offices and established agents in distant communities.

Insurance companies were extraordinarily careful in selecting investments for their capital. Because a well-managed company set its premiums high enough to more than offset any claims, it could tie its capital up in long-term projects. Real estate was generally considered the soundest investment. Early companies tended to be heavily capitalized, though, so they could also provide funds for other enterprises.

Insurance company capital, banknotes, federal securities, shipping profits, all of these could be devoted to other purposes. Money was always more available in the Northeast, especially for upper-class borrowers. Some capital was recycled through a series of similar ventures, but many individuals and companies were willing to consider innovative concepts if the return looked good. Changing economic conditions sometimes altered the economic picture so much that even very cautious investors took the plunge on new enterprises.

PULLING IT ALL TOGETHER: FRANCIS CABOT LOWELL

The United States possessed many of the societal, financial, and technical elements essential for industrialization long before it occurred. A final key factor was required: the entrepreneurial genius to combine machines, capital, labor, and markets. These characteristics finally came together in a self-sustaining way after the turn of the century.

Many early American industrial planners hoped to create an American alternative to the British textile industry. The United States could never be self-sufficient as long as it shipped raw cotton to England and then paid premium prices to reimport it as finished cloth. Samuel Slater had stolen some spinning secrets, but the British retained their technological supremacy through the use of power looms. Well into the nineteenth century, Great Britain's superiority at weaving enabled her goods to be sold in the United States at or below the cost of most domestically manufactured cloth. To compete, Americans would have to develop a more efficient production system than that of their trans-Atlantic rival.

The integrated textile factory Francis Cabot Lowell constructed during the War of 1812 accomplished that objective. He started out with a distinct advantage over other potential industrialists. He was already a successful merchant and a prominent member of the commercial class as well as the Harvard-educated social elite of Boston. While President Jefferson's 1807 embargo and succeeding trade policies were stifling the normal shipping and trade activities in Massachusetts, Lowell skillfully devised an industrial alternative. In 1810 he began a long visit to the British Isles where he visited a great many textile mills. He observed the employment of machinery and labor there and returned to the United States with a fully formed plan.

Like any other industrial entrepreneur, Lowell had to gather capital, devise a management strategy, establish a production system, hire a labor force, and find a market for his output. He began by forming a corporation. He and a couple of associates obtained a charter from the Massachusetts legislature in 1813 for the Boston Manufacturing Company. Its initial working capital of $100,000, soon expanded to $400,000, was an unprecedented capitalization for a manufacturing venture. Lowell was able to retain control of the company because he had the complete trust of the friends among the Boston aristocracy who purchased all of the company's one hundred shares. The entrepreneur had a hand in everything, but he relied heavily on two other "Boston Associates." Lowell's brother-in-law, Patrick Tracy Jackson, served as the company's chief manager, while Paul Moody, a brilliant mechanic with weaving experience, handled the technical aspects.

THE SOCIETY FOR ESTABLISHING USEFUL MANUFACTURES

The dramatic failure of the Society for Establishing Useful Manufactures (S.U.M.) in the 1790s proved just how crucial proper timing could be. The ambitious endeavor was clearly a case of too much too soon. The ubiquitous Alexander Hamilton was a major sponsor of the society formed in 1791 as the first chartered business corporation in New Jersey. William Duer, the eclectic speculator, served as the society's first governor. It sold shares for $100 each, hoping to raise at least half a million dollars to finance the construction of a manufacturing center in the state. It staked a claim to a water power site at the future location of Paterson and looked overseas for skilled textile workers interested in immigrating.

Despite Hamilton's patronage, the society lapsed into dormancy in 1796. Duer obviously contributed to that decline when his personal bankruptcy triggered the Panic of 1792. Unfortunately, other directors of the company also exhibited extravagance and mismanagement. Pierre L'Enfant, fresh from designing his grandiose plan for the District of Columbia, was far less able to handle the mundane task of laying out canals and workshops along the Passaic River. The foreigners hired to share their expertise with American workers proved to be either incompetent or disinterested after arriving in New Jersey. The small cotton spinning mill the S.U.M. finally built ended up relying on child labor. Although Paterson later became a mill town noted for its silk production, the society persisted in name only. Industrialization would have to await better economic times, sounder management, and more rational strategies.

The Boston Associates purchased a paper mill at Waltham, Massachusetts, to gain access to a reliable source of water power. There Lowell and Moody set up a workshop to construct both spinning and weaving machinery incorporating many innovations. This was to be installed in an operating mill next door. The shop employed many mechanics and craftsmen to repair and improve that equipment as well as to construct additional machinery to sell to others setting up their own mills. Machinery sales were as important to the firm as its textile output.

Lowell made his most stunning innovation, however, in deciding to combine all of the textile processing functions under one roof, something no other industrialist had conceived of doing. He installed the water-powered equipment his shop made in the proper order for an orderly production flow. Raw cotton delivered to the factory was carded, spun, and loomed into finished cloth ready to be marketed. The economies of scale and elimination of wasted time and movement in his integrated mill enabled the Boston Manufacturing Company to produce its material at extraordinarily low cost.

The machinery was so sophisticated that it did all of the difficult tasks, so unskilled workers could run it efficiently. Lowell had visited utopian theorist Robert Owens's factory in Scotland and had borrowed from it the concept of hiring young women. Conservative New England farm families were initially suspicious of this idea, but the clean, orderly dormitories at Waltham supervised by mature, responsible matrons reassured them. Lowell never intended for the farm girls he hired to become permanent laborers. He expected them to leave after staying a couple of years and earning enough for a dowry. He hoped his factory would thus avoid the labor exploitation and oppression he had observed in England.

With hundreds of yards of cloth pouring from his mill, Lowell needed to find a market. The ideal sales agent was a fellow Boston Brahmin named Nathan Appleton who had superintended the original capitalization of the Boston Manufacturing Company. Appleton arranged for a commission house in which he owned an interest to sell all of Lowell's cloth at a 1 percent commission. The fabric sold well, as did the machinery, so the company was able to declare a 17 percent dividend in 1817. Its annual sales increased tenfold to more than a third of a million dollars in the next five years. Lowell personally took a hand in trying to preserve his market by lobbying in Washington while Congress debated the wisdom of imposing higher protective tariffs on imported textiles.

Francis Cabot Lowell died at the age of 42 in 1817, before the full impact of his innovations had been realized. Future entrepreneurs adopted not only his production and labor policies but also benefited from the machinery and patents his company developed. Factories modeled after his "Waltham System" sprang up all over Massachusetts and its environs. Lowell had thus helped redraw the economic map of the United States. While industrialization lagged in the rest of the country, it assumed increasing importance in New England, ultimately overshadowing the region's shipping and mercantile activities.

Had Lowell lived to observe the consequences of his entrepreneurial pioneering, he would probably have been most distressed at the failure of his labor strategy. The supply of New England farm girls quickly proved inadequate to the rapidly growing demand for textile workers. Factory owners therefore hired young women from nearby Canada and impoverished Ireland, but soon these sources were exhausted as well. Destitute immigrant families began filling the mills. Workdays grew longer, conditions more oppressive, and supervision harsher as employers devoted their attention to increasing output at any cost. Living and working conditions in squalid New England mill towns came to resemble those dreary industrial villages Lowell had observed in England and had hoped to exclude from America. Succeeding generations of workers were fated to pay a heavy price for the efficiencies of industrial mass production.

EXTERNAL AND INTERNAL CONSTRAINTS ON GROWTH

A leading reason why Lowell had turned to manufacturing was the disturbed economic situation in the United States after 1807. Shipping had traditionally been the primary source of wealth in New England, but the lucrative Atlantic trade had fallen victim to the conflicts that resulted from French Emperor Napoleon Bonaparte's ambition to dominate Europe. His arch enemy, England, was the world's leading seafaring nation, and the Royal Navy clamped down on any American merchant vessels even suspected of aiding France. The British also impressed American sailors into the harsh discipline of their own navy.

President Thomas Jefferson responded to these outrages with an embargo he though would convince the Europeans of their dependence on American trade. But his policy idled thousands of American ships and severely curtailed economic activity throughout the United States. The embargo thus roused more resentment at home than abroad. None of the successive federal measures induced the British to abandon their search and seizure policies. These and other factors led to the American war declaration against England in 1812, but neither side gained the upper hand in three years of intermittent fighting. Having at last deposed and exiled Napoleon, the Europeans inaugurated a century of peace in 1815, and the United States gratefully ratified a treaty that ended its conflict with England.

The restoration of world peace seemed to bode well for the future. The boom the United States enjoyed after 1815 resembled its experiences following the Revolutionary War. Because they had similar roots, of course, one could safely predict that this period of prosperity would end in a rather abrupt economic readjustment. This second time around, though, the prosperity lasted nearly four years, long enough not only to disarm pessimists but also to guarantee that when the fall did occur it would be long and hard.

Some of the prosperity stemmed from a dramatic revival of international trade. American shippers and merchants rushed to recapture their traditional share of the world's maritime traffic. Along with the carrying trade, fishing, whaling, and the shipbuilding industry itself revived. So attractive were these activities that they diverted New Englanders' attention from manufacturing and bolstered the influence of the mercantile class. British businessmen were equally excited about the reopening of trans-Atlantic trade, and they found more than enough goods to fill their vessels. The wartime blockages had created huge inventories so that, in a replay of 1783, thousands of tons of manufactured goods were dumped on the American market. Low prices and easy credit terms encouraged merchants and consumers to buy excessively. This behavior inevitably harmed the domestic manufacturers who had prospered in the war-protected markets at home, and many marginal producers in America went out of business.

For the moment the United States had plenty of money and goods to exchange for its imports. European crop failures as well as pent-up demand for American staples guaranteed premium prices for all types of agricultural produce. Cotton and tobacco led as usual, but foreign buyers paid well for wheat and other foodstuffs. The high prices offered for exports and the low ones requested for imports benefited people all over the country. Many farmers were doing so well that they substantially expanded their operations.

JOHN JACOB ASTOR

The reopening of trans-Atlantic trade in 1815 gave John Jacob Astor the opportunity to complete his dominance of the American fur trade, a business that had already made him a wealthy man. Like Stephen Girard, with whom he had many dealings, Astor had humble European origins. The son of a poor German butcher, he left home as a teenager to work in his older brother's music business in London. Four years later, he headed for New York, arriving in 1784 with seven flutes and $25 he had saved. He continued to buy and sell musical instruments for many years even as he was establishing the foundations of his fur trading enterprise.

To get the lay of the land, Astor tramped through upper New York State and the Ohio country and even made contacts in Montreal, the Canadian fur capital. He relied on his wife Sarah, an astute manager and businesswoman in her own right, to run his affairs in New York City. After Jay's Treaty had assured the withdrawal of British troops from the Northwest Territory in 1794, Astor became the leading fur trader in the United States. Acting as the middleman between western trappers and London buyers, he had amassed a fortune of $250,000 by 1800.

That was the year that he sent his first shipload of furs to China and sold the cargo for a $50,000 profit. He continued this lucrative trade, but the distances were so extreme he hatched a bold plan to establish a trading post on the West Coast. With four minor partners, he formed the Pacific Fur Co. in 1810. It planned to send ships from New York with Indian trade goods to exchange for furs at Astoria, the company's outpost at the mouth of the Columbia River in Oregon. The furs would bring a good price at Hong Kong, and the ships could trade in European ports on the way back to New York.

The project had an inauspicious beginning when the arrogant captain on the company's first trading voyage ignored Astor's firm instructions to deal cautiously with the Indians. First he thoroughly alienated the local population. Then he allowed many Indians to swarm on board his ship where he traded knives for their furs. Shortly after they began attacking the crew with their newly acquired weapons, the powder magazine exploded, killing almost everyone on board. Other troubles plagued Astoria as well, and Astor concluded, after a few months, that the costs were too high to sustain the venture. The company sold its property at a great loss to the British-owned Hudson's Bay Co. in 1813.

The fighting during the War of 1812 did clear British traders out of the western United States, though, leaving the field open for Astor. He used government contacts to obtain special privileges and protection. By 1820, he controlled virtually all of the fur trade in the country through his American Fur Company. Astor had formed that organization under a New York corporation charter in 1808, and he remained virtually its sole owner. When he sold it in 1834, it was the largest company in the United States.

John Jacob Astor had no need for the business at that point because he had been systematically buying real estate in Manhattan for years. When he died at the age of 85 in 1848, he left $20 million to his heirs, virtually all of it to his son. That constituted by far the largest personal fortune in the history of the United States. Although he is remembered most for his fur trading activities, the bulk of his estate had derived from his astute land purchases.

The rising agricultural prospects fueled a new round of land speculation in the South and West. Thousands of families poured into the fertile cotton lands of Mississippi and Alabama. Waves of pioneers also spilled into Indiana and Illinois in the Northwest Territory now that British and Indian alliances no longer discouraged settlement. Despite the speed of settlement, speculators kept well ahead. Land companies with extravagant plans and shaky finances optimistically contracted for tracts far beyond the frontier line.

Wartime experiences had meanwhile caused a rather important change of heart among the Republican party members who now controlled the federal government. The ghost of Alexander Hamilton might well have written President James Madison's State of the Union message in December 1815. The Republican president called for higher tariffs to protect domestic manufacturers from foreign competition, federal financing for internal improvement projects, and the reestablishment of a central bank. In a rare mood of consensus, Congress quickly implemented these suggestions. It raised import duties on commodities like cotton textiles to encourage domestic production. A new federal bank to replace the one that had expired in 1811 was chartered. In exchange for this charter, the new bank was to give the government a "bonus" of $1.5 million that Congress earmarked for the financing of canal and highway projects.

All three of these moves were destined to generate political controversy in the years to come. Trouble flared up first over the Bonus Bill of 1817 which was to provide federal funding for a proposed canal linking the Hudson River with Lake Erie. Even though he had spoken in favor of the idea in 1815, President Madison concluded that his dedication to a strict construction of the Constitution forced him to veto the bill. The New York State government therefore had to shoulder full responsibility for financing the Erie Canal. Madison's decision acted as a precedent for the federal government's refusal to finance internal improvements projects right through the Civil War. But his acceptance of the tariff and banking bills did not prevent their reconsideration in the future. Emotional tariff disputes rocked the nation in the 1820s, and many Americans were convinced that the Second Bank of the United States had set off the financial catastrophe that overwhelmed the nation in 1819.

The depression that began that year was the most severe peacetime economic blow the United States had suffered since the Revolution. Although the American people were deeply shocked at the Panic of 1819, plenty of warning signs existed for those perceptive enough to read them. Domestic manufacturers, for example, had been complaining bitterly over British dumping for some time. Vast sums of money had been flowing into unwise investments. Indeed, much of the postwar prosperity rested on insecure foundations.

The high prices paid for American agricultural exports were representative of the underlying weakness. This inflation stemmed largely from pent-up demand so that, once European inventories of cotton, tobacco, and other American products had been replenished, their prices were bound to fall. Cotton prices broke dramatically, dropping by more than half by 1819, and other commodities suffered similar declines. American farmers found themselves overextended and indebted for lands and equipment they could no longer afford.

The agrarian troubles inevitably punctured the land speculation bubble. Far too much land financed with unreliable bank notes glutted the market. The general price deflation that set in after 1819 wiped out the paper value of land held for speculation as well as reducing the returns on any real estate sold. Land prices dropped in half or even more as farmers lost their ability to buy. The land speculators' losses also drained off eastern capital funds, spreading the misery to all sections of the country.

Many of those searching for a scapegoat for these troubles focused on the Second Bank of the United States. It had indeed performed poorly since it opened in Philadelphia in the spring of 1817. The bank's charter authorized a capitalization of $35 million, but generous funding arrangements allowed investors to finance some of their stock purchases without putting up specie. At times, the bank was functioning with just $2 million in its specie reserves, far too little to support its extensive operations. The bank's incompetent president, William Jones, allowed the home office and its many branches a free hand. The branches behaved according to local custom: those in the financially conservative Northeast were very cautious in issuing bank notes, those in the expanding South and West showed no restraint. Regardless of which branch issued the notes, the bank maintained a policy of redeeming all of them at face value, so currency speculators bought depreciated western notes at a discount and converted them at par in the East.

An expanding money supply made sense whenever the level of economic activity was also rising. When the economy began to slow, a downward adjustment in the money supply would be prudent. Jones tardily recognized the damage his lax policies had caused, so he abruptly reversed course, withdrawing notes from circulation as quickly as possible. Langdon Cheeves soon replaced Jones as president of the bank, and he pursued an even more restrictive monetary policy. Many Americans concluded that the bank's sudden deflationary policy was the primary cause for the rapid, unsettling price reductions around the country. In fact, price declines were inevitable given the external and internal recessionary forces mentioned above.

A recent analysis of the bank's activities suggests that it deserves even less blame for the financial crisis. Robert H. Timberlake, Jr.'s thoughtful study of the origins of central banking in the United States argues that the Treasury Department, not the bank, provoked the dramatic deflation that occurred after 1817. During the War of 1812, the Treasury had issued millions of dollars worth of interest-bearing notes to finance military campaigns. Private banks then used these government bills to supplement the specie they held in reserve. The size of a bank's reserves dictated the amount of currency it could safely issue. The expanding supply of treasury bonds therefore permitted a startling increase in the number of private bank notes issued, inevitably fueling inflation. Federal revenues remained high after the war ended, though, so Treasury Secretary William Crawford used the surplus to retire outstanding treasury obligations. But his laudable policy of reducing the national debt also eliminated much of the backing for the country's paper money, triggering deflation and ultimately a depression. Crawford's activities escaped public notice, though. Even as they victimized the Second Bank of the United States, they were giving it a bad name.

Hostility toward it specifically, toward all forms of central banking, and toward banks in general persisted long after the Panic of 1819. Such emotions were understandable given the severity of the depression. So dismal were prospects for all types of American enterprise that some pessimists gloomily predicted that James Monroe might be the last president of the United States. Fortunately, the nation's resource base and the energy of its people enabled it to survive this depression. Invigorating growth and innovative development in the next forty years caused the American people quickly to forget the bleakness they had faced in 1819.

READING SUGGESTIONS

Among general works, Curtis P. Nettles's *The Emergence of a National Economy, 1775-1815* (1962), mentioned earlier, is even more useful for this period. In *Economic Growth of the United States 1790-1860* (1964) Douglass C. North incorporates more quantitative material than does Nettles. The leading expert on American business history is Thomas C. Cochran, the author of *Frontiers of Change: Early Industrial America* (1981). Elisha P. Douglass takes a sector-by-sector approach in *The Coming Age of American Business* (1971). Drew R. McCoy's *The Elusive Republic: Political Economy in Jeffersonian America* (1980) comments on the societal and political conditions that influenced economic and business development through the War of 1812.

Charles A. Beard's *An Economic Interpretation of the Constitution of the United States* (1913) set off a continuing debate on the subject of the motivations of those who framed this key political document. Both Robert E. Brown (*Charles Beard and the Constitution* [1956]) and Forest McDonald (*We the People: The Economic Origins of the Constitution* [1958]) come to quite different conclusions than did Beard. Merrill Jensen's *The New Nation: A History of the United States During the Confederation Period 1781-1789* (1958) overturned the traditional interpretation of that era as one of profound crisis.

Alexander Hamilton has fascinated historians of every era. Joseph E. Charles's *Origins of the American Party System* (1956) offers a penetrating critique of the political consequences of Hamilton's proposals as do Clinton Rossiter (*Alexander Hamilton and the Constitution* [1964]) and John C. Miller (*Alexander Hamilton, Portrait in Paradox* [1959]). Broadus Mitchell's *Alexander Hamilton: The National Adventure 1788-1804* (1963) looks at his financial program from an economic historian's viewpoint. Forrest McDonald claims in *Alexander Hamilton* (1979) that fame rather than personal wealth was his chief motivation. The most thorough study of early banking practices is Bray Hammond's *Banks and Politics in America: From the Revolution to the Civil War* (1957). In *The Origins of Central Banking in the United States* (1978), Richard H. Timberlake, Jr., is less critical than Hammond of people like William Jones who were caught in no-win situations.

A most enjoyable book is A. M. Sakolski's biting critique of the early land speculators. *The Great American Land Bubble* (1932) discusses the expansive plans of frontier schemers as well as speculators' lobbying and skullduggery in New York and other settled areas. Shaw Livermore's *Early American Land Companies: Their Influence on Corporate Development* (1939) stresses the links between land speculation and structural changes from the colonial to the post-Revolutionary period. Another entertaining book is by Samuel Eliot Morison, whose *Maritime History of Massachusetts* (1921) carries the story well into the nineteenth century.

Rolla Milton Tryon discusses the foundations of American manufacturing in an older but very informative work, *Household Manufacture in the United States 1640-1860* (1917). Joseph Stancliffe Davis's *Essays in the Earlier History of American Corporations* (2 vols., 1917) describes the S.U.M. and other corporate activity through 1800. George Heberton Evans, Jr., picks up the story at that point in his largely quantitative *Business Incorporations in the United States 1800-1943* (1948*). The Philosophy of Manufactures* (1982) by Michael Brewster Folsom and Steven D. Lubar is a collection of intriguing primary documents.

Some of the early tinkerers are portrayed in Roger Burlingame's *The March of the Iron Men* (1938). Harold Livesay's *American Made: Men Who Shaped the American Economy* (1979) presents delightful essays on many innovators including Eli Whitney. For more detailed accounts, consult *Eli Whitney and the Birth of American Technology* (1956) by Constance M. Green, and Jeanett Mirsky and Alan Nevins's *The World of Eli Whitney* (1962). In *The Entrepreneurs* (1974) Robert Sobel includes an essay on Francis Cabot Lowell, and Sigmund Diamond portrays Stephen Girard in *The Reputation of American Businessmen* (1955).

Chapter 4

ENTERPRISE IN AN EXPANDING NATION 1819-1860

The expansion of the United States in the four decades following the Panic of 1819 created a great variety of opportunities for enterprise. The population continued to grow rapidly due to natural increase and European immigration. The introduction of new technology and substantial capital investment in transportation reduced costs and speeded up travel and communication. The tender shoots of industrialization planted in the Northeast thrived and spread, stimulating factory and market growth. Business operations became increasingly complex, involving many more workers and much larger marketing areas.

Agriculture continued to occupy center stage though, and most Americans lived and worked in rural settings. The Cotton Kingdom spread westward even more energetically than did the diversified farming economy of the Middle West. Agricultural products continued to supply the majority of American exports, and the processing of such goods kept domestic mills and factories humming. Even so, the land's great potential remained only partially exploited. Because agriculture was still labor intensive, the persistent shortage of workers acted as a major constraint. Farming techniques did change in this period, but the relatively slow adoption of scientific and mechanized practices meant that agricultural productivity rose at a moderate pace.

The vast increases recorded in overall agricultural output in these years resulted primarily from the dispersion of population by means of a rapidly improving transportation system. Canal fever swept the United States in the 1820s after the opening of the Erie Canal. Other manmade waterways could link a few trading centers effectively, but railroads quickly proved to be a more versatile mode of transportation. The railroad craze began in the 1830s and took off in the following decade, offering ambitious entrepreneurs seemingly limitless rewards. The construction, management, and operation of railroads became the nation's leading large-scale enterprise, and the methods developed to cope with it influenced and shaped manufacturing and other industrial organizations.

Political controversy meanwhile arose between those who favored greater federal participation in economic affairs and the Jacksonian Democrats who were content with more limited governmental activity. Because the Democrats won most of the political battles, they were blamed for a serious economic breakdown that began in 1837. A business panic in that year brought the more flamboyant speculators to their knees, and several years of depression followed.

Hard times were soon forgotten in the enthusiasm for national expansion that blossomed in the 1840s. The nation's size expanded dramatically with the annexation of Texas and the incorporation of the Oregon, New Mexico, and California regions. The discovery of gold near Sacramento in 1848 attracted an enormous rush of prospective miners and hangers-on who quickly populated the Far West. Land speculation and generally prosperous times once again stimulated overextension. An inevitable readjustment came in the wake of yet another financial panic in 1857. The northern economy in particular struggled to right itself through the end of the decade.

Emotionalism concerning slavery had already begun to overshadow economic concerns for Americans in both the South and the North. Tempers had flared over whether slavery should be admitted to the western territories as early as 1820. Opposing sectional attitudes significantly hardened in succeeding years. The U.S. failure to find a universally acceptable method for dealing with slavery would ultimately tear the Union apart. It is appropriate, therefore, to begin the discussion of this chapter with an examination of southern agriculture and its interrelationship with slavery.

THE COTTON KINGDOM

As it had in the colonial and early national periods, the South continued to produce a great variety of agricultural commodities in the first half of the nineteenth century. Tobacco remained the major source of farm income in the border states of Kentucky, Virginia, and Maryland where a shorter growing season discouraged the cultivation of cotton. Along the South Carolina and Georgia coastline, rice plantations generated sizable fortunes. Hemp was a major commercial crop in parts of

Kentucky just as sugar was in the Louisiana bayou country. Corn grew everywhere, often interspersed with fields devoted to locally popular export crops.

Despite the region's diversity, cotton clearly ranked as the South's leading staple. At mid-century, 74,000 plantations were producing five bales or more annually. By contrast, only 16,000 plantations specialized in tobacco, 2681 in sugar, and a scant 551 in rice. Several factors made cotton so popular. It was less perishable than other southern crops and relatively easy to transport. Short-staple cotton thrived on flat lands or hillsides anywhere in the lower South that enjoyed two hundred or more frost-free days a year. Because no special tools or equipment were needed to plant, cultivate, or harvest the crop, even a single-acre plot could be profitable. Most attractive of all, of course, was the apparently inexhaustible demand for the versatile fiber.

Cotton farming techniques depended upon the type of workers involved, the location and size of land parcels, and, most importantly, the number of hands available during the picking season. Cotton seeds were broadcast liberally on tilled earth in March. After the seeds had sprouted, the fields were "scraped" to eliminate excess plants and weeds, and the resulting rows had to be hoed repeatedly right through the summer. The plants bolled out in July or August. Because they ripened at different times, picking occurred almost continuously for the next four or five months.

The best field hands could pick a couple of hundred pounds in a single day, but the average was much lower for most adults and lower still for the children and oldsters drafted into the picking crews. Every plantation of any size maintained its own gin and press to clean and bale the cotton immediately. Bales weighed approximately 450 pounds in this era, and they could be stored without serious deterioration for at least a year and often much longer. Wagons hauled the bales to the nearest waterway to be rafted or shipped to major cotton ports like New Orleans, Mobile, or Savannah for transfer to ocean-going vessels.

The many tasks associated with managing a plantation left its owner little time to superintend the shipping and selling of his cotton. Just as colonial tobacco growers had relied on British, Scotch, or New England merchants to market their crops, cotton planters depended on outside businessmen or "factors" to do the same for them. The factorage system involved a network of commission agents throughout the Cotton Kingdom working either independently or for distant mercantile houses located in the southern cotton ports or New York, Boston, and London. A factor typically charged the grower a 2.5 percent commission on the sale of his output. Factors might also serve as purchasing agents for the preoccupied planters, collecting commissions of from 2 to 10 percent on the price of the goods they supplied. A planter wishing to expand or suffering from a temporary financial setback could borrow from a factor as well, paying interest either in money or cotton. As with most middlemen, the factors were often unpopular with their clients even though they provided essential business services.

The factors also collected and distributed marketing information. Cotton dominated the United States export trade in this period. From 1820 to 1850, it accounted for anywhere from 46 to 63 percent of the annual value of all American exports. The 180 million pounds grown in the South in 1821 represented just under 29 percent of the whole world's production. Thirty years later the United States produced 990 million pounds of cotton or almost 70 percent of the world's output. American output and sales nearly doubled in the succeeding decade. As Figure 4-1 illustrates, Great Britain consistently purchased nearly two-thirds of the American crop. Most of the rest supplied textile factories in the northeastern United States.

The figure also shows that cotton prices averaged thirteen cents a pound in the 1820s, and about a half a cent less in the 1830s. They declined substantially late in that decade, though, and hovered around eight cents a pound in the troubled

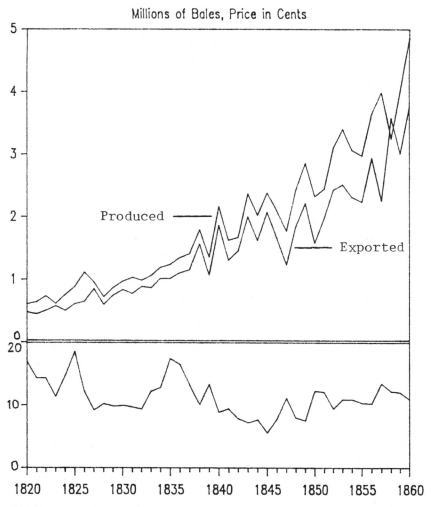

FIGURE 4-1 Cotton: Production, Exports, and Prices (From tables in Matthew B. Hammond, *The Cotton Industry: An Essay in American History*, Part I [New York: Macmillian, 1897], p. 357.)

1840s, a figure lower than many growers' production costs. Some contemporary analysts and historians claim that this decline proved that the Cotton Kingdom and its associated slavery system were bound to disappear even without a civil war and emancipation process. But price levels rebounded in the 1850s. The average of 11.5 cents a pound through the decade was high enough to assure reasonable returns for all but the most inefficient growers.

Fluctuating prices, rapid soil depletion, and limited amounts of cleared land encouraged many planters, accompanied by their slaves, to relocate to the south and west. Georgia consistently produced at least twenty percent of the nation's cotton crop, and the state's population nearly tripled from 1820 to 1850. The other two major cotton-producing states, Alabama and Mississippi, grew even faster. Texas and Arkansas experienced cotton-based booms in the 1850s. Westward migration of slaves accounted for much of their population growth. By 1850 many counties along the Gulf Coast and the adjacent rivers had more black inhabitants than white. Because half of the slaves in the United States were engaged in cotton cultivation, the plantation system naturally had a predominant influence on their lives.

THE ENSLAVED LABOR FORCE

Plantation slavery was the most familiar example of what southerners referred to as their "peculiar institution," but masters of four or fewer slaves owned half of the black population. Many of these slaves worked as household or personal servants. Other blacks living in towns and cities learned crafts such as carpentry or barbering which their owners could use directly or hire out for a fee. Some of these workers were even allowed to keep any surplus earnings their labor brought. A few industries like the Tredegar Iron Works in Richmond, Virginia, employed blacks as well. Estimates of the size of the skilled slave labor pool in the South before the Civil War differ widely, with the most optimistic claiming it to be as high as 30 percent of the total black population. The number of blacks who truly deserved to be classified as skilled craftsmen was probably much smaller.

As with the white population, agriculture absorbed the energies of most of the slaves. Many of those owned individually or in small groups worked on farms throughout the South supplementing the endeavors of the typically large white families. In southern society, ownership of a black servant or farm laborer brought prestige to his master, so many yeomen farmers were eager to purchase one or more slaves even if their labor was not absolutely essential. The tasks agricultural workers performed on farms differed little from the chores of the white family members. Slaves often ate with the family at a common table and were otherwise treated like the hired hands on northern farms.

Living and working conditions on the plantations were usually quite different but subject to great variety depending upon the land's location and the staple crops it produced as well as intangible factors like an overseer's personality. Some plantation slaves were given specific tasks to perform without direct supervision.

More often the workers were assigned to gangs under the leadership of a black or white foreman or overseer. The supervisor was responsible for making sure his gang completed one project or job before moving on to the next.

A large plantation was a complex micro-economic unit within which each slave had a specific job. Central to the success of the whole operation was the prime field hand, a strong, healthy man in his late teens or twenties who performed the many arduous tasks essential to bringing in the crop. Older slaves and children might be herdsmen, stableboys, or household servants. Youngsters also might learn skills from the plantation's resident craftsmen. Women did maintenance tasks such as cooking, sewing, washing, and gardening for most of the year. When picking season arrived, of course, all available workers regardless of age or sex headed for the cotton fields.

The prosperity of the labor system reflected the vitality of the plantation economy. After remaining fairly constant for many years, slave prices began to rise in the 1850s. A prime field hand sold for about $800 at the beginning of the decade; a similar slave might cost as much as $2000 or more in 1859. Whites who were willing to pay such premium prices for black laborers obviously had no intention of abandoning the slave system. Some felt that slave prices were too high because demand was overreaching supply and called for a reopening of the slave trade from abroad. Most southerners would not favor such a regressive step, but buyers exhibited their faith in the future worth of their slaves by continuing to invest large sums in them right through the 1850s.

The question of whether the high slave prices were justified is intertwined with the larger issue of just how profitable and efficient the plantation system was. Some analysts take it almost as an article of faith that slave labor could never be as efficient or productive as free labor. The need to enforce discipline, the expense of supervising the work force, the absence of capitalistic incentives, even the expenses associated with feeding and housing unproductive young and old slaves were cited as factors contributing to this inefficiency. As soon as southern planters realized how high these indirect costs were, some argue, they would sell or free the slaves and then hire them back as less expensive free labor.

A key point often overlooked in the historical debate is that beliefs are often far more important than realities in dictating human behavior. Whether they were attacking or defending slavery, individuals had become highly emotional by the 1850s. While a modern quantitative analysis might "prove" that slavery as a system was inherently unprofitable, no one was capable of conducting such an exercise in the nineteenth century. As long as slave maintenance costs appeared on the surface to be lower than the workers' ability to produce, the system would persist. And maintenance costs could be quite minimal on a large, well-managed plantation producing virtually all of its own food and shelter.

Few Americans North or South believed that slavery would shortly disappear of its own accord. High cotton prices and unending demand encouraged more, not less, exploitation of slave labor. The southern economy was so healthy, in fact, that it survived the Panic of 1857 and the depression that followed with hardly a

SOLOMON NORTH ON SLAVE LABOR

Although he had lived as a free man in New York for thirty years, Solomon Northrup was captured in Washington, D. C., and spent more than a decade as a slave before managing to escape. This selection from his autobiography describes the working conditions at the Bayou Beouf cotton plantation in Louisiana in the 1840s.

When a new hand, one unaccustomed to the business, is sent for the first time into the field, he is whipped up smartly, and made for that day to pick as fast as he can possibly. At night it is weighed, so that his capability in cotton picking is known. He must bring in the same weight each night following. If it falls short, it is considered evidence that he has been laggard, and a greater or less number of lashes is the penalty.

An ordinary day's work is two hundred pounds. A slave who is accustomed to picking, is punished, if he or she brings in a less quantity than that. There is a great difference among them as regards this kind of labor. Some of them seem to have a natural knack, or quickness, which enables them to pick with great celerity, and with both hands, while others, with whatever practice or industry are utterly unable to come up to the ordinary standards. Such hands are taken from the cotton field and employed in other business. Patsey, of whom I shall have more to say, was known as the most remarkable cotton picker on Bayou Beouf. She picked with both hands and with such surprising rapidity, that five hundred pounds a day was not unusual for her. . .

. . . The hands are required to be in the cotton field as soon as it is light in the morning, and, with the exception of ten or fifteen minutes, which is given them at noon to swallow their allowance of cold bacon, they are not permitted to be a moment idle until it is too dark to see, and when the moon is full, they often times labor till the middle of the night. They do not dare to stop even at dinner time, nor return to the quarters, however late it be, until the order to halt is given by the driver.

The day's work over in the field, the baskets are "toted," or in other words, carried to the gin-house, where the cotton is weighed. No matter how fatigued and weary he may be—no matter how much he longs for sleep and rest—a slave never approaches the gin-house with his basket of cotton but with fear. If it falls short in weight—if he has not performed the full task appointed him, he knows he must suffer. And if he has exceeded it by ten or twenty pounds, in all probability his master will measure the next day's task accordingly. So, whether he has too little or too much, his approach to the gin-house is always with fear and trembling. Most frequently they have too little, and therefore it is they are not anxious to leave the field.

(From Solomon Northrup, *Twelve Years a Slave* [Auburn, NY: Derby and Miller, 1853], reprinted in Gilbert Osofsky, ed., *Puttin' On Ole Massa* [New York: Harper and Row, 1969], pp. 314-15.)

tremor. Furthermore, white southerners had become so accustomed to the institution that they could not conceive of blacks and whites living in the same region without slavery to define and segregate them. Right up to the Civil War–and long afterward, for that matter–southerners considered slavery a necessary, profitable, and rational system for generating agricultural wealth and structuring a biracial society.

WESTERN LANDS

The westward migration of settlers in the North paralleled the advance of the cotton frontier in the South. Land was the primary attraction in both areas. The Panic of 1819 broke the back of the surge of speculation that had followed the Treaty of Ghent, however, and land sales remained sluggish for another decade and a half. So many purchase contracts had fallen into arrears that the federal government canceled all credit arrangements in the Land Act of 1820. This same piece of legislation reduced the minimum parcel size from 160 to 80 acres and the base auction price to $1.25 an acre, where it would remain for the rest of the century. The $100 required for a minimum purchase lay beyond the means of most pioneers, though, so a further parcel reduction to 40 acres was authorized in 1832 to bring land ownership within the reach of many more settlers.

Potential farmers lacking the cash to buy land resorted to various alternatives. Tenancy became common as overextended landholders offered to rent idle acreage to anyone willing to put it into production. Some farmers borrowed to pay for desirable properties, but interest rates sometimes went as high as 50 percent or more. A more attractive option with a long history was preemptive settlement on unoccupied lands beyond the survey line. Squatters who had devoted their time, money, and energy to improving such lands were reluctant to lose them to higher bidders when the government finally held its auction. Some squatters formed claim associations made up of neighbors who intimidated outsiders at the sales to insure that the land went to those who had already worked it. The federal government formally recognized squatters' rights in the Preemption Act of 1841 which protected current residents from having land sold out from under them.

Rising wheat and corn prices in the mid-1830s helped set off another round of frenzied land speculation. Figure 4-2 clearly illustrates this boom. Federal land sales totaled over $17 million in 1836 alone, compared to an annual average of less than one million throughout the 1820s. The boom collapsed in conjunction with the Panic of 1837, and sales ran around $2 million per year through the 1840s. Transfers increased once again as the nation's boundaries expanded to the west and

south in the late 1840s. Excessive land speculation then played its now all too familiar role in helping set off the Panic of 1857.

Military land warrants complicated settlement and provided ample opportunity for fraud. The federal government had encouraged enlistments in every war
by rewarding volunteers with warrants or scrip they could exchange for public
lands. After compensating those who had fought in the Mexican War (1846-1848),
vote-seeking congressmen approved retrospective land grants to veterans or their
heirs of virtually any military service all the way back to the Revolution. The land
warrants issued for retrospective bounties in the 1850s amounted to over 45 million
acres, compared to approximately 27 million previously distributed.

Only a minority of those who claimed their land warrants actually used them
to settle on new lands. Most sold them, particularly after legislation in 1850 allowed title to these warrants to be assigned freely. Individuals or companies that

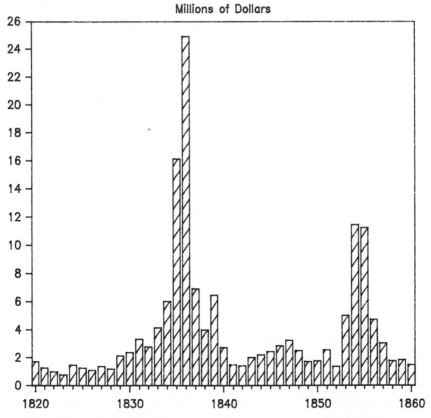

FIGURE 4-2 Receipts from Public Land Sales. (From U.S. Bureau of the Census, *Historical
Statistics of the United States* [Washington, DC: Government Printing Office, Y-263, 1960].)

used them for bulk transfers of land or continued speculation constituted a lively market. Prices fluctuated daily according to perceptions about the supply and demand of both the warrants themselves and the land they represented. Almost 40 percent of Iowa's fertile acreage went from public to private ownership through military bounty warrants. The corruption and uncertainty connected with this business convinced many Americans that homesteads should be distributed free to actual settlers. Veterans were given preferential treatment in the 1862 Homestead Act, but Civil War soldiers did not earn land warrants.

The purchase of land represented only a fraction of the investment a settler had to make in a potential farm. In wooded areas of the country, professional clearing could cost ten dollars an acre or more, so many individuals did that back-breaking work themselves. The trees thinned out as the line of settlement reached the prairies in the 1840s, but there the root-infested soil had to be worked by "sod-busters" who charged anywhere from two to five dollars an acre. Fencing, housing, equipment, seed, livestock, and subsistence for oneself and one's family until the farm came into full production absorbed additional capital. Many years might pass before a Midwestern farm turned a profit. Planters who relied on slaves to do the clearing and building in the Southwest naturally achieved quicker returns.

Wheat and corn were the two major field crops in this period. Wheat grew throughout the United States, but commercial production centered in the Northeast and Midwest. Pennsylvania, New York, and Virginia were still major producers in 1850, but Ohio, Indiana, and Illinois were already overshadowing them. Wheat farming would continue migrating westward through the nineteenth century. As the nation's preferred bread crop, wheat consistently commanded a higher price than corn. A hardier crop that usually produced more bushels per acre, corn was also more versatile, feeding both people and livestock. The leading corn producing states in the 1840s were Illinois, Ohio, Missouri, Indiana, Tennessee, and Kentucky. Much of the surplus corn in the upper Midwest fed livestock and was therefore marketed indirectly in the form of beef and pork.

Cattle and swine were raised in all rural areas. The East supported more dairy than beef cattle, so the coastal cities depended on westerners to provide them with meat. Overland cattle drives had originated in the colonial period and continued to be profitable. The Scioto River Valley in Ohio and, later, the Blue Grass region of Kentucky supported numerous feedlots. Cattle would be bought from farmers, fattened on corn, and then turned over to drovers for the trek east to Pittsburgh and beyond. Smoked or salt pork and beef also rode flatboats down the internal river system to New Orleans.

Although a few resourceful individuals imported purebred stock from Europe hoping to improve American breeds, most farmers were indifferent to livestock quality in this period. A similar disinterest characterized plant-breeding and farming practices. Despite the circulation of publications touting modern agricultural techniques, American farmers were slow to adopt new methods even when they promised to increase productivity and profits.

Advertisement for a McCormick Reaper. (State Historical Society of Wisconsin)

The same could be said for farm mechanization. Jethro Wood patented an ingenious iron plow in 1819 that incorporated several replaceable parts. But, like Eli Whitney and his cotton gin, Wood could not control his invention, so a good many imitations appeared. John Deere took the process a step further, fashioning a plow out of saw steel in 1838. After years of experimentation, he established a factory in Moline, Illinois, to manufacture his plows. It was only when they proved superior to other models in cutting cleanly through the clinging soil of the Great Plains that he found a lucrative market.

Cyrus McCormick achieved financial success with his reaper at about the same time. Labor-intensive wheat harvesting with scythes and cradles severely limited a farmer's ability to plant as much wheat as he could cultivate. Both Mc-Cormick and Obed Hussey devised successful horse-drawn harvesting machinery in the 1830s, but two decades passed before farmers began buying reapers on a large scale. The only type of machinery that caught on in the first half of the nineteenth century were mechanical threshing devices. Threshers were too expensive for most individual farmers to buy, so they shared the costs with their neighbors or relied on centralized threshing operations to process their grain.

How can one explain the growing prosperity of American agriculture in the absence of improved breeds, mechanization, and inexpensive labor in the Midwest? One key factor was the transportation revolution that began in the 1820s. Steam navigation, canals, and railroads cut shipping costs so much that farmers could earn increasing returns for their produce even if the market prices remained stable. Im

CYRUS McCORMICK

The technical problems facing anyone designing a mechanical harvesting machine were daunting. Tough wheat stalks quickly dulled cutting edges, the fields themselves were seldom level, rocks broke teeth and wheels, and the clatter of the machinery spooked the horses and mules harnassed to it. But the potential market was so enormous that many individuals invented mechanical reaping machinery. Obed Hussey was the most famous rival of Cyrus McCormick, but that grim and determined Virginian ultimately prevailed by designing not only a capable machine but a national marketing and distribution system as well.

Cyrus served his mechanical apprenticeship alongside his father, an inveterate tinkerer living on a large farm in Virginia's Shenandoah Valley. Robert McCormick actually built a reaper of his own as well as hemp breakers and other mechanical devices. But young Cyrus surpassed his teacher when he built the prototype of his own reaper in 1831 at the age of twenty-two. He did not get around to patenting his device until 1834, though, and then spent many years in a fruitless iron-mining enterprise. It was not until the early 1840s that he returned to his Virginia shop and began to advertise his reaper. He sold six in 1842 and twenty-nine in the following year, most of them to local customers.

To succeed in this business, Cyrus McCormick had to reach more potential customers. The center of American wheat production was migrating westward with the frontier, so he decided to relocate in Chicago in 1848. There he built a huge factory that incorporated all of the mass production techniques that Eli Whitney and others had pioneered. The plant built 1500 machines in 1849 and steadily increased its output until it had tripled by 1858. Demand for the machinery soared when the Union armies enlisted hundreds of thousands of farmers, so production figures in the 1860 rose accordingly.

Solving the production problems was an easier task in some ways than developing an effective sales strategy. Fully aware that his reapers were prone to accidents and breakdown, McCormick had originally tried to identify local mechanics willing to repair them for all his customers. As the factory's output grew, these informal arrangements evolved into a nationwide network of franchised dealers. Each local proprietor agreed not only to sell, repair, and stock parts for the machines, but also to handle the inevitable credit arrangements. A McCormick reaper cost $130 in the 1850s, a sum well beyond the reach of all but a handful of potential customers. McCormick himself served as a lender of last resort, and farmers often owed him a million dollars or more for machines they had bought on time.

Primarily remembered as the inventor of a machine, Cyrus McCormick deserves full credit for his pioneering in the areas of marketing and distribution. Thousands of other entrepreneurs adopted the techniques he developed. The most obvious descendants of his system are the automobile dealerships that sell, repair, and finance cars around the world today

provements in the nation's transportation system thus encouraged agricultural production and regional specialization at the same time they were altering traditional trading patterns.

SHIPPING DEVELOPMENTS

Between 1820 and 1850 the speed of travel in the United States increased remarkably. About the best a wagon traveling on a sound roadway could do was two miles an hour. By 1850 steamboats and freight trains were averaging ten miles per hour, a fivefold increase. The great clipper ships could knife through the water at over 20 knots, and express trains went faster still. Shipping charges also declined dramatically. It cost about twenty cents a ton-mile to transport goods overland from Buffalo to New York City in 1820. A similar load using either the Erie Canal or the Erie Railroad in the late 1840s traveled for two or three cents a ton-mile. These reductions in time and cost resulted from substantial improvements in river and ocean-going vessels as well as the development of alternatives like canals and railroads.

The United States had always enjoyed a high ranking among the world's seafaring nations, and by mid-century its merchant marine nearly equaled that of the world's leading sea power, Great Britain. Low construction costs in the United States were a definite spur to this growth. Easy access to high quality building materials more than offset the generally higher wage rates that prevailed on this side of the Atlantic, allowing ships to be built in the United States for about thirty-five dollars per ton of displacement as compared to around sixty dollars overseas. As the seas became safer and markets more available in the century of peace that followed the Napoleonic wars, larger ships made sense. The average size of a merchantman tripled between 1820 and 1850. Naval architects also began designing longer, leaner hulls for trading ships. The change produced higher speed operation without impairing cargo capacity or crew efficiency. American skippers and crewmen earned reputations for sobriety and common sense, so shippers around the world were attracted to use their vessels.

Innovative sailing schedules also contributed to improved performance. Trading vessels had traditionally pursued erratic voyages in search of full cargos and favorable markets. In 1818, the Black Ball Line introduced its packet ship strategy: vessels would sail on a set schedule between New York City and Liverpool, England, whether or not their holds or cabins were full. Shippers and passengers appreciated the predictability of this regular operation which was so profitable that other companies soon offered similar service. By 1845 over fifty trans-Atlantic packets were operating, with at least three sailings a week from New York.

Attempts to establish overseas packet service from Boston and other cities were less successful, so New York strengthened its position as the major international shipping center in the United States. At the same time, the packet concept became popular in the coastal trade. Sloops or schooners operating on regular schedules carried passengers and freight up and down the Atlantic shores and into the Gulf of Mexico. All sorts of goods including cotton from the South were distributed in this booming ocean trade.

Irregular or tramp voyages handled the rest of the nation's shipping needs. Just as they had in colonial times, merchants engaged in particular branches of trade often operated their own ships. Other voyages were financed through partners' shares or conducted by company fleets. Owners and companies often granted their captains considerable latitude, even allowing them to use a percentage of the cargo space for their own dealings. This inducement permitted an enterprising captain to profit on the side at the same time it gave him an incentive to seek out the best deals for all of the ship's business.

In the mid-1840s, United States sailing ship design achieved its highest expression with the building of the clippers. These long, sleek ships with towering

An American clipper ship. (The Harry T. Peters Collection, Museum of the City of New York)

expanses of sails and relatively limited cargo space broke one speed record after another. They dominated the China trade because the valuable cargo loaded there justified their higher operating expenses. As specialized vessels, though, they presented little competition to the vast flotilla of conventional sailing ships.

Steam posed little threat to sail either. The enormous supplies of fuel that early ocean-going steamships consumed fatally limited their cargo capacities. One of the more successful experimental voyages in the late 1830s, for example, involved a ship loaded with 750 tons of coal carrying just 500 tons of paying cargo. Until more fuel-efficient engines were developed, steamboat navigation would be profitable only in a coastal or river setting. Fuel was readily available along the inland waterways, especially in the early years when most boilers burned wood. River boats seldom encountered rough seas either, so they could be cheaply constructed and provide extensive cargo capacity. Their obvious advantage over other vessels was their ability to travel up and down stream with equal ease, regardless of wind and water currents. Hundreds of steam-powered vessels plied the rivers, bays, and coastal waters, carrying passengers and freight with comfort, speed, and predictability. The typical eastern steamboat was a comparatively narrow vessel

Cornelius Vanderbilt. (Library of Congress)

CORNELIUS VANDERBILT

Both friends and enemies alike called Cornelius Vanderbilt the "Commodore" long after he had switched most of his attention to railroading. It was an appropriate nickname for a man who had started his career in transportation as an unlettered ferryboat operator in Staten Island. Just sixteen in 1810, young Cornele borrowed $100 from his father to buy a sailboat. He found plenty of passengers and cargo to keep his tiny vessel flitting about the busy New York Harbor. During the War of 1812, the shrewd young captain obtained contracts to provision some of the forts established to protect the city from invaders. His endeavors proved so profitable that Vanderbilt emerged from the conflict as the owner of several boats employed primarily in coastal and river commerce.

In a surprising move, this independent shipowner sold all of his vessels in 1818 and signed on as a captain for Thomas Gibbons, a struggling steam ferry operator. One of his main problems was that New York had granted the Fulton-Livingston combine a monopoly of ferry service so that Gibbons's activities were technically illegal. Fine points of the law never bothered the rough, hard-drinking Vanderbilt who welcomed any excuse for a brawl. Within a year, he had put Gibbons's operation in the black and was encouraging the embattled entrepreneur to add more ships to his fleet. In the famous *Gibbons* vs. *Ogden* case in 1824, the Supreme Court struck down the monopoly legislation and cleared the way for Gibbons to expand legally.

Four years later, Vanderbilt abruptly changed jobs again, forcing his wife to sell the very successful hotel she had run in New Jersey and to move with most of their thirteen children back to New York City. For the next twenty years, the Commodore dominated the coastal trade. Absolutely ruthless in competition, he whittled down his own rates until he had beggared his opponents into bankruptcy or forced them to sell out to him. At the same time, he was designing and having built increasingly elaborate and beautiful ships for the comfort and enjoyment of his passengers.

The California Gold Rush gave Vanderbilt another opportunity to undercut the opposition. Other shipowners were sending their vessels down to the Isthmus of Panama where mules carried goods and people to the other side. To establish a competing service, Vanderbilt obtained a charter from Nicaragua. His Accessory Transit Co. built some canals and roads to facilitate travel across the southern part of that country, and Vanderbilt had eight new ships constructed to link his pathway with San Francisco on the west and New York on the east. Because his route lopped a full two days off the travel time between the coasts, it was heavily used. Vanderbilt's many maritime activities earned him the enormous fortune that financed his extensive railroad buccaneering after the Civil War.

sporting wheels on both sides and a deck-mounted boiler. Low pressure engines remained in service well into the 1830s and their high superstructures with elaborately decorated walking beams were an impressive sight.

Mississippi steamboats evolved along different lines. Because shallow water was a constant worry along the great river and its tributaries, flat bottoms and shallow drafts were essential. The paddle wheels migrated to the sterns of these vessels for increased maneuverability and protection from river obstacles. Mississippi steamboats took full advantage of their broad deck space, piling a couple of stories of cabins and cargo space on top. High pressure engines quickly took hold in the West because they offered more reserve power and could use the muddy river water. These engines also increased the likelihood of boiler explosions, particularly when river skippers tied down their safety valves while racing with rivals. Floods, floating ice, sand bars, embedded trees or snags, and low water also contributed to the dangers and delays of river traffic.

The rapid spread of steamboating on the western rivers stimulated all sorts of enterprise. Rafts or flatboats had traditionally carried agricultural produce down river to New Orleans where the crude vessels were broken up and sold as scrap lumber. Flatboat traffic actually increased in the 1830s and 1840s once the farmers

Labor and Commerce in the Old South. (Library of Congress)

who floated downriver could rely on steamboats to give them speedy return trips. Shallow-draft steamers penetrated far up the Mississippi and the Missouri River networks, stimulating farm production and population growth in Illinois, Wisconsin, Iowa, and beyond.

The steamboat business itself offered substantial profits. Individuals or partnerships owned many of the riverboats in much the same way that ocean-going vessels were financed. The investment required was relatively modest since construction costs for a standard boat ran around $20,000. Many costly and elaborate vessels were built, of course, usually for corporations which sold stock and operated fleets. Some of these companies even offered packet service, but the bulk of the traffic consisted of tramp steamers on the prowl for passengers and cargo. The nation's expanding canal network meanwhile funneled both people and produce to the natural waterways and did their part in stimulating inland shipping.

THE CANAL CRAZE

The concept of connecting rivers and coastal areas with manmade waterways captured the imagination of the American people. The first major project, the Erie Canal, looked so promising as it neared completion in the early 1820s that dozens of other canal-building projects were undertaken throughout the country. Some 1277 miles of artificial waterways were in service by 1830, and that figure had risen to 3326 ten years later. Construction continued after 1840 at a more leisurely pace and, by mid-century, more canal mileage was being abandoned each year than was opening for service. The meteoric rise and decline of the canal craze followed a typically American pattern of overenthusiastic adoption of a concept with only limited feasibility.

Part of the blame lay with the Erie Canal: no other project ever matched its phenomenal success. It ran along a remarkably level route, served a rich hinterland, quickly paid off its investment, and enjoyed enlightened management. Proposals for using the Mohawk River Valley as a canal route had begun circulating even before the turn of the nineteenth century but costs were the major stumbling block. Hope for federal financing died when President Madison vetoed the Bonus Bill in 1817. De Witt Clinton and his fellow enthusiasts therefore switched their lobbying efforts to the New York State Legislature. That body created a Canal Board made up of state officials, including Governor Clinton himself, to administer the project. The legislators also increased some taxes and authorized government loans to finance the building of the waterway. In return, the state was to receive all revenues associated with the operation of the canal.

The Canal Board issued hundreds of subcontracts, some for segments as short as a quarter of a mile. That allowed a great many people to benefit from the public funds allocated for the work. Because formal engineering training was unknown in the United States, the contractors literally learned on the job. Lacking power shovels or heavy earthmoving equipment, workers used spades and wheelbarrows supplemented by plows and scrapers. Stone construction was favored over timber or

The Erie Canal. (New York Public Library, The T.N. Phelps Stokes Collection)

earthworks, and one of the self-taught engineers on the project developed a patentable cement that hardened under water, the forerunner of concrete.

The board wisely let the first contracts for the central section where the geography was most favorable, allowing the first ninety-five miles of the canal to open in the fall of 1819, just over two years after the groundbreaking. Tolls collected from boats using the completed portion of the canal helped fund construction of the western and eastern extensions. The ditch reached Albany in 1823, and the completed canal opened for business in October 1825. It ran 40 feet wide and 4 feet deep for 363 miles from Lake Erie to the Hudson River. Eighty-three locks raised and lowered boats over the 675 vertical feet traversed, and 18 aqueducts carried them over rivers and valleys. A separate 22-mile-long canal linked the Hudson to Lake Champlain in the north, drawing all parts of the state together with a water network.

A tow-path for the horses or mules that pulled heavily laden vessels ran the length of the canal. All of the boats were privately owned, either by individuals or companies. Some companies ran passenger packets back and forth, but most vessels were freighters. The major commodity carried was wheat or wheat flour, but virtually anything and everything including immigrants and livestock rode canal boats in both directions. The 3000 boats using the canal in the mid-1830s created so much congestion that the board decided to increase the size of the waterway to seventy feet wide and seven feet deep. The expansion project was not completed until the 1860s, and the canal did not achieve its peak tonnage until 1880. Revenue from the tolls quickly paid for the canal's $7,143,789 initial cost and provided financing for its operation, expansion, and repair for years afterward.

Pennsylvania residents, jealous of the benefits flowing to their commercial rivals in New York City, were determined to build a rival canal from Philadelphia to Pittsburgh. Begun in 1826, the Pennsylvania Main Line Canal was completed eight years later. Even though it included more than twice as many locks as the Erie, the Portage Railroad had to be built to cross the mountainous backbone of the state. This complex of inclined planes, tracks, and winches hauled segmented canal boats over the top piece by piece. It represented an unavoidable bottleneck that naturally reduced the canal's overall carrying capacity, and it suffered from financial crises and railroad competition as well. The Main Line Canal and its impractical, overextended feeder canal system nearly bankrupted the state government which had spent more than $65 million on public works projects by 1860.

Other states also suffered near fatal attacks of canal fever. Indiana joined Pennsylvania in teetering on the verge of financial collapse after its extensive canal system generated revenues equal to only about one-third of its construction costs. Most New England canals were unprofitable as well. Virginia sponsored one major canal project up the James River and west toward the mountains. It also cooperated with the state of Maryland and the federal government in providing funds for the famous Chesapeake & Ohio Canal. The C & O was larger than most other canals and solidly built, but these advantages delayed its completion. It ran parallel to the Potomac River, reaching Cumberland, Maryland, in 1850, just four years before the Baltimore & Ohio Railroad rendered it redundant.

A few projects paid off handsomely. Ohio built two successful north-south canals connecting Lake Erie with the Ohio River, one in the east serving Cleveland and the other for Toledo in the west. Illinois spent exorbitant amounts to link Lake Michigan and the Illinois River in 1848, but it is one of the few manmade waterways still in use. Several privately financed eastern canals paid good dividends, particularly those that carried coal from the Pennsylvania anthracite fields to seaboard cities.

Even the most successful canals had several disadvantages. They could operate only on a seasonal basis due to freezing, flooding, or drought. No matter how large a canal might be, locks created delays and dictated the maximum size of the boats it could handle. Speed was limited to four miles per hour or less, so perishable goods could not be shipped. Most jurisdictions caved in to the persistent lobbying of those the major canals bypassed and ended up throwing away enormous sums on inefficient feeder lines. But the key factor undermining the profitability of canals was the nearly simultaneous development of railroads which, though they had their own set of drawbacks, soon proved themselves superior to canals.

EARLY RAILROADS

The initial legislation concerning railways treated them like turnpikes. It was assumed, for example, that companies chartered to construct them would make their

Classic American-style wood-burning locomotive. (Sante Fe Railway Photo)

profits off tolls they collected from privately owned vehicles using the tracks. Traffic management considerations quickly convinced the railroad companies that they must own and operate all the rolling stock. Because they had to rent cargo space and passenger accommodations on a continuing basis, a railroad was a more complex business than a canal company. In addition to surveying routes, constructing roadbeds, laying rails, and establishing yards, it also had to buy and maintain locomotives and cars and superintend an on-going transportation operation.

The first railroad builders had to make a number of basic decisions about both construction and operations. They first had to choose from among a number of proposed types of rails. Granite blocks with grooves cut in them were solid and level, but so rigid that they quickly wore out rolling stock. Wooden rails were flexible enough but wore out rapidly. Fastening an iron strap along the top to reduce wear seemed advisable until it broke loose and curled up, ready to destroy anything passing over. Some roads continued to use these strap rails right through the Civil War even though cast iron T-rails, later made of steel, had been developed in the 1830s. This flexible, long-wearing design became the world's standard.

A prospective railroad baron also had to decide how far apart to lay his rails. Many of the first locomotives were imported from England, and the rails were therefore laid to match. British wagon wheels had traditionally been set at a standard width of five feet. When the 3.5 inches the two wheels themselves occupied was subtracted, the distance between the tracks came to 4 feet 8 1/2 inches. This gauge became quite common throughout most of the Northeast and was adopted as standard in the United States after the Civil War. Until that standardization, however, rails and equipment varied considerably and prevented interchangeability of rolling stock.

The precursors to steam railroads were tramways using either horses or stationary steam winches to haul cars. Well into the 1830s railroad companies kept teams of horses on hand to step in when their primitive steam locomotives inevitably broke down. Technological improvements came along quite rapidly, though, as American manufacturers responded to the challenge of building powerful, high-pressure locomotive engines. Because roadbeds in the United States involved many more curves than their British counterparts, Americans installed a four-wheel bogie truck in front of the large-diameter driving wheels to guide the locomotive along the tracks. Sanding systems were also developed to increase the friction between the drivers and sloping or icy rails. Cow catchers—to prevent damage to the locomotive, not to protect stray animals—were another distinctly American requirement.

Winning public acceptance was, in some cases, as difficult as overcoming technological obstacles. Some Americans genuinely feared that speeds of thirty miles per hour or more could be fatal to passengers and crew. Others opposed railroads for safety and pollution reasons. Canal fever blinded many Americans to the advantages railroads offered. New Yorkers were perhaps the most extreme opponents because they had invested so much in their expanding canal system. For some time, in fact, railroads that paralleled sections of the Erie Canal had to pay to the state the same tolls for the freight they carried that boat owners did. Fear that railroad competition might bankrupt the canals was hardly irrational. As early as 1835 the Boston & Lowell Railroad was carrying freight twenty times faster than the Middlesex Canal could, and the canal company shortly went out of business.

Regional competition with waterways sometimes had the opposite effect, acting as a stimulus to railroad construction. The longest road in the United States when it was completed in the early 1830s, the Charleston & Hamburg Railway linked South Carolina's coastal port with the Savannah River. Charlestonians had built it to siphon Georgia's cotton away from its normal route down river to Savannah. Construction of the Baltimore & Ohio began in 1828—earlier than any other major railroad—because Baltimore businesses felt their port could not compete with New York and Philadelphia, both being linked by canals to the interior. After seriously considering the construction of a canal from Boston to the Hudson River, the Massachusetts state government decided instead to charter the Boston & Worcester Railroad Co. It completed a connection with the Erie Canal in the early 1840s. Many other shorter lines were also designed to tie canals, rivers, and seaports together.

Four hundred railroads were chartered in the 1830s. Although the Panic of 1837 significantly dampened enthusiasm for canal projects, railroad building continued at an average rate of over 400 miles a year, bringing a total of 2808 miles of track into operation by 1840. Most of this mileage was scattered about in bits and pieces, but the end of the canal boom encouraged even faster growth in the next ten years. The Middle West lacked the population and resources to fund such expensive internal improvements projects and the South lagged behind as well, so most

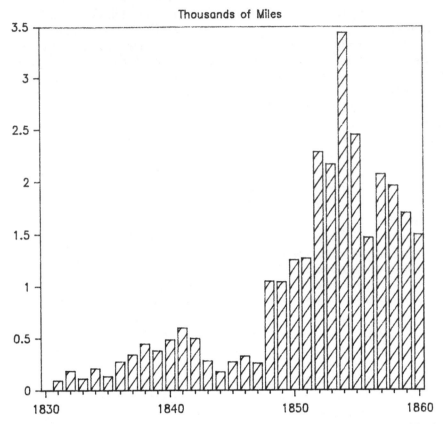

FIGURE 4-3   Miles of Railroad Built. (From U.S. Bureau of the Census, *Historical Statistics of the United States* [Washington, DC: Government Printing Office, Q-43, 1960].)

of the building in this decade was concentrated in the Northeast. A desire to unite the eastern seaboard with the Ohio River was the major motive for the development of the four major east-west lines in this region.

As noted above, the Baltimore & Ohio had optimistically set off toward that goal in 1828, but its progress was very slow. By 1832 it had only reached Frederick, Maryland, forty miles inland. It constantly had to compete with the Chesapeake & Ohio Canal for funding and state favor, and the Panic of 1837 hurt as well. Its management wisely decided to send branches to Philadelphia and Washington long before it achieved its western objective. The B & O did not reach the Ohio River port of Wheeling in western Virginia until 1854.

Like the C & O in Maryland, the Erie Canal exerted such a powerful influence in New York State that proponents of parallel rail lines faced stiff opposition. The Erie Railroad got off to a shaky financial start in the late 1830s, and it finally began substantial operations in the following decade. Its route along New York's southern border from New York City to Buffalo looked fairly direct on a map, but it passed through hilly and mountainous country that complicated and delayed construction. Even so, the Erie reached the lake for which it was named in 1851, two years before the New York Central opened its statewide service across the level terrain further north. The latter company had strung together ten shorter intercity lines in making its way from the Hudson River to Lake Erie.

Although destined to become the busiest of the four major east-west trunk lines, the Pennsylvania Railroad was actually the last to be chartered. The Main Line Canal and its connector railroads already provided passenger and freight service from Philadelphia to the West. As in New York the state legislature was reluctant to charter an obvious competitor to its publicly owned canal system. Plenty of money became available to finance the project once it won approval in 1846, so construction moved ahead much faster than on any of the other trunk lines. It reached the Ohio River at Pittsburgh in 1852.

Impressive as it was, the construction that took place in the 1840s was dwarfed in the next decade. Some 30,000 miles of track were in service in 1860, more than three times the 9000 in operation as of 1850. Capital invested in American railroads had also tripled, surpassing the billion-dollar mark before the decade ended. Construction continued in all sections of the country, though New England had the least need for it because its major rail arteries had already been completed. Mileage in the Middle Atlantic region doubled, while the South, which had lagged somewhat in the 1840s, quadrupled the track in service by 1860. The biggest boom occurred in the Old Northwest, with Ohio, Indiana, and Illinois leading the way. By 1860 Ohio boasted a more extensive railroad network than any other state, and Illinois ranked second.

Having crossed the Appalachian barrier, the major race was to reach Chicago and tap the rich Midwestern hinterland. The Pennsylvania Railroad took over the Pittsburgh, Ft. Wayne & Chicago line to establish through service from Philadelphia to Lake Michigan. Other companies linked the New York trunklines with Cleveland and points west through northern Ohio and Indiana. Two major roads crossed Michigan on the way to the same Chicago terminus, offering passengers and shippers alternative carrier and route choices. Eleven different roads eventually converged on Chicago and made it the central hub in the northern railroad network. The B & O meanwhile headed to the southwest to establish a tie through Cincinnati to St. Louis in 1857.

While the comprehensive railroad network provided convenient service to virtually all of the citizens living in the Midwest, the southern roads were less comprehensive. By 1860 only one connected route carried passengers from the east coast to the Mississippi by way of Richmond and Memphis. Several roads did stretch north from the Gulf to river ports in the border states. The southerners' failure to complete an integrated railroad system prior to 1861 would have fateful consequences when they needed to move troops and supplies during the Civil War.

Laying additional track was only one way that rail service improved in the 1850s. The Erie Railroad first used telegraphy to regulate train movement up and down its tracks in 1851. All railroads faced with handling complex traffic flow quickly followed suit. A few roads experimented with night passenger service in primitive sleeping cars, anticipating the introduction of the popular Pullman model that appeared after the Civil War. A traveler could also purchase a through ticket at his point of departure even though his trip might involve several train changes as he crossed the country and entered different companies' service areas. All of these innovations added to the complexities of management in what was rapidly emerging as the major business enterprise in the United States.

THE RAILROAD BUSINESS

State governments had quickly recognized the boost canals could give their economies, and railroads promised similar tangible and intangible benefits to the regions they served. The indirect returns from transportation projects often outweighed the value of the stock dividends and interest payments they made. Even a railroad company that failed to turn a profit year after year could still serve its customers in vital ways. Railroads stimulated production on local farms, brought freight from distant locations at low cost, and linked communities to one another and the outside world. State and local governments therefore rushed to support railroad projects.

They offered some encouragement through favorable charter provisions. As noted in the previous chapter, corporations had become common long before the first railroad promoters requested authorization to build. Crucial to any railroad charter was the power of eminent domain that allowed them to obtain the real estate they needed. Some state legislatures also granted corporations the exclusive right to lay rails along particular routes. Charters might also include short- or long-term tax exemptions, and most avoided restricting the number and types of securities a corporation could issue. Some railroad companies were even permitted to establish banks. Occasionally a charter limited profit margins or rate charges, but these were often evaded or unenforced.

Governments also financed much railroad construction. The absence of federal support until the 1850s left this responsibility to state and local authorities. States contributed over $100 million of the approximately $350 million that went into railroad construction and equipment nationwide from 1830 to 1850. The total invested by city and local governments may have been even larger. Public financing therefore provided the majority of all the money spent on American railroading in its first two decades. Private corporations spent most of the state money funneled into the industry in this period. Sometimes funds were granted outright as for the Erie Railroad which needed two separate transfusions of state money to stay in business. More often the financing became available when a state treasurer bought blocks of stocks or bonds of railroads expected to benefit the local economy.

Some governments even built railroads themselves, just as New York had done with the Erie Canal. State projects could be relatively minor like the railroad sections incorporated into the Pennsylvania Main Line Canal, but others were quite substantial. The state of Georgia dedicated fully one quarter of its total expendi-

RAILROAD LAW OF NEW YORK, ACT OF APRIL 2, 1850

This general incorporation law noted the steps necessary for individuals to form a railroad company. Section 10 outlines the limits on a stockholder's liability.

SECTION 1. Any number of persons, not less than twenty-five, may form a company for the purpose of constructing, maintaining, and operating a railroad for public use in the conveyance of persons and property, or for the purpose of maintaining and operating any unincorporated railroad already constructed for the like public use; and for that purpose may make and sign articles of association, in which shall be stated the name of the company; the number of years the same is to continue; the places from and to which the road is to be constructed, or maintained and operated; the length of such road as near as may be, and the name of each county in this State through or into which it is made, or intended to be made; the amount of the capital stock of the company, which shall not be less than ten thousand dollars for every mile of road constructed, or proposed to be constructed, and the number of shares of which said capital stock shall consist and the names and places of residence of thirteen directors of the company, who shall manage its affairs for the first year, and until others are chosen in their places. Each subscriber to such articles of association shall subscribe thereto his name, place of residence, and the number of shares of stock he agrees to take in said company. On compliance with the provisions of the next section, such articles of association may be filed in the office of the Secretary of State, . . . and thereupon the persons who have so subscribed such articles of association, and all persons who shall become stockholders in such company, shall be a corporation by the name specified in such articles of association and shall possess the powers and privileges granted to corporations. . .

SECTION 10. Each stockholder of any company formed under this act shall be individually liable to the creditors of such company, to an amount equal to the amount unpaid on the stock held by him, for all the debts and liabilities of such company, until the whole amount of the capital stock so held by him shall have been paid to the company. . .

(Reprinted in Henry M. Flint, *Railroads of the United States* [Philadelphia.: John E. Potter and Co., 1868], pp. 426-28.)

tures to railroads in the 1830s and then raised its ante to more than a third in the 1840s. When no private promoters appeared interested in linking Atlanta with

Chattanooga, Tennessee, the government began building the Atlantic Railroad in 1836 and completed it fifteen years later. This road continued to operate as a Georgia government enterprise for another twenty years. The midwestern states of Illinois, Indiana, and Michigan were conspicuous for their expenditures on state-run railroad projects. These were typically sold to private companies after they had proven their worth.

Smaller jurisdictions followed the lead of state governments in financing railroad development. To gain a commercial advantage over its rival, Albany, the city of Troy, New York, built and operated the Troy & Schenectedy Railroad. When the state capital emerged victorious in this competition, Troy had to sell its enterprise at a great loss. Such direct involvement was rare. A city's contribution usually came in the form of stock and bond purchases, land grants for yards or rights of way, or gifts of lumber and other building supplies.

Congress approved its first federal land grant for railroad construction in 1850. Proceeds from the sale of certain federal lands had been earmarked for specific purposes from time to time, but the proposed Illinois Central Railroad was the first major project to break the long-standing opposition to federal aid for internal improvements. This ambitious project connected Chicago with the southern Illinois city of Cairo at the junction of the Ohio and Mississippi Rivers. When the full 700 miles of track had been laid, it constituted the longest railroad in the United States. A connecting road south to New Orleans also received federal allocations of six sections of land for each mile of track put in service. The land adjacent to the tracks naturally attracted much higher bids than did other parts of the public domain. The government therefore doubled the minimum auction price on the alternating sections it retained to compensate for revenue lost when it gave the rest to the railroads. A number of federal land grants in succeeding years assisted railroad-building efforts.

Private investors put up the rest of the money railroads absorbed before the Civil War. Local businessmen who recognized the advantages regular rail service could bring to their enterprises were prime investors in the railroads that served their communities. Railroad promoters knew that an offer to serve a particular town would stimulate investment from local sources. Formal and informal groups exhorted their members and their neighbors to contribute. Merchant groups in Baltimore and Charleston contributed generously to the financing of the companies building roads in their vicinity. The Baltimore money pouring into the B & O Railroad naturally competed with the tax revenues the Maryland state government was sinking into the Chesapeake & Ohio Canal.

Railroad stocks replaced canal shares as the most popular sellers on Wall Street in the 1840s. Once basic rail service had been established along the East coast, speculators and investors in that region began buying the stocks and bonds of more distant railroad companies. American railroad securities also sold well in England and other European countries. Banking on the naïveté of far-off investors, some unscrupulous promoters issued excessive amounts of stock for small or nonexistent roads.

DANIEL C. McCALLUM'S SUPERINTENDENT'S REPORT

*While serving as general superintendent of the New York and Erie Railroad
in the 1850s, Daniel C. McCallum developed a comprehensive management
scheme which was to serve as a model for other railroads and industries.*

Under the circumstances, it will scarcely be expected that we can at once
adopt any plan of operations which will not require amendment and a reasonable time to prove its worth. A few general principles, however, may be regarded as settled and necessary in its formation, amongst which are:

1. A proper division of responsibilities.
2. Sufficient power conferred to enable the same to be fully carried out, that
    such responsibilities may be real in their character.
3. The means of knowing whether such responsibilities are faithfully exe-
    cuted.
4. Great promptness in the report of all derelictions of duty, that evils may be
    at once corrected.
5. Such information, to be obtained through a system of daily reports and
    checks that will not embarrass principal officers, nor lessen their influence
    with their subordinates.
6. The adoption of a system, as a whole, which will not only enable the Gen-
    eral Superintendent to detect errors immediately, but will also point out
    the delinquent.

ORGANIZATION

The following comprises a list of the principal officers acting directly under
the General Superintendent, with powers and duties arranged with reference
to obtaining the results proposed.

1. Division and Branch Superintendents.
2. Masters of Engine and Car Repairs.
3. Car Inspectors.
4. General Freight Agent.
5. General Ticket Agent.
6. General Wood Agent.
7. Superintendent of Telegraph.
8. Foreman of Bridge Repairs.

(Reprinted from *Reports of the President and Superintendent of the New York and Erie Railroad to the Stockholders, for the Year Ending September 30, 1855*, in Alfred D. Chandler, ed., *The Railroads: Pioneers in Modern Management* [New York: Arno Press, 1979], pp. 34-36.)

A good many railroad ventures failed to live up to the promises of their advocates. Stock dividends in the late 1840s averaged 4 or 5 percent while some bonds offered interest payments twice as high. Weak companies sometimes sold additional securities to obtain cash to fatten their dividend payments rather than to spend on capital improvements. A popular method for skimming profits from funds earmarked for expansion or improvements was to create a construction company separate from the railroad's operating company. Railroad officials often retained all of the construction company's stock for themselves. They profited enormously when this organization negotiated padded or inflated building contracts with the parent company.

The separation between construction and operation was just one example of the growing division of a railroad's management responsibilities. Unlike a farm, mine, or factory which involved supervision of a limited number of workers doing similar tasks, a railroad could have hundreds of employees handling divergent jobs sprinkled over an extensive area. The growing size and complexity of railroad operations forced them to develop innovative management structures. Daniel McCallum, superintendent of the Erie Railroad, described the diversified organizational structure he had developed in 1855, and many other companies used it as a model for their own organizations. Typically, the board of directors met only intermittently to set overall goals, leaving branch supervisors, engineers, conductors, and foremen to make key decisions relating to the railroad's day-to-day operation. This dispersion of decision-making responsibilities could give employees with little or none of their own capital invested in the company a great deal of authority over other people's funds.

Some years ago economic historian Walt Rostow postulated a theory of economic growth that identified a series of specific developmental stages. In his view, the year 1843 marked the beginning of the "take-off" stage in the United States when industrialization entered a period of self-sustained growth. Essential to such an industrial take-off was a "leading sector," one which galvanized the economy, absorbed substantial financial and entrepreneurial resources, and encouraged growth in secondary industrial sectors. Rostow identified railroads as the leading sector in this country, but others have criticized some of Rostow's conclusions. Some data, for example, suggest that the stimulation railroads gave to secondary sectors like the iron and coal industries may have been less pronounced than he claimed. Even so, the concept of railroading as a leading sector remains a useful one from a business perspective. As other large-scale enterprises appeared, they quickly adopted the methods of financing and operation the railroads had pioneered. Furthermore, the improved transportation network that steamboats, canals, and railroads created definitely encouraged urbanization and regional specialization in manufacturing and related industries.

THE CONTINUING INDUSTRIAL EVOLUTION

The switch from household or shop manufacturing to integrated factories did not occur overnight. Many people continued to hand make items at home well into the nineteenth century, especially in rural and frontier areas. Skilled carpenters and joiners in woodworking shops made the bulk of the nation's furniture. Cobblers fitted shoes to individual customers. Blacksmiths capable of fashioning and repairing utensils and tools were in constant demand. Although Rochester and Baltimore developed enormous grain-milling complexes, most flour mills continued to serve local customers. The dispersion of the rural population and the extent of the nation's settled area discouraged the centralization of many functions.

Industrialization did move ahead in other sectors, however. As the improving transportation network brought down distribution costs, it expanded the potential market for many entrepreneurs. Larger markets, in turn, encouraged more investment in enterprises which could mass produce commodities at lower costs than similar handmade items. The transportation revolution thus paved the way for regional specialization. Able to distribute their output nationwide, certain cities or districts could consolidate capital, labor, raw materials, and expertise in specific enterprises.

Rising customer expectations also fostered centralized production. Individual craftsmen working at home or in shops without modern machinery simply could not manufacture some items. A blacksmith at his country forge, for example, could hardly build a steam locomotive or, for that matter, shape a smooth-running set of flanged railroad wheels. Larger production units equipped with plenty of power and machine tools were essential. In addition to their fascination with gadgets and inventions, American tinkerers and mechanics were constantly experimenting with ways to streamline manufacturing processes and increase productivity.

Factories differed in a number of ways from the shops and mills they replaced. Substantial capital was required just to get a factory started. The company was expected to provide buildings, machinery, raw materials, and power, while the workers supplied their own labor and expertise in return for wages. Factories often combined several steps or processes under one roof, although full integration on the Waltham pattern was relatively rare before the Civil War. Many companies filled specific customers' orders just as craft shops did. A railroad might develop a list of specifications for the locomotives it wanted to buy and submit it to a manufacturer who would strive to meet these requirements. Other factories emphasized the making of massive numbers of identical items, and their production frequently ran well ahead of demand.

The textile mill that the Boston Associates built at Waltham was a model establishment. It returned such attractive dividends on invested capital that the corporation constructed copies of it at many other sites. The Associates built so many factories, in fact, that by 1850 they handled about one-fifth of all the textile manufacturing in the United States. Virtually all of the mills were located in New England, exemplifying the regional specialization in the textile business. Half of all the factory-made cloth in the United States came from Massachusetts and Rhode Island. Philadelphia, at the heart of the most substantial and diversified manufacturing region in the country, was also a major textile producer. Its factories specialized in higher grade cloth and, in the late 1840s, they moved into carpet manufacturing as well.

The development of sewing machinery stimulated further demand for cloth. Although a couple of other tinkerers had devised similar processes, Elias Howe independently developed and patented a machine in which the thread ran through a hole in the pointed end of the needle. This thread made a lock stitch with another one carried on a revolving bobbin below. Howe lacked the capital to merchandise his invention, though, opening the way for Isaac Merritt Singer. As a penniless mechanic, Singer had designed a machine with a flat sewing table and a presser foot to hold the cloth in position. After years of patent litigation, the manufacturers of sewing machinery formed a "combination" to pay both Howe and Singer appropriate royalties for their innovations. Singer then created a company with a remarkably successful sales strategy based on the maintenance of local service facilities. Singer sewing machines were soon being marketed all over the world.

The most widespread and long-lived fashion development in American history began inadvertently. A dry goods merchant named Levi Strauss took a diversified shipment of cloth to the California gold fields in the 1850s and quickly sold everything except the tough denim fabric used for tenting. The mildness of the California climate made tents unnecessary. Strauss observed that the miners' wool and cotton trousers rapidly deteriorated in their rough outdoor life, so he had the heavy cloth sewn and riveted into ill-fitting trousers. They sold out immediately. He ordered more denim from the East and established a permanent factory to produce his popular heavy-duty garments, now universally known simply as "levis."

Several other individuals' names became associated with products or processes they developed in this period. Charles Goodyear was obsessed with finding a commercial use for natural latex. Heat melted it into a sticky mess; cold made latex brittle and crumbly. Goodyear was so poor that he did some of his experimentation while confined to a debtor's prison. He finally discovered vulcanization when he accidentally spilled sulfur into a pan of heated latex. Vulcanized rubber retained its softness and flexibility at extreme temperatures, making it a useful material for a number of industrial and domestic uses.

Cooking and sealing foods to preserve them for later consumption had a long history, but several developments in this period lay the foundations for a commercial packaged-food industry. A machine that fabricated tin cans appeared in 1847, and these durable containers were soon preserving items as diverse as Columbia River salmon and garden vegetables. In 1856 Gail Borden perfected a method for

SINGER AND HOWE BATTLE OVER THE SEWING MACHINE

Before Elias Howe and Isaac Merritt Singer worked out a mutually beneficial royalty scheme, they carried on a publicity war asserting their exclusive rights to the invention. The following items appeared in the classified columns of New York papers in the summer of 1853. The first is from Howe, the next is Singer's rebuttal, and the last is Howe's cautionary notice.

The Sewing Machine.−It has been recently decided by the United States Court that Elias Howe, Jr., of No. 305 Broadway, was the originator of the Sewing Machines now extensively used. Call at his office and see forty of them in constant use upon cloth, leather, etc., and judge for yourselves as to their practicability. Also see a certified copy, from the records of the United States Court, of the injunction against Singer's machine (so called) which is conclusive. He has a suit now pending against the two-needle machines, so called, and is about commencing suit against all others offered to the public except those licensed under his patent. You that want sewing machines, be cautious how you purchase them of others than him or those licensed under him, else the law will compel you to pay twice over.

Sewing Machines.−For the last two years Elias Howe, Jr., of Massachusetts, has been threatening suits and injunctions against all the world who make, use or sell Sewing Machines−claiming himself to be the original inventor thereof. We have sold many machines−are selling them rapidly, and have good right to sell them. The public do not acknowledge Mr. Howe's pretensions, and for the best of reasons. 1. Machines made according to Howe's patent are of no practical use. He tried several years without being able to introduce one. 2. It is notorious, especially in New-York, that Howe was not the original inventor of the machine combining the needle and shuttle, and that his claim to that is not valid. . . Finally−We make and sell the best SEWING MACHINES−the only good ones in use; and so far from being under injunction, we are ready to sell and have perfect right to sell our Straight Needle, Perpendicular Action Sewing Machines−secured by two patents in the United States−at the very low price of $100, at our offices in New-York, Boston, Philadelphia, Baltimore and Cincinnati.

ALL PERSONS ARE CAUTIONED against publishing the libelous advertisements of I. M. Singer & Co. against me as they will be prosecuted to the fullest extent of the law for such publications. I have this day commenced action for libel against the publishers of the said Singer & Co.'s infamous libel upon me in this morning's *Tribune*. . .

(Reprinted in Ruth Brandon, *A Capitalist Romance: Singer and the Sewing Machine* [Philadelphia: Lippincott, 1977], pp. 90-91.)

evaporating and storing milk in unrefrigerated cans. Two years later John L. Mason patented a screw-top glass jar that was a boon for both home and commercial canners. These developments would shortly prove vital to the feeding of the vast Union and Confederate armies.

All of these products and processes depended to a degree upon the increasing quality and sophistication of the nation's metalworking capabilities. Iron production in the United States became industrialized, although not as quickly as it had in Great Britain. Part of the lag stemmed from the continuing American preference for iron processed with charcoal. Since colonial times, charcoal furnaces had produced pig iron at hundreds of locations throughout the country. Blacksmiths preferred this type of metal because it was both malleable and easy to weld. It also proved suitable for many railroad uses. Knowledge of chemistry was rudimentary at that point, though, and techniques such as hammering and puddling produced iron of variable quality. Coke-fired furnaces in England were meanwhile producing a somewhat inferior product at a substantially lower price. Abundant deposits of coking coal existed in western Pennsylvania, but its high sulfur content discouraged its use until later.

The major industrial ironworks in the United States clustered along the East Coast in the vicinity of Philadelphia. An exception was the Tredegar Iron Works, founded in 1838 in Richmond, Virginia, and destined to become the leading metalworking plant in the South. Raw materials for the iron industry could be found almost anywhere. The opening of the Sault Sainte Marie Canal in the upper Great Lakes in 1855 allowed the abundant iron resources along Lake Superior to be tapped, and they were supplying half of the nation's ore by 1860.

Railroads absorbed as much as 30 thirty percent of the iron produced in the 1840s, and it was the chief ingredient in machinery. As refining techniques improved, innovative uses for the metal were developed. Iron facings for city buildings were installed, and the iron ships constructed along the Delaware River were lighter and more durable than their wooden counterparts. Steel began appearing in the United States in the 1840s, much of it destined for the small arms factories whose products enjoyed a worldwide reputation for craftsmanship and quality.

American manufacturers were equally adept at fashioning machinery and tools for factories. Francis Cabot Lowell had recognized the importance of cleverly designed and well-constructed machinery. The company Eli Whitney had founded continued to devote its resources and ingenuity to developing new and better machine tool applications. Samuel Colt invented his revolver while working at the Whitney establishment, and he applied the principles he had learned there when he built his own factory. The many Connecticut brassworks that had sprung up in the early part of the century continued to thrive, turning out a vast assortment of products ranging from simple buttons and pots to intricate clocks and nautical instruments.

By 1860 the industrialization of the urban areas between Boston and Baltimore was well advanced. At that point 140,000 factories were in operation, employing well over a million workers. Most were quite small, with fewer than ten workers each, but larger firms had come into being with extensive financial backing and hundreds of employees. Few factories could match the railroads in these respects, but they had already begun to grapple with similar organizational problems. America's industrial entrepreneurs had to become skilled managers, developing or adapting new techniques for dealing with their production, finance, and distribution problems.

THE MANAGEMENT OF BUSINESS

Shops and factories employing a handful of workers posed few management problems. The owner might be a craftsman himself who participated in the work while assigning other tasks to his employees. The shop could also double as a sales outlet. Cabinet makers or tailors, for example, often made and sold their wares on the same premises. The limited amount of capital required could be obtained from a single lending agency or by reinvesting profits.

As the size and complexity of an industrial enterprise increased, the management functions became differentiated. Historian Thomas C. Cochran has identified three types of business specialists that most industries required. Fundamental to any operation were foremen or plant managers who dealt directly with the workers, superintending the day-to-day tasks. Other individuals, those with expertise in the realms of banking, accounting, real estate, and the like handled company finances. Finally, most enterprises relied on persons skilled at external relations like sales or promotion. Because few individual businessmen were expert in all areas, industrial management became increasingly specialized.

The larger the factory or railroad, the less contact occurred among those carrying on their specialized functions. At the production level, the trend toward separation and specialization of tasks extended to the workers themselves. They might belong to a work crew headed by a foreman who submitted bids on particular jobs within the factory. As a carry-over from the independent shop era, this sort of internal contracting was quite common in the first half of the nineteenth century, but it faded in the face of more centralized management decision-making and increasing job specialization. The distinction between production and finance also became more pronounced. Separate financial offices assumed the responsibility for raising, allocating, and dispersing company's funds. If a company's output was large enough, it might employ its own sales force. Traveling salesmen called *drummers*—they were supposed to be out drumming up business—became common figures throughout the United States, going from town to town with their models, samples, and catalogs.

External supports were available for firms, both small and large, which did not care to or could not handle their own distribution. Just as factory jobs became differentiated, so too did the activities of merchants. Growing markets allowed some businessmen to specialize in particular commodities or lines of goods that they obtained at import auctions or in large lots from domestic factories. In most large northeastern cities by the 1840s, mercantile specialists had largely supplanted the general merchants of earlier times. As these agents refined and extended their control over particular segments of the trade, the traditional import auction system disappeared as well. Nearly 3000 commission houses were operating in New York City alone at mid-century and handling consignments of goods from factories and importers for a percentage of their value. Sometimes they sold items directly through their own retail outlets; more often they acted as jobbers supplying other retailers throughout the country.

Although small town and rural merchants continued to operate general stores, cities supported a variety of specialty stores. Food, books, dry goods, and hard

---

ALEXANDER T. STEWART

As a child growing up in his native Ireland, Alexander Stewart gave no indication that he would achieve phenomenal business success. After visiting New York, however, he returned to Ireland to claim a $5000 inheritance and invested most of it in fine handmade Irish lace. He brought it back to America where, at the age of twenty in 1823, he opened a small shop on lower Broadway. Stewart's business never stopped growing. He always paid cash for anything he bought but did extend credit to buyers. His cash-only policy protected him from swings in the business cycle. When other textile merchants went broke during the Panic of 1837, he was able to buy their stock at auctions and then resell it later at substantial profits.

To handle his expanding dry goods trade, Alexander Stewart created America's first true department store in 1846. He built a large building in which he conducted both wholesale and retail trade in all grades of cloth from coarse burlap to the finest silks and satins. Depending upon which fabric they wished to buy, customers were directed to the appropriate section or department of the store that specialized in it. An expansion in 1850 made his establishment the largest store in New York, and he became the proprietor of the largest retail emporium in the world when he opened a new building in 1862. It had cost nearly $3 million and employed 2000 people in its myriad departments.

The marketing mogul had meanwhile bought controlling interests in many textile mills in the Northeast to supply his store, and he maintained overseas offices and warehouses to collect goods for import. His prominence in the industry inevitably won him contracts as a major supplier to the Union Army during the Civil War. His annual income exceeded $2 million at the height of his wartime endeavors. In addition to investing in hotels, theaters, and other manufacturing and mercantile properties, he donated heavily to a variety of charities. Stewart's success as a merchant thus placed him in company with the nation's leading industrialists and financiers.

ware sold at their own retail outlets. Further specialization took place within prod-uct lines: some merchants handled coarser fabrics, for example, while others dealt only in costly silks and other high-grade imported textiles. Ambitious dealers could expand the extent of their market reach or the number of related items they handled.

In addition to relying on external sales mechanisms, many companies turned to outside agencies for financing. They might borrow from banks or, if their char-ters permitted, offer stock for sale through brokers. After its formal organization in 1817, the New York Stock Exchange rapidly expanded its influence, serving as the leading marketplace for American securities of all kinds. Ambitious entrepreneurs with expansive plans were eager to have their shares traded on Wall Street although many alternatives existed. "Curb sales" took place outside the exchange itself in New York City, and several other commercial cities supported more or less struc-tured exchange mechanisms to bring buyers and sellers together.

Speculators and investors were naturally interested in the soundness of the companies that issued stocks and bonds, and the companies themselves needed in-formation about potential customers, suppliers, and rivals. Some hired investiga-tors, usually lawyers in distant locations, to assess the credit worthiness of an indi-vidual or firm. This technique was used extensively in the 1820s by the Baring Brothers in England who handled much of the European investment in American enterprises. The firm took the process a step further in the next decade when it sent regular employees traveling around the United States to investigate the soundness of potential investments. The British firm developed this information for its own use but did share it with favored clients.

The American public's growing interest in business and investment evalua-tions encouraged Lewis Tappan to open the Mercantile Agency in New York in 1841. His agents collected credit information all over the country to provide his customers with valuable business intelligence. Tappan made his service available to anyone willing to pay for it, and the knowledge that his agency was gathering such information encouraged businesses throughout the United States to keep their affairs in order.

Because the nation's commerce increasingly involved transactions in distant cities and towns, rapid and reliable communication was essential. Fortunately, a portrait painter named Samuel F. B. Morse patented a magnetic device for trans-mitting messages instantly over long distances in the late 1830s. Like so many other inventors, he struggled for several years before finally taking in Ezra Cornell and Alfred Vail as partners. They used their resources to build a demonstration line between Baltimore and Washington, D.C., in 1844. In a matter of a few years, telegraph wires were linking all of the major cities, and businessmen quickly rec-ognized the usefulness of this system for transmitting orders and keeping up with market information.

The telegraph also made news reporting much more timely. Journals of varying quality and circulation had served the major cities for years. Commercial reporting had always helped to sell papers, but now editors were recognizing the market potential of an appeal to popular interests. Cheaper mass circulation news-papers continued to carry some commercial news, and a few specialized business and technical journals served the particular needs of manufacturers and investors. One crucial function some publications performed in this era was regular reporting on the fluctuating market value of the thousands of different private bank notes in circulation. The financial anarchy that settled over the country in the late 1830s was, to a degree, a consequence of the political decisions that affected all forms of enterprise in this period.

THE BUSINESS ENVIRONMENT

Although the Constitution had assigned Congress authority over internal and exter-nal trade policies, there was relatively little government interference in economic affairs during the first half of the nineteenth century. Indeed, key Supreme Court decisions reinforced private property rights and discouraged government meddling. The *Dartmouth College v. Woodward* case in 1819 is representative. Chartered as a private entity in colonial days, the college sued to maintain its independence when the state of New Hampshire attempted to revoke its charter and run it as a public institution. Led by Chief Justice John Marshall, the court ruled that the state could not set aside the earlier charter, thereby establishing a precedent for the invi-olability of other charter privileges.

Two subsequent cases dealt with the sensitive matter of monopoly rights. The first was the *Gibbons v. Ogden* case, in which the justices had canceled New York's attempt to create a monopoly of steam ferry services. The court reinforced this doctrine in the 1837 *Charles River Bridge v. Warren Bridge* case. The Charles River Bridge Company had objected when the Massachusetts legislature issued a charter to a second company offering to span the Charles River. The Court con-cluded that the first company's charter did not imply exclusive rights in this in-stance.

While most Americans seemed content with the federal government's limited scope, a noisy few insisted that it should erect high tariffs to "protect" what they saw as the country's "infant industries" from foreign competition. Although the is-sue generated an enormous amount of rhetoric, tariff rates generally remained low. Petty partisan politics created the infamous Tariff of Abominations in 1828, but a compromise in 1833 gradually scaled down its higher duty levels. They dropped still lower as a result of the Walker Act in 1846. Despite all the controversy, no one ever conclusively proved that adjusting the rates either up or down had any major impact on the growing industrial community in the United States.

Another economic issue that provoked high political drama was the "bank war" that President Andrew Jackson declared. The Second Bank of the United States, or B.U.S., had received a twenty-year charter in 1816. Its first president, William Jones, had failed to win admirers for the institution, and his successor, Langdon Cheeves, did little to improve its reputation. Cheeves maintained rigid control over the bank's branches and carefully restricted the ratio of notes issued to specie reserves. When Nicholas Biddle replaced Cheeves as president of the bank in 1823 he discovered about half of all of the specie in the United States stored in its vaults.

An intelligent Pennsylvania aristocrat, Biddle ran his institution with flair and rationality. It admirably performed its duty of collecting the federal government's revenues and paying its obligations at no cost. The bank also issued its own notes redeemable in hard currency at its main office in Philadelphia or at any of its many branches around the country. Because of its sound specie reserve policy, these notes were readily accepted at face value for both public and private transactions.

Hundreds of state-chartered banking corporations also issued notes backed by the specie and government securities they held in reserve. Sound notes maintained their face value in the vicinity of their issuing bank's redemption office where they could be exchanged for hard currency on demand. But when state bank notes surfaced at remote points, merchants were far less willing to honor them. Private bill brokers made a business of buying a distant banks' notes at a discount and then returning them to the issuing institutions for full redemption. With its branches located throughout the United States, Biddle's bank performed this same service. The possibility that B.U.S. officers might at any moment appear with a large bundle of notes to redeem encouraged all private banks to maintain reasonable reserves.

Despite its efficiency and stability, the B.U.S. under Biddle alienated many Americans. Its redemption activities exposed slipshod banking practices and put pressure on insecure or mismanaged firms. Speculators objected because its actions helped stabilize the price of money and credit so that ambitious or unscrupulous operators could never count on using devalued currency to pay their debts. Other critics distrusted all banks and all banknotes, convinced that hard currency alone was the only safe type of money.

Although he kept his views to himself for some time, President Andrew Jackson eventually emerged as a dedicated hard-money man, distrustful of all banks and of Biddle's institution in particular. Partisan politics played a major role in his campaign to destroy what he termed "The Monster." Friends of the bank could not muster enough votes in Congress to override Jackson's veto of an 1832 rechartering bill. Biddle gamely struggled to keep his institution viable for the next few years, but it closed permanently in 1837.

It was not alone. A major financial panic struck in that year. Thousands of firms became insolvent; speculators saw their ambitious plans destroyed; the common people suffered a debilitating deflation in the prices of commodities they wished to sell. Many Americans laid the blame squarely at Jackson's feet. His anti-bank campaign had initially led to an expansion of the money supply which encouraged speculation. Then his dedication to hard money and rigid adherence to the gold standard had apparently so restricted the expansion of the money supply that deflation was inevitable.

Over the years, a number of other explanations for the financial gyrations of the 1830s have been advanced. Some insist that complex international trade patterns were primarily responsible. Others consider the Panic of 1837 a predictable, unavoidable manifestation of longterm business cycles. Excessive land speculation, particularly a remarkable burst of buying in 1835 and 1836, has also been singled out for blame. No doubt all of these factors played important parts in toppling the United States into an extended period of hard times. Despite a minor rally in 1838 and 1839, the slump persisted and hit bottom in the early 1840s.

Fortunately, the country's financial structure slowly recuperated, in part because private enterprise had developed ways of handling some of the positive and protective functions Biddle's bank had previously performed. Back in the 1820s a private institution in Boston called the Suffolk Bank had begun acting as a central clearing house for the notes of other New England banks. In the 1830s the New York legislature began requiring the banks it chartered to contribute to a Safety Fund which insured the value of their notes. Most private banks operated responsibly anyway; a few unscrupulous or foolish wildcatters stimulated far more distrust of banks in general than they deserved. Although thousands of different types of private banknotes circulated, offering varying degrees of soundness and redeemability, after 1855 deposits in American banks actually grew faster than did the amount of paper currency in circulation. To deal with this shortage, demand accounts which allowed depositors to write checks were introduced, and they made for a more elastic money supply.

Some of the prosperity that developed in the early 1850s obviously resulted from western gold mining. So many people rushed to California and nearby Nevada that the vast majority were fated never to find any of the precious metal. Furthermore, many of those who did quickly lost it to merchants, cardsharps, claim jumpers, and assorted parasites. Even so, the bonanza was truly staggering. Federal government purchases kept the market price of gold hovering around twenty dollars an ounce, and as much as $50 million worth was gleaned from the California diggings in some years. When the mining fever abated, the new Californians found themselves in an extraordinarily pleasant environment that offered all sorts of agricultural and commercial potential. The Golden State rapidly established its credentials as a mecca for adventurers, speculators, and plain folk seeking a better life.

The nationwide period of prosperity ended abruptly in 1857. Banks headed the list of standard scapegoats blamed for this panic, and many of them did contribute to its severity. Reckless land speculation had inevitably accompanied the development of the Midwestern railroad network, creating an inevitable glut of land in comparison to the available supply of settlers. The railroads themselves were victims of their own overly optimistic building plans. Some western roads never did generate enough revenue to justify their construction costs. Factories and farms typically produced far more than the American people alone could consume, and the resulting exports of the surplus brought much of the world's excess gold and silver into the United States. Combined with that from the western bonanza, this specie stimulated excess banknote issues, railroad construction, and land speculation.

External forces also played familiar parts in undermining the nation's economic health. The Panic of 1857 was a worldwide phenomenon, with the United States as much a victim as an instigator of the global instability. The Crimean War that broke out in 1854 consumed huge quantities of capital and manpower. Of particular significance for the United States, it increased the demand for agricultural products. World price levels for food and other staples naturally rose and encouraged American producers to overextend. The end of the conflict in 1856 sharply reduced the overseas demand for American exports, with the key exception of cotton. Postwar European retrenchment affected the business climate on this side of the Atlantic as well. The depression lingered for several years, casting a pall over the northern economy but leaving the South virtually untouched.

That circumstance reinforced the southerners' conviction that their system was inherently superior to that of the North. This smugness was all the more galling to northerners given the growing emotionalism of the abolition and freesoil movements. The Panic of 1857 and the subsequent depression thus intensified the hostility between North and South and focused further attention on the actual and perceived efficiencies and profitability of the slave system. Political emotionalism and moral outrage in both sections was fated to draw the United States into its bloody civil war. The conduct and outcome of that struggle would profoundly alter the nature and prospects of American enterprise.

READING SUGGESTIONS

George Dangerfield wrote two books on all aspects of the earlier years covered in Chapter 4: *The Era of Good Feelings* (1952), and *The Awakening of American Nationalism 1815-1828* (1965). Another well-written survey of the first half of the nineteenth century is Charles M. Wiltse's *The New Nation 1800-1845* (1961). Robert Sobel offers a lighter historical treatment in *Conquest and Conscience: The 1840s* (1971).

The most detailed coverage of the agrarian South appears in Lewis Gray's *History of Agriculture in the Southern United States to 1860* (2 vols., 1933), but Harold D. Woodman's *King Cotton and His Retainers* (1968) is a more recent analysis of the topic. In *History of the Old South* (2nd ed., 1966), Clement Eaton paints a sympathetic portrait. Percy W. Bidwell and John I. Falconer, in *History of Agriculture in the Northern United States, 1620-1860* (1925), provide thorough coverage similar to that of Gray. Paul W. Gates's *The Farmer's Age 1815-1860* (1960) looks at agriculture in both the North and the South.

One of the best studies on slavery is Kenneth M. Stampp's *The Peculiar Institution* (1956) which emphasizes its many negative consequences. Stanley M. Elkins's *Slavery: A Problem in American Institutional and Intellectual Life* (2nd ed., 1968) is equally critical. Eugene D. Genovese produced a very controversial but quite interesting analysis in *The Political Economy of Slavery* (1961). Robert

Fogel and Stanley Engermann attempt to apply quantitative methods to the study of slavery in *Time on the Cross* (1974). The many critical reviews and studies that have appeared since its publication, however, suggest that the book be consulted with great caution. A more respected general study by August Meier and Elliott M. Rudwick is *From Plantation to Ghetto* (1965).

George R. Taylor takes a very detailed look at both transportation and industrial developments in *The Transportation Revolution 1815-1860* (1951). Edward C. Kirkland views the same topics from a regional perspective in *Men, Cities, and Transportation: A Study in New England History, 1820-1900* (2 vols., 1948). Two books on the application of steam power to water transportation are Louis C. Hunter's *Steamboats on the Western Rivers* (1949) and James T. Flexner's *Steamboats Come True* (1944). Ronald E. *Shaw's Erie Water West: The Erie Canal, 1792-1854* (1966) is an excellent scholarly account. A more general survey of the canal craze appears in Madeline S. Waggoner's *Long Haul West: The Canal Era, 1817-1850* (1958). Carter Goodrich's *Government Promotion of American Canals and Railroads 1800-1890* (1960) is especially useful on finances and chartering practices, as is the very thorough book by Frederick A. Cleveland and Fred Wilbur Powell, *Railroad Promotion and Capitalization in the United States* (1909). John F. Stover's *American Railroads* (1961) is probably the best overview of nineteenth-century railroading.

A brief work on how the Northeast became highly industrialized by the 1850s is Thomas C. Cochran's *Frontiers of Change, Early Industrialism in America* (1981). Walt W. Rostow discusses the general mechanisms for that process in *The Stages of Economic Growth* (1960). A variety of industries are examined in the very readable *The Coming Age of American Business, Three Centuries of Enterprise, 1600-1900* (1971), by Elisha P. Douglass.

Like Hamilton, Andrew Jackson has been the subject of widely conflicting accounts. An impressive revisionist view is provided by Peter Temin in *The Jacksonian Economy* (1969) which downgrades the importance of the bank war and Jackson's hard-money attitudes. Although Robert V. Remini's *Andrew Jackson and the Bank War* (1967) came out before Temin's work, it is a sound monograph. Two other solid works look specifically at the bank: Alexander Wilburn's *Biddle's Bank, The Crucial Years* (1967), and Walter Buckingham Smith's *Economic Aspects of the Second Bank of the United States* (1953). The books by Bray Hammond and Richard H. Timberlake, Jr. mentioned in the reading notes for Chapter 3 should also be consulted.

Chapter 5

ACHIEVING INDUSTRIAL MATURITY 1860-1890

While campaigning in 1858, Abraham Lincoln called the United States "a house divided against itself" and explained that, "I do not expect the Union to be dissolved—I do not expect the house to fall—but I do expect it will cease to be divided. It will become all one thing, or all the other." Since neither the Southerners nor the Northerners would peacefully accept the other's political control, a war had to be fought to determine which region's philosophy would dominate. No one anticipated how long and devastating the struggle would be. The South was literally torn limb from limb before it surrendered. The war interfered with and dictated human endeavor as no previous political event had done, and it temporarily or permanently affected many aspects of the free enterprise system.

Simultaneously, the war created new opportunities and reshaped older ones. Lavish government expenditures, amounting to as much as one-fourth of the nation's material output, directed capital and resources in novel directions. The continuing crisis also called forth new methods for solving problems on a massive scale, some of which would be quickly adapted to postwar endeavors. Buoyed by the wartime demand, the victorious North emerged from the conflict seemingly more prosperous and dynamic than ever. The capital collected to finance the war effort flowed directly into the hands of entrepreneurs eager to invest in land, railroads, and factories.

That bloom of prosperity faded when the collapse of Jay Cooke's financial house in 1873 spread panic throughout the country. The severe depression that followed revealed many serious flaws in the American economy. And, though the United States slowly waded out of this morass, cyclical recessions and investor caution in the 1880s prevented a revival of the prosperity mood of the late sixties. Disappointed and impatient Americans banded together in political coalitions dedicated to simplistic cures like free trade or more protectionism, increasing the money supply or restricting it, and promoting or opposing the consolidation of industry. The obvious lack of consensus here prevented decisive political action of any kind.

Hard times hurt some more than others. Railroading remained the nation's most prominent industrial activity, but cutthroat competition, particularly in the overbuilt Northeast, dampened enthusiasm and cut profits. Steel and oil producers experienced abrupt shifts in demand and prices for their output. Shrewd operators like Andrew Carnegie and John D. Rockefeller took advantage of their competitors' hard luck to advance and consolidate their own interests.

The depression was especially trying for those at the lower end of the social scale. It stranded millions of optimistic immigrants in miserable, dangerous, and low-paying jobs in bleak industrial cities. Workers who tried to improve their relative positions through organization and collective bargaining often succeeded best at alienating their employers. Yet many of these industrial workers were better off than millions of rural residents battling to make ends meet. Northern farmers blamed high railroad charges and low commodity prices for their plight, while those in the South found themselves locked in an increasingly restrictive economic and social bind. Whether black or white, Southerners endured hardships throughout this period as a direct legacy of the waste and dislocations of the Civil War.

THE LOST CAUSE

The American people discovered that sliding into a war was far easier than getting out again. Had either the southern secessionists or northern unionists realized all of the horrors in store, they might have worked much harder to reach a peaceful compromise. The South ultimately lost its slave system, wasted hundreds of thousands of lives, destroyed its economy, denuded its landscape, and profoundly altered its society. Such devastating consequences shocked the southern cavaliers who marched off to war confident that, in a fair fight, the Confederacy would win.

But nothing about this war was fair from start to finish. No rules restricted the number of soldiers or the amount of money and materiel; nothing arbitrarily limited the length of the conflict. In the long run—and that was what mattered—the North had infinitely more to pour into its war effort than did the South. The states that stayed in the Union had more than 22 million inhabitants compared to just nine million in the Confederacy. And one-third of that number were slaves whom the whites considered unsuitable for combat. Industrialization had occurred so unevenly in the United States that 85 percent of its factories were located in the North. Furthermore, these factories were better financed and more efficient than southern establishments, producing more than 90 percent of the nation's manufactured goods. For decades wealth had been flowing from south to north so the

Union had ample supplies of specie and other monetary instruments. The North's capital and industrial resources enabled it to replace and expand its military hardware and logistical support throughout the conflict. When the South lost mechanical or heavy equipment like locomotives or cannons, it simply had to do without them.

Stockpiled goods sitting in warehouses were of no use to an army; they had to be moved. Here again, the North was far better off, possessing more than twice as many miles of track as the Confederate states in 1860. The cheap construction typical of southern railroads had caused frequent interruptions of service even in peacetime, and the war naturally intensified these problems. Because virtually all of the combat occurred within the borders of the Confederacy, many of the roads were completely destroyed. Northern commanders meanwhile learned how to use their integrated rail network to carry supplies wherever needed. The Union also exploited its predominance at sea. Rapid conversion of merchant vessels and construction of new ships made the United States Navy a formidable force. Union soldiers and sailors cooperated in capturing control of vital southern rivers early in the conflict, further hindering the transportation and distribution of both military and civilian goods throughout the South.

The seceded states began the struggle fatefully short of material resources. Weapons and ammunition had to be imported from abroad on blockade-running ships or scrounged from fallen Yankee troopers. As the Union blockade tightened and Confederate victories grew rarer, the South had to rely on its internal resources. The efforts of a Pennsylvanian named Josiah Gorgas whom President Jefferson Davis installed as his army's chief of ordnance were crucial. Gorgas established arsenals and powder mills throughout the South. The region had plenty of coal, iron, and other raw materials to supply these installations so that, by 1863, Gorgas had sufficient weapons and ammunition for all the troops the Confederacy could field.

The resources used to arm its soldiers left the Confederacy less able to meet other military and civilian demands. The few private textile mills in the South simply could not supply the hundreds of thousands of uniforms desired. Reversing the industrial revolution, household spinning wheels and hand looms were dusted off and put back into service. Cottage industries also produced shoes, harnesses, wagons, and other scarce items. Farming changed, too, with the acreage devoted to food crops increased at the expense of staples like tobacco and cotton.

The feebleness of King Cotton proved quite unnerving. Secessionist agitators had confidently assumed that the South's customers around the world would rally to the rebel cause. Just as the oil-exporting countries essentially blackmailed the industrialized nations in the 1970s, cotton growers in the 1860s expected to dictate global economic developments through their control of the world's most important industrial raw material. But bumper crops in 1859 and 1860 had stuffed European warehouses with raw cotton. British mills were able to continue drawing from this stockpile until 1863, by which time the southern cause was clearly doomed. Furthermore, the war itself discouraged new cotton planting and reserves from earlier crop years filtered away through the blockade to Europe or the battle lines to the North. Finally, the Confederate government's decision to peddle cotton-backed bonds abroad not only reduced the available supply, it also failed to produce needed specie.

The bond sale fiasco was all too typical of the Confederacy's fumbling attempts to raise revenue. Southerners had always hated taxes, so the Confederate Congress was slow to impose them. A resort to paper money was inevitable. Slowly at first, then with increasing abandon, printing presses spewed out Confederate notes that promised redemption two years after the South had won its independence. With no specie reserves to give them even a semblance of soundness, the bills rapidly depreciated in value just as the Continental notes had during the Revolutionary War. A combination of commodity scarcities and excess paper money triggered debilitating inflation. On the eve of Lee's surrender, a buyer in Richmond would have had to offer at least $1000 for a barrel of flour—if one could be found to purchase at all. The Confederate notes of course became completely worthless when the government that had issued them ceased to exist.

When the fighting ended, the war-weary Southerners assessed the damage their massive, self-inflicted wound had caused. Much of the South had been reduced to a condition similar to that found along the frontier. Advancing and retreating armies had burned down or damaged cities and towns; foragers and raiders had ruined farm crops and buildings. The veterans who straggled back to what was left of their homes often had to begin their lives all over again.

Blacks living in the South had few guideposts to the future. President Lincoln had begun the emancipation process with his proclamation on January 1, 1863. Within the year, Congress had approved the Thirteenth Amendment to the Constitution, and abolition became the law of the land when the necessary three-fourths of the states had ratified it. Although Lincoln toyed with the idea of compensating slave owners for their financial losses, he found little support among his fellow Northerners. The estimated $2-4 billion of capital invested in slaves evaporated as completely as the value of Confederate notes.

The freedmen, as the former slaves were called, gained political and legal independence but lacked the economic support necessary to enjoy it. The only significant federal initiative was the Freedmen's Bureau which acted as a general relief agency for the destitute of both white and black races. The bureau also experimented with a labor contract system. Many landowners were eager to hire field hands, intending to work their plantation fields with work gangs as they had before the war. But the contract system broke down quickly when neither side seemed capable of meeting its commitments.

An alternative was sharecropping, in which an individual agreed to farm a tract of land and pay its owner a portion of the resulting crop. A landlord typically collected about one-third of the output. This system inevitably splintered farming operations into small units. The demand for agricultural labor in the South drew poor whites as well as blacks into sharecropping. Tenants farmed one-third of the southern acreage in 1880 and fully two-thirds at the end of the century. The inefficiencies of this dispersed, labor-intensive system held southern agricultural productivity well below that of the North.

The smaller farm units could not support the factors who had supplied antebellum plantations and handled their bulk shipments to New York and London. Local storekeepers now stepped in as middlemen. Operating in a cash-poor economy, they relied on barter for direct sales and extended credit to regular customers. Because the only collateral most croppers had to offer was part of their harvest, store credit was drawn against that output. A storekeeper placed a lien on a farmers's crops in return for supplying food, tools, seed, feed, and other necessities. The interest charged for these services could run high, sometimes reaching 50 or even 100 percent. By imposing high interest rates and juggling their books, storekeepers could easily prevent their clients from paying off their indebtedness and thereby force them to accept a new lien on the next year's crop. The crop lien system ultimately impoverished everyone connected with it since the fortunes of the

FIGURE 5-1 Cotton Production and Exports. (From tables in Matthew B. Hammond, *The Cotton Industry: An Essay in American History*, Part I [New York: Macmillan, 1897], p. 357.)

shopkeepers themselves were inextricably linked to those of the unmotivated farm workers they preyed upon.

Sharecropping and crop liens discouraged agricultural diversification just as effectively as the prewar plantation structure had. Landlords and lienholders demanded payment in cotton, the one crop independent farmers could not readily market or consume themselves. The South therefore remained tied to its traditional staple crop despite unfavorable price fluctuations and variable demand. As Figure 5-1 illustrates, postwar cotton production soon surpassed its prewar level, and cotton also recaptured its leading position among American exports.

Where cotton would not grow, croppers planted tobacco, rice, or sugar for market as well as corn and wheat to feed themselves. Georgia and Florida expanded their production of fruit in these years, much of it for canning and shipping all over the country. Southern logging and mining increased in importance as the discouraging returns from farming made them comparatively more attractive. Overall, the South continued to function much as it had before the Civil War as a largely dependent economic area, resembling a mercantile colony of the more industrialized and productive North.

Southern factories had produced less than 10 percent of the United States's industrial output before the Civil War and that ratio had changed very little by 1900. Because the nation as a whole had vastly increased its industrial capacity, however, southern manufacturing had actually risen rather dramatically as well. The processing of agricultural staples was the most common industrial endeavor. Northern capital helped finance the construction of cotton textile mills in the South, particularly after 1880. Sugar refining and grain milling also continued as major industries. Abundant coal and iron deposits in northern Alabama stimulated the growth of Birmingham, which soon came to resemble its British namesake as a manufacturing center. Southern mills were processing one-fifth of all the iron and steel produced in the United States by 1890.

The extension and integration of the southern railroad network encouraged the concentration of industries. At first the reconstruction of damaged lines absorbed most of the available capital. Later funds were directed to new projects that established better linkages and encouraged trade and travel throughout the Southeast. An overdue decision in 1886 to establish the standard gauge throughout the region made its rails and rolling stock compatible with those elsewhere and facilitated cheap and convenient service to all parts of the country. The growth of certain inland cities depended upon the rising importance of land transportation as a competitor to the South's traditional reliance on water-borne commerce. As the hub of ten different railroads, Atlanta symbolized the ideal of the "New South": vigorous, expanding, and proud, a far cry from the fire-ravaged skeleton General William T. Sherman had left behind in 1864.

Except for isolated spots of urbanization and industrialization like Atlanta and Birmingham, though, the South lagged behind the rest of the country. The inefficiency and motivational problems of its stagnant agricultural economy acted as

JAMES B. DUKE

The Dukes of Durham, North Carolina, rose from postwar poverty to global prominence exploiting the traditional southern staple, tobacco. Washington Duke had two sons, Benjamin and James Buchanan Duke, the latter named for the president who was elected in the year of his birth, 1856. When Washington Duke returned from serving in the Confederate Army in 1865, he had just fifty cents in his pocket, but the scavengers who had looted his farmstead had overlooked a small store of tobacco. With his sons' help, Duke prepared the tobacco, packaged it under the brand name "Pro Bono Publico," and peddled it in the southern part of the state. It sold well, encouraging Duke to set up a processing facility and become a tobacco merchant.

In 1874 he brought his sons into a partnership, W. Duke, Sons & Co., and continued to expand. The major tobacco products at that point were plugs for chewing and leaf for pipes, and the leading distributor was the firm of Blackwell & Carr whose Bull Durham brand had achieved popularity around the world. Recognizing the difficulty of competing against an established power, James Duke decided to concentrate on manufacturing and selling cigarettes. In 1878 he helped perfect the Bonsack machine capable of rolling 120,000 cigarettes in a day. Because the major market was in the North, the Dukes opened a branch plant in New York City in 1884, and budgeted huge sums for advertising. In 1889 they were producing half of the cigarettes sold in the United States.

Like so many other Gilded Age entrepreneurs, James Duke hated the inefficiency and costs that competition levied on his industry. His rivals were meanwhile so disturbed at his success that they approached him with a buy-out offer. Duke countered with a plan to form a trust that would include all of the major cigarette manufacturers. The resulting American Tobacco Co., formed in 1890 with Duke as its president, controlled 90 percent of the growing cigarette market. It was only the first of several consolidations Duke arranged. Around the turn of the century he superintended the creation of comprehensive business structures for the cigar, chewing tobacco, and even tobacco retailing businesses. The most successful southern businessmen of his generation, he left a fortune of $100 million, most of it to endow the university that bears his name.

a drag on the productivity of farm workers. Wage levels barely approached half of those for comparable work in the Northeast. The South was a fairly discouraging place in which to live and work in this period. In losing the war to preserve its racial system, however, it had definitely stimulated growth and enterprise in its enemy's economy.

NORTHERN WARTIME PROSPERITY

The economic picture in the North started out as bleak as its battlefield record. More businesses closed in 1861 than had done so in the panic year of 1857, though the capitalization of these firms was considerably smaller than that of the prewar bankruptcies. Many of the failures naturally involved enterprises with close ties to the South. Banks holding southern states' securities, merchants specializing in the cotton trade, even New York sugar factors suffered adversely. The composite southern indebtedness to the North in 1860 was about $150 million, and most of it became uncollectable after the fighting began.

The northern economy recovered quickly. By 1863 it experienced a full-scale business boom that would persist through the end of the conflict and into the Reconstruction years afterwards. Historian Allen Nevins defined four categories of causes for this prosperity. First, western farms were remarkably productive in the early 1860s just when European demand for wheat and other commodities was reaching record levels. A second factor stimulating business activity was the mass of war contracts the Union government issued as it expanded its military efforts. Simultaneously, protective tariffs far higher than necessary for revenue purposes allowed manufacturers to set premium prices. Nevins fourth category of prosperity factors includes the adoption of new technologies and methodologies which increased individual and sector productivity. Perhaps a fifth factor should be added: the impact of inflation. The huge sums added to the nation's money supply throughout the conflict boosted prices for goods and contributed to the impression of prosperity.

Agricultural production did indeed rise dramatically during the war, and some of this bounty directly fed wartime demand. Even hay turned out to be vital to armies relying on four-legged transportation. The price for hay rose as high as $35 a ton and the demand never slackened. In addition to its military uses, hay also fueled urban transit systems involving horsecars and wagons. Another mundane product in high demand during the conflict was lumber used both as fuel for railroads and homes and as the nation's chief building and rebuilding material. Sales of fuel and feed enabled farmers to earn significant returns from their woodlots and pastures alone.

The secession of the southern states cut the North off from some of its normal sources of supply. The inevitable shortage of cotton revived the woolens industry. Many northern textile mills modified or bought new machinery to process wool, and the sheep population in the North nearly doubled in response to the premium prices offered for fleeces. Wool processors tried to limit these price increases by calling for reductions in the tariff rates to encourage the importation of wool from Australia and other foreign sources.

Wartime demand was only partially responsible for the boom in wheat production. Vast new tracts of land were cultivated, and the resulting bumper crops created unprecedented surpluses. Fortunately, European grain production fell far below normal from 1860 to 1862, so thousands of tons of American wheat and other cereal grains flowed overseas. These shipments generated higher prices for northern wheat farmers and simultaneously compensated for the reduction of cotton exports in the United States trade balance.

Producing such plenty at the same time hundreds of thousands of farmers and farm hands were enlisting in the armed forces encouraged the widespread adoption of agricultural mechanization at last. The reapers, mowers, threshers, seed drills, and other implements that had formerly been considered luxuries now invaded the midwestern landscape. The value of all the reapers and mowers produced in 1864 came to $15 million compared to only $3.5 million in 1860. Here the Civil War generated a permanent change: farm mechanization proved so beneficial that it became the norm.

The union government bought unprecedented amounts of equipment and clothing. Unfortunately, the various bureaus within the War and Navy Departments issued contracts independently of one another and without adequate coordination or supervision. On the whole, the commission agents and suppliers were reasonably honest, but a few unscrupulous ones took advantage of the federal windfall to supply defective or inferior goods. Some of the first backpacks purchased, for example, were glued together out of a cheap, pressed fiber fabric called "shoddy." Many came apart at the seams when packed or disintegrated in the first rain shower. Many other supplies were equally shoddy. Often the Union soldier's only comfort was his knowledge that rebel troopers had worse equipment or none at all.

Both the procurement process and the suppliers became more efficient as the war persisted. The army's demand for uniforms helped set the ready-made clothing industry on its feet. Before the war only poorer individuals wore the ill-fitting manufactured clothing available. Sewing machines improved the quality of stitching and enabled workers to produce many more garments in a given period. The development of power cutting machinery and detailed patterns created the potential for better fitting. A few entrepreneurs set up integrated clothing factories capable of economies of scale and better quality control. Even so, much of the industry continued to operate in the traditional putting-out manner where workers collected pre-cut cloth and sewed it at home on their own machines.

The ready-made shoe business became more progressive. In the late 1850s, Gordan McKay bought Lyman R. Blacke's patent rights to the machine he had designed to sew together shoe parts. McKay added further innovations before leasing his machinery to manufacturers in return for royalties on the footwear they produced. By 1863 over 200 of McKay's complex machines were turning out a total of 2.5 million shoes per year. The leasing policy McKay developed was retained when his operation became the United Shoe Machinery Company that monopolized this specialized branch of manufacturing for decades. So many Americans became accustomed to wearing ready-made shoes and clothing during the war that they continued to buy them afterward, thus assuring sustained growth in these industries.

Constant demand and high protective tariffs helped American metals and machines to sell well during the war. The North had always been amply supplied with iron ore and forges. Coal mining boomed as well to feed the smelting and fuel needs of the industrialized Union. The North's highly sophisticated machine tool industry proved an invaluable asset. Although surprisingly few major weapons innovations were adopted during the war, northern factories were remarkably competent at churning out standard items with greater and greater efficiency. The federal arsenals at Harper's Ferry and Springfield had jointly produced only 22,000 rifles a year before the war. At its wartime peak, the Springfield facility alone was completing more than 200,000 weapons annually. With the cooperation of dozens of privately owned factories, the Union could manufacture 5000 rifles a day on a regular basis compared to the 300 that the southern weapons industry could muster on its best days.

When not debating war issues, the Republican politicians controlling the federal government approved several key domestic bills. The 1862 Homestead Act, for example, allowed settlers to stake out 160-acre tracts anywhere in the public domain, title passing to the claimant for slight improvements in the land and the payment of a nominal registration fee. Congress also authorized the famous transcontinental railroad land grants that would extend access to markets and resources nationwide. The Contract Labor Act of 1864 enabled manufacturers to recruit workers in Europe, a gesture aimed at reducing domestic labor costs.

Wage levels did climb during the war but nowhere near as rapidly as inflation. By 1864 the consumer price index had risen approximately 75 percent over its 1861 level while wages were up barely 20 percent. That meant that the workers' real wages—the value of their take-home pay compared to the prices of goods—had actually declined almost a third. Farmers, too, suffered from a decline in their real income despite the high prices paid for their produce. Not surprisingly, the comparatively poor compensation for both agricultural and industrial labor contributed to many a young man's decision to enlist in the armed forces.

These factors also meant that the wartime prosperity was in many ways illusory. Conditions seemed better than they actually were. Substantial increases in the money supply and high employment rates that government spending induced had a lot to do with generating this impression of prosperity. At the same time, the federal government's financial policies were complex and confusing and, as usual, intricately involved with the ever-controversial issues of money and banking.

THE WAR'S FINANCIAL LEGACY

The Lincoln administration spent approximately $3.3 billion during the four years of the Civil War, more money than the federal government had appropriated in the seven decades since the adoption of the Constitution. The funds came from three major sources. Taxes brought in a little over $600 million, paper currency (greenbacks) were issued in the amount of something over $400 million, and federal borrowing accounted for around $2.3 billion. The decision to tap each of these revenue streams had important consequences that persisted for many years.

The Union government imposed every sort of tax imaginable. By 1864, it had quadrupled many prewar tariff rates to bring the average customs duty to nearly 50 percent. Traditional excise taxes on such items as liquor and tobacco rose correspondingly. Congress also instituted a battery of taxes that hit raw materials, processed parts, and final products. To avoid this piecemeal taxation, some manufacturers brought related processes under one roof to integrate production. Personal income was taxed for the first time in American history. It began as a modest bite of 3 percent, but the top rate had risen to 10 percent on incomes above $10,000 by the end of the war.

Like almost everyone else, Lincoln's Treasury Secretary, Salmon P. Chase, anticipated that there would only be a brief military showdown in 1861 and then a rapid return to normal. He therefore decided to pay for the early campaigning by selling short-term federal bonds. These sold quickly because of their attractive interest rate of 7.3 percent, a figure chosen because it generated an interest payment of two cents a day for every $100 invested. This first round of government borrowing absorbed most of the available capital, though, forcing Chase to work a lot harder to sell the bonds needed to finance the continuing war.

The government eventually issued a bewildering array of bonds with widely divergent interest rates and terms running as long as forty years. Recalling Robert Morris's role during the Revolution, Jay Cooke became known as the financier of the Union war effort. A colorful, energetic, personable man, he had helped bankroll Chase's futile effort to win the presidency. As a bond seller, Cooke put in a remarkable performance. He advertised widely, hired 2500 agents, and staged popular entertainments to publicize the bond sales. Because he wanted to convince everyone, not just the wealthy, to invest in war bonds, he directed his ballyhoo at all levels of society. His marketing methods eventually sold a billion dollars' worth of federal securities.

While Cooke tapped the public's purse, Congress went after the banking community. It replaced its initial, flawed legislation with a second National Banking Act in June 1864. That established procedures for the creation of a nationwide system of federally chartered and regulated banks. To qualify for a national bank charter, a financial institution had to buy at least $30,000 worth of Union bonds and agree to keep one-third of its capital reserves in that form. The

JAY COOKE'S CAMPAIGN TO SELL UNION WAR BONDS

Rather than restrict his sales pitch to the wealthy, Cooke inaugurated a nationwide campaign to convince all Americans that they should lend their government money. This broadside was part of his campaign.

TO FARMERS, MECHANICS AND CAPITALISTS!

You have a solemn duty to perform to your government and to posterity!

Our gallant army and navy must be supported by every man and woman who has any means, large or small, at their control. The United States Government, to which we owe our prosperity as a nation, security of person and property of every sort, calls on each individual to rally to its support—not with donations or gifts—though who could withhold them—BUT WITH SUBSCRIPTIONS TO HER LOANS, based on the best security in the world, the untold and scarcely yet tried resources of this mighty Continent, which were developing rapidly when the rebellion broke out, and to maintain which, AS A PRICELESS HERITAGE TO POSTERITY, this defence against rebellion is made.

There is no miscalculation, and can be no failure—the cost has been counted, and the burthen will be light to us, and gladly borne by posterity. What our Revolutionary Fathers are to us, WE will be to coming generations, if we fail not in our plain and simple duty!

The owner of every foot of ground, of every house and workship, owes a debt of service in the field, or of his means in this noble work!

Talk not of Taxes! they secure the Loans. Take the Loans! and the Taxes will fall more lightly—and they supply the ready, present and required means to strike the death blow at rebellion and the foul disturbers of the Nation's peace!

Talk not of Rulers! They are the ministers of GOD! who rules the world and the destiny of this mighty Nation! Our first duty is to God—our next to our country—fail not of either!

Your nearest patriotic Bank or Banker will supply this loan, on which so much depends!

(Reprinted in Henrietta M. Larson, *Jay Cooke: Private Banker* [Cambridge: Harvard University Press, 1936], pp. 129-30.)

government's major objective here was to encourage the sale of its bonds to bankers with ready access to capital. The law also required national banks to maintain relatively large cash reserves on their deposits and meet other performance guidelines.

To sweeten the package, the government permitted cooperating institutions to issue notes redeemable at face value at any national bank in the United States. The federal bonds on deposit would provide the backing for these notes, and they could be issued in amounts up to 90 percent of a bank's bond-holdings, but no more than $100,000 in all. A new Treasury official called the comptroller of the currency would allocate to each bank its currency quota. Energetic politicking caused the comptroller's distribution scheme to be highly inequitable: New York and New England banks were assigned the right to issue $170 million national bank notes out of the total of $300 million Congress authorized.

Because few bankers initially applied for federal charters, Congress levied a 10 percent tax on all private bank notes. Taking out a national bank charter was the only way to avoid this tax, so institutions began signing up by the hundreds. The package of federal regulations that governed national banks' behavior gave the United States a more stable private banking system than it had enjoyed since the 1830s. The national bank notes they issued meanwhile increased the money supply and, for a time, exerted inflationary pressures. In the long run, though, the legislated maximum of $300 million proved restrictive, and, once the government began retiring its outstanding bonds, the backing for them began to disappear and force a cut in their total circulation.

Because the revenue from taxes and bond sales fell short of the government's needs, Congress decided to issue paper money, the expedient that had such disastrous consequences in the Revolution and the War of 1812. The first of three separate authorizations of $150 million "United States Notes" was approved on February 25, 1862. Although the law proclaimed them legal tender for all public and private debts, wary creditors tried to avoid accepting these "greenbacks" for payment just as their predecessors had shunned Continental bills. The government gave only the vaguest of hints that it ever intended to redeem them with specie, so the value of greenbacks fluctuated according to the fortunes of the Union war effort.

The United States continued to experience difficulties as a result of its wartime financial legacy right through the end of the nineteenth century. Some parts of the mixed money supply seemed completely beyond human control. Neither government officials nor private financiers could, for example, determine how much gold would be circulating in the United States at any given moment. The accepted medium of international exchange, gold set import and export prices even as its relationship to other types of American currency varied. Until the late 1870s, the amount of gold available for monetary purposes in the United States hovered around $100 million, most of it residing in Treasury vaults. From time to time, the government issued certificates to represent its gold holdings, and these circulated much more conveniently than the specie itself. With their distinctive orange printing on the back, these certificates could be redeemed at subtreasuries for gold coins on demand, so they circulated at face value.

That made them far more acceptable than the greenbacks whose value compared to gold continued to fluctuate after the war. As they did whenever a discrepancy in prices occurred, speculators moved in, buying and selling gold with green-backs in hopes of making a killing. The Gold Room on Broad Street, adjacent to the New York Stock Exchange, became the center of frenzied bidding whenever shifts occurred in the ratio between gold and greenbacks.

Jay Gould's attempt to corner the nation's entire gold supply in 1869 was one of the most audacious speculative schemes in American history. A dour, secretive financier chiefly involved in railroad investments, Gould hatched his gold corner plan ostensibly to stimulate grain shipments to the East Coast over the Erie Rail-road he controlled. If he could cause the price of gold to rise in comparison to greenbacks, European buyers might spend their suddenly more valuable gold on massive purchases of American grain.

The drive began when Gould joined several others in a speculative pool that placed "buy" orders for millions of dollars worth of gold at elevated prices. The group planned to meet these contracts later, after their actions had created a tempo-rary shortage of specie on the market—a shortage should drive gold prices higher still. When they entered the market, gold was selling at 135, a price that reflected about a 35 percent premium compared to greenbacks. Gould's move quickly pushed the price to over 160. Other speculators, unaware of the pool's inflationary campaign, thought that the price would surely break long before they actually had to deliver any specie, so they eagerly signed "sell" orders for gold at these unusu-ally high prices.

The nearby federal subtreasury held millions in specie, but Gould had bribed President Ulysses Grant's brother-in-law, Abel R. Corbin, by transferring valuable gold receipts to his account. In return, he expected Corbin to convince Grant to keep the government's gold locked up. But Gould secretly learned that the Presi-dent intended to release the government gold anyway, so he reversed field and be-gan selling his vast paper holdings—some to his own business partner, Jim Fisk. When the New York subtreasury did flood the market with so much extra specie that no one could corner it, the price actually fell below 135, wiping out the for-tunes of many of the innocent and not-so-innocent speculators involved in the op-eration. Gould's timely bailout had left him several million dollars ahead of the game, though.

The reckless speculation on the disparity between the price of gold suggested that the unbacked paper money ought to be entirely withdrawn from circulation, a move that would significantly reduce the nation's overall money supply. When the economy tumbled into the severe depression of the 1870s, however, many Ameri-cans blamed their troubles on a relative shortage of currency, so, like Daniel Shays had done in the 1780s, they advocated the issuance of even more paper money. Facing a concerted political campaign from Greenbackers, the fiscally conservative Republicans agreed to a compromise that left the existing greenbacks in circulation but ruled out any further issues. They also insisted that the U.S. Treasury must "resume" gold payments on January 1, 1879. If the government promised to re-

THE GOLD CORNER

Having observed the bidding in the Gold Room, James Medbery wrote this description of the action on "Black Friday," September 24, 1869.

The paramount question now was, How would gold open? They had not many minutes to wait. Pressing up to the fountain, around which some fifty brokers had already congregated, a bull operator with resonant voice bid 145 for twenty thousand. The shout startled the galleries. Their margins were once more in jeopardy. Would their brokers remain firm? It was a terrible moment. The bears closed round the aggressors. Yells and shrieks filled the air. A confused and baffling whirl of sounds ensued, in which all sorts of fractional bids and offers mingled, till '46 emerged from the chaos. The crowd within the arena increased rapidly in numbers. The clique agents became vociferous. Gold steadily pushed forward in its perilous upward movement from '46 to '47, thence to '49, and, pausing for a brief twenty minutes, dashed on to 150½. . . . At 11 of the dial gold was 150½; in six minutes it jumped to 155. Then the pent-up tiger spirit burst from control. The arena rocked as the Coliseum may have rocked when the gates of the wild beasts were thrown open, and with wails and shrieks the captives of the empire sprang to merciless encounter with the ravenous demons of the desert. The storm of voices lost human semblance. Clenched hands, livid faces, pallid foreheads on which beads of cold sweat told of the interior anguish, lurid passion-filled eyes—all symptoms of a fever which at any moment might become frenzy were there. The shouts of the golden millions upon millions hurtled in all ears. The labor of years was disappearing and reappearing in the wave line of advancing and receding prices. With fortunes melting away in a second, with five hundred millions of gold in process of sale or purchase, with the terror of yet higher prices, and the exultation which came and went with the whispers of fresh men entering from Broad Street bearing confused rumors of the probable interposition of the government, it is not hard to understand how reason faltered on its throne, and operators became reckless, buying or selling without thought of the morrow or consciousness of the present.

(James K. Medbury, *Men and Mysteries of Wall Street* [New York: Fields, Osgood & Co., 1870], pp. 264-65.)

deem any greenbacks turned in for gold at face value, the paper notes would become effectively as good as gold.

This compromise disappointed those eager to increase the nation's money supply. Once the price of greenbacks had stabilized, easy money advocates switched their support to a call for more silver coinage. Earlier, a persistent scarcity of that metal had kept most people from selling it to the government at its traditional established price ratio of sixteen ounces of silver to one of gold. During the Civil War, silver virtually disappeared from circulation, forcing people to use

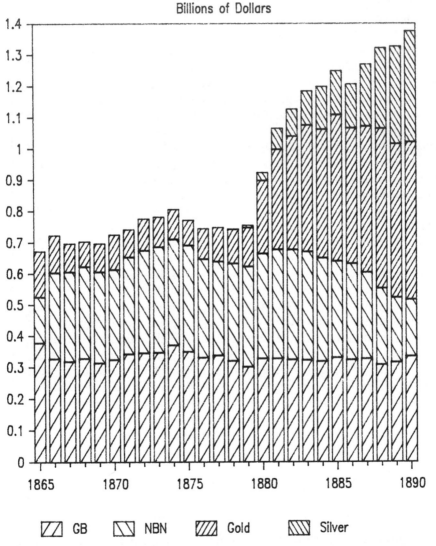

Billions of Dollars

FIGURE 5-2   Currency in Circulation 1860-1890. (From Historical Statistics of the United States, X 285-88, 297-98.)

GB = Greenbacks; NBN = National Bank Notes.
*Gold and silver figures include certificates as well as coins and specie.

ungummed postage stamps in place of coins. Huge silver mining strikes after the war, however, forced the market price well below the Treasury's fixed standard. Now the miners joined the easy money advocates in a cry for the "free and unlimited coinage of silver at sixteen to one." Congress responded with the Bland-Allison Act of 1878 that ordered the Treasury to purchase between two and four million ounces of silver per month. It could either mint it into silver dollars or print silver certificates to be redeemed in specie at its offices. Because few Americans wanted to be burdened with the bulky coins, the Treasury ended up with literally tons of silver dollars occupying every conceivable storage space. Even so, the coins and certificates that represented them were legal tender, and they added considerably to the amount of money circulating during the next twelve years.

Figure 5-2 illustrates the complex structure of the money supply in the years after the Civil War. The value of the greenbacks in circulation remained almost constant, and the supply of national banknotes started out at a similar level but gradually declined as the federal bonds that backed them were retired. The increase in silver and silver certificates resulted from the operation of the Bland-Allison Act after 1878.

The real surprise was the dramatic increase in the amount of gold that began circulating about the same time. Part of this bonanza resulted from shifting world trade patterns. In the late seventies, the United States began regularly exporting far more merchandise than it imported. Foreign buyers made up the disparity by transferring gold to American accounts. The infusion of both gold and silver into the domestic money supply may well have been a major factor in helping the United States begin its economic recovery after 1878.

How the available money was distributed also had important consequences. Most of the new wealth the war effort had created or collected fell into the hands of northern industrialists, bankers, and war profiteers. A comparatively small group of entrepreneurs committed to industrialization were thus ideally positioned to draw upon and exploit the growing wealth of the whole United States.

ROBBER BARONS OR CAPTAINS OF INDUSTRY?

Kansas Populists apparently were the first to call the aggressive businessmen of the late nineteenth century Robber Barons, each trying to control a particular sector of the economy. Stories about brooding, ruthless entrepreneurs like Jay Gould or flamboyant financial swashbucklers like Jim Fisk gave credence to this unflattering image. John D. Rockefeller, Andrew Carnegie, J. P. Morgan, and Cornelius and William Vanderbilt fought pitched battles involving millions of dollars worth of property and potential monopolies for the victors. Their critics charged them with extralegal if not downright criminal behavior in amassing their wealth and power.

The prevailing attitudes in succeeding years added to or altered the historical perceptions of the tycoons and business practices of the post-Civil War United States. Henry Demarest Lloyd's caustic portrait of John D. Rockefeller in *Wealth Against Commonwealth* (1894) strengthened the already negative public view of the great oil magnate. Progressive reformers in the early twentieth century were highly critical of monopolistic practices and centralized business control and, consequently, anyone who participated in or promoted them. In the depths of the Great Depression of the 1930s, Matthew Josephson's entertaining and unflattering portrait of *The Robber Barons* (1934) fit right in with the prevailing view that greedy and insensitive businessmen had brought on the current economic catastrophe.

Many writers have tried to reverse or at least soften this unpleasant stereotype, but the negative image persists. Economic historians like Allen Nevins and Edward C. Kirkland sketched much more flattering portraits of the Americans who guided the nation through the maturation of its industrial revolution. More recently, Maury Klein has contended that even Jay Gould had a positive influence on American industrial development. These historians argue that Gilded Age businessmen ably shouldered the complex task of bringing order out of chaos. Their brilliant business sense enabled them to integrate diversified processes and innovative production and management techniques into efficient, large scale industries. The centralized control they exercised eliminated waste and duplication; their coordination of interstate enterprises canceled destructive competition. Their defenders consider the sizable personal fortunes these individuals accumulated along the way either as secondary to their passion for setting the economy in order or as reasonable compensation for creating structures far more productive than earlier ones.

As in most historiographical controversies, the truth lies somewhere in between. Those who ran roughshod over workers or greedily looted companies fully deserve the Robber Baron label. But many entrepreneurs did appear more interested in developing orderly management and efficient operation of industrial and financial organizations than in personal aggrandizement. Despite the unpopularity of railroad promoters and operators among midwestern farmers, they doubtless received earlier and better service from the private sector than they would have under a state-run system. Nothing, of course, can justify the elaborate rebates to favored shippers or the excessive dividends that railroad companies paid their stockholders. The overall situation was obviously far too complex to fit any stereotype; individual entrepreneurs should be judged on the basis of their own merits or failings.

A separate evaluation of each person's behavior, however, would leave unanswered the question of whether their activities accelerated or impeded the development of a modern, industrialized economy. Some feel that the oppressive labor conditions the entrepreneurs countenanced and the profits they skimmed off for themselves more than offset the benefits of any industrial or business improvements they introduced. Admirers of their entrepreneurship, on the other hand, insist that the increased productivity and output that their streamlined management stimulated simply would never have occurred otherwise. Here again, the evidence is conflicting. While some industries made great progress in this period, economic conditions in general were quite dismal. Indeed, the overall rate of economic growth in the last third of the nineteenth century was somewhat lower than that for the thirty years preceding the Civil War.

Another possible avenue for analysis would be to investigate whether the industrialization process had to go the way it did—toward monopolization and the creation of a few enormous personal fortunes. In fact, regardless of their individual wealth or positions, most Americans in the late nineteenth century shared a common set of beliefs that probably would have driven the country in the same general direction even if one or more of the notorious entrepreneurs had never lived.

Many of these beliefs were, of course, extensions of the economic, political, and social concepts that had been popular in the United States for a century or more. Ever since the Revolution, Americans had accepted the premise that each individual possessed fundamental rights that, under ideal circumstances, should allow for full personal fulfillment. The prevailing faith in classical economic principles and a laissez-faire government also had deep historical roots. As long as they held these beliefs, Americans were not likely to criticize anyone for successfully exploiting the system even if it led to huge personal fortunes or business consolidation.

One of the most popular writers of the period was Horatio Alger who churned out more than a hundred books to entertain and inspire the nation's youth. All had essentially the same theme: a youngster who worked hard and remained true to high principles would achieve material success and wellbeing. Although his heroes sometimes received surprise inheritances rather than direct compensation for being diligent or honest, Alger's message was just what all Americans wanted to believe. The hope of rising from rags to riches encouraged farmers to head west in search of new homesteads, rural children to seek opportunities in the growing cities, and European peasants to gamble everything on a trip to the New World.

The successful prophet is one who tells the people what they already believe, and no philosophy could have been more timely than Social Darwinism. Englishman Herbert Spencer actually formulated his social theories almost a decade before Charles Darwin published his famous book on biological evolution, *The Origin of Species* (1859). But it was the popularity of Darwinism that promoted the spread and acceptance of Spencerianism. Both Darwin and Spencer felt that evolution—which they equated with progress—resulted from struggles in the natural world. Only the most talented or capable could survive and reproduce. Thus talented people prospered while the weak or the dull lost out.

Acceptance of Social Darwinism logically led to two important conclusions. First, no artificial obstacles should be placed in the path of those striving for success through entrepreneurial activities. If some individuals were inherently more capable than others, neither society nor government should interfere with this preordained inequality. Such a conclusion led to a second key tenet of Social Darwinism: those who did achieve prominence must be God's chosen people. Indeed, John D. Rockefeller's claim that "God gave me my money" represented a sincere belief on his part. Whereas others might resent or envy the entrepreneurial elite, Social Darwinists considered their success proof of divine planning.

As one of the most successful businessmen of all, Andrew Carnegie happily accepted this positive judgment and added a nuance of his own by outlining his concept of a "stewardship of wealth." Because Providence had arranged for certain individuals to amass sizable fortunes, Carnegie maintained, they should be free to dispose of their wealth as they saw fit. They alone should be the stewards of their wealth, doling it out to heirs or philanthropies as they chose. Taxation or other arbitrary confiscation of this wealth would never do; no government could be as wise in the disposition of a fortune as the one who had created it in the first place.

Not all Americans, not even all businessmen, accepted Social Darwinism and favored the strictly laissez-faire system it prescribed. As generation succeeded generation on subsistence farms or in bleak factories, the elitist society Spencerianism sanctioned became increasingly unpopular. Yet the United States remained a land of opportunity for so many that it discouraged the development of any substantial socialistic orientation. As long as most Americans believed in the importance of maintaining economic freedom, they were unlikely to call for the restraint of even the most aggressive or ruthless entrepreneurs. The Gilded Age therefore nurtured a number of extraordinarily talented, energetic businessmen whose individual initiative paid handsome rewards indeed.

THE STEEL KING: ANDREW CARNEGIE

From a childhood as an impoverished Scottish immigrant, Andrew Carnegie rose to majority ownership of the largest steel manufacturing combine in the world, an accomplishment that dwarfed that of any of Horatio Alger's fictional heroes. The embodiment of the Social Darwinist ideal, Carnegie vocally advocated the concepts of Herbert Spencer whom he counted among his many friends. Most Americans knew the Steel King as a generous philanthropist who financed the building of public libraries in thousands of communities throughout the United States and abroad. Both Carnegie's charity and his humble origins insulated him from the criticism other exorbitantly successful industrialists aroused.

He clearly did not take after his father, a linen weaver whose skills the industrial revolution had made obsolete. The elder Carnegie never regained a sense of personal worth after moving his family to Pittsburgh in 1848 when Andy was thirteen. The lad's ambitious and domineering mother, on the other hand, continued to exercise a powerful influence on Carnegie until her death in 1886. Even so, much of young Andrew's spirit, inquisitiveness, and industriousness were inborn.

Although he later bragged that his first job had been as a humble bobbin boy in a textile mill earning only $1.20 per week, he won quick promotion to a better paying position. The tedium of the work in the textile industry drove him to seek outside employment as a telegraph messenger boy. While awaiting assignments, he learned to "read" the messages off the wire by ear, a feat few could perform at that time. Promoted to the position of telegraph operator, he studied accounting at night. The superintendent of the Pennsylvania Railroad's Western Division, Thomas A. Scott, then hired the talented young man as his personal secretary and telegraphic clerk at the handsome salary of $35 a week in 1852.

Carnegie's intelligence and drive made his thirteen years with America's leading railroad a success story in themselves. He absorbed all of the intricacies of

Andrew Carnegie. (Library of Congress)

business management that would prove to be so useful to him in managing his iron and steel operations in the future. He also made hundreds of business contacts through his boss and the railroad's dynamic president, J. Edgar Thomson, a master at creating an effective bureaucratic structure. When Tom Scott became general manager of the system in 1855, he took his valued assistant to Altoona with him, but four years later Carnegie was back in Pittsburgh in Scott's former position as superintendent of the bustling Western Division. There Carnegie spent the Civil War years, honing his business and organizational skills.

He also engaged in private speculation. After taking his first plunge with a borrowed $600, he never looked back, making one brilliant investment decision after another. He cashed in on the western Pennsylvania oil boom in the early 1860s with timely land purchases in the region. When Theodore Woodruff showed him designs for a railroad sleeping car, Carnegie instantly recognized its market potential and helped the inventor sell the cars through his railroad contacts. Convinced that durable iron bridges would also be brisk sellers, he established a partnership that became the Keystone Bridge Company. This firm was ideally situated to take advantage of the reconstruction of the southern railroads and the expansion of tracks in the North. Carnegie left the Pennsylvania Railroad for good in 1865 to become a peripatetic salesman, arranging bridge-building contracts for his company and selling bonds to finance these projects both in the United States and Europe. His annual income topped $50,000 in 1868, and he continued to accumulate the capital he would need for his move into steel manufacturing in the early 1870s.

At that point, the iron and steel industry in the United States was a basically inefficient hodgepodge of relatively small mining, puddling, and rolling operations whose technology had scarcely advanced since the Revolutionary War. In the 1850s, William Kelly had patented a process for piping cold oxygen into a furnace to burn out impurities in the ore. Later, Englishman Henry Bessemer devised enormous converters that used a similar process to turn out huge ingots of steel. Kelly fought the introduction of the Bessemer system into the United States until 1868 when both sides agreed to share their patent rights. At about the same time, the technique for transforming the bituminous coal so plentiful in western Pennsylvania into sulphur-free coke had been perfected, and mines along the upper Great Lakes were ready to ship thousands of tons of rich iron ore. These developments combined with the postwar railroad building boom convinced Carnegie that the time was right to build a huge, modern steel plant in the United States.

Ever wary of bankers and corporations, Carnegie handled all of his major undertakings through partnerships, with himself serving as the leading partner. He personally contributed $250,000 of the $700,000 invested in the organization he helped form in 1872. His chief ally, William Coleman, paid $100,000 for his shares, and seven other partners including Carnegie's former railroad associates Tom Scott and Edgar Thomson each put up $50,000.

Coleman found an ideal site at Braddock, Pennsylvania, where both the Pennsylvania and the Baltimore & Ohio Railroads competed for cargos with barges on the Monongehela River. The partners hired a brilliant engineer named Alexander Holley to construct an enormous mill named for Edgar Thomson. When the country toppled into its worst depression to date in 1873, Carnegie withdrew his investments in other enterprises to get the cash he needed to buy out several of his overextended partners and complete the construction of the plant. When it opened in 1875, therefore, Carnegie personally owned more than half of the company's stock. The Edgar Thomson Steel Works was an outstanding success from the very beginning, its ten Bessemer converters pouring out high grade steel at a cost of about $56 a ton, well below the prevailing market price of $70.

Never satisfied even with success, Carnegie constantly searched for improved processes and new techniques to reduce his production costs. He skillfully created a centralized bureaucracy for his firm, modeled after those he had observed in railroading. He relied on detailed accounting procedures to identify those parts of his operation that either cost too much or caused delays. Because he refused to declare dividends on his stock, he always had plenty of money to spend on conversion, modernization, and technological improvements. He never balked at replacing men with machines and thus reducing his dependence upon skilled workers. One of Carnegie's real gifts was his ability to locate able managers. Holley was superb at designing and housing equipment, and "Captain" Bill Jones turned out to be an equally masterful plant manager, enthusiastically solving day-to-day crises and drawing maximum effort from his workforce.

Carnegie's willingness to integrate was a key factor in his operation's efficiency. Rather than maintain separate facilities or, worse yet, subcontracting ore-reduction and other intermediate steps, Carnegie's mills handled a number of pro-

TWO VIEWS OF ANDREW CARNEGIE

Andrew Carnegie's autobiography provides one explanation of his rise from rags to riches. Matthew Josephson wrote a far less flattering description of Carnegie's methods in The Robber Barons *during the Great Depression of the 1930s.*

(Carnegie) To make a ton of steel, one and half tons of iron stone had to be mined, transported by rail a hundred miles to the Lakes, carried by boat hundreds of miles, transferred to cars, transported by rail one hundred and fifty miles to Pittsburgh; one and a half tons of coal must be mined and manufactured into coke and carried fifty-odd miles to Pittsburgh. How then could steel be manufactured and sold without loss at three pounds for two cents? This, I confess, seemed to me incredible, and little less than miraculous, but it was so.

. . . The price of steel rails when we began was about seventy dollars per ton. We sent our agent through the country with instructions to take orders at the best prices he could obtain; and before our competitors knew it, we had obtained a large number—quite sufficient to justify us in making a start.

So perfect was the machinery, so admirable the plans, so skillful were the men selected by Captain Jones, and so great a manager was he himself, that our success was phenomenal. I think I place a unique statement on record when I say that the result of the first month's operations [of the Edgar Thomson Steel Co.] left a margin of profit of $11,000. It is also remarkable that so perfect was our system of accounts that we knew the exact amount of the profit. We had learned from experience in our iron works what exact accounting meant. There is nothing more profitable than clerks to check up each transfer of material from one department to another in process of manufacturing.

(Josephson) With a few scathing words on a postcard or telegram [Carnegie] would spur on the best of his men by a system of "unfriendly competition" for which he became celebrated and dreaded.

"We broke all records for making steel last week," his managers would telegraph him. And he would answer at once: "Congratulations! Why not do it every week?" Or one manager would report a huge order received and filled, and his reply would be: "Good boy—Next!" Or they signaled him: "Lucy Furnace No. 8 broke all records today," giving the figures. And Carnegie returned: "What were the other ten furnaces doing?"

There was no satisfying the man. Nor was there any peace for his workers and partners, driven alternately by generous money rewards or tongue-lashings. Some of them . . . whose jealousies and rivalries were played upon incessantly by the domineering master, did not speak to each other for years. Others would rebel at Carnegie. Jones would send in his resignation with almost "rhythmic periodicity" only to be tempted back by handsome gifts and apologies. But most of them turned their anger at the Carnegie taunts into renewed and fiercer efforts to surpass each other's labor, while Andy, as one of them said, "drove the whole bandwagon."

(Andrew Carnegie, *Autobiography of Andrew Carnegie* [Boston: Houghton Mifflin, 1920], pp. 204, 226-27; Matthew Josephson, *The Robber Barons* [New York, Harcourt, Brace & World, 1934], pp. 256-57.)

cessing functions under one roof. Just as Francis Cabot Lowell had done with his textile mill, Carnegie reduced or eliminated middleman charges through vertical integration. He bought ore deposits along the Great Lakes, a coke-producing company in Pennsylvania, and the entire town of Conneaut, Ohio, to serve as a lake port for the transshipment of his raw and finished materials. He also expanded horizontally in 1883 when he purchased the Homestead Steel Mill, the most advanced plant in the United States at that point. Carnegie's many holdings allowed him to produce steel without depending on any outside suppliers. And, because both the size and the management of his operations were superior to those of any of his competitors, he always had lower production costs.

Carnegie's masterful sales ability increased his competitive edge. To develop and serve clients around the world, Carnegie spent much of his time abroad. He operated out of a headquarters in New York City and only rarely visited his Pennsylvania mills. The latter he left to the management of others, most notably Henry Clay Frick after 1883. This hardnosed businessman had become a major partner when Carnegie bought the Frick Coke Co. with shares in his own company. Frick had accumulated virtually all of the high-grade coal deposits around Connellsville, Pennsylvania, during and after the Civil War, and his company was operating more than a thousand coke ovens at the time of Carnegie's takeover. As the firm's second largest stockholder and a brilliant entrepreneur in his own right, Frick was the ideal manager for the whole complex.

If Frick had a weakness, it lay in the realm of labor relations. Carnegie always prided himself on being the working man's friend—even though that friendship did not lead to larger pay packets. The Steel King experimented with three eight-hour shifts a day for a couple of years in the 1880s but felt he must abandon the system as long as the other major steel mills maintained two twelve-hour shifts. Carnegie's typical response to labor agitation was to close down operations until the workers agreed to accept his offer. He twice ordered Frick to make concessions to the workers in the late 1880s, but he deliberately left for Scotland in 1892 just before a new three-year contract was slated for negotiation at Homestead.

This time around, Frick had no intention of giving in. The Amalgamated Association of Iron and Steel Workers had enrolled only a small minority of the Homestead workers, but most of the rest heeded the union's strike call anyway. They captured control of the plant and sealed it off from company officials, so Frick hired three hundred pugnacious strikebreakers from the Pinkerton's Detective Agency. These thugs attempted to assault the plant by making an amphibious landing from rafts on the Monongahela, but the strikers fended them off after a bloody battle. The Pennsylvania national guard finally restored the plant to company control, but not before an outside agitator had shot and stabbed Frick. The wounded Frick grimly carried on his vendetta against the workers, winning respect as a martyr to the principle of private enterprise. Soon the strike collapsed and fatally undermined the influence of the Amalgamated Steel Workers union. Although Carnegie publicly expressed anguish over the confrontation, his company continued paying the same low wages that other mills did right through the 1890s.

Anticipating that the railroad market would become glutted, Carnegie diverted much of his production to structural girders and sheet steel. When the Panic of 1893 broke or weakened many other steel manufacturers, Carnegie continued to prosper. The exploitation of vertical integration, a coordinated and centralized business structure, innovative production methods, and generally astute management made Andrew Carnegie one of the richest men in the world when he sold out in 1901. He spent the remaining years of his long life disbursing much of that wealth through foundations and charitable grants. Acting as the sort of benevolent steward of wealth he had described earlier, he felt fully competent to dispose of the money his acumen and drive had generated.

CREATING THE FIRST TRUST: JOHN D. ROCKEFELLER

A secretive and aloof man, John D. Rockefeller seemed perfectly at ease with the contradictions in his character. He combined a sincere Baptist faith and a devotion to regular charitable contributions with an intense drive and ruthlessness in his business dealings. His vast holdings fell under the control of the nation's first trust in the early 1880s, an event that revolutionized and stimulated business consolidation at the same time it roused widespread envy and fear of monopoly.

Like Carnegie, many of the adult Rockefeller's attributes made their first appearances in his boyhood. His father was an avid speculator and talented patent medicine salesman who delighted in teaching his children the value of a dollar. He charged them the prevailing interest rate on any money they borrowed and insisted that they respect contracts. John D.'s mother meanwhile instilled piousness, sobriety, and determination. After a couple of moves from the boy's western New York birthplace, his family settled in the outskirts of Cleveland, a brawling lakeport on the make in the early 1850s. Rockefeller spent a lonely adolescence at the local high school where most of his classmates came from the city's wealthier families. After graduating, he attended a commercial college and developed his lifelong fascination with numbers and accountancy.

At the age of seventeen, Rockefeller tramped the city streets for weeks, contacting every conceivable employer before the commission firm of Hewitt & Tuttle hired him as a bookkeeper. During his three years there, he participated in all aspects of the lucrative business. The firm collected commissions for handling bulk orders and arranging shipments. It also provided loans and helped locate buyers for the products of both farms and factories. A commission agency's success in those days depended upon timely buying decisions and preferential treatment from railroads and shipping companies. Rockefeller left Hewitt & Tuttle in 1859 to invest his savings and $1000 borrowed from his father—at 10 percent interest—in a partnership with Maurice B. Clark. Their commission business especially prospered from Union government contracts for food and supplies during the Civil War. The partnership dissolved in 1865, leaving Rockefeller relatively wealthy and already dabbling in oil.

Just as the Civil War was shutting down the whaling industry, a far more accessible and less expensive lighting source began flowing from the oil fields of western Pennsylvania. Colonel Edward Drake adapted the technology for tapping water laying beneath salty earth to drive a shaft into a rich pool of crude oil in 1859. This primitive oil well was so successful that thousands joined in a California-style rush to exploit the bonanza in black gold. Petroleum previously skimmed

John D. Rockefeller. (Rockefeller Archive Center)

from streams and natural outlets had been used primarily for lubrication, but new refining techniques came along just in time to utilize fully this abundant natural resource. Refiners separated crude oil into a host of useful products, the most marketable of which was kerosene. As a fuel for lamps, it sold readily both at home and abroad.

Rather than enter the brutally competitive drilling and pumping business, John D. Rockefeller and a new partner, Samuel Andrews, bought an established refinery for $72,000. Because a rudimentary distillery could be erected at relatively little cost, refineries had sprung up in the oil regions themselves, in nearby Pittsburgh, and in the vicinity of New York City, the major overseas shipping point. Each of these locations had inherent advantages over Cleveland, but Rockefeller intended to make the Ohio lake port a major refining center.

His strategy emphasized three principles: high volume, market control, and trustworthy associates. He hounded local bankers into lending him enough money to keep his refinery going full blast by making bulk purchases of crude oil at a discount. He brought his younger brother into the partnership and sent him to New York City. There William Rockefeller kept watch on the crucial overseas market, telegraphing his brother of any price fluctuations. The partners in Cleveland used this information to expand their refining and shipping operations. To attract still more outside capital, they decided to incorporate their business as the Standard Oil Company of Ohio. Because he retained ownership of the largest block of the corporation's stock, John D. Rockefeller could dictate company policy. Among other decisions, he insisted that dividends be kept to a minimum so that profits could be reinvested.

The company's success rested in part on its skill at obtaining favorable transportation rates. Railroad and shipping lines customarily offered reduced freight rates to large or repeat customers. Rebates kept these arrangements secret. The transportation company would publish standard rates for the shipment of specific types of freight and actually charge them to all its customers. Favored shippers, however, would then get some of their money back in the form of a secret rebate. A railroad manager burdened with substantial, continuing overhead costs was particularly prone to promise rebates to encourage a bulk shipper to use his system instead of another.

Henry Flagler, another of Rockefeller's trusted associates, handled most of the company's railroad rate negotiations. Two major east-west trunk lines maintained connections through Cleveland: the Erie, by way of the Atlantic & Great Western, and the New York Central, using the Lakeshore Railroad's tracks (Figure 5-3). Each road wanted Standard Oil's trade and was willing to bargain for it. The head of the Lakeshore finally agreed to pay a substantial rebate in return for Flagler's promise that his company would ship sixty carloads of refined oil east every day.

Standard Oil's total refining capacity at that point would scarcely have filled twenty cars a day, though, so Rockefeller set out to tie in additional refiners. He

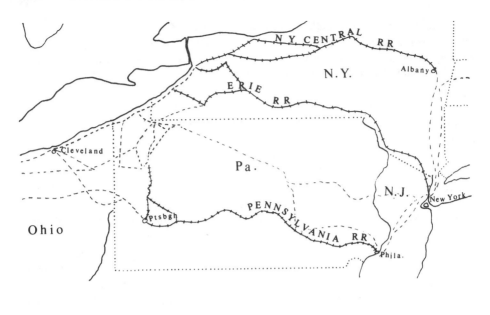

Trunk Lines ⊢⊢⊢⊢⊣ Connector Roads – – – – Oil Regions

FIGURE 5-3 Railroads Linking Cleveland to the Oil Regions and the East Coast, 1864.

did so under the guise of a charter for a corporation that existed in name only: the South Improvement Co. He convinced one Cleveland refiner after another to sell out to this company or face certain bankruptcy due to his favorable rebate from the Lakeshore Railroad. Even when Rockefeller offered a fair market price for their properties, many of those who sold out felt aggrieved. In a single month, Rockefeller engulfed twenty-three companies, eighteen of them located in Cleveland. He then controlled enough refining capacity to meet the daily shipment figure Flagler had promised.

Rockefeller's broader ambition to capture control of refineries all over the Northeast temporarily derailed when their owners banded together against his predatory raids. Crude oil producers also became so alarmed that they refused to sell to the South Improvement Co., thus cutting off its access to raw materials. To evade the producer's boycott and disarm his rival refiners, Rockefeller abandoned that corporate facade completely and ran his holdings as elements of Standard Oil. That company participated briefly in the National Refiners' Association, a pool designed to control output and maintain price levels by allocating quotas to all refiners.

The Panic of 1873 discouraged such voluntary cooperation and drove many individual refiners toward bankruptcy. Rockefeller responded to the crisis by borrowing extensively to purchase additional properties at depression prices. He often made few alterations in their outward appearances. By leaving a firm's officers,

TWO VIEWS OF JOHN D. ROCKEFELLER

The first selection offers Rockefeller's own rationalization for buying out competitors with the South Improvement Co. The second comes from William Demarest Lloyd's bitter critique of the man written in 1894.

(Rockefeller) In speaking of the real beginning of the Standard Oil Company, it should be remembered that it was not so much the consolidation of the firms in which we had a personal interest, but the coming together of the men who had the combined brain power to do the work which was the actual starting-point. Perhaps it is worth while to emphasize again the fact that it is not merely capital and "plants" and the strictly material things which make up a business, but the character of the men behind these things, their personalities, and their abilities; these are the essentials to be reckoned with.

Late in 1871, we began the purchase of some of the more important of the refinery interests of Cleveland. The conditions were so chaotic and uncertain that most of the refiners were very desirous to get out of the business. We invariably offered those who wanted to sell the option of taking cash or stock in the company. We very much preferred to have them take the stock, because a dollar in those days looked as large as a cart-wheel, but as a matter of business policy we found it desirable to offer them the option, and in most cases they were even precipitate in their choice of the cash. They knew what a dollar would buy, but they were very skeptical in regard to the possibilities of resurrecting the oil business and giving any permanent value to these shares.

(Lloyd) One of the Cleveland manufacturers who had sold was asked why he did so by the New York Legislature. They had been very prosperous, he said; their profits had been $30,000 to $45,000 a year; but their prosperity had come to a sudden stop.

"From the time that it was well understood in the trade that the South Improvement Company had . . . grappled the entire transportation of oil from the West to the seaboard . . . we were all kind of paralyzed, perfectly paralyzed; we could not operate. . . . The South Improvement Company, or some one representing them, had a drawback of a dollar, sometimes seventy cents, sometimes more, sometimes less, and we were working against that difference."

It was a difference, he said, which destroyed their business. . . .

His firm was outside the charmed circle, and he had to choose between selling and dying. Last of all, he had an interview with the president of the all-conquering oil company, in relation to the purchase of their works. "He was the only party that would buy. He offered me fifty cents on the dollar, on the construction account, and we sold out. . . . He made this expression, I remember: 'I have ways of making money that you know nothing of.'"

For the works, which were producing $30,000 to $45,000 a year profit, and which they considered worth $150,000, they received $65,000.

"Did you ascertain in the trade," he was asked, "what was the average rate that was paid for refineries?"

"That was the figure. . . . Fifty cents on the dollar."

"It was that or nothing, was it not?"

"That or nothing."

(John D. Rockefeller, *Random Reminiscences of Men and Events* [Garden City, NY: Doubleday, 1933], pp. 94-95; Henry Demarest Lloyd, *Wealth Against Commonwealth* [New York: Harper, 1894], pp. 51-53.)

operations, and even its brand names unchanged, Rockefeller concealed just how extensive his empire had become. In fact, he was well on the way toward achieving a comprehensive horizontal integration of the refining business in the United States. He wisely left the drillers to squabble among themselves. Any price cuts that resulted from their competition benefited Rockefeller most since they had to sell almost all of their crude to Standard or its affiliates.

Rockefeller was meanwhile assembling a second tier of horizontal integration in the industry by investing in railroad tankcars. These had recently been developed for bulk shipments of oil, replacing the more expensive and fragile wooden barrels. Rockefeller had a serious rival, though, in Joseph D. Potts' Empire Transportation Company. A subsidiary of the Pennsylvania Railroad, it was well funded and extraordinarily aggressive. Because the company owned 1500 tankcars, Potts could offer competing railroads massive regular freight allotments. But Standard Oil had accumulated a 3000-car fleet, and the devastating consequences of the depression of the late 1870s drove Potts to the wall. The Pennsylvania Railroad suffered a costly strike in 1877 that eroded its financial support for the transportation company. Rockefeller then bought its cars and equipment and was able to "even" the traffic, something the railroads had wanted all along. He negotiated agreements with the four major east-west roads that allocated a fixed percentage of his shipments to each of them.

A final chink in Rockefeller's entrepreneurial armor was his conviction that his tankcar monopoly guaranteed him permanent control over all oil shipments. This confidence seems somewhat surprising since some of his own companies were using short pipelines to move crude from the oil regions to his Cleveland refineries. Pipelines were just one of a number of innovations Standard adopted rather tardily. Rockefeller typically waited to buy the rights to novel methods and processes until others had brought them through the costly experimental stage.

He therefore reacted rather sluggishly to a challenge from the Tidewater Pipe Line Company in the late 1870s. With the support of the Pennsylvania Railroad

First Standard Oil Refinery in Cleveland.

and the state legislators at Harrisburg, neither of whom favored Rockefeller's Ohio-based oil combine, Tidewater began laying a pipe from the oil regions to Williamsport in central Pennsylvania. There crude oil could be pumped into tankcars for shipment further east on the Reading Railroad. As the project neared completion, Rockefeller responded characteristically with an offer to buy the whole company. Repulsed, he tried to deny the Reading Railroad access to any tank cars. Finally, even though it would compete with his tankcar monopoly, he began punching his own pipeline through the Pennsylvania mountains parallel to the Tidewater Company's route. Unfortunately for the pipeline company, the major railroads became involved in cutthroat rate competition that caused them to charge Standard almost nothing to haul its tankcars. The beleaguered Tidewater stockholders finally had to sell out to the only buyer—the Standard Oil Company.

In 1879, Rockefeller and his associates were doing approximately 90 percent of all the refining in the United States. While their operations continued to expand, new oil discoveries and the relatively low cost of building competing refineries continually threatened their control over the industry. One of the group's chief hindrances at that point was the cumbersome and splintered organization and management that had evolved. Rockefeller definitely needed to formalize and streamline his operations on a national scale.

A brilliant lawyer named Samuel C. T. Dodd helped Henry Flagler devise just such an effective national organization. First they had to find a legal way to sidestep restrictions in the state chartering laws which usually prohibited any corporation from owning property outside its home state's boundaries. Obviously, no single state-chartered corporation could manage all of Rockefeller's diverse properties, so Dodd arranged for a separate Standard Oil company to be incorporated in each state to consolidate and manage all operations within its borders. He then established a board of trustees in New York City to coordinate the activities of these separate companies. Stockholders who turned over their shares in the various Standard Oil companies to the board received trust certificates in return. To satisfy the state laws, the board technically held these shares only "in trust," but the major decisions for all of the Standard Oil companies were made at the trust's offices at 29 Broadway. Although he let others organize this system, John D. Rockefeller personally owned four-ninths of all of the stock transferred to the trust. He arranged to have himself chosen one of its nine trustees, and his influence and vast holdings made his opinions predominant.

The Standard Oil Trust immediately began streamlining the operating procedures and developing efficiencies of production and organization that the earlier jumble of companies could never have achieved. Its success naturally attracted the attention of other entrepreneurs similarly hampered by state laws. Trustee arrangements soon appeared in other sectors like tobacco, sugar refining, and other processing operations. Trusts also roused public concern because they appeared to be well beyond the control of any political or legal restraints. Sufficient criticism arose to prod Congress into passing the Sherman Antitrust Act in 1890. Although this move made it appear likely that the federal government would step in and control these huge interstate business combines, the real impact of the legislation remained unknown until it could be tested in the courts.

The possibility of legal action never concerned Rockefeller and his cronies. The profits from their near monopoly of refining allowed the Standard Oil trustees to expand vertically. John D. became almost fanatically interested in purchasing oil leases for the reserves discovered in Ohio and Indiana, even though their high sulfur content required very complex distillation processes. In addition to expanding backwards to assure a supply of raw materials, the company also engaged in an aggressive marketing campaign. Standard Oil tank wagons roamed city streets, peddling kerosene by the gallon and putting thousands of independent distributors out of business. In 1890 Rockefeller conservatively estimated that the value of his personal assets stood at $37 million, the kernel of a fortune that would ultimately be measured in the hundreds of millions.

Rockefeller repeatedly insisted that accumulating money had never been his chief aim. Instead, he prided himself on his ability to coordinate a vast industry. His distaste for destructive competition compelled him to expand continually to reduce its effect. He wanted to prevent surprises, essentially to control the future. He insisted that each participant in the industry should be content with a reasonable share of the larger whole, and he struck quickly against any individual or company that appeared likely to shatter the equilibrium he sought. The only way he could ultimately guarantee that balance was to own or control almost everything. Not surprisingly, few Americans agreed that he, or any other individual for that matter, should dominate any industry that thoroughly so Rockefeller was fated to become one of the most unpopular entrepreneurs of the period.

RAILROADS: A TROUBLED LEADING SECTOR

The use and abuse of railroads clearly contributed to the success of both Carnegie and Rockefeller. The Steel King's apprenticeship with the Pennsylvania Railroad taught him how to organize and manage a huge business operation at the same time it introduced him the people he would later use as customers. Steel rails were one of his chief products throughout his career. Rockefeller relied on rails to carry his crude and refined oil. His company's success at gaining preferential treatment from the railroads helped him outearn and eventually buy out his rivals. Of course, the railroads also served the common man. Americans used them to move to new jobs, to send goods to distant customers, and to transport resources from remote stockpiles. A city needed reliable rail service to grow, and the extension of the tracks throughout the West encouraged settlement in the territories.

To meet the growing demand for transportation service after the Civil War, the size of locomotives, the length of trains, the capacity of freight cars, and the number of trains operating each day escalated. Railroads carried 10 billion ton-miles of freight in 1865; the figure for 1890 was 79 billion ton-miles. Much of this freight flowed over newly-opened routes. Figure 5-3 illustrates the sensitivity of railroad construction to the economic health of the United States. The Panic of 1873 cut construction sharply, and a recession in the mid eighties caused another dip. Despite these temporary slowdowns, the total mileage in service nearly tripled in the quarter century following the war, rising from 35,000 to over 93,000 miles.

New tracks went down all over the country, but the construction of the transcontinental railroads attracted special attention. Shortly after the southern congressmen stormed out of Congress to join the Confederacy, the northerners left behind authorized major federal land grants to two railroad companies. The 1862 act was then amended in the companies' favor two years later so that each railroad would receive twenty sections of the public domain in alternating strips along its completed right of way. Congress also provided loan guarantees to help the companies find financing for construction. The guarantee amounted to $16,000 for

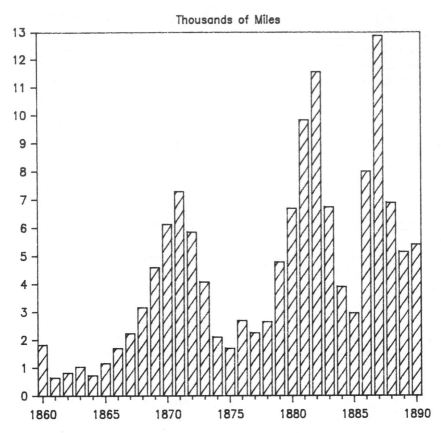

FIGURE 5-4   Miles of Railroad Built. (From U.S. Bureau of the Census, *Historical Statistics of the United States* [Washington, DC: Government Printing Office, Q-15, 1960].)

each mile of track laid across level terrain, it doubled to $32,000 in hilly country, and it jumped to $48,000 in the mountains which lay across much of the route.

The Union Pacific Railroad Company was formed to take up the land grant and build across Nebraska toward the West. Promoter Thomas C. Durant managed its business affairs while General Grenville M. Dodge acted as chief engineer, superintending the actual construction of the road. Employing as many as 10,000 men at a time, the company could lay several miles of track each day, qualifying it for more land and additional loans. The haste with which the road was built inevitably produced sloppy workmanship, so money and effort continued to be expended long after its official "completion."

A separate organization, the Central Pacific Railroad, simultaneously assumed the much more difficult engineering task of pushing rails eastward from Sacramento, California. Four local businessmen dominated the company. Leland

Joining the tracks at Promontory Point, Utah, May 10, 1869, (Library of Congress)

Stanford, Collis P. Huntington, Charles Croker, and Mark Hopkins eventually became the most powerful entrepreneurs in the Golden State. An extreme scarcity of labor on the West Coast encouraged the company to import thousands of Chinese workers to cut the roadbed through the Sierras and beyond. It also had to ship most of its tools, rolling stock, and the rails themselves by sea around Cape Horn. After many months, the two roads had come close enough to connect, but both continued to survey and grade rights of way parallel to one another hoping to earn more land and loans. Congress finally ordered them to join their tracks near Promontory Point in the Utah Territory. On May 10, 1869, officials from both companies ceremoniously celebrated the completion of the nation's first transcontinental railroad by driving home a symbolic golden spike—and then prying it right back out again so it could be returned to California for display.

The success of this enterprise encouraged construction along other transcontinental routes. The Northern Pacific received an extraordinarily generous land grant of forty sections per mile, but the territory it traversed was quite barren. Civil War financier Jay Cooke became so overextended trying to fund this project that his firm went bankrupt in 1873 and set off a severe nationwide business panic. Work on the line was not completed for another decade. Other entrepreneurs ran the Southern Pacific Railroad along the lower border of the United States. Finally, a small road linking Atchison and Topeka in Kansas built southwest to Santa Fe, New Mexico, on its way to connecting Los Angeles with Chicago as the Santa Fe Railroad system.

The new construction and the rising demand for rail service stimulated a number of innovations. The railroads began operating on "standard" time in the four zones that Congress eventually prescribed for everyone in 1918. Major roads also quickly adopted automatic knuckle couplers and the air braking system George

---

J. J. HILL

James Jerome Hill dreamed of making a fortune trading in the Orient so he left his Canadian home in 1856 at the age of eighteen hoping to find a berth to China. He never made it, getting only as far west as St. Paul, Minnesota. There he worked as a clerk for a riverboat firm and later established himself as an independent forwarding and transportation agent. His business activities led him to explore much of the surrounding territory, and he became convinced that the Red River Valley was prime agricultural land.

He also naturally became familiar with the railroad situation in the region. The Northern Pacific had frittered away its federal land grants and fallen into receivership in 1873. The St. Paul & Pacific Railroad was doing poorly as well even though it held claims to five million acres of land. Its peculiar funding arrangement dictated that all of its stocks must be sold in Holland, but the Dutch stockholders were so disillusioned that they were ready to entertain any reasonable offer. Hill convinced three other wealthy men to join with him in a partnership that bought a controlling interest in the railroad in 1878.

It thrived under Hill's management. He insisted on rebuilding it to high quality standards and then extending it only to logical markets. Hill surveyed much of its westward progress personally, and moved at just the right pace to keep the road solvent. He also advertised in Europe and elsewhere to encourage settlers to move into the territories his tracks were serving. Many therefore considered him an "empire builder," so extensive and pervasive was his influence in the Northwest. His tracks reached Great Falls, Montana, in 1887 and his ultimate objective, Everett, Washington, on the Pacific Coast in 1893. He had meanwhile reassembled his many properties under a single corporate structure in 1890 named the Great Northern. In the 1890s, he also gained control of the rival Northern Pacific Railroad. At that point he was recognized as one of the United States's great rail barons, and he would play a key role in the consolidation and development of integrated and lucrative railroad networks.

Westinghouse had invented. These mechanisms not only simplified train make-up and movement, they protected thousands of brakemen from serious injury or death. Mechanically and electrically controlled block signals also improved safety records as did the installation of stronger steel rails and bridges. Specialty cars of all types appeared. Oil tankers, cabooses, hoppers, and refrigerator cars moved freight more efficiently; Pullman sleeping coaches and dining cars increased passenger comfort.

Unfortunately, many railroad owners, managers, and operators showed little concern about comfort or efficiency; they were in the business solely to make money. Competition interfered with this objective. Freight rates had to be set very low to undercut parallel lines. Rebates like those granted to Standard Oil were commonly offered to attract and hold customers. Some railroads went even further, paying preferred customers "drawbacks," essentially rebates taken from the fares their rivals paid. A shipper who received rebates on his own freight and drawbacks on his competitors' obviously enjoyed an unbeatable advantage. The roads also issued thousands of passes to favored travelers like government officials, providing free transportation for them at the expense of paying passengers.

To avoid the loss of revenue such favors caused, railroad companies tried to establish reliable cooperative arrangements. Pools had no legal standing, but many companies conspired to fix rates and allocate traffic so as to guarantee higher returns for all. Most pools evaporated rather quickly, though, because one or more participants simply could not resist seeking advantages by extending special favors. The only sure way to stifle such independent action was to draw all the roads serving the same region into an integrated system. Even then, others might build "nuisance" roads nearby and then demand exorbitant prices when the combine moved to buy them.

Gilded Age railroadmen often became involved in convoluted financial and legal tangles. Cornelius Vanderbilt initially looked like a winner when he began devoting his shipping fortune to railroading after the Civil War. He was well into his sixties when he bought control of two small railroads linking Albany with New York City. As he well knew, the New York Central Railroad needed to use their tracks to reach the great seaport. When Vanderbilt suddenly refused to handle any shipments from the Central in 1867, the value of the larger road's stock tumbled, allowing the tycoon to buy enough shares to gain control of the whole system. After the dust settled, only the frail Erie Railroad blocked Vanderbilt's domination of all rail transport between Manhattan and the Great Lakes. He immediately began buying Erie shares, planning to extend his control over that company as well.

A seasoned veteran of many a stock battle, Vanderbilt behaved somewhat naively in taking on the current management of the Erie: Daniel Drew, Jim Fisk, and Jay Gould. Aware of Vanderbilt's takeover plans, these scoundrels gleefully sold him thousands of shares—brand new ones, in fact, that they were printing fresh daily under the questionable legal premise that they represented convertible bonds. Unable to obtain a controlling percentage of this inexhaustible flow of Erie stock, Vanderbilt had a judge he had bribed issue an injunction ordering the company to

WILLIAM VANDERBILT ON THE RAILROAD BUSINESS

William H. Vanderbilt more than doubled the $100 million he inherited from his father Cornelius through ruthless speculation in railroads. In a candid interview with newsmen in the fall of 1882, he revealed much about his own and his fellow financiers' attitudes. The following interchange began when a reporter asked if lower passenger rates might be anticipated.

"The passenger traffic is only a small part of the business of the railroads. No lower rates could be made to pay between New York and Chicago. Why, sir, do you know that not over one hundred fifty passengers are sent from Chicago to New York per day over all the eastbound roads? Of course, if any one road could afford to have all this business, it could afford to carry them for fifteen dollars a head."

"Does your limited [to Chicago] pay?"

"No; not a bit of it. We only run it because we are forced to do so by the action of the Pennsylvania road. It doesn't pay expenses. We would abandon it if it were not for our competitor keeping its train on."

"But don't you run it for the public benefit?"

"The public be damned! What does the public care for the railroads except to get as much out of them for as small a consideration as possible! I don't take any stock in this working for anybody's good but our own, because we are not. When we make a move, we do it because it is in our interest to do so, not because we expect to do somebody else some good. Of course, we like to do everything possible for the benefit of humanity in general, but when we do, we first see that we are benefiting ourselves. Railroads are not run on sentiment, but on business principles, and to pay, and I don't mean to be egotistic when I say that the roads which I have had anything to do with have generally paid pretty well!"

(Reprinted in Wayne Andrews, *The Vanderbilt Legend* [New York: Harcourt, Brace, 1941], pp. 193-94.)

stop printing any more. For good measure, Vanderbilt then passed out retainers to the members of the New York Assembly, who promptly voted 83 to 32 in favor of a law to support the injunction.

To avoid these legal restraints, the Erie wrecking crew packed up its printing equipment and fled to the friendly shores of New Jersey. Within a matter of hours, the state legislature at Trenton issued a new charter for the railroad company whose property and operations lay wholly in New York. This New Jersey charter allowed the company to continue printing stock certificates, but Fisk pined for the gaiety and glitter of Broadway. He convinced Gould to return to Manhattan where the financier was promptly arrested. But Gould had taken the precaution of bringing a large satchel full of greenbacks out of which he made bail and bought a ticket to Albany. Soon his satchel was empty and the New York Assemblymen were reconsidering their position. They ended up voting 101 to 6 to permit the Erie to carry on as before. A disgusted Vanderbilt abandoned the field, leaving the way clear for Fisk and Gould to complete their looting of the Erie.

A jealous suitor of one of the many women Fisk had dallied with shot and killed the flamboyant businessman a couple of years later, but Gould continued to collect railroad properties all over the country. He hoped to draw together an integrated system stretching from coast to coast but never succeeded in achieving that goal. Along the way, he made literally thousands of enemies ranging from the workers who objected to the wages and working conditions on his railroads all the way to rival speculators like Vanderbilt. Gould seemed to relish his notoriety, though, and he had accumulated one of the largest personal fortunes in the United States at the time of his death in 1892.

Speculators like Gould were all too common in the Gilded Age, raking off profits and letting assets deteriorate. Thomas Durant, head of the Union Pacific Railroad, and some of his associates had formed a subsidiary called the Credit Mobilier to perform the actual construction of the road. Although the establishment of separate construction and operating companies was a common practice in this period, the Credit Mobilier was unusually profitable. Proceeds from land sales and guaranteed loans flowed into the company, but far less trickled out to pay for the work performed. Estimates of the amount that the stockholders of the construction company siphoned off for themselves ranged as high as $40 million. The matter became a major political scandal when investigators discovered that a number of congressmen had received blocks of Credit Mobilier stock, presumably in return for supporting government appropriations beneficial to the company.

This sort of behavior was just one cause for the widespread hostility toward railroads in the late nineteenth century. Few roads were solidly built and efficiently managed; scavengers and incompetents could buy or bully their way into control of even the most public-spirited companies. Protests also arose over unfair freight rates, overcapitalization, sloppy or dangerous operating procedures, and monopoly or oligopoly control. Even so, the railroads greatly extended access to markets and thereby allowed for the concentration of industries and substantial populations in cities.

URBAN PROSPECTS AND PROBLEMS

Urbanization was nationwide. The South lagged somewhat, but major marketing and commercial centers developed throughout the Northeast, the Midwest, and along the West Coast. Chicago grew the fastest, climbing from a population of

100,000 in 1860 to over a million in 1890. Many other cities competed strenuously for population, industries, railroads, and influence.

Building a city was a major enterprise or, to be more accurate, a series of enterprises. The owners of farmhouses and outbuildings usually did most of the structural and finishing work, but the building trades shaped the urban environment. Construction companies organized and financed like other industrial firms hired carpenters, masons, plumbers, and other specialists to work together. Completed buildings could be rented or sold to other landlords. More than half the buildings in New York City in the 1890s were rental units, ranging from crammed, oppressive tenements to luxury headquarters for the thousands of businesses located there.

The structure of cities changed over time. Communities in the United States usually began as concentrations of wooden buildings. Despite the catastrophic fires that swept many of the major cities in this period, cheap, highly flammable lumber continued to be widely used. Bricks were also popular for houses and smaller commercial buildings, so brickyards and clay pits could be found near every major city. Plentiful and easily shaped brownstone faced thousands of row houses in New York, Boston, Chicago, and other cities, although they usually had brick sidewalls or wooden skeletons. The preferred building materials for major downtown commercial structures were marble and granite, and the demand for them kept New England's quarries busy.

The congestion and the high cost of downtown lots encouraged architects to design taller buildings. Elisha Otis developed a steam-powered elevator to carry passengers and freight vertically, but brick or stone walls could only go as high as their load-bearing strength permitted. William LeBaron Jenney overcame this structural limit when he designed the first "skyscraper" in the 1880s with a steel girder skeleton to suspend floors and walls. The Brooklyn Bridge, opened in 1887, was a massive yet graceful structure of steel girders and cables, and it served as a model for other bridges all across the country. The swing to steel construction in the cities took up some of the slack in Carnegie's industry as the overbuilt railroads slowed their own building drive.

Some of the leading financiers and railroad barons in the United States invested in urban transit systems. Jay Gould was able to monopolize New York City's system in the 1880s with his access to the capital needed to update or replace outmoded equipment. Horse-drawn omnibuses, many running on rails, had provided mass transit earlier in the nineteenth century. The horsecars gave way to more technologically advanced—and substantially more expensive—cable cars, elevated railways, and electric trolley car systems as the century drew to a close. Elevated railroads were designed to relieve surface traffic congestion, but the noise and pollution of their steam engines were decided drawbacks. When Frank J. Sprague constructed an entire electric trolley car system for Richmond, Virginia, in 1887, he set off a surge of investment and construction throughout the country. Electric streetcars could flow with the traffic on busy streets, and they offered clean and quieter service on elevated tracks. In the 1890s, Boston began burying its electrified railways below ground, and soon other cities were planning similar subway systems.

Trolley cars exploited the electric power that Thomas Edison had popularized. Perhaps the most prolific and admired of American tinkerers, he had first tackled the problem of finding a reliable alternative to the temperamental carbon arcs that produced a harsh, bluish light principally used for street illumination. After extensive experimentation he devised a long-burning incandescent lightbulb. It worked both outdoors and indoors, where it could replace smelly and dangerous kerosene lamps and the gas lighting systems more progressive cities had installed. To demonstrate the potential of the new power source, Edison constructed the Pearl Street generating station that lit New York's Broadway in 1882. This was only the first of a number of electric utility operations in which Edison played both a technical and an entrepreneurial role.

Edison's popularity had one unfortunate consequence: he stubbornly insisted that direct current electricity was the only safe type. Most Americans relied upon Edison's expert opinion, to the exasperation of his chief rival, George Westinghouse, an ardent advocate of alternating current. Direct current had so limited a range that generating plants would have to be built anywhere it was to be used. Alternating current, on the other hand, could be transmitted over great distances at high voltage and then stepped down through transformers for safe commercial or residential use. Many years passed before the transmission advantages and greater energy potential of alternating current overcame Edison's frenzied publicity campaign against it.

Edison lost on another front as well. Although he obtained 1093 patents, none was as financially rewarding as the telephone patent Alexander Graham Bell obtained. Instantaneous voice communication would greatly facilitate businesses affairs involving broad customer and regional bases, so the invention proved quite timely. Bell's associates, particularly Theodore M. Vail, quickly established effective and efficient manufacturing, service, and switching facilities. The American Telephone and Telegraph Co. was formed in 1885 to handle long distance service. It engulfed the Bell System in 1900 to become one of the most profitable near monopolies in American history until a court battle dismembered it in 1982.

While the Bell System was the popular choice for telephone service, bitter controversies raged over who would provide and profit from other city utilities. Some of these were run directly as public services like the government programs that provided water supplies for New York, Philadelphia, and other cities. In other cases, the mayor or aldermen would award a franchise to a private concern. Profit-hungry individuals or syndicates with regional or national financing could step in to provide utility services, just as Gould dominated New York's transit system in the 1880s.

Some businessmen grew wealthy overcharging city dwellers for utility service, but others saw them primarily as customers. The concentration of people in urban areas led to important changes in the marketing of consumer products. The cities contained thousands upon thousands of dependent individuals, none of whom came anywhere near the level of self-sufficiency that pioneers and many farm families could achieve. The wage earners, renters, and specialized craftsmen and businessmen who made up the urban population were therefore prime prospects for merchants and salesmen.

Older cities like Boston, New York, and Philadelphia had well-developed shopping districts for retail customers, and the large number of potential buyers encouraged specialized merchandising. Some merchants dealt exclusively in dry goods, shoes, groceries, or hardware. In larger cities, whole blocks or districts were given over to the buying and selling of a single type of commodity, a phenomenon that has persisted in our own time in the form of auto rows, produce, garment, and financial districts, and the fast-food "miracle miles" that line the nation's highways.

At the same time, cities were also fostering diversified merchandising in the form of department stores. A. T. Stewart's dry goods emporium had pioneered this approach before the Civil War, and the concept spread and became much more elaborate in the late nineteenth century. Wherever they sprang up, department stores shared some common characteristics. They set fixed cash prices for their goods rather than permitting the bargaining common in general stores. The volume of trade these retailers conducted enabled them to negotiate directly with manufacturers and thereby obtain goods more cheaply than they would have through jobbers, wholesalers, and other middlemen. Reduced wholesale costs, in turn, permitted them to advertise lower retail prices to draw in customers.

Department stores appeared in every major city. Even though his earlier retailing ventures had failed, R. H. Macy decided to open a dry goods store in New York City in 1858. To expand his offerings, he invited other specialty retailers to operate self-contained departments within his larger establishment. Adam Gimbel began his business career at a trading post in Indiana. He later built diversified retail stores in Milwaukee and elsewhere, but it was his son who made the move to New York City in 1910. Marshall Field worked with several partnerships in Chicago to earn enough capital to buy complete control of a successful department store business in 1881. His philosophy that "the customer is always right" won public confidence and repeat patronage. William Filene in Boston, J. L. Hudson in Detroit, David May in Denver, and I. Magnin in San Francisco also started their department store operations in this period.

WORKING-CLASS AMERICA

Most of the millions who gathered in the cities hoped to achieve some degree of economic independence, but that goal eluded many who worked in factories. As industrialists invested more capital in machinery, they needed less skill in their

JOHN WANAMAKER

The founder of the first modern department store, John Wanamaker was a resourceful and innovative merchant. After holding a number of minor positions in his native Philadelphia, he got married at the age of 22. To be a good provider, he went into partnership with his wife's brother in a haberdashery in 1861. The firm did so well it ultimately became the largest retail men's clothing store in the United States. The ambitious entrepreneur used his profits to open other stores as well.

In 1876 John Wanamaker topped his earlier successes by converting an old Pennsylvania Railroad freight depot into an enormous emporium stocking all sorts of goods. Popularly known as the "Grand Depot," it served hundreds of thousands of customers, many of them attracted to Philadelphia by the Centennial Exhibition in that year. Shortly afterward, Wanamaker opened another huge store in which he hoped to install a collection of independently managed speciality shops. He ended up stocking and operating the various departments himself in what soon became one of the largest department stores in the United States.

As early as 1865, Wanamaker was offering a money-back guarantee on his goods. He typically bought in bulk and therefore could advertise lower prices than other retailers. He never stinted on his advertising budget, being particularly effective in the use of newspaper campaigns. Unlike many other aggressive entrepreneurs, Wanamaker was quite paternalistic to his employees, providing them with training opportunities and other fringe benefits unusual in that era. After serving as Postmaster General in the Benjamin Harrison administration, Wanamaker continued to expand his operations, even buying A. T. Stewart's old store in New York in 1896.

workers. To perform simple, routine tasks as cheaply as possible, managers and foremen recruited people with little training and limited expectations. In some regions and industries, that led to the hiring of ill-paid women and children. Textile mills, particularly those built in the reconstructed South, made extensive use of female and child labor. The ready-made clothing industry in the North put semiskilled seamstresses to work for long hours in crowded sweatshops.

The millions of immigrants who entered the United States in the late nineteenth century represented a major source of cheap, unskilled labor. The flow of immigration fluctuated according to the economic health of the United States. Relatively few of the newcomers managed to become independent farmers, tradespeople, or shopkeepers. Those who arrived penniless at coastal ports had to take whatever low-paying jobs they could find. Immigrants with mining or

John Wanamaker. (Library of Congress)

metalworking expertise were often hired and transported to company towns in the interior. More than half of the miners and over 40 percent of the iron and steel workers employed in the United States in 1870 were foreign-born.

The constant influx of immigrant labor insured far from ideal working conditions in industrial America. Through the First World War, the average workday for all Americans lasted ten hours, with a six-day week being standard. Twelve-hour days and seven-day weeks were considered essential in some industries like steel. Other employers demanded even more. Ironically, a shorter workday became the norm in some factories because the managers noted that their employees lost efficiency and had many more machinery-damaging accidents during the eleventh or twelfth hour of toil. Wage rates rose somewhat in the late nineteenth century but never kept pace with workers' increasing productivity.

Pensions, workmen's compensation, job tenure, and other fringe benefits were seldom even discussed much less implemented. Some employers congratulated themselves for providing company housing or running a store for their workers. All too often, though, impoverished laborers had no more success in paying off their debts to a company store than southern farmers did their lienholders. Patronage of these stores was unavoidable where employers paid their workers in scrip, redeemable only for the overpriced goods and supplies they stocked. At its worst, the system amounted to industrial peonage, destructive of worker morale and well-being.

While individual workers were powerless, some advocated organizing to fight for better treatment as a group. A few trade unions had exercised limited local influence since the 1830s. The most effective were those containing highly skilled members like the typographers and railroad workers who patched together rudimentary national organizations prior to the Civil War. Afterwards, other skilled workers established links with colleagues in other parts of the country, but they seldom included more than a fraction of the labor force in any industry. Economic hardships like the depression that followed Jay Cooke's Panic in 1873 further discouraged labor organizers. Workers were far more willing to accept unsatisfactory working conditions if unemployment was their only alternative.

Extraordinarily callous actions on the part of the eastern railroads nevertheless ignited a nationwide workers' protest. Robert A. Ammon, a brakeman for the Pennsylvania Railroad, secretly formed the Trainman's Union, hoping to draw all railroad workers into a single bargaining unit. In the summer of 1877, the Baltimore & Ohio and then the Pennsylvania Railroads cut wages and altered their train structures to reduce the number of crews needed. Members of a Trainman's Union local retaliated by halting B & O traffic through West Virginia. Stoppages quickly extended along both lines. Pittsburgh suffered the most extensive damage from strikers and rioters who ran berserk for nearly two weeks. Dozens of individuals died as the strife spread throughout a nation disillusioned with the power and arrogance of the railroad companies. In many cases, they regained control of their properties only with the assistance of militia units and federal troops.

Despite its futility, the strike of 1877 stimulated interest in collective action. The Noble and Holy Order of the Knights of Labor stood ready to exploit these sentiments. It had begun in 1869 as a secret society, cloaked in ritual. Secrecy made sense in an era when employers blacklisted labor organizers and hired Pinkerton's operatives to spy on their workers. When machinist and politician Terence V. Powderly became the organization's Grand Master Workman in the late 1870s, however, he opened its doors to all workers, regardless of their skill level, race, or sex.

Powderly's organization really began flourishing after some of its members won impressive concessions from Jay Gould in 1885. Deeply involved in other delicate financial maneuvering, the financier gave in to the demands of the striking Knights. Membership in the national organization quickly mushroomed to three-quarters of a million, far more than it could effectively manage. Gould meanwhile cleared for action and provoked another walkout early in 1886. He ruthlessly broke this strike and fired the troublemaking Knights. Faith in the national union's capabilities declined markedly in the wake of this defeat. It plummetted still further when opponents incorrectly charged it with complicity in the 1886 Haymarket bombing in Chicago which had been the work of radical agitators.

The decline of the Knights of Labor left a clear field for the American Federation of Labor. A carpenter named Peter J. McGuire and two cigarmakers, Adolph Strasser and Samuel Gompers, firmly believed that an organization containing unskilled workers could never succeed. They formed the American Federation of Labor (AFL) in 1886 to provide craft unions with a safe haven from the undisciplined mob under Powderly. The federation functioned as a coordinating body for a coalition of formerly independent craft unions. Elected as the first president of the AFL in 1886, Samuel Gompers held that office until his death in 1924 except for one year in the 1890s. So moderate as to appear conservative, he detested strife and strikes. Instead, Gompers campaigned to earn

Samuel Gompers. (Library of Congress)

recognition of his union affiliates as bargaining agents for the "bread and butter" issues of higher wages, shorter hours, and better working conditions. In the end, his leadership was much more effective than a dynamic approach might have been, given the fundamental American antipathy for radicalism in any form. The American Federation of Labor therefore grew slowly but steadily in influence and respectability.

No such organization developed among the majority of working Americans who still engaged in agricultural pursuits after the Civil War. Although the absolute number of farmers in the United States continued its historic increase, agriculture was definitely losing ground relative to industry. By 1890 farmers constituted only 42 percent of the nation's workforce operating four and a half million farm units. Even so, the majority of all American goods shipped overseas still originated on farms. Agricultural productivity rose each year as new technology and methods improved output and increased labor efficiency.

Advances in processing and marketing methods helped stimulate this productivity. The postwar cattle industry, for example, quickly fell under the control of a few technologically oriented entrepreneurs. Recognizing that the shipment of live cattle to eastern customers was costly, burned weight off the animals, and inflicted damage on the finished product, Gustavus Swift developed a complex but effective alternative. He built stockyards and mechanized slaughter houses adjacent to midwestern feedlots to process fattened beef cattle immediately. Swift shipped the resulting "dressed beef" carcasses east in insulated box cars, kept cool with block ice at first and mechanical refrigeration later. Railroads equipped with standard livestock cars initially refused to haul his loads, but the quality of his product and aggressive sales campaigns gradually broke down their resistance. Other meatpacking concerns like Armour, Nelson Morris, Cudahy, and Wilson followed Swift's lead. They integrated vertically by owning or leasing ranches, feedlots, slaughter houses, refrigerated cars and storage houses, and even retail outlets. Although meatpacking remained an oligopoly, critics referred to it as the "Beef Trust" in the 1890s and charged that it was inflating consumer prices at the same time it forced stockgrowers and feeders to provide them with meat at low cost.

Mechanization also made vast wheat farms in the Northern Great Plains feasible. To prosper in this arid region, a farmer had to harvest hundreds of acres each season. Horses harnessed together in hitches of as many as forty animals powered huge implements. Forward-looking farmers had also begun using powerful steam tractors to pull gang plows, seed drills, and combines or to run stationary threshing machines. Unusually heavy rains fell in that part of the country after 1875, encouraging hundreds of thousands of native-born farmers and immigrants to settle there. The land magnet was so strong, in fact, that Iowa and Illinois actually lost population to the states and territories further west.

The efficiency and productivity of industrial mass production encouraged experimentation along similar lines in agriculture. One of the most dramatic and extensive enterprises developed when receivers of the financially troubled Northern

Pacific Railroad sold huge tracts carved from the road's federal land grants. Corporations bought and farmed much of this land. Oliver Dalyrample emerged as the most prominent manager of what were enthusiastically labeled "bonanza farms" in Minnesota and North Dakota. To cultivate thousands of acres at a time, the farms adopted factory techniques like hiring hundreds of wage workers to operate scores of machines. In their best years, the industrialized bonanza farms produced grain for half what it would bring when sold. Unfortunately for the bonanza farmers and all others drawn out to the Great Plains, weather patterns shifted abruptly after 1887, and a decade of drought set in. Half the population of western Kansas abandoned its farmsteads between 1888 and 1892, and Dalrymple himself surrendered to the elements in the mid-nineties.

Agriculture would remain depressed through the end of the century. Protest movements ranging from local grange organizations to massive alliances promoted schemes to revive the health and prosperity of the farming community. Their proposals included the alteration of tax structures, government control or even ownership of railroads and grain elevators, increasing the money supply with greenbacks or silver coinage, and a federal commodity marketing program. None of these concepts evoked much sympathy outside of the farm belt. Many of them would, however, be incorporated into the Progressive movement, a generalized reaction to the real or perceived flaws in the industrial business structure that would sweep the United States in the coming years.

READING SUGGESTIONS

No topic in American history has attracted more attention than the Civil War, and several important articles are collected by Ralph Andreano, ed., in *The Economic Impact of the Civil War* (1962). Another compilation of comments on pre- and postwar developments is David T. Gilchrist and W. David Lewis's *Economic Change in the Civil War Era* (1965). In *Money, Class, and Party* (1959), Robert P. Sharkey focuses on economic developments during the conflict. Allen Nevins's monumental study, *The War for the Union* (4 vols., 1960-1971), contains excellent discussions of the domestic responses to the war and the government's organizational, financial, and contractual activities. More specialized and extraordinarily detailed is Paul W. Gates's *Agriculture and the Civil War* (1956). Bray Hammond, in *Sovereignty and an Empty Purse: Banks and Politics in the Civil War* (1970), examines the Union's financial problems, and Henrietta M. Larson looks at the life of the great bond salesman in *Jay Cooke: Private Banker* (1936). George E. Turner describes the importance of transportation in *Victory Rode the Rails: Railroads in the Civil War* (1953). Two comprehensive surveys of the Confederacy are Clement Eaton's *A History of the Southern Confederacy* (1954), and Emory Thomas's *The Confederate Nation* (1971).

The philosophical setting for postwar enterprise is discussed in Richard Hofstadter's *Social Darwinism in American Thought* (1944); Sidney Fine's

Laissez-Faire and the General Welfare State (1966); and Edward C. Kirkland's *Dream and Thought in the Business Community, 1860-1890* (1956). Kirkland also wrote a detailed economic history of the period—*Industry Comes of Age: Business, Labor and Public Policy, 1860-1897* (1961).

No one escapes criticism in Matthew Josephson's *Robber Barons: The Great American Capitalists* (1934), written in the depths of the Great Depression. Although it portrays Carnegie as insensitive and grasping, other accounts are more balanced. Harold C. Livesey's *Andrew Carnegie and the Rise of Big Business* (1975) is a brief survey, while Joseph Frazier Wall's *Andrew Carnegie* (1970) is an exhaustive study. The personable steel monger's autobiography is witty and entertaining.

The competitiveness of the oil industry is evident in two general works: *The American Petroleum Industry: The Age of Illumination, 1859-1899* (1959) by Harold F. Williamson and Arnold R. Daum, and *Pioneering in Big Business 1882-1911* (1955) by Ralph Hidy and Muriel Hidy. A bitter critique of John D. Rockefeller's role in that industry is Henry D. Lloyd's *Wealth Against Commonwealth* (1894). Less emotional but hardly less critical is Ida M. Tarbell's *History of the Standard Oil Company* (2 vols., 1925) which originally appeared as a series of muckraking articles in *McClure's Magazine*. The oil magnate gave his own version of the truth in *Random Reminiscences of Men and Events* (1933). His most authoritative and detailed defense appears in Allen Nevins's *Study in Power: John D. Rockefeller, Industrialist and Philanthropist* (2 vols., 1953).

John Stover's *American Railroads* (1961) is the best shorter survey of the topic. Books by distinguished business historians are Thomas C. Cochran's *Railroad Leaders, 1845-1890, The Business Mind in Action* (1953) and an excellent compilation of sources and commentary, *The Railroads: The Nation's First Big Business* (1965), edited by Alfred D. Chandler, Jr. Two other reliable works are George Rogers Taylor and Irene D. Neu's *The American Railroad Network: 1861-1890* (1956) and Julius Grodinsky's *Transcontinental Railway Strategy, 1869-1893* (1962). More controversial are two books by Robert Fogel: *The Union Pacific Railroad: A Case of Premature Enterprise* (1964); and *Railroads and American Economy Growth: Essays in Economic History* (1964). In the latter, Fogel suggests that canals and other alternatives could easily have satisfied the nation's transportation needs had railroads never been invented. The "empire builder of the Northwest" is the focus of *James J. Hill and the Opening of the Northwest* (1976), by Martin Albro. Julius Grodinsky is far less sympathetic to his subject in *Jay Gould: His Business Career 1867-1892* (1957) than is Maury Klein in *The Life and Legend of Jay Gould* (1986).

The impact of urbanization on the American people is a major theme in three thoughtful works: Arthur M. Schlesinger, Sr., *The Rise of the City, 1878-1898* (1933); Howard Chudacoff, *The Evolution of American Society* (1981); and Alan Trachtenberg, *The Incorporation of America: Culture and Society in the Gilded Age* (1982). The plight of the industrial workers is delineated in Melvin Dubovsky's *Industrialism and the American Worker* (1975) and Stanley Buder's

Pullman (1967). The founder of the AFL is the subject of Stuart Kaufman's *Samuel Gompers and the Origins of the American Federation of Labor* (1978).

Chapter **6**

THE CONSOLIDATION OF THE BUSINESS SYSTEM 1890-1914

Republican party spokesmen had warned for decades that if Democrats won control of the federal government, dire consequences would follow. Just as the Republican Cassandras predicted, a major business panic and a sharp economic decline occurred just after the Democratic party swept the 1892 elections. Congressional implementation of President Grover Cleveland's tariff and monetary policies did nothing to prevent further bankruptcies and unemployment. The restoration of conservative Republican leadership under William McKinley in 1897 then appeared to steer the United States on a more promising course, the beginning of three decades of general prosperity.

Beneath this simplistic partisan explanation for the nation's economic rebound flowed deep economic and social currents that were altering the character of American enterprise. Along with his countrymen, President Cleveland was a victim of the dislocations and realignments that accompanied the final stages of the American transformation from an agrarian society into the leading industrial nation in the world. The people had to accommodate to a new order the founding fathers had never anticipated.

One of the United States's traditional guiding principles, for example, had been faith that unrestrained competition would maximize the nation's economic potential. In the 1890s entrepreneurs were actively seeking ways to avoid competition and the inevitable waste and uncertainty it caused. They devoted their best business and legal talents as well as considerable capital to consolidating industries, drawing rival enterprises together into vast combines, and restructuring these giants into efficient, profit-making operations. Holding companies, trusts, labor unions, and professional associations grew in size and influence as the American people attempted to rationalize their activities on a nationwide basis.

This orgy of consolidation occurred in conjunction with the emergence of a mass consumption society. Industrialists took up the challenge of producing more sophisticated and attractive consumer products. To do so they had to develop new techniques of manufacturing; to sell 'the goods, they had to employ innovative advertising and marketing methods. The rapid technical evolution and public acceptance of the automobile symbolized consumerism, and no individual had a greater impact in that area than Henry Ford. A pioneering automaker, he developed marketing, manufacturing, and employment policies that would serve as models for future consumer industries.

Many Americans were far from comfortable with consumerism and consolidation. As thousands of independent businessmen abandoned their enterprises for positions in larger corporations, those outside worried that monopolists and oligopolists might ignore or overwhelm the rights and desires of individuals. Government intervention and regulation therefore seemed essential to protect the people from huge, callous corporations. Reformers in the early twentieth century laid the foundations for the mixed economy of the present-day United States with its combination of private enterprise and substantial government activity. Although a mixed economy seems somewhat antithetical to traditional American concepts, it developed as a natural reaction to the consequences of a century of laissez-faire policies. The massive business combines of the 1890s were the products of the full flowering of the free enterprise system.

MERGER MANIA

Business consolidation profoundly altered the character of American enterprise. A handful of railroad combinations collected most of the revenues in that industry and a single holding company, United States Steel, performed 60 percent of all basic iron and steel fabrication in the country. Similar monopolistic or oligopolistic trends were apparent in other sectors. In the eyes of many Americans, this centralized control, much of it under the management of finance capitalists rather than stockholders or industrialists per se, threatened to destroy completely the free enterprise system that had offered opportunities to so many in the past.

Several factors encouraged the binge of business concentration. The completion of the national railroad network combined with telegraphic and telephonic communication gave businessmen speedy and reliable access to customers everywhere. The size of the national market promised rich rewards for anyone capable of serving it. To supply all the potential customers, industrialists had to develop high volume production. By consolidating their enterprises into larger units, manufacturers could achieve substantial cost reductions through the efficiencies of scale. The building of a high volume, mechanized factory required so much capital that access to leading investment banking houses seemed essential.

The potential for market control also made consolidation attractive. The larger an enterprise grew, the larger its share of the market was likely to be. The Standard Oil Trust had graphically illustrated the advantages of near monopoly control in one sector. Rockefeller and his associates could dictate nationwide price levels for all of the products they sold. Huge combines could also smooth out uncertainties in costs and demand. Destructive and inefficient competition was unavoidable in a free enterprise system, but a combination like U. S. Steel could easily dominate its rivals. Freed from the pricing restraints an open market exercised and capable of reducing costs through mass production, big businesses promised attractive profits for investors.

Despite their public pronouncements praising the ideal of free enterprise, business leaders had long been seeking security through combination. The mechanisms they used evolved and changed in response to public opinion, inventiveness, and government restrictions. Pools had been popular in the 1870s. Those who provided similar products or services would assign shares of the market to each firm based on its size or historical sales record. A pool member could then charge higher prices without worrying that a competitor would steal its business. Aggressive entrepreneurs like Rockefeller and Carnegie disliked pools, and they cooperated with others as little as possible. Their rivals, on the other hand, were eager to tie powerful operators into restrictive pools. By the 1880s, however, pooling agreements had become subject to both legal and popular disapproval. Though secret agreements continued to be made, more formal and public control arrangements needed to be developed.

One such mechanism has already been described: the trust that managed the Standard Oil properties. Trusts became popular for reducing competition in the late 1880s, in part because creating one required little capital. Stockholders of independent companies simply allowed a board of trustees to operate several properties for the greater good of all. The prices of the stocks of companies operating as component parts of a trust often rose dramatically. The 1890 Sherman Act referred to trusts specifically as possible targets for litigation, though, so this device lost much of its appeal.

Besides, an attractive alternative had just been introduced. Although the Sherman Act suggested that the federal government might sometime play a larger role in business affairs, incorporation laws remained the prerogatives of the separate states. New Jersey led the way in revising its general incorporation statutes in the late 1880s. The key change was to lift the traditional prohibition against a corporation's owning stock in an out-of-state company. A New Jersey corporation could now own and manage property all over the United States. A new creature had been born: the interstate holding company. Some holding companies functioned like regular operating or manufacturing companies on a larger scale; others existed solely as management devices, owning controlling shares of several operating companies and coordinating their activities to benefit the whole organization.

Delaware and other states quickly liberalized their incorporation laws along similar lines, but New Jersey's strategic location just across the Hudson River from New York City and across the Delaware River from Philadelphia made it a popular spot for incorporation. More than half of the major business combinations assembled from 1887 through 1903 maintained their legal headquarters in New Jersey.

Most holding companies followed the same general pattern. Stockholders of operating companies were encouraged to exchange their shares for the holding company's preferred stock, issued in sufficient volume to represent the total real assets of the combine. The holding company also distributed common stock, often in excessive amounts, to these same stockholders who could hold it or sell it on the exchanges. The common stock thus represented a premium for joining the combine, while the preferred stock supposedly protected their equity in the company. Common stock lacking direct backing in the form of corporation assets was referred to as "watered stock."[1] If the holding company fulfilled its organizers' optimistic projections, the value of the combine's assets would eventually rise high enough to squeeze the water out of the common stock.

The holding company format was so attractive that several established giants reshaped themselves in the new image. The Sugar Trust deliberately reorganized its refining monopoly in an effort to avoid an antitrust suit. Federal officials decided to prosecute the combine anyway, but the Supreme Court delivered a surprising ruling in the 1895 E. C. Knight Co. case. The justices concluded that refining was essentially a manufacturing process rather than commerce – the transfer of goods from one owner to another. Consequently, they decided that the Sherman Act's injunction against restraining interstate commerce did not apply to sugar refining, regardless of the company's dominance of the industry. This ruling seemed to clear the way for consolidation of manufacturing and processing enterprises. The formation of a new holding company, Standard Oil of New Jersey, to replace the older trust in 1899 was one of many such reorganizations.

The most famous of the holding companies was United States Steel. Finance capitalist J. Pierpont Morgan was the proud father of the world's first billion-dollar supercorporation. He had taken the first step in the late 1890s by helping several elements of the steel industry consolidate in an effort to compete with Carnegie. The most effective grouping involved wire and tubing manufacturers who refused to buy any of their raw materials from the Steel King. Carnegie retaliated by threatening to buy or build his own secondary processing plants to undercut his rivals' prices. Faced with this potentially ruinous competition, they urged Morgan to arrange an accommodation.

He found the 65-year-old Carnegie willing to retire from the business – for the right price. Morgan agreed to pay $492 million to Carnegie and his associates for

---

[1]This term had a rural origin. Unscrupulous cattle drovers or feeders would force their thirsty livestock to drink excessively just before they were weighed for sale. The unfortunate buyer then ended up paying for water rather than beef. While watering livestock was generally considered unethical, watering corporation stock became a widely accepted technique for generating operating funds and rewarding insiders.

their diversified holdings. He transferred the stock for these and dozens of other plants and processors to the United States Steel Corporation, a New Jersey holding company. The new firm issued more than $1.4 billion worth of common and preferred stocks and bonds although it controlled only $682 million worth of real assets. Thus more than half of the financial package was pure water. By controlling a majority of all the steel business in the United States, the corporation could dictate prices and, in the long run, reap sufficient profits from its operations to wring all of the water out of its securities by 1920. Morgan's fee for establishing the company reputedly ran to more than $60 million.

Consolidation fever also swept the nation's traditional leading sector. Too many railroads had been built, so that almost one-fourth of them were in receivership after the Panic of 1893. But the stocks of these troubled companies could be purchased at ridiculously low prices so banking concerns and wealthy individuals could assemble large blocks of shares. Some buyers insisted that their primary interest was to create viable, efficient transportation systems, but many others were clearly out to milk the weakened industry of additional profits. All too often the distinction between these objectives faded anyway as some of the self-proclaimed builders looted their properties as mercilessly as did the unscrupulous speculators.

Although he definitely qualified as a system builder, Edward H. Harriman made millions in the process. Starting from the solid base of the Illinois Central Railroad, he exploited his contacts with the financial house of Kuhn, Loeb & Co. to assemble enough capital to buy a controlling interest in the bankrupt Union Pacific Railroad in 1897. In the next four years, he rehabilitated the pioneering transcontinental line and established vital links between it and several others roads including the Southern Pacific. That gave him control of all rail traffic in the southwestern United States. With his profits he also bought into the New York Central, the B & 0, the Chicago and Northwestern, and even the Pacific Mail Steamship Company to extend his transportation empire to the Far East.

Harriman's only serious rival in the West was James J. Hill, builder of the Great Northern and owner of a controlling interest in the Northern Pacific. Drawing on J. P. Morgan's resources, Hill took over the Chicago, Burlington & Quincy Railroad early in 1901 and thereby gained direct access to Chicago. Unable to halt the Burlington deal, Harriman decided to outflank Hill by secretly buying Northern Pacific shares. When Hill and Morgan found out, they began buying as well, driving the price for a Northern Pacific share from $110 to over $1000 in a couple of weeks. At that point, the brokers discovered that they had accepted orders to deliver 78,000 more shares than actually existed. Both Harriman and Hill had technically purchased more than a majority of the railroad's stock. Recognizing the threat these maneuvers posed to the stock exchange system, the rivals agreed to assign all of their rights to a gigantic holding company. The Northern Securities Company thus came into being to operate the Northern Pacific, the Great Northern, and the Burlington (see Figure 6-1).

The company also gave Hill just as effective control of the Northwest as Harriman had in the Southwest. The railroad empire Jay Gould had begun continued to expand after his death, adding western and eastern links to its holdings centered

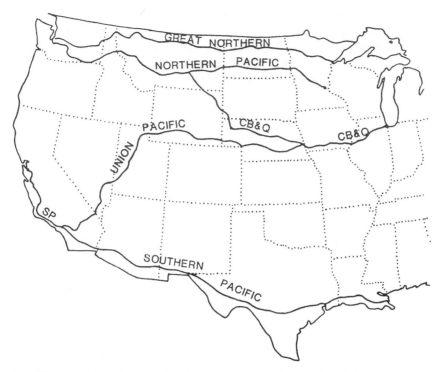

FIGURE 6-1 Railroads involved in the Northern Securities Co. Negotiations.

in the Mississippi Valley. Another group of speculators pulled together a rival midwestern system centered on the Chicago, Rock Island & Pacific Railway. So recklessly did they proceed that they had all but destroyed the Rock Island line by 1914. The Vanderbilt group still ran the New York Central as the center of the major system in the Northeast, and the Pennsylvania Railroad had extended its reach well into the Midwest. In the Southeast, J. P. Morgan folded a number of properties into his Southern Railway system. In 1906, these seven systems operated two-thirds of the track in the United States and collected 85 percent of all railroad earnings. Furthermore, the close association among the Hill, Morgan, and Vanderbilt interests constituted an even greater concentration of control over the nation's leading transportation system.

Not every consolidation was successful, nor was railroad operation necessarily the chief objective. A syndicate including Harriman, George J. Gould, and James Stillman, president of the National City Bank, decided to buy a controlling interest in the conservatively run and prosperous Chicago & Alton Railroad. Through a variety of maneuvers they raised its capitalization from $34 million to nearly $115 million while actually investing only $18 million in improvements. Even though more than half of the final capitalization was water, the syndicate members netted clear profits of over $23 million. These antics left the railroad in very poor physical condition and burdened with an exorbitant outstanding indebtedness it could scarcely service out of its limited revenues.

Sometimes a reasonable plan deteriorated despite the best of intentions. Consolidating the railroads in New England into a single, efficient system seemed a sensible enough objective. The New Haven Railroad served as the keystone for a plan to purchase or control not only the steam railroads in the region but also several urban trolley systems and coastal shipping firms. At the end of a decade, however, the New Haven's $93 million capitalization had more than quadrupled, and much of that money had been thrown away buying overpriced short lines and connectors. An Interstate Commerce Commission report estimated that waste and mismanagement of the system had cost it between $60 and $90 million. The most surprising aspect of this case of incompetence was that the nation's most respected banker, J. P. Morgan, had brought it about.

FINANCE CAPITALIST: J. P. MORGAN

John Pierpont Morgan had a head start toward wealth, having been born in 1837 into a solid upper-middle class home in Hartford, Connecticut. Grandfather Pierpont was a respected Boston clergyman, Grandfather Morgan a successful real estate and insurance promoter in Hartford. The future tycoon's father, Junius Spencer Morgan, gained international prominence when British multimillionaire and humanitarian George F. Peabody took him on as a partner. When Peabody died, Morgan assumed control of his partner's affairs and became the leading American banker in London. His stature allowed him to demand top fees for underwriting and marketing millions of dollars worth of American railroad and industrial stocks in Europe.

His father's career drew young J. P. Morgan from a mundane childhood in Connecticut to an exclusive school in Geneva, Switzerland, and then to the prestigious German university at Göttingen. This European training distinguished Morgan from other American financiers, giving him a cosmopolitan polish as well as ready access to foreign capital. His business career began when he returned to New York City to handle his father's affairs on this side of the Atlantic. In many ways he remained in his father's shadow until the old man died in 1890. It was Junius, for example, who arranged for Charles H. Dabney to become J. P. Morgan's senior partner in New York, and who later urged his son to form a partnership with the powerful Drexel family of Philadelphia.

The young Morgan established contacts in the New York banking community and made careful investments of his own. During the Civil War, he was implicated in a scandal involving some carbines that a profiteer had bought from the government for $3.50 each and then sold back to the army for $22.00. Morgan had arranged the credit for the purchase, collecting a 50 percent premium on a five-week loan. He also dived into the rough and tumble of gold speculation. As the conflict drew to a close, though, he deliberately set out to develop a reputation for reliability and respectability. He avoided the flamboyance and impetuousness so characteristic of other Gilded Age speculators and quietly built a sizable personal fortune through his lending and securities underwriting activities.

He discovered his true calling in 1885. Having inherited control of the New York Central Railroad from his father, William Vanderbilt set out to destroy the archrival Pennsylvania Railroad's regional monopoly by building a competing line through southern Pennsylvania. The Pennsy counterattacked by opening construction on the West Shore line along the Hudson River and, not incidentally, adjacent to J. P. Morgan's country estate. Morgan brought the rivals in this foolish and costly warfare together on his huge yacht, *Corsair.* There he browbeat them into agreeing that the New York Central should take over the West Shore and surrender its blackmail line to the Pennsylvania. Morgan collected a substantial fee for his services as mediator and established his reputation as an effective organizer dedicated to eliminating destructive competition in the chaotic railroad business.

Over the years he developed a standardized approach for salvaging weak or insolvent companies. Having taken control of a faltering or bankrupt railroad, he would wring the water out of its stock, issue new low-interest bonds to pay off older ones at high rates, and demand additional capital from the stockholders. Next he would consolidate the road with its competitors or, if that was impossible, negotiate traffic and rate agreements with them to assure reasonable profits for all. Such agreements often had to be kept secret since they violated even the lax legal codes of the period. Morgan became an ardent advocate of the holding company mechanism to manage large systems. To assure continuing prosperity for a salvaged road, he insisted that he or one of his trusted lieutenants be given a place on the board of directors to monitor the company's future behavior. His minimum fee for such reorganization service was half a million dollars, but few objected because his reputation for sound and conservative management stood in marked contrast to that of many of his fellow bankers and speculators. Investors flocked to buy securities in the companies Morgan had reorganized. Indeed, his popularity with stockholders grew almost in direct proportion to his unpopularity among those who felt victimized by the companies he controlled.

Two obstacles prevented him from completing his plan to rationalize the entire United States railroad system: his rivals and his other ambitions. Sharp operators like E. H. Harriman, backed with Rockefeller money, who pursued their own megalomaniacal passions presented Morgan with tough competition. Furthermore, he never devoted his full attention to railroads. He was constantly seeking opportunities to add to his personal wealth; he maintained an increasingly influential position in the international banking community; and he enjoyed an opulent, leisurely lifestyle.

Morgan certainly cast a large shadow in New York society. He owned a succession of enormous yachts—one of them was converted into a navy gunboat in the Spanish-American War—and he dispensed gold cups to his yacht-racing colleagues. He invariably took three months off each year to travel. He loved Egypt so much that he had a special steamer built for his annual cruises up the Nile. He also roamed Europe seeking valuable paintings and manuscripts to add to his elegant library in Manhattan. A large, stocky man with a penetrating gaze and an enormous red nose, the result of a chronic skin disease, he intimidated almost everyone he met. His arrogant personality, his lavish lifestyle, and his pervasive control over the hated railroads earned him the dubious distinction of succeeding Jay Gould as the most unpopular financier in the United States.

While some of his unpopularity reflected envy, many Americans sincerely considered him too powerful. He could manipulate not only the stock exchanges but the very credit of the United States government itself. President Grover Cleveland became concerned when, in the depression of 1893, federal gold reserves fell well below their traditional minimum of $100 million. He reluctantly asked Morgan to sell United States Treasury bonds abroad in exchange for specie. This move angered the many Americans who favored free silver and appalled those who considered Morgan a scoundrel. His efforts did, however, shore up the nation's credit rating, and he made sure he collected his usual commission for his services. His extensive international connections also made him the logical agent to conduct major financial exchanges. For example he handled the $20 million Spain received from the United States for relinquishing control of the Philippines after

J. Pierpont Morgan. (Courtesy of Morgan Guaranty Trust Company of New York)

the Spanish-American War in 1898. Later he distributed the $40 million in royalties the federal government had earmarked for the stockholders of a French company for its early work on a canal through Panama.

The financier's interests were so broad-ranging and complex, in fact, that no human being, not even Morgan himself, could manage them all effectively. One indication of his fallibility was the Northern Pacific fiasco in 1901 when he and J. J. Hill barely staved off disaster. His pet creation, United States Steel, staggered along for years under its enormous burden of watered stock. Morgan repeatedly made heroic gestures to bolster the sagging price of the company's stock. He also wreaked havoc in his effort to consolidate the New England railroads. An international shipping firm he sponsored was equally ill-fated. That fact that one of the ships this combine constructed was the *Titanic* was all too appropriate.

Despite such failures, J. P. Morgan reached the zenith of his career as a finance capitalist during the Panic of 1907. Investment capital seemed very scarce at that point because of the millions of watered shares the wave of business consolidation had generated. This shortage had already played a major part in the recession of 1903. Four years later, one overextended brokerage house or bank after another tottered toward insolvency as investors and depositors rushed to withdraw their funds. For once Morgan found himself well insulated from this frenzy, but he recognized the desirability of limiting the financial damage as quickly as possible. He imperiously summoned leading bankers and brokers to his library and ordered them to lend money to institutions on the verge of ruin. Bowing to Morgan's leadership, the financiers created an emergency stockpile of capital to distribute to the neediest cases, and the panic faded. His admirers felt that Morgan's dramatic intervention had prevented a potential collapse of the entire U.S. banking and capital structure.

Always sensitive to any opportunity for personal gain, however, he had executed a brilliant coup at the height of the panic. He learned that the financial house of Moore & Schley was in serious trouble because of its excessive purchases of shares in the Tennessee Coal, Iron, and Railroad Company, a formidable southern rival of Morgan's beloved United States Steel. He dispatched his company's boss, Judge Elbert Gary, to Washington to convince President Theodore Roosevelt not to use the antitrust law against U. S. Steel if it bought the Tennessee enterprise. Gary convinced the anxious president that Moore & Schley would collapse and set off another devastating round of bankruptcies if it was not rescued. Morgan then brought the competing company under his own firm's control at the modest cost of $45 million, far below the billion dollars the company's assets were estimated to be worth. Both Morgan and Roosevelt were outraged and embarrassed when President William Howard Taft invoked the Sherman Act in 1911 and sued U. S. Steel over the merger anyway.

Morgan's behavior in 1907 strengthened the widespread belief that he headed a "Money Trust" made up of international bankers and financiers. Although no formal organization existed, the influence Morgan and a few of his friends wielded did seem excessive even to jaded veterans of the Gilded Age. Public concern about

TWO VIEWS OF J. P. MORGAN

Morgan made a powerful impression on all who encountered him. Both of these selections describe the banker during the Panic of 1907. The first is by Herbert Satterlee, J. P.'s son-in-law. The other is a secondary account of his behavior while the bankers made their rescue plans in his library.

(Satterlee) Any one who saw Mr. Morgan going from the Clearing House back to his office that day will never forget the picture. With his coat unbuttoned and flying open, a piece of white paper clutched tightly in his right hand, he walked fast down Nassau Street. His flat-topped black derby hat was set firmly down on his head. Between his teeth he held a paper cigar holder in which was one of his long cigars, half smoked. His eyes were fixed straight ahead. He swung his arms as he walked and took no notice of anyone. He did not seem to see the throngs in the street, so intent was his mind on the thing that he was doing. Everyone knew him, and people made way for him, except some who were equally intent on their own affairs; and these he brushed aside. The thing that made his progress different from that of all the other people on the street was that he did not dodge, or walk in and out, or halt or slacken his pace. He simply barged along, as if he had been the only man going down the Nassau Street hill past the Subtreasury. He was the embodiment of power and purpose. Not more than two minutes after he disappeared into his office, the cheering on the floor of the Stock Exchange could be heard out in Broad Street.

(Burr) It was not the custom of the master of the Library to be present during the general plans which preceded actual decisions. In a small, adjoining room, he sat with his cigar, the patience-cards spread before him, if a picture caught his eye that hung a thought askew, he rose to straighten it. When the time came to lay results before him, he would stroll in, tall, heavy, powerful and standing on the hearth-rug, state his will. . . . Sometimes a sheet of paper would be handed him, on which each man present had set down either his resources or his needs, Glancing at this, he was likely to tear it up and go back to his patience-cards without a word. All then, was to do over again. . . It was late when the question of the Trust Companies came up. Morgan was perfectly frank about them.

"Why should I get into this?" he asked. "My affairs are all in order. I've done enough. I won't take all this on unless − " he ended, with a gesture which the others perfectly understood to mean, "unless I get what I want out of it."

(Herbert L. Satterlee, *J. Pierpont Morgan: An Intimate Portrait* [New York: Macmillan, 1939], p. 479; Anna Robeson Burr, *The Portrait of a Banker: James Stillman* [New York: Duffield & Co., 1927], p. 235.)

the concentration of business and industry had risen high enough by 1912 to provoke a congressional investigation. Morgan spent two days explaining and justifying his behavior before the Pujo Committee, but his testimony failed to convince the American people of his unselfish patriotism. The committee discovered no Money Trust per se, but it did uncover a mass of interlocking directorships and financial arrangements that allowed a small group of individuals to control many of the major industrial and financial firms in the United States. The presence of Morgan representatives on dozens of boards of directors made him appear extraordinarily powerful. In fact his personal authority was less extensive than most people believed and, for that matter, than Morgan himself desired.

By 1912, federal control seemed to offer the best hope for creating effective and fair industrial and financial structures. The heyday of the free-wheeling capitalism Morgan personified had passed, a fact the old man seemed to recognize himself. His health failed rapidly after his testimony before the Pujo Committee, and he died early in 1913. He left a fortune of $77.5 million, a sum so much smaller than most people believed he had amassed that it provoked John D. Rockefeller to say, "And to think that he wasn't even a rich man."

REACHING OUT TO THE CUSTOMERS

J. P. Morgan had outlived his time in another sense: most of his consolidation activities involved the basic industrial enterprises that had predominated in the late nineteenth century. Many of these enterprises manufactured producers' goods like steel or coke that required further processing before reaching individual consumers. By the turn of the century, the maturing American industrial system was increasingly concerned with satisfying consumer demands. A rapidly growing population of relatively prosperous urban customers attracted the attention of many entrepreneurs. The age of mass consumption had dawned.

This new emphasis required changes in production and marketing techniques. Factories that turned out consumer goods, for example, tended to be smaller and more labor intensive than those in the producers' goods industries. By 1900 basic steel manufacturing had become so automated that a few employees could operate huge plants. Consumer goods generally needed more finishing work that only larger workforces could accomplish. Craftsmen skilled in upholstering, carpentry, glazing, and metal fabrication assembled early automobiles literally by hand. The garment industry would remain labor intensive for decades. Even though 95 percent of all men's clothing in the United States was ready-made by 1900, automation had hardly extended beyond mechanical cloth cutters. Individuals still did most of the work at their sewing machines.

The expanding use of electric power in this period also encouraged the building of smaller and more geographically dispersed factories. A major energy innovation occurred in 1895 when a power station began tapping the force of Niagara Falls. Its alternating-current electricity could travel as far as five hundred miles through high-voltage wires. Its success encouraged the building of other hydroelectric power stations. Even more crucial to the spread of electric power was George Westinghouse's decision in 1896 to obtain patent rights to build steam turbine generators modeled after those already in service in England. Monster steam generating plants soon dwarfed the output of the Niagara Falls station and allowed utility companies to supply inexpensive energy for private and commercial use virtually anywhere in the United States.

Tinkerers were meanwhile developing new devices to use electricity. Some were consumer products like the electric flat iron introduced in 1893. A few years earlier, an Italian immigrant named Nikola Tesla had designed an efficient alternating current motor by reversing the flow of electricity through a brush generator. Soon electric motors of all sizes were powering tools and other factory equipment. These electric tools and machines ran much more consistently and reliably than the ones attached by leather belts and pulleys to mechanical steam engines.

The consumer economy encouraged the production of goods ahead of orders. Even a confident manufacturer like Andrew Carnegie worked hard to line up enough advance business to fill his production schedules. Manufacturers of consumer goods could not rely on customer requests since buyers tended to be fickle if they could not get immediate delivery. Because inventories of finished goods therefore had to be maintained, styles or special features reflected a manufacturer's reading of popular taste rather than being dictated by individual consumers as they had in the age of the artisan. Because the national marketplace consisted of millions of potential buyers, no producers needed to concern themselves with a particular individual's preference. Instead, they worked to convince customers that what their factories produced was just what the buyer really wanted. In short, the product had to be advertised.

Advertisements had been appearing in newspapers and handbills since colonial times, but the business of touting products and services became much more sophisticated and specialized after the Civil War. The size and layout of newspaper promotions changed markedly; multiple-column or even full-page ads crowded out the discrete one-column-inch notices of earlier days. Elaborate claims, decorative illustrations, and fancy type faces drew the reader's attention. Some publishers depended almost exclusively on advertising revenues, selling their newspapers for as little as a penny an issue to generate the large circulation their advertisers desired. As the nineteenth century drew to a close, advertising invaded even the most staid literary magazines. By 1900 slick mass-circulation magazines like *Colliers* and *The Saturday Evening Post* were attracting millions of readers with their elaborate illustrations and common touches. Billboards and barns sported sales pitches as well. The consumer age was inevitably an era of ballyhoo.

At first proprietors or sellers wrote their own ad copy, but advertising gradually developed into a separate enterprise. The early professional advertising agents often collected fees from the newspapers they served, but it obviously made more sense to bill advertisers directly. As the business became more competitive, agencies hired professional writers and artists to design attractive displays and campaigns for their clients. By the turn of the century, progressive agencies were conducting rudimentary market surveys as well, testing product and slogan appeal be-

---

FRANCIS W. AYER

An extraordinarily ethical businessman named Francis W. Ayer founded one of the first major advertising agencies in the United States. At a time when advertising solicitors had a reputation for being inept at best and scoundrels at worst, Ayer maintained a record-keeping system that enabled him to account fully for all of his expenditures. When he opened the agency in Philadelphia in 1869, the 22-year-old entrepreneur named it after his school-teacher father, Nathan W. Ayer. The firm initially had just two members: Francis to do the legwork and his father to keep the books.

The agency's first customers were religious publications that relied on advertising to offset their production and distribution costs. Very quickly, however, Ayer shifted to serving the advertisers themselves and to maximizing the impact of each dollar spent. As the firm grew and took on partners, it became involved in many aspects of the trade like developing trademarks and brand names, drafting catchy slogans, and designing attractive pictorial displays. A client could go to N.W. Ayer & Son confident that it could create a complete advertising campaign.

Like many other entrepreneurs, Ayer was successful in other lines as well. He was president of a Philadelphia bank from 1895 to 1910. For many years he also conducted breeding experiments with beef cattle he imported for his large farm in New York State. When he retired from business, he retreated to his farm where he continued his livestock research. Meanwhile, his pioneering advertising agency continued to serve as a model of a respectable yet highly successful member of a growing industry.

---

fore committing themselves to a specific sales strategy. The business grew quickly. J. Walter Thompson started his own small agency in 1864; when he retired in 1916 its annual billings of $3 million made it the largest in the world.

Local department stores had pioneered in aggressive consumer advertising and their success convinced manufacturers and processors to mount campaigns of their own. Many advertised products differed from their competitors in name only, and manufacturing a better or different product was often less important than simply convincing your customers that you had done so. One way to appeal to a nationwide market was to develop a memorable brand name. The United States Patent Office had registered just 121 trademarks by 1870; in 1906 the number exceeded 10,000 and continued to climb as their value as marketing devices became appreciated. The cost of registering and protecting a brand name could only be justified if the product received wide distribution. In many cases, advertising created the market. Customers were no longer satisfied with a local merchant's assurances; they wanted nationally advertised products like Pear's Soap, Smith Brothers' Cough Drops, or Carter's Little Liver Pills. Retailers were quite willing to stock such items, knowing they would sell themselves without additional advertising expense.

Chain stores applied the brand-name concept to retailing itself, assuring customers of reliability through their size and regional or national reputations. Many retail chains began when a successful speciality store operator decided more customers could be reached by opening branches in different locations. Some chains eventually consisted of hundreds or even thousands of links. The larger a chain grew, the more power it had to negotiate low wholesale prices from its suppliers. The resulting savings could then be passed on to retail customers or retained as profits. Some chains developed and sold house brands identical to nationally advertised products but less expensive since their costs did not involve independent advertising and promotional expenses.

The pioneer enterprise using this retailing approach began humbly enough when George Huntington Hartford and George F. Gilman bought imported tea by the shipload to sell at discount prices to customers belonging to their mail-order club. Their Great American Tea Company had enough business in the 1850s to justify the opening of retail stores in New York City. These sold quality goods at low prices through bulk purchases, a strategy they could easily extend to other foods. They diversified into a general grocery business: The Great Atlantic & Pacific Tea Company, founded in 1859. Soon A & P stores were opening in many cities and towns, charter members of the premier grocery chain in the United States in the twentieth century.

Chain stores could also stock other product lines. Frank Winfield Woolworth had worked in several retail stores before one of his employers gave him the responsibility of selling a consignment of mixed goods for five cents apiece. The promotion was so successful that Woolworth borrowed $300 worth of merchandise and opened his own store devoted exclusively to five-cent items. That strategy proved too limited in customer appeal, though, so he tried again with both five- and ten-cent items. When he had paid off his creditors, he began an ambitious expansion program. There were seven F. W. Woolworth stores in 1886, and the chain grew to twenty-five in 1895 and fifty-nine in 1900. In 1911 the founder combined his own stores with those belonging to a number of his former partners into a massive company operating nearly six hundred outlets.

James Cash Penney got a later start on his chain that would eventually surpass Woolworth's in both size and sales volume. Penney started his business career with a tiny dry goods store in a small Wyoming town in 1902. His success formula emphasized high turnover and minimal wages. A hardworking, fundamentalist Christian who would tolerate neither smoking or drinking among his workers, J. C. Penney won their loyalty and industriousness by promising that his best employees could become partners in the venture. Because each new partner owned a share of the store he managed, profit margins tended to remain very high. The chain grew rather slowly at first, consisting of just twenty-two stores in 1911, but Pen-ney's sound business sense insured that his company would continue expanding.

While chain stores were catering to city and town dwellers, other retailers used catalogs to reach rural customers. Aaron Montgomery Ward left his position at a Marshall Field's store in 1872 to set up a mail-order business. Starting with a one-page list of items, his enterprise grew into one of the world's major retailing firms. Richard W. Sears was a comparative latecomer. To provide a repair service for the watches he sold, he hired a watchmaker named Alvah C. Roebuck. Sears then broadened his mail-order product line and brought Roebuck in as a full partner. After several false starts, the partnership had expanded its offerings into a catalog that ran to over 500 pages in 1895. To handle its enormous volume of trade, the company constructed the largest business building in the world in Chicago in 1906.

Franchised dealerships provided another way to reach thousands of distant customers. As noted earlier, Cyrus McCormick had authorized agents to sell his reapers throughout the wheat-growing regions in the antebellum period. The Singer Sewing Machine Company had created a similar network of dealers for its products, and the concept seemed particularly suited to machinery that required skilled after-sale service. Dealerships were therefore ideal for the automobile industry when it began marketing its complex products.

AUTOMAKER FOR THE COMMON FOLK: HENRY FORD

In the late nineteenth century, tinkerers around the world began installing small gasoline, steam, or electric engines on carriages. Because so many experiments were conducted, a number of individuals could justifiably claim to have shared in inventing the automobile. While Europeans built most of the early cars, Charles Duryea is usually credited with constructing the first successful gasoline-powered automobile in the United States. Other American designs quickly surpassed these primitive vehicles.

By 1900 dozens of groups were building automobiles in northeastern cities. The early machines were expensively handcrafted, so only wealthy buyers could afford them. Because the high production costs suggested that automobiles would remain luxury items in the foreseeable future, some makers devoted as much or more attention to woodwork, upholstery, and decoration as they did to engineering matters. Manufacturing efficiency hardly mattered if only a few units were to be sold. Just a handful of companies managed to complete more than a hundred automobiles in a year, and all of these firms bought many parts and components from specialty producers. Henry M. Leland, who later built Cadillac cars, first earned his reputation for high quality merchandise by producing precisely ground gears for many different cars. The most prolific early manufacturer was Ransom E. Olds. His comparatively inexpensive car attracted enough buyers to justify a greater division of labor and more streamlined production techniques. His company was selling as many as 4000 Oldsmobiles a year in the early 1900s, but, even so, he was barely tapping the potential market.

It was left to Henry Ford to recognize the full commercial possibilities of the American love affair with the automobile. He designed and built a car cheap enough to attract millions of buyers, and, even more important, he devised a manufacturing system capable of satisfying that enormous demand. Ford thus became the chief architect of the bustling mass consumption society. Production techniques developed at his plants transformed manufacturing of all types in the United States and around the world.

Ford's humble origins and his simplistic, Populist faith in the value of hard work turned him into a cult figure of sorts. Born into a struggling farm family in Michigan in 1863, he never liked agricultural work and preferred instead to tinker with machinery. He was such a good natural mechanic that his neighbors brought their tools and implements to him for repair. After serving an apprenticeship as a machinist, he took a position with the Detroit Edison Co., which supplied the city with electric power. There his practical talents earned him promotion to the position of chief engineer, and he worked for the company for over a decade.

He practiced his true calling in his spare time, constructing experimental automobiles in a shed behind his house. The first Ford car made its debut in 1896, and a couple of improved models appeared shortly afterward. These successful cars and a nationwide burst of interest in automobiles convinced Ford he could find financial backing for full-time automaking, so he resigned from the electric company in 1899. He contributed his engineering talents to two different companies and also worked on racing cars. He hired a daredevil bicyclist named Barney Old-

Henry Ford. (Courtesy of Ford Motor Co.)

field to drive "999," Ford's most famous racer. With Oldfield at the tiller, the car beat those of more well-known makers by more than half a mile in a five-mile run.

This remarkable performance attracted the attention of Detroit industrialist Alex Y. Malcomson who invited Ford to join him in what would become an equally remarkable business venture. They formed the Ford Motor Company in 1903 and issued stock with a par value of $100,000. Each founder retained 25.5 percent of the shares so they could jointly control the business. The company actually started operating with just $28,000 in cash; most of its assets consisted of Ford's engineering genius and an arrangement with John and Horace Dodge. In return for some of the company's stock, the Dodge brothers agreed to cancel their lucrative contract to supply engines to Ransom Olds and make them instead for Ford-built cars. Malcomson also insisted on bringing James Couzens into the firm to oversee its day-to-day business affairs.

Nothing distinguished the Ford Motor Company at that point from any of a hundred other struggling automakers in the United States. It did have a brilliant designer in Ford, though, and he engineered and built a series of cars priced in the mid-range for the times. The original Model A was followed by Models B, C, F, K, N, R, and S. Ford added to his company's prestige by personally piloting his 1904 Model B in a world speed record setting run of 91 miles per hour. These models sold well enough to earn the company a comfortable profit from the very start. Its net worth had risen to more than a million dollars by 1907, but Ford was unhappy. He wanted to abandon the expensive car market and build cheap ones instead. He got his opportunity when Malcolmsen and some of the other original investors sold out. Couzens ended up with 11 percent of the company's stock, but now Ford held 55.2 percent, giving him uncontested personal control of his company.

Ford had eliminated the internal obstacles to his production strategy, but he still faced an external legal threat. After toying with the concept for many years, George Selden had filed papers in 1895 with the United States Patent Office describing a gasoline-powered self-propelled vehicle. Although Selden never actually built a working example, he claimed credit for inventing the automobile. The Electric Vehicle Co. took up his claim and sued Henry Ford for patent infringement in 1903. The company also organized the Association of Licensed Automotive Manufacturers to collect royalties from the automakers who acknowledged Selden's rights. The ALAM warned dealers against representing an "unlicensed" manufacturer like Ford, and it also published advertisements designed to intimidate potential buyers. The ultimate insult came when Ford was told that his company was neither substantial nor respectable enough to qualify for an ALAM license. Ford and his business manager Couzens determined to defeat this attempt at monopoly. After years of expensive advertising campaigns, litigation, and appeals, the Ford Motor Co. won its case in 1911, rendering the Selden patent void and destroying the ALAM. The victory of the embattled independent automaker over the arrogant establishment added greatly to Ford's popularity with his chief customer, the common folk.

By that time, Ford had already completed the initial steps in his spectacularly successful production and marketing strategy. It began with the design of a basic automobile for the mass market. Introduced in late 1908 and designated the Model T, the car had a simple, durable four-cylinder engine that used belts and pulleys for a transmission. Perched on a three-point leaf-spring suspension, the vehicle had a high center of gravity that enabled it to go almost anywhere in a country with only a few paved or all-weather roads. It could negotiate potholes and plow through muddy ruts, and it consistently won hill-climbing contests against cars costing three or four times as much.

The machine was attractive enough in its own right, but its $825 price tag made it an unbelievable bargain. Occasionally, the price for a new Model T shifted slightly higher, but the general trend over the next twenty years was downward until it fell below $300. Almost every time Ford announced a price reduction, demand for his versatile little vehicle rose dramatically. He also used other pricing gimmicks to boost his sales. In 1914, for example, Ford promised that if more than 300,000 Model T's sold in the next year, every buyer would receive a rebate of from $40 to $60. The company ultimately sent out checks totaling more than $15 million to 308,313 buyers at the end of the period.

The Model T had such an enormous market appeal just as it was that few technical improvements needed to be made over the years. The last Model T to roll off the assembly line was basically the same machine as the first one built, so Ford had plenty of time to devote his mechanical skills to developing a full-scale mass production system. The use of standardized, fully interchangeable parts was essential. Another logical move was to expand his company's operations to encompass the manufacture of many of the components that went into the finished cars.

Swamped with orders, the company's major goal was to speed up production through constant experimentation with reorganizing and streamlining the flow of the work. The increasing volume of production at Ford encouraged considerable diversification of individual tasks. Just as Adam Smith had predicted more than a century earlier, the factory's productivity increased every time it hired more workers and assigned them more specialized tasks. Even so, the Ford operation resembled other factories making machinery like bicycles and farm implements until the company moved into its enormous new manufacturing complex at Highland Park, a suburb of Detroit.

Those roomy quarters permitted even more elaborate reorganization of the manufacturing process. Henry Ford wandered through his huge factory looking for ways to boost productivity, and his remarkable technical skill led him to suggest many changes that eliminated waste and delay. He was intuitively applying the same principles that Frederick W. Taylor had championed for years under the name of "scientific management." Its premise was that if workers eliminated unnecessary or awkward movements, their speed would inevitably increase. A popular industrial consultant, Taylor conducted time and motion studies of each worker to determine the most efficient method for accomplishing each task. The Ford management simply took the concept of Taylorism several steps further.

TWO VIEWS OF THE FORD ASSEMBLY LINE

Henry Ford describes his assembly-line process in the first selection, taken from his autobiography. The second selection, written in the 1930s, takes a more critical look at the same process.

(Ford) The first step forward in assembly came when we began taking the work to the men instead of the men to the work. We now have two general principles in all operations—that a man shall never have to take more than one step, if possibly it can be avoided, and that no man need ever stoop over.
     The principles of assembly are these:
                    1.   Place the tools and the men in the sequence of the operation so that each component part shall travel the least possible distance while in the process of finishing.
                    2.   Use work slides or some other form of carrier so that when a workman completes his operation, he drops the part always in the same place—which place must always be the most convenient place to his hand—and if possible have gravity carry the part to the next workman for his operation.
                    3.   Use sliding assembling lines by which the parts to be assembled are delivered at convenient distances.
     The net result of the application of these principles is the reduction of the necessity for thought on the part of the worker and the reduction of his movements to a minimum. He does as nearly as possible only one thing with only one movement.

(Leonard) The belt was tireless. A larger part of the foreman's job was to watch each man, and if he were not working at the extreme limit of his capabilities, to order his belt to be speeded up. The foremen in turn were spied on from above. Ever-increasing demands were made on each department. If a man were observed to leave the plant at the end of the shift with a too springy step or a smile on his lips, he was transferred to another job which corrected this condition. The men were treated as if they were mere containers of labor, like gondola cars of coal. They arrived full; they left in the evening as empty of human vitality as the cars were empty of coal. The trolleys which crawled away from Highland Park at closing were hearses for the living dead. . . .
     There was another point, too, which touched Ford's own personal philosophy. He believed that work, no matter how dull, was an end in itself, not a means toward various small, irrational, human satisfactions. He wanted his men to follow his own example and lead lives of hard work and simple-minded rural Puritanism. If they left his plant in a state of complete physical,

spiritual, and mental exhaustion, they were more apt to keep out of mischief when the evening whistle blew. This, Ford learned to say later, was Americanism.

(Henry Ford, *My Life and Work* [Garden City, NY: Doubleday, 1923], p. 80; Jonathan Norton Leonard, *The Tragedy of Henry Ford* [New York: Putnam's, 1932], pp. 25-27).

The final major revision in the manufacturing process took shape after Clarence Avery had been hired in 1912 to run time and motion studies. The first successful experiment involved the assembly of magnetos, devices that generated electricity to fire an engine's spark plugs. Instead of having workers walk along an assembly line, appropriate parts were placed on a moving belt, timed to pass in front of assemblers just as rapidly as they could work. Determining the optimum speed for this moving assembly line naturally involved a lot of trial and error, and bringing needed components to it at the proper moment also created problems. But once the necessary adjustments had been made, productivity soared: the average amount of labor time expended per unit dropped to one-fourth what it had been with the old stationary assembly line. Moving belts were soon installed on the lines building engines and other parts. These proved to be so efficient, in fact, that the flow of components began to swamp the vehicle assemblers on the main floor. The last step was obvious. Ropes were attached to pull the chassis past teams of workers, each assigned to install a specific part. The manufacturing process speeded up enormously when the whole operation converted to moving assembly lines.

In a single year, the time required to assemble a Model T fell from twelve hours to an hour and a half. Labor costs naturally dropped correspondingly, allowing Ford to continue reducing his prices. With a plant capable of producing hundreds of thousands of cars in any given year, Henry Ford emerged as the undisputed giant of the industry. Indeed, as Figure 6-2 illustrates, his sales in the early twenties sometimes exceeded those of all his competitors combined. His system's success revolutionized manufacturing. Moving assembly lines and other cost-cutting processes developed at the Ford Motor Co. became standard features not only in other automobile plants but also in every sort of consumer industry.

Henry Ford had designed a phenomenally successful consumer product and then superintended the development of a revolutionary process to manufacture it. The final step was to restructure the business aspects of his operation. The Dodge brothers had already left the firm to build a car of their own. Differences of opinion and temperament had strained relations between Ford and Couzens for many years, and Ford's quixotic peace mission to Europe during the early months of the First World War finally embarrassed Couzens into resigning from the company's management. Recognizing the intrinsic value of their founders' shares, however, no one disposed of them. As investments they were somewhat disappointing because Henry Ford plowed a lot of his profits right back into the company to finance

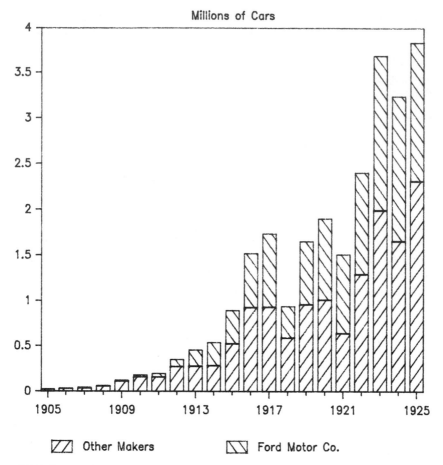

FIGURE 6-2   Automobile Production 1905-1925. (From Ralph C. Epstein, *The Automobile Industry* [Chicago: A.W. Shaw Co., 1928], pp. 314, 324.)

further expansion. In 1916 the Dodges sued Ford for failing to distribute appropriate dividends on the company's stock. When a judge eventually ordered him to
pay the dividends, Ford determined to "shuck the parasites" who interfered with his
plans. He toyed with the idea of establishing a new enterprise to build a car even
cheaper than the Model T. Certain that he could do so and thereby undermine the
value of their investment, the remaining stockholders in the Ford Motor Company
reluctantly surrendered their shares. The company's founder, his wife, and his son
ended up owning all of the stock in an industrial complex conservatively valued at
half a billion dollars.

Despite his phenomenal personal wealth, Ford continued to consider himself
a man of the people. He railed against capitalists and bankers, and managed to
avoid borrowing from them except when he temporarily needed cash to buy out the

parasites. He saw his main purpose in life as benefiting mankind by providing as large a number of people as possible with inexpensive, reliable transportation. Throughout his career, he also viewed himself a humane and generous employer. But consideration of Ford's relationship to his workers should be placed in the context of the demographic and structural changes occurring in the American labor force in this era.

THE LOT OF THE WORKERS

Although the nation's population grew less rapidly after 1890 than it had earlier, more than 100 million people were living in the United States in 1915, up from just over 60 million in 1890. As usual much of this growth represented natural increase, the comparative prosperity of the early twentieth century encouraging couples to have several children. Always a restless group, many of these people moved about. While the absolute number of Americans living in rural settings rose slowly through this period, the urban population grew much more rapidly.

The cities felt the brunt of the wave of immigration. Prosperity attracted unprecedented numbers of new arrivals after the turn of the century; more than a million individuals entered the country in several years. Railroad and steamship company advertising convinced some foreigners to come, labor contractors brought over others, but most came on their own, hoping to share the high standard of living Americans enjoyed. Many immigrants financed their passage with money earlier travelers had remitted from the New World. Thousands of single young men came to the United States intending to save as much as possible from their wages and then return to live in the old country in comfortable circumstances. Native-born workers complained that these "birds of passage" accepted minimal wages and terrible working conditions that lowered the standards for all.

Those who planned to remain in the United States and become citizens had difficulty fitting in if they had come from countries which had previously sent few people to the United States. The "new immigration" involved hundreds of thousands of people streaming in from central, southern, and eastern Europe. In America, they often found themselves confined to less desirable neighborhoods and menial jobs. The discrimination and segregation that defined relations between southern blacks and whites had its counterpart in the hostility new immigrants encountered in the Northeast. The steel, mining, and auto industries attracted predominantly non-English-speaking workforces, a fact that complicated training and managing them. On the basis of little hard evidence, employers and conservative union leaders considered foreigners less reliable than native-born workers and more likely to participate in radical, communistic, or socialistic agitation.

The 1894 Pullman Strike offered convincing proof that labor organizers should avoid any hint of radicalism. As depression set in after the Panic of 1893, the Pullman Company halted production of its more expensive sleeping cars. It decided to continue building freight cars at a loss, though, to prevent any competitor from gaining control of the market. To cut operating losses, the company reduced the wages it paid the employees who lived in the model company town of Pullman, located just south of Chicago. Rents there remained unchanged. Many workers found themselves earning less at the factory than they needed to pay for their housing. George Pullman refused to scale the rents downward, though, claiming that they and the wage levels were parts of two separate business arrangements.

The workers were members of the American Railway Union that had been founded by Eugene Debs, a railroad brakeman and a labor activist. Convinced that the separate railroad brotherhoods had splintered the workers' bargaining leverage, Debs invited anyone working in the industry, regardless of position or degree of skill, to join his organization. Under this broad definition, the Pullman workers who assembled railroad cars qualified for membership. When they went on strike, ARU members staged a boycott, refusing to handle trains that included any car built at George Pullman's plant. This tactic interrupted rail service all across the United States. Railroad managers retaliated by coupling United States mail coaches on trains hauling Pullman cars so they could complain that the ARU boycott was interfering with the delivery of the mail, a federal offense. President Cleveland accepted this interpretation and his attorney general dispatched federal troops to confront the strikers. Hundreds of injuries and many deaths resulted.

While the army battled the strikers, their leaders became mired in judicial proceedings. Debs and his associates were charged with violating the Sherman Antitrust Act. This law declared illegal "every contract, combination in the form of trust or otherwise, or conspiracy, in restraint of trade or commerce among the several states . . ." The ARU could be seen as a "combination" or "conspiracy" whose boycott was "restraining" interstate commerce. When the union's leaders would or could not halt the boycott, they were jailed for violating a court order calling upon them to end the strike. Debs emerged from his six-month prison term an outspoken socialist, a position he would maintain for the rest of his life. The strike had burned itself out and destroyed the union in the process.

If the courts and the government were going to support management so firmly, union organizers recognized the need to move cautiously. Conservative unions that took that approach did remarkably well during the period of industrial consolidation running from 1897 through 1904. Total union membership ballooned from less than half a million to more than two million, with American Federation of Labor affiliates accounting for 80 percent of that total. While the AFL under Samuel Gompers preferred to coordinate the activities of craft unions with highly skilled workers, it did admit and support some industrial organizing groups.

The most prominent of these was the United Mine Workers. Its dynamic leader, John Mitchell, organized the workers in the bituminous mining regions of Pennsylvania and, through carefully orchestrated strikes, forced the mine operators to negotiate with the union. In 1902, the union attempted to duplicate this success in the anthracite fields, calling a protracted strike that riveted national attention and caused President Theodore Roosevelt to attempt to mediate. The president found Mitchell to be far more tactful and reasonable than the mine owners. Their spokesman, George Baer, did little to endear himself to the public when he claimed that "The rights and interests of the laboring man will be protected and cared for not by labor agitators but by the Christian men to whom God has given control of the property rights of the country." Roosevelt eventually prevailed upon J.P. Morgan to coerce the mine owners into a more reasonable posture. The crisis passed without the owners recognizing that the union had a right to bargain collectively.

The organizing drive lost momentum after 1904 partly because of the National Association of Manufacturers' aggressive campaign to preserve the open shop system. Originally founded in 1895 to stimulate industrial exports, the NAM achieved much greater prominence with its antiunion drive. Furthermore, the unions were losing one court battle after another as conservative judges insisted upon ruling in favor of property rights. Particularly galling was the continued citation of antitrust legislation to outlaw or discourage union initiatives. Even though unionization staged something of a comeback beginning in 1910, some blamed the conservative philosophy of the AFL and the railroad brotherhoods for the general lack of union influence.

A few advocated far more aggressive tactics. The American labor force had always harbored a radical fringe, ranging from anarchists willing to plant bombs to humane socialists like Eugene Debs. But most Americans ignored the distinction between Debs's Socialist party and the much more radical International Workers of the World. The IWW first gained a foothold in oppressive mining and lumber camps in the West. Linked to European communists and socialists, the "Wobblies" never developed a wide following in this country. The IWW reached the peak of its influence in 1912 after successfully defending the rights of embattled textile workers in Lowell, Massachusetts. A widely publicized defeat the very next year involving silk weavers in Paterson, New Jersey, tarnished its image. The organization's support declined even more dramatically when its leaders proclaimed the First World War a capitalists' conspiracy and urged pacifism or revolution.

The absence of respected, aggressive unions and of public concern for the workers' plight in general meant that working conditions improved very little throughout this period. Long hours, low wages, job insecurity, few pension plans, marginal safety regulations, and almost no workman's compensation programs were the rule. Some dedicated Progressive reformers did manage to push through a few feeble local and state licensing and safety inspection laws as well as legislation designed to reduce the exploitation of child and female labor. By and large, though, the workers remained at the mercy of the whims of their employers.

Henry Ford was one employer who claimed to be concerned with his workers' welfare. The steady demand for his Model T's that had encouraged him to expand and reorganize his company's production system naturally affected his workforce. The Ford plant rather quickly abandoned the haphazard piecework payment system and the often dictatorial authority of shop foremen for standardized hourly pay rates and centralized hiring and personnel policies. The moving assembly lines proved to be both a blessing and a curse. While they simplified each task so that an unskilled worker could begin productive work almost at once, the line moved relentlessly, regardless of human fatigue, inattention, or boredom. While the moving assembly line was being perfected at the Ford plants in 1912 and 1913, they suf

Moving assembly line for Model T Fords. (Courtesy of Ford Motor Co.)

fered a very high rate of labor turnover, a problem common throughout the rapidly changing auto industry. The proponents of scientific management who became aware of the human engineering problems associated with revolutionary production systems took a few tentative steps to deal with them.

The Ford Motor Co. apparently intended to buy a solution. It announced a dramatic incentive plan early in 1914, promising to pay its workers a standard wage of five dollars a day. Because that was more than twice the average daily wage for autoworkers in Detroit, the proposal had broad repercussions. Some of Ford's competitors lambasted him for raising workers' expectations far above other companies' ability to pay. Other critics claimed the move was designed to enable Ford to hire and retain only the most efficient workers in his plants. With such a topnotch labor force, he could presumably speed up his assembly lines and thereby increase his output and reduce his per unit labor costs despite the higher pay scale. Whatever motivated the decision, the policy turned out to be extraordinarily popular with workers. Thousands of unemployed or poorly paid laborers rushed to Detroit from all over the United States. With a substantial number of workers already on the line, the Ford Motor Co. could hire only a small fraction of this army of job-seekers, leaving a good many of them stranded, out of work, and homeless in the dead of a bitter Michigan winter. Over the long term, the five-dollar-day did seem to reduce labor tensions at the plant—even as the assembly lines ran faster and faster.

At about the same time, the company established its Sociological Department to investigate the working and living habits of its employees. Headed by a clergyman, its ostensible goals were to improve and uplift the workers as well as to help recent immigrants adjust to American life. Because the department's moralism reflected Henry Ford's personal disapproval of drinking and smoking, a good many of his employees considered the agency arrogant and intrusive. But thousands of workers willingly submitted to it in order to qualify for the five-dollar wage which, not incidentally, enabled a good many of them to buy Model T's of their own.

Another group of workers who enjoyed comparatively better times in the years leading up to the First World War were the farmers. As noted earlier, the total number of rural residents continued to increase during this period, and many of them moved into previously unsettled areas. The 1890 Census report had claimed that no identifiable frontier line could be drawn anymore, but land rushes in Oklahoma, settlement in western Texas, and migration to the Great Plains and the Far

---

ROSE KNOX

Around the turn of the century, many farms were becoming highly specialized and therefore increasingly dependent upon commercial or industrial processing of their commodities. Indeed, a successful business might develop around a single product. To generate customer loyalty and demand, however, a promoter might have to go beyond brand name identification. Innovative uses for basic food products could dramatically increase their marketability. No one could have done more than Rose Knox to make gelatin a standard item in virtually every kitchen in the United States.

Rose Markward had been born in Ohio before the Civil War but moved with her parents to Gloversville, New York, seeking employment. While working in one of the community's many glove factories, she met Charles Briggs Knox, a glove salesman, and the couple married in 1883. Charles saved enough to buy a gelatin processing business in Johnstown, New York, in 1890. The profits from that venture financed expansion into the hardware, newspaper, and electric power business. When Charles died in 1906, however, Rose sold everything but the gelatin company.

From the very beginning, she had proven to be an astute entrepreneur. In her own kitchen at first and later in a modern research facility, she tested recipes to find new uses for her company's product. She published the best recipes in cookbooks and printed them on the sides of her packages of Knox Gelatin. She also wrote advertising copy that made her a familiar figure to generations of housewives. Her company grew rapidly. Its $300,000 value in 1915 was triple what it had been when she had inherited it nine years earlier. She remained president of the Charles B. Knox Gelatin Co. into her eighties. She was still serving as chairman of the board at the age of 92 in 1949 when *Collier's* magazine designated her "America's foremost woman industrialist."

West created thousands of new farms and ranches. Agricultural productivity continued its historic rise during these years, although at a somewhat slower rate than it had earlier. The expanding, increasingly urbanized domestic market for agricultural products helped offset the inevitable cyclical declines in overseas demand.

One of the most encouraging developments was the gradual recovery of prices from the depressed levels of the late nineteenth century. Some of this increase reflected a general rise in all consumer prices, but, even so, many farmers found themselves relatively better off than they had been for decades. Many Americans later praised the first fifteen years of the twentieth century as the golden age of American agriculture, and the price levels of farm products in the years 1910 to 1914 became benchmarks. The concept of parity which has been an integral part of federal price support programs since the 1930s began as an attempt to guarantee farmers the same relative buying power they had enjoyed in the five years prior to the First World War.

Ironically, this golden age in many ways constituted the final stage of the type of agricultural economy that had existed since colonial times. The population of draft animals escalated, for example, as implements of all sorts were harnessed to natural horsepower. Stationary steam engines and clumsy steam tractors provided most of the rest of the motive power on farms; lightweight, maneuverable gasoline-powered tractors would not appear in large numbers until the 1920s. Land-grant colleges and agricultural experiment stations propounded scientific farming doctrines, but traditional practices persisted throughout much of the country. The farm population was denied access to many of the technological advances and improvements available to city dwellers. The relative agricultural prosperity nevertheless dampened rural interest in the political concepts that had fueled the Populist protests of the 1890s. It was left to the urban-based Progressive reform movement to revive, modify, and implement these concepts.

THE PROGRESSIVE REACTION

The period around the turn of the twentieth century has sometimes been called the "Organizing Age." This seems an appropriate label for years that saw the rise and consolidation of huge industrial combines, the expansion of national labor unions, and the growth of interest in government regulation and control of the economy. The simultaneous appearance of these trends was hardly coincidental; all of these attempts to order and restructure the United States were interrelated. Individuals and groups worried about losing control over their destinies as the scope of American enterprise expanded and encouraged the formation of giant businesses that even their own managers found difficult to guide. All sorts of proposals appeared, aimed at restoring human authority over bloated, impersonal institutions. The bulk of these suggestions fell under the general heading of Progressive reforms.

Progressivism was an extraordinarily broad, loosely defined reform sentiment that arose around the turn of the century and crested just before the First World War. Historians have devoted considerable time and energy to defining Progressivism and then to classifying which individuals met their definitions. Little consensus has emerged because Progressivism seems to have reflected a generalized feeling that the American economy was slipping out of control and ought to be curbed. The business community so favored certain reforms, for example, that some claim the Progressive impulse actually resulted from clever businessmen manipulating public sentiment to accomplish goals they never could have achieved otherwise. The idealistic reformers who saw themselves engaged in a crusade against evil and corrupt special interests would have stoutly denied such an allegation, but business support was certainly essential to much of their success.

While an individual's occupation or wealth might cause one set of programs to appear more attractive than another, by 1912 most Americans seemed convinced that the government should play a much larger role in the management of the nation's affairs. There were three major areas of concern. Because the railroad industry had matured by the turn of the century, it had encountered obstacles and roused so much political opposition that railroading was subjected to the most comprehensive set of Progressive regulations. A second target of reform, closely related to the railroads, were the huge business and industrial combines that had recently taken shape. The perennial American political dilemma of creating an appropriate and responsible monetary and banking structure presented the Progressives with their third major challenge.

The drive to regulate the railroads was the most effective of these reform initiatives. Responding to complaints from farmers and other shippers, Congress had created the Interstate Commerce Commission in 1887. The executive branch ignored this agency during its early years, though, and judicial rulings trimmed its authority almost to the vanishing point. As the new century dawned, the nation's shippers mounted a lobbying campaign which, combined with popular resentment against railroad practices, encouraged Congress to give the ICC more power. The Elkins Act of 1903 prohibited any railroad from deviating from its published rate schedules. The commission was to insure that all customers, regardless of the size of their shipments, paid identical rates; rebates and drawbacks were explicitly outlawed. A good many railroad owners and managers welcomed this federal protection from competitors who had been paying secret premiums to entice shippers.

The Elkins Act only whetted the appetites of the Progressives. President Theodore Roosevelt made more and broader regulation a key plank in his 1904 reelection platform, and several Progressive Republicans won seats in Congress to help him make good on his pledge. The resulting Hepburn Act of 1906 authorized the ICC to investigate and adjudicate any complaints of unfair charges. Conservatives insisted, however, that any challenged rates could be collected until the commission delivered a final ruling. Furthermore, if a railroad objected to that ruling, it could take the matter to court where the burden of proof lay with the commission. A backlog of cases soon developed, delaying decisions and allowing railroads to continue charging rates the commission would later rule unfair.

The reform impulse had grown strong enough by 1910 to enable the Progressives to push through much broader regulatory legislation. The Mann-Elkins Act extended the commission's authority to certain public utilities and other common

MR. DOOLEY COMMENTS ON "THE BIG FINE"

Journalist Peter Finley Dunne editorialized through the voice of an amiable Irishman named Mr. Dooley. The following selection discusses the huge fine that U.S. District Court Judge Kenesaw Mountain Landis levied on Standard Oil of Indiana in 1907 for continuing to collect rebates from railroads after the Elkins Act had made them illegal. To Mr. Dooley's disappointment, no doubt, John D. Rockefeller evaded both the fine and a prison term through appeal.

"That was a splendid fine they soaked Jawn D. with," said Mr. Dooley.

"What did they give him?" asked Mr. Hennessy.

"Twenty-nine millyon dollars," said Mr. Dooley.

"Oh, great!" said Mr. Hennessy. "That's a grand fine. It's a gorjus fine. I can't hardly believe it."

"It's thrue, though," said Mr. Dooley. "Twenty-nine millyon dollars. Divvle th' cent less. I can't exactly make out what th' charge was that they arrested him on, but th' gin'ral idee is that Jawn D. was goin' around loaded up to the guards with Standard Ile, exceedin' th' speed limit in acquirin' money, an' singin' "A charge to keep I have" till th' neighbors cud stand it no longer. The judge says: "Ye're an old offender an' I'll have to make an example iv ye. Twenty-nine millyon dollars or fifty-eight millyon days. Call th' next case, Misther Clerk.

"Did he pay th' fine? He did not. Iv coorse he cud if he wanted to. He wuddent have to pawn annything to get th' money, ye can bet on that. All he'd have to do would be to put his hand down in his pocket, skin twenty-nine millyon dollar bills off iv his roll and 'hurl them at th' clerk. But he refused to pay as a matter iv principle. 'Twas not that he needed th' money. He don't care f'r money in th' passionate way that you an' me do, Hinnissy. Th' likes iv us ar as crazy about a dollar as a man is about his child when he has on'y wan. Th' chances are we'll spoil it. But Jawn D., havin' a large an' growin' fam'ly iv dollars, takes on'y a kind iv gin'ral inthrest in thim. He's issued a statement sayin' that he's a custojeen iv money appointed by himsilf. He looks afther his own money an' th' money iv other people. He takes it an' puts it where it won't hurt thim an' they won't spoil it. He's a kind iv society f'r th' previntion of croolty to money."

(Peter Finley Dunne, *Mr. Dooley Says* [New York: Scribner's, 1910], pp. 158-60.)

carriers in addition to railroads. The big change, though, lay in its rate-setting responsibility. Rather than wait for railroads to publish rate schedules and then review them, the ICC set the rates itself. If a railroad considered the agency's decisions unfair, it could sue, but the burden of proof now lay with the railroads, and the ICC's schedules would prevail while the case made its slow progress through the courts. Despite the breadth of the new regulations, they met with little industry opposition because they offered railroad companies protection from unfair competition and helped insulate them from many customer complaints.

The Progressives were also interested in regulating or controlling companies or business structures that fell outside the purview of the ICC. Some reformers firmly believed that only by breaking up big business combinations could the government "restore" competition and free enterprise. The authorization for this trust-busting approach resided, of course, in the Sherman Antitrust Act of 1890. The executive and judicial branches were so reluctant to invoke it that almost any business combine could find a precedent or work out an accommodation to avoid dismemberment. Indeed, its first prominent use had been against the Pullman strikers in 1894.

A couple of court rulings had finally begun to put some punch into the antitrust drive even before President Theodore Roosevelt sent a shockwave rumbling through the corporate world in 1902. Dismayed at the unsettling effects of the speculative warfare over Northern Pacific Railroad stock, he ordered his attorney general to sue the Northern Securities Company. Because a small group of individuals was using that holding company to control virtually all rail traffic west of the Mississippi, Roosevelt considered it a clear example of what the Sherman Act outlawed: a combination in restraint of interstate trade. The Supreme Court agreed in 1904 and ordered the company dissolved. As a result, the railroad shares the holding company possessed were returned to their original owners. Even without the holding company apparatus, Harriman, Hill, Rockefeller, Morgan, and their associates could and did continue to operate the western railroads pretty much as they wished.

Despite its relatively minor effect on railroad operations, the Northern Securities suit was extraordinarily popular. This, in turn, encouraged the Roosevelt administration to institute more than forty similar legal proceedings, including antitrust suits against Standard Oil and the American Tobacco Co. Roosevelt's successor showed even more dedication to trustbusting. President William Howard Taft ordered twice as many actions begun, the most famous being the case against United States Steel for its 1907 takeover of the Tennessee Coal, Iron, and Railway Co.

Although the government won many of its suits, the Supreme Court diluted the impact of the Sherman Act in its rulings against the oil and tobacco combines in 1911. It distinguished between mere bigness or the degree of monopoly control a corporation enjoyed and the use it made of this power. A single company might own or control a majority of the assets and output in a given industry, but as long as the court considered its behavior reasonable, it need not be broken up. The judicial "rule of reason" infuriated many Progressives, and they called for more specific restrictive legislation to strengthen or supercede the Sherman Act.

Democratic Presidential nominee Woodrow Wilson responded to these sentiments in his 1912 New Freedom platform by advocating detailed antitrust legislation that would leave no room for legal or judicial equivocation. After he was elected, Congress set to work on a complex bill that would outlaw a number of specific practices. Corporations that engaged in these activities risked antitrust prosecution and dissolution. In a characteristically Democratic party gesture, the act also exempted labor unions from antitrust litigation. Framing such a comprehensive and complex measure took so long that the Clayton Antitrust Bill was not ready for Wilson's signature until the fall of 1914.

By that time Progressive thinkers had moved beyond a simplistic trust-busting philosophy. They recognized that large-scale industrialization was there to stay. Rather than splinter big businesses into small, inherently less efficient units, many reformers now favored the development of federal guidelines to regulate them for the benefit of all. President Wilson became convinced of the wisdom of this approach as well, and the result was the creation of the Federal Trade Commission in the fall of 1914. The FTC performed similar functions for industrial and commercial operators that the ICC did for transportation. It collected data, investigated complaints about unfair practices, and issued guidelines for corporate behavior based upon its own research and current interpretations of the antitrust legislation. Astute managers consulted with the commission before they expanded or consolidated. With the FTC providing advice and enforcement and the Clayton Act specifying what they could and could not do, corporations operated in a much more defined setting after 1914.

The Progressives tried to bring similar order to banking and monetary affairs, the third major area of reform. In 1896 Democratic and Populist party presidential candidate William Jennings Bryan had centered his campaign on a strident call for the free coinage of silver. But Republican William McKinley won convincingly and support for silver faded. The 1900 Gold Standard Act reconfirmed the nation's intention to maintain a specie basis for its currency. Gold from the abundant deposits in South Africa and the Yukon had combined with a string of favorable U.S. trade balances to increase the nation's bullion stockpile in the early 1900s.

The Panic of 1907, however, convinced many Americans that the money supply still lacked sufficient elasticity to serve the nation's needs. It also suggested that a federal monetary policy might be preferable to the whims of private bankers and the free market expansion and contraction of currency. Some of the fluctuation in the money supply could be traced to the fact that a national bank's holdings of federal securities determined how many banknotes it could issue. Commercial paper appeared to be an attractive supplement to the government bonds. Increased business activity would normally generate a rise in corporate borrowing and, therefore, the amount of commercial paper the banks held. If it could serve as backing for the issue of more bank notes, the money supply could be expanded in conjunction with increases in business activity.

The panic also demonstrated the difficulty sound financial institutions could encounter in gathering enough ready cash to handle unusually heavy withdrawals. J. P. Morgan's insistence that private financiers create a fund to shore up beleaguered banks was a temporary solution, but no one could guarantee that the same strategy would work in the future. A more systematic pooling of reserve funds seemed advisable. The Aldrich-Vreeland Act of 1908 represented a step in that direction. It called upon private bankers to form voluntary associations to act as clearing houses for their members, thus strengthening each other's liquidity. It also authorized national banks to issue notes backed by sound commercial paper as well as state and local government securities. These were clearly seen as stopgap measures, however, so the legislation also created the National Monetary Commission to study alternatives for a permanent solution.

Senator Nelson Aldrich, a Rhode Islander with close family connections to the Rockefellers, chaired the commission. It presented a lengthy report in 1912 that called for the establishment of a single central bank to store other banks' reserves and to monitor their operations. As a conservative Republican, Aldrich naturally felt that private bankers should own and operate the institution. The Progressives, on the other hand, harbored a general distrust of big business so they preferred to have the federal government control the monetary system. The rural conservatives and former Populists who figured prominently in the Democratic party's congressional majorities thought the Aldrich proposal sounded too much like a revival of the central bank that Democratic President Andrew Jackson had dismantled eighty years earlier. Antipathy toward the eastern banking establishment still ran deep in the rest of the country.

With President Wilson's guidance, Congress sculpted a complex compromise in the 1913 Federal Reserve Act. Twelve reserve-holding banks were to be established, each serving a separate geographical region or district. Private banks would purchase their stocks in order to supply the necessary investment capital. Each would also collect reserves from all banks in its district, creating a substantial stockpile of funds that could quickly be dispatched to any bank experiencing an unusual demand for withdrawals. The central bank could also act as a lender of last resort. It would "rediscount" its loans to other banks and could move the discount rate up to discourage or down to encourage additional borrowing. Finally, the reserve banks would issue federal reserve notes backed by government securities of all types as well as sound commercial paper.

The management of the system also represented a compromise. The regional banks were to select directors representing both the banking community and the general public. Each board of directors would have considerable latitude in setting discount rates and deciding how many notes to issue in accordance with its reading of the monetary requirements of its district. In a bow to Progressive sensibilities, though, a Federal Reserve Board located in Washington, D.C., would oversee the operations of the whole system. Five of its members were to represent private interests, while the secretary of the treasury and the comptroller of the currency served as government watchdogs. This cumbersome system with its overlapping layers of control seemed to work well enough during and after the First World War, but it stumbled badly when severe economic adversity struck in 1929.

In addition to creating regulatory structures for railroads, corporations, and banking, the Progressive reform movement exploited the government's power to protect individual Americans. Although federal efforts at labor legislation were disappointing, state and local authorities developed many effective protection programs for workers. Federal concern for consumers was most obvious in the passage of both the Pure Food Act and the Meat Inspection Act in 1906. These early efforts laid the groundwork for subsequent labor and welfare programs.

American entry into the war in 1917 blocked further legislative moves. It also interfered with a full application of the principles underlying the Federal Reserve System, the Federal Trade Commission, and other Progressive instrumentalities. The postwar years would see a reversion to a conservative orientation within the United States that would continue to undermine the effectiveness of the reforms. It took the debilitating shock of the Great Depression of the 1930s to revive the Progressive concepts and encourage a broad implementation of them.

READING SUGGESTIONS

A classic survey of the years covered in this chapter is Samuel P. Hays's *The Response to Industrialism, 1885-1914* (1957). More recently, Robert Wiebe took a penetrating look at the organizing spirit of the period in *The Search for Order, 1877-1920* (1967). Other sound overviews are Robert Higgs's *The Transformation of the American Economy, 1865-1914* (1971); Carl Degler's *The Age of the Economic Revolution* (1977); Thomas C. Cochran and William Miller's *The Age of Enterprise* (1942); and Harold U. Faulkner's *The Decline of Laissez Faire 1897-1917* (1951). Charles Hoffman looked at one decade in detail in *The Depression of the Nineties: An Economic History* (1970).

Ralph L. Nelson takes a comprehensive look at consolidation in *Merger Movements in American Industry, 1895-1956* (1959). The chief architect of that phenomenon is portrayed sympathetically by his son-in-law in Henry L. Satterlee's *J. Pierpont Morgan, An Intimate Portrait* (1939). The great investment banker appears in a less favorable light in three other biographies: Frederick Lewis Allen, *The Great Pierpont Morgan* (1949); Edwin P. Hoyt, Jr., *The House of Morgan* (1966); and Andrew Sinclair, *Corsair: The Life of J. Pierpont Morgan* (1981).

John B. Rae analyzed the early auto industry from two perspectives: *American Automobile Manufacturers* (1959) and *The American Automobile* (1965). Another general work is James Flink's *The Car Culture* (1975). The first of an exhaustive three-volume study of the automotive genius is *Ford: The Times, The Man, The Company 1865-1915* (1954) by Allan Nevins and Frank Hill. A far less awesome but favorable description appears in Roger Burlingame's *Henry Ford* (1955). For a less flattering portrait, consult *The Legend of Henry Ford* (1948) by Kieth Swados.

Dozens of books have been written about the political aspects of the Progressive movement, among them Richard Hofstadter's classic, *The Age of Reform* (1955). Robert Wiebe concerns himself with its impact on enterprise in *Businessmen and Reform: A Study of the Progressive Movement* (1962). Both the books that Gabriel Kolko wrote on Progressivism, *Railroads and Regulations, 1877-1916* (1965) and *The Triumph of Conservatism* (1963), conclude that business interests exploited the reform spirit to achieve ends beneficial to themselves. Craig West focuses on one area of reform in *Banking Reform and the Federal Reserve, 1863-1923* (1977). A recent look at the whole subject is Thomas McCraw's *The Prophets of Regulation* (1984).

Chapter 7

THE MATURATION OF THE CONSUMER SOCIETY 1914-1929

President Calvin Coolidge concisely expressed the prevailing attitude in the 1920s when he proclaimed that "The chief business of the American people is business." Many felt that the "Prosperity Decade" represented the full flowering of the free enterprise system. Thousands of business consolidations occurred involving many of the largest enterprises in the country. The organizers and executives who created and managed these combines were popular heroes and role models for young Americans. Consumers were the focus of most of the entrepreneurial attention. Automobiles, radios, ready-made clothing, home appliances, packaged foods, and countless other products flooded the market to entice buyers. Euphoria about business prospects, profits, success, and the future pumped stock prices to unprecedented heights. Americans from all walks of life aspired to become tycoons through investments.

And then it all collapsed. The stock market had ridden the wave of prosperity for so long that few expected it ever to crest. Speculation had become a national mania, blinding even the "experts" to the economy's underlying weaknesses. The dramatic plunge of stock prices in late 1929 set the tone for a long, debilitating decline into the worst depression in United States history.

The jobless veterans of the American Expeditionary Force who gathered in Washington to seek relief discovered little sympathy for their earlier sacrifices.

Memories of the Great War had become so vague that no one seemed sure just how or why the United States had become involved. Even before the United States had entered the European conflict, though, foreign and domestic demand for American industrial and agricultural products had begun generating profits for the nation's farmers, manufacturers, shippers, and financiers. After the American entry, the federal government imposed controls on all aspects of domestic enterprise. Never before had the American people functioned under such centralized dictation, and they eagerly looked forward to its termination. Yet the war stimulated the American economy all across the board, building the industries and creating the pent-up demand for consumer goods that laid the basis for the Roaring Twenties.

THE UNITED STATES AND THE GREAT WAR

Although the American people had learned of the assassination of Austria's Archduke Francis Ferdinand in Sarajevo in late June 1914, the announcement of an Austrian ultimatum to the Serbian government four weeks later came as a shock. In a matter of days, all of the major European countries had become engaged in a costly and destructive conflict well deserving its contemporary name, the Great War. President Wilson immediately proclaimed that the United States would remain strictly neutral. But the war dragged on year after year, making the wealth and productive capabilities of the United States increasingly attractive to the belligerents. During that same period, empathy and propaganda were tearing away the cloak of impartiality the United States had donned. Neutrality may have been the official posture, but sympathy for embattled England and France gained strength daily.

The economic seeds for the swing away from neutrality had taken root long before the war's outbreak. American capital had begun flowing overseas in the late nineteenth century, most of it in the form of investments in Mexico, Canada, and the Caribbean. Simultaneously, the profitability of American enterprises attracted European money to our shores. An international balance sheet in 1914 would have shown $6 billion worth of European-held shares in American companies offsetting approximately $3 billion in United States investment abroad. Traditionally this country's most important trading partner, Great Britain had sunk the largest amount of foreign capital into United States enterprises, but French and German investors had bought millions of dollars worth of American stocks as well. On the eve of the war, fear arose that a crash sale of these European-held stocks would force all share prices downward and possibly break the back of the American financial markets. To prevent it the New York Stock Exchange closed its doors on July 31, 1914, and did not reopen except for limited trading until April 1, 1915.

Uncertainty over what neutrality actually meant also clouded the international trade picture. The official policy did not prevent Americans from selling munitions and other military supplies to the warring parties because other nations, including both Great Britain and Germany, had previously permitted neutrals to trade with belligerents. The most eager customers were England and France who, unfortunately, quickly ran through their available cash. As the allies converted their foreign exchange into dollars to purchase needed supplies, the United States turned into a net creditor nation virtually overnight. In mid-August, Secretary of State William Jennings Bryan decreed that Americans could not make any further loans to those at war. While the moralistic Bryan clung to this position through October, the more pragmatic President Wilson considered an appeal from the House of Morgan for greater flexibility.

When the elder J. P. Morgan had died in 1913, his banking concern passed to his son and namesake. Some doubted that the heir could follow in the footsteps of the great investment banker, but personal and business connections with the British and the French placed the younger Morgan in an enviable position. Both the allied governments hired his firm to handle all their wartime buying in the United States. Morgan asked Wilson whether he could extend credit to these two longstanding trading partners if they ran out of cash. The president realized that an abrupt end to the foreign orders might undermine the United States economy, so he agreed that Morgan and his colleagues could allow England and France to continue buying American goods without immediately paying for them.

No one initially expected the war to last very long, but as it extended into 1915, administration officials warned the president that a severe depression could result if England and France stopped purchasing American goods. The credit arrangements Wilson had approved could no longer sustain the allies' demands; they needed to borrow money directly. To avoid what he now believed would be devastating economic consequences, Wilson permitted allied bonds to be sold in the United States. J. P. Morgan & Co. immediately distributed $500 million worth of British war bonds to American customers. The allies eventually negotiated more than twice that amount in additional direct loans, bringing the total of both credits and loans from American sources to around $2.3 billion by April 1917.

Wilson's approval of the loans may have violated his pledge of neutrality, but it definitely stimulated prosperity in the United States. War-related orders kept exporters hopping at the same time domestic demand remained high. Global food shortages pushed farm prices in 1916 even higher than they had been during agriculture's Golden Age from 1909-1914. Railroads struggled to haul mountains of goods to eastern distribution centers. Shipowners could assume the risks of earning high profits by fitting out voyages themselves or selling their vessels at huge markups to others willing to take the gamble. Workers cited the resulting inflation as a cause of their striking for higher wages.

An emotional debate about the defenses of the United States itself erupted. Some favored a massive army and navy buildup to guarantee the nation's peace and freedom; others complained that such preparations would only draw the United States into the war. Still others considered American participation the only honorable course. Bowing to militaristic pressures, President Wilson called for greater national preparedness. Congress appropriated funds for a substantial increase in the standing army and a three-year naval building program. Beginning in the summer of 1916, these packages applied further inflationary pressure to the already overheated economy.

The American preparedness drive intensified the logistical nightmare. Domestic and foreign orders mushroomed without any priority system to structure the processing of raw materials into finished goods. The Council of National Defense, established in August 1916, made a stab at relieving this congestion, but it lacked enforcement powers. Despite the allocation problems, companies supplying war materials to the United States and foreign governments benefited immensely.

By January 1917 the German government had concluded that it must halt the flow of goods from the United States to England. It therefore declared unrestricted submarine warfare on all vessels, regardless of nationality, that traded with Great Britain. After German torpedoes had begun sinking American ships, President Wilson decided he must send a war message to Capitol Hill on April 2, 1917. The Great War had already acted as a tonic for the American economy and given a boost to speculators and businesses all over the country, but the official entry of the United States would have even more pronounced effects on American enterprise.

The Wilson administration took some time to develop rational approaches to solve its financial, material, and manpower problems. Collecting the money fortunately proved to be far less difficult and disruptive in this war than had been the case in earlier conflicts. Ratified in 1913, the Sixteenth Amendment made personal income taxation constitutional. Shifting the rate schedules upward was a simple legislative matter. At the height of the war, the government collected as much as 70 percent of the highest incomes. Excise taxes, excess profits taxes on corporations, and tariffs also generated revenue. Together, taxes and other revenues provided approximately $10.7 billion of the $31.5 billion the United States spent on the war.

It borrowed the rest. Several war bond drives took place, complete with publicity, propaganda, and ballyhoo. Individuals bought $17 billion worth; corporations and banks purchased the remainder. As their vaults filled with bonds, the banks could issue more notes based on them. The number of banknotes in circulation increased nearly 500 percent and exerted a substantial inflationary effect. As long as the Federal Reserve system insured that the notes had appropriate backing, however, the system was far sounder than the printing of greenbacks that had snarled United States finances for years after the Civil War. The federal government lent around $9.5 billion to its wartime allies and spent most of the remainder of its revenue and borrowings on wages, supplies, and equipment for the armed forces.

Twentieth-century warfare demands plenty of material support. The United States was already the most productive country in the world; its major problem lay in organizing and coordinating its capabilities effectively. At first army and navy orders competed with each other and, worse still, the several bureaus within each department also fought among themselves. No one could properly evaluate and allocate the stream of purchase requests and orders designated "priority" that were pouring out of Washington.

Selling America on the war. (Library of Congress)

The War Industries Board was created in July 1917 to sort out these conflicting demands. The supply chaos continued, though, until President Wilson restructured the board and lent it his full executive authority. He centralized its control under Bernard Baruch, a brilliant businessman he had named chairman of the board. His responsibilities included creating new facilities to produce needed goods, converting existing plants to vital war production, establishing levels of priority among the thousands of government orders, allocating raw materials and components to those engaged in war work and, most important, making all industrial purchases for the allied governments and the American armed forces.

With such an extensive mandate, Baruch instructed, examined, cajoled, and manipulated American industry. In the process, the board eliminated excessive production and wasteful duplication by developing standards for thousands of products ranging from war materials to civilian goods as mundane as typewriter ribbons and plows. Bargaining with producers enabled the board to establish reasonable prices for many raw materials and producer's goods which, in turn, influenced but did not fix prices for consumer goods.

The federal government was also interested in promoting efficiency in transportation. The United States Railroad Administration took charge of all of the nation's railroads. Each received what amounted to rent in proportion to its share of the whole industry's revenues during the previous three years. The Railroad Administration's total control allowed it to operate 230,000 miles of track as a single, coordinated system. Its success can be seen in the record of freight car usage. Before American entry into the war, the railroads had suffered from serious shortages of cargo-carrying capacity, sometimes amounting to as much as 100,000 cars. By late 1918, despite the enormous wartime demand, the Railroad Administration had

BERNARD BARUCH CONFRONTS THE AUTOMOBILE INDUSTRY

In his autobiography, Bernard Baruch claims that he encountered serious opposition to the War Industries Board's actions only from the American automobile and steel industries. In this passage, he describes how he dealt with the automakers.

The heads of all the great companies were present, with the exception of Henry Ford. They listened with ill-concealed impatience as we explained WIB's plans to curtail immediately the production of automobiles by seventy-five per cent, and employ the facilities thus freed for war production. . . .

This reasonable speech made no impression. John Dodge led the attack by giving me a personal dressing down. He did not want any white-haired, white-faced Wall Street speculator telling him how he ought to conduct his business, he said among other things. . . .

The other auto manufacturers, in terms less emotional than Dodge, made it equally clear that they were prepared to ignore WIB. They informed me that they had stocked all the steel and coal they needed and could proceed in spite of us. During a lull in the argument I made up my mind on what had to be done to meet this challenge to our authority.

"Just a moment, gentlemen," I said as I picked up the phone and put in a call to McAdoo at the Railroad Administration. With the auto people listening to me, I said, "Mac, I want you to take down the names of the following factories, and I want you to stop every wheel going in and going out."

The automobile men looked at me, astonished and outraged, as I read off the names of Dodge, General Motors, Ford, and other plants. This effect was heightened as I put in a call to Secretary of War Baker. "Mr. Secretary, I would like you to issue an order to commandeer all the steel in the following yards," I said. Then I called Fuel Administrator Garfield and asked him to seize the manufacturers' coal supplies.

That did it. Billy Durant, head of General Motors, said, "I quit." The others capitulated soon after, but not before some had tried to bring political pressures to bear.

(Bernard M. Baruch, *Baruch: The Public Years* [New York: Holt Rinehart and Winston, 1960], pp. 60-61.)

a surplus of freight cars on hand due to its efficient use of rolling stock. The centralized system continued to operate until March 1, 1920, when the railroads reverted to private control.

The government's success in railroad management contrasted sharply with its experience in shipping. The United States Shipping Board had been set up in 1916 to revitalize the American merchant marine that had been deteriorating since the Civil War. Delays and bottlenecks prevented the first ship constructed completely under the board's auspices from entering service until December 1918, a month after the war ended. Fortunately, it was much more capable at utilizing the many existing ships it commandeered.

PIERRE S. DU PONT

Several generations of du Ponts lived and worked at the gunpowder mill that Eluthere du Pont had founded at Wilmington, Delaware, in 1799. Pierre S. du Pont, a great grandson of Eluthere, was born into this tradition-bound family in 1870. His father was killed in 1884 when his dynamite works exploded, so Pierre was left as the head of a large family of brothers and sisters. He joined a couple of cousins in attending MIT, but returned to work for the family business after graduation.

He discovered it to be an anachronistic, inefficient operation because it had never really been forced to compete. Throughout the nineteenth century, the very effective Gunpowder Trade Association had controlled the market absolutely and assigned shares to each manufacturer. Pierre felt frustrated in this environment, but could make no changes until 1902 when the old guard decided to sell the firm. Pierre and his cousins Alfred and Coleman insisted on taking control instead. They gave the retiring owners bonds and issued themselves stock in the reorganized firm, a plan that required no actual cash transfers.

Pierre quickly emerged as a business genius. He introduced modern cost accounting procedures and designed market forecasting techniques so effective that many other businesses adopted them. He also built a a modern research facility to develop and test new products. Under his leadership, the du Pont company integrated vertically to cut its production costs and horizontally until it had gained a 60 percent control of the gunpowder business. That was enough to trigger an antitrust action in 1907 that led to a major reorganization in 1913 and the divestiture of some properties and assets.

Even so, the company was ideally positioned to benefit from the wartime demand for its products. Under Pierre du Pont's careful scrutiny, it expanded its powder-making facilities and diversified into plastics, dyes, and other products that would continue to have markets after the war ended. Between 1914 and 1918 the firm collected $238 million in net profits on sales of $1.1 billion. Pierre du Pont considered his work completed in 1920, and, intending to retire, he relinquished control to other family members. The fortune he had accumulated was so vast, however, that it bought control of the ailing General Motors Corporation, forcing him later to superintend a thorough reorganization and reorientation in the auto industry.

In all some 5000 agencies large and small oversaw or managed various aspects of the war effort. For the first time in history, the American economy was marshaled in a coordinated fashion that eliminated much of the destructive competition that is inherent in a free enterprise system. Federal officials did show considerable concern, however, that orders and opportunities be funneled to the private sector whenever possible. Consequently, a number of American enterprises, especially those that made products used directly in combat, profited enormously.

Along with other chemical manufacturers, the Du Pont company took advantage of the activities of the federal government's Alien Property Custodian. Among the many German-owned items this agency seized were the patents that had elevated the German chemical industry to a position of world dominance. Du Pont now began manufacturing a wide range of chemicals, moving aggressively into the lucrative dye business. Freed from patent restraints, the country had by 1920 become essentially independent of external chemical suppliers. American glassmakers took similar steps to capture the market for high quality optical and other specialized types of glass that German, Austrian, and other European producers had formerly monopolized.

In addition to such obvious beneficiaries of war orders like Du Pont and the nation's two leading small arms manufacturers, Winchester and Remington, other industries chalked up substantial profits. Steel manufacturers could scarcely keep up with the demand from the makers of weapons, ships, and vehicles. Adequate supplies of coal were deemed so crucial that a special government agency, the Fuel Administration, stepped in to allocate supplies for civilian, industrial, transportation, and military uses. Coal's relative scarcity encouraged many customers to switch to petroleum products. The demand for all these items pushed prices up and boosted producers' profits.

Overall the United States put in a creditable performance. The country emerged from the conflict richer, stronger, more confident, and far more respected around the world than it had been in 1914. The rather short duration of its actual participation in the fighting prevented a resolution of all the management and production problems, but it also insulated the American people from the despair that demoralized the Europeans. Even so, the cataclysmic events altered many individual lives and affected groups in a variety of ways.

THE PEOPLE IN WAR AND PEACE

In the summer of 1917, a selective service system began registering men between the ages of 17 and 45, and it ultimately drafted more than two million into the armed services. Another two million volunteered, leaving significant vacancies in both industry and agriculture. Many women took jobs in industries that had never previously considered hiring them, and blacks received similar treatment. The prospect of finding better-paying jobs in northern industrial cities encouraged some 400,000 blacks to move out of the rural South.

Unionized workers did better than any group except farmers. Samuel Gompers and his American Federation of Labor were outspokenly partisan even before the United States joined the allies. When his country went to war, the aging labor leader issued a no-strike pledge. Thousands of work stoppages occurred anyway, but virtually all were short-lived. A 1912 law had mandated an eight-hour day, 44-hour week for all government-contract work. So much production came under federal contracts during the war that these rules became quite common, with workers who exceeded the limit on hours qualifying for higher overtime pay. The Department of Labor had been estimating changes in the cost of living for some time, and unionized workers expected and to a large degree received raises that caught their wage levels up with the rising cost of living. In that respect, the experience of wage earners contrasted sharply with that of salaried workers who generally received no raises at all. The federal government itself failed to adjust salary levels upward, leaving most white-collar workers much worse off financially at the end of the war.

The United States looked forward to the new year with great optimism after Germany surrendered on November 11, 1918, but the labor movement was headed for grave disappointment. The rise of communism around the world, most frighteningly in the form of Bolshevism in the Soviet Union, lay at the heart of the problem. Fear of foreign rabble-rousers or subversives soon developed into a full-blown Red Scare. Anyone who attempted to assert the rights of the working class in such an atmosphere risked being branded as an agent of Bolshevism in America.

While a very small group was committed to overthrowing capitalism in the United States, the vast majority of workers wanted only to improve their relative positions within the existing structure. Their first objective was to protect the better working conditions and higher wage rates they had gained during the war. The rather tepid assistance the federal government had provided evaporated quickly once the emergency had passed, so the unions found themselves on their own. About four million workers participated in 3600 strikes of greater or lesser magnitude in 1919. A few of the early walkouts did win concessions but, as the strikers' militancy rose, so did employers' resolve to resist. Played out in the gloom of the Red Scare, the strikes and violence that accompanied them caused a great deal of disillusion with organized labor.

A massive steel strike in the fall of 1919 was a case in point. Although many other industries had long since gone to an eight-hour work day, steel producers continued to demand back-breaking twelve-hour shifts. Low wages kept unskilled steelworkers well below the poverty line. William Z. Foster headed the Steelworkers Organizing Committee which drew thousands of disgruntled laborers into an industrial union. After enrolling one-fourth of the nation's steelworkers, Foster called a strike that halted about 90 percent of the steel production in the United States. Judge Elbert H. Gary, the head of U. S. Steel, not only refused to recognize the union, he claimed that Foster and his colleagues were foreign agitators and communists. Public support swung behind Gary as the personification of American free enterprise fending off Bolshevism. The impoverished strikers began to break ranks and filter back to their oppressive jobs, and the strike faded away without accomplishing any of its objectives.

A key factor for both sides in this confrontation was the sizable percentage of steelworkers who were non-English-speaking immigrants. Employers charged them with behaving in an un-American manner at the same time their very foreignness impeded labor organizers' efforts to inform them of the exploitation they suffered in comparison to other workers. After the 1919 Red Scare, labor leaders joined upper-class and nativist critics in opposing the continued immigration of millions of foreign workers to the United States. Minor limitations already prohibited the entry of certain people classed as undesirable, but in 1921 numerical quotas were assigned to each country. The National Origins Act of 1924 reduced the quotas still more, and they remained virtually unchanged until 1967.

Stringent immigration limitations could not prevent the deterioration of organized labor's influence in the 1920s. Union membership had reached an all time high of over 5 million just after the war. It then entered a debilitating decline, dropping to 3.6 million in 1923 and sliding all the way down to 2.9 million a decade later. As usual, the cautious, conservative craft unionists who constituted the backbone of the American Federation of Labor suffered the least deterioration in their strength.

The National Association of Manufacturers publicized the "American System" whose basic tenet was a firm commitment to the open shop principle. The courts bolstered this campaign by decreeing that yellow-dog contracts were legal. These forced workers to swear that they were not union members. If a worker who had signed a yellow-dog contract then agitated for unionization, he faced the prospect not only of losing his job but of being prosecuted for breach of contract. Known labor agitators were blacklisted, their names circulated among employers to prevent them from finding jobs. In most respects then, the 1920s was a very discouraging time for unionists.

Slowly rising wages in that decade also undermined unionization's appeal, although changes in pay levels tended to lag behind changes in prices. Workers therefore did relatively worse during the brief postwar boom when their wages slowly crept upward chasing the more exuberant price inflation. When prices plummeted in the summer of 1920, though, wages did not immediately fall. Those who held on to their jobs then found that their pay bought them much more than it had earlier. And, because prosperity returned relatively quickly in late 1921, wage levels never did fall as far as prices had, leaving employed workers slightly ahead of the game.

The farmers, as usual, swung through a more exaggerated cycle of prosperity and depression. When the fighting broke out overseas, the European nations drafted many of their farmers into army service. With battles raging across farmlands, they had to step up purchases of American commodities. Agricultural prices inflated rapidly and would probably have gone far higher had not the Food Administration intervened beginning in 1917.

An internationally reknowned mining engineer named Herbert Hoover headed this agency charged with encouraging agricultural production and conservation, keeping price escalation within bounds, and eliminating uncertainties over production and prices associated with speculation. The Food Administration also bought all of the food for the allies, the army, the navy, Belgian relief, and the Red Cross. Because these purchases amounted to about 40 percent of all United States sales, whatever the agency was willing to pay essentially dictated the market price for all customers. Hoover tried to set price levels that would guarantee farmers sufficient profits to encourage them to increase production. Commodities like sugar and grain required elaborate price-fixing mechanisms. The Food Administration's Sugar Equalization Board, for example, purchased literally the entire cane sugar crop from Cuba, Louisiana, and Hawaii as well beet sugar from the western states at whatever price it deemed necessary to keep the producers in business. It then sold sugar at an average or "equalized" price to all customers.

Despite Hoover's best efforts, prices for agricultural products continued to climb because output remained almost flat while demand rose daily. Prices had already jumped 50 percent between 1913 and early 1917, and they rose a similar percentage during the twenty months of American participation in the war. This unusual spurt of agrarian prosperity encouraged farmers to borrow and expand in anticipation of continuing high demand. Instead, prices for farm goods fell precipitously when the postwar boom sputtered out. Corn that had sold for $1.88 a bushel in August 1919 brought only forty-two cents a bushel by the end of 1921. The collapse was so dramatic, in fact, that most commodity prices rolled back not only below wartime levels but all the way to where they had stood in 1913. A general price break in the United States was partially responsible, but the disappearance of the European market compounded the farm crisis. Both the British and German governments called upon their farmers to strive for national self-sufficiency so that neither country could ever again be subjected to the blackmail of food embargoes or interruptions of overseas shipments.

The rapid decline in American agricultural commodity prices had devastating consequences. Farmers had traditionally relied on steadily increasing land values to compensate for poor crop years. But the wartime demand had artificially boosted land prices at the same time it was encouraging farmers to borrow to gain control of greater acreage. The 1920 price collapse wiped out their ability to make mortgage payments. Nearly half a million independent farmers lost their land and became tenants or abandoned farming altogether. Those who managed to hang on to their property continued to suffer. Land prices fell all through the 1920s, eliminating much farm equity. For the first time in history, the total amount of land under cultivation in the United States declined. Simultaneously, mechanization, improved seed and livestock, and wiser management boosted agricultural productivity 26 percent in the decade.

Beleaguered farmers experimented with individual and cooperative mechanisms hoping to improve their positions. California and Florida growers irrigated huge citrus groves and distributed their fruit from coast to coast through marketing cooperatives. Dairy farmers also joined cooperatives, the most prominent of which was the enormous Land O'Lakes Creameries which boasted attractive packaging, quality controls, and effective advertising. Some attempts to diversify were ill-advised. The substitution of wheat cultivation for cattle grazing on the Great Plains had particularly tragic results. Not only did the nation suffer from a constant over-supply of grain throughout the 1920s, but the plowing up of the root networks of natural prairie grasses freed the topsoil so it could blow away during the intense duststorms of the drought-ridden 1930s.

Many disheartened farmers looked to the federal government for salvation. A few arrangements were devised to help farmers get credit from banks otherwise reluctant to supply them with capital. In the mid-twenties, Congress also approved the McNary-Haugens Bill that would have federal officials sell surplus agricultural commodities abroad at the same time they "equalized" domestic prices. It was too radical a concept for a conservative Republican president, so Calvin Coolidge twice vetoed the proposal. The age-old malady continued to plague American farmers: they were simply too productive for their own good. Each farm family was bound to try to maximize its income by expanding its own production. The result in the 1920s was a debilitating agricultural depression in which low prices left farm operators and workers considerably worse off than their urban, industrial counterparts. Many farmers concluded that urban America cared very little if at all about their troubles. They were quite correct because the non-agricultural sectors were basking in a heady business boom in the 1920s.

THE PROSPERITY DECADE

Folksy Ohio Senator Warren G. Harding was anything but a great orator, but he did add the word "normalcy" to the political lexicon while running for president on the 1920 Republican ticket. When he called for the United States to return to normalcy, he was referring to conditions as they had existed around the turn of the century. In "the good old days," it seemed, businesses had consolidated and operated without encountering Progressive harassment or international interference. Harding's ideological bent was apparent in his cabinet choices. He appointed aluminum magnate Andrew Mellon, one of the wealthiest men in the United States, to head the Treasury Department and Herbert Hoover, an advocate of associationism among producers, to superintend the Commerce Department. Both men retained their posts after Harding's sudden death in 1923 just before scandals involving his friends and associates became public. Sober, taciturn Vice President Calvin Coolidge took over as the very model of public and private rectitude. Coolidge defined his mission as reducing government intrusion into individual and entrepreneurial activities. The prosperity that so many Americans enjoyed during his administration seemed ample justification for Coolidge's laissez-faire attitudes.

Several artifacts of Progressivism prevented a complete retreat from regulation. The Federal Trade Commission, for example, had barely been established when the war intervened. When it was finally ready to investigate allegations of restraint of trade and monopoly practices, conservative Republican presidents were busy replacing key Progressive members of the commission. A conservative majority had developed by 1925, so the FTC slackened its efforts to monitor existing or potential monopolistic behavior. Similar personnel changes stripped other agencies of their Progressive orientation and regulatory zeal.

The Commerce Department meanwhile emerged as a most active federal agency. Herbert Hoover had already applied his superb administrative skills to the Belgian Relief program and the Food Administration. Now he intervened personally in all sorts of areas including foreign relations and monetary and fiscal policy. An advocate of trade associations, he encouraged manufacturers and distributers to cooperate voluntarily in establishing fair prices and trade practices for all. Such actions could lessen the costs of competition without raising the likelihood of antitrust suits. Cooperation among producers also helped Hoover continue the healthy wartime trend toward the standardization of many products. By developing a common threading standard for light bulbs, for example, the Commerce Department allowed customers to purchase a bulb from any manufacturer to fit into their lamp sockets. Standardization aided producers as well because it eliminated duplication and encouraged streamlined production. Business leaders therefore applauded the commerce secretary's proposals and cooperated with them as long as they appeared beneficial.

Standardization was only one technique that made production and marketing more efficient in the Prosperity Decade. The businesses that had geared up for war production often had to make do with fewer workers. To cope with this labor shortage, many relied on new or modified machinery to perform many tasks. Factory owners who installed such equipment discovered that it could pay for itself by increasing the speed and reliability of their operations. Industrial automation continued to spread after 1918 in part because companies had ample investment funds available from their war profits. Another motivating factor was the decline in the number of cheap unskilled workers available in the United States once immigration restrictions had been imposed.

Combining many smaller units of production into larger ones capable of greater economies of scale also boosted industrial productivity. Consolidation and reorganization therefore ran rampant, especially since the business community now faced only the mildest of governmental and legal constraints. Financiers and industrialists used holding companies as the major tools in their binge of business concentration. Some of the most efficient combinations were the fully integrated industrial operations. Single-sector industrial combines were quite common in the 1920s, and, by avoiding middleman charges at each step, these vertically integrated companies could be quite competitive. On the other hand, some of the largest and most influential organizations were non-operating holding companies like United States Steel. These companies existed primarily to hold controlling blocks of shares in companies that actually produced goods or provided services. A few corporations were hybrids, running some operations directly out of their central headquarters at the same time they managed other plants and subsidiaries less directly through an internal holding company structure.

Powerful combines that wielded enormous power over the market and resources naturally provoked some criticism, but the 1920 Supreme Court ruling in the long-running U. S. Steel antitrust case reassured those planning more consolidation. Even though the monster holding company controlled well over half of all of the steel production in the United States, the justices cited their rule of reason to allow it to continue functioning without alteration. Clearly a combine would have to be remarkably ruthless and unprincipled to earn judicial censure.

Businesses could operate even more freely outside the country. The Webb-Pomerene Act of 1918 specifically permitted American corporations in competition with one another inside the United States to join forces in foreign operations. If business leaders from other countries had established cartels to control particular sectors of international commerce, American companies could either join these or create competing international combines. Cartels were especially prevalent in controlling the distribution of and, consequently, maintaining elevated prices for raw materials found in only a limited number of locations. Two American sulphur companies combined forces with the major external supplier, an Italian firm, to dominate the world's supply of this basic chemical. They jointly worked out global marketing agreements that divided the world into exclusive sales areas for each participant.

The round of business consolidation had thoroughly reshaped large-scale American enterprise by 1929. At that point, half of all the corporate assets in the United States belonged to the country's two hundred largest business corporations. Most of them were either wholly or partially holding company operations. Their convoluted structures allowed managers to issue bewildering varieties of stock, to loot subsidiaries of assets, to conceal from stockholders and the general public the actual financial condition of their properties, and to stage secret assaults on rivals. Simultaneously, the prosperity of the late 1920s had lulled investors into bidding up the prices of stocks without any knowledge of their real worth. Speculators often cared very little about the soundness of the companies offering shares for sale anyway; they acted chiefly in response to arbitrarily declared dividends and daily price variations on the stock tickers.

Individuals equipped with the skills or insider knowledge necessary to comprehend what was really going on earned a great deal of popular respect in the Prosperity Decade. Their swashbuckling speculations were simultaneously admired, imitated, and feared. One such figure was Sam Insull whose personal fortune was rumored at one point to exceed $170 million. The public also stood in awe of Oris P. and Mantis J. Van Sweringen. These brothers started out modestly enough in the real estate business in Chicago before the war. Afterwards, they began taking advantage of the fact that many small railroads were in deep financial trouble. The Van Swearingens bought controlling interests in them at bargain prices and folded them into more efficient consolidated systems. The Vaness Corporation served as the capstone of their holding company pyramid which, like Insull's combine, had several layers. Just before the 1929 stock market crash, the Van Sweringens were reputed to be worth more than $120 million and to control a railroad empire with $3 billion in assets.

Insull and the Van Sweringens focused their attention on particular sectors of the economy, but other tycoons built incredible fortunes speculating across the board. Harry F. Sinclair had started out in oil, but he increased his vast fortune substantially through gambles on the stock exchange. The General Motors Corporation bought the seven Fisher brothers' automobile body manufacturing concern

SAM INSULL

The dubious distinction of suffering the most colossal financial collapse in American history fell to an English immigrant named Sam Insull. He began his business career as a clerk for a firm of auctioneers in London. The British representative of Thomas A. Edison then hired him as a secretary and was so impressed that he arranged for Insull to go to America to work for the boss.

Although he was just twenty-two in 1881 when he took over as Edison's private secretary, Insull soon became the inventor's advisor and business manager. When Edison sent him to Schenectedy, New York, to manage a struggling generating plant, Insull turned it into a profitable, efficient operation. He then moved to Chicago in 1892 to deal with another ailing firm, Chicago Edison. He convinced the owners of its rival, Commonwealth Electric Company, to accept his management as well, and he combined the two into Commonwealth Edison in 1907. As its president, Insull obtained a forty-year exclusive franchise to supply the city of Chicago with electric power. Meanwhile, he imported an English compound steam turbine system that was so efficient and powerful it revolutionized electric power generation throughout the United States.

Had Insull stopped at that point, he would probably be recognized as a modestly successful entrepreneur. Instead, he began pulling together smaller utility companies and facilities with the help of a holding company called Middle Western Utilities. Although it eventually served nearly two million customers in thirty-nine states, it lacked financial stability. Infected by the free and easy attitudes of the 1920s, Insull created several other holding companies and piled them on top of each other in so confusing and haphazard a manner that no one including Insull could manage the complex. And yet his empire seemed inordinately profitable. The stock price for Insull Utilities Investments rose from $30 a share to $147 in just eight months in 1929.

After the stock market crash in that year, however, it became clear that Insull had been paying dividends on existing stocks with the money he got from sales of new shares. That strategy could only work in an expanding bull market, hardly the circumstance that prevailed in the early thirties. He did manage to stave off the inevitable reckoning for two full years before his holdings lapsed into receivership. As much as $750 million in investment funds had simply disappeared. And so, it turned out, had Insull. He fled to Europe and dodged extradition for two years before being arrested in Istanbul and turned over to American authorities. Although he escaped conviction for mail fraud and embezzlement, he was inundated with wave after wave of civil suits until his death in 1938. No other individual did more to discredit the business leadership in the United States than Sam Insull.

for a huge sum that the brothers then used to pull off one grand speculation after another on Wall Street. At the same time, the man who had earlier bought them out joined them in this high risk business. General Motors founder William C. Durant lost control of his corporation in 1920 and had to spend the subsequent years orchestrating one spectacular financial coup after another that built his personal fortune up to an estimated $100 million by the end of the decade. This fabulous wealth in securities and other paper investments probably meant less to Durant than the success of the great corporation he had fathered. General Motors was, in fact, an ideal example of the elaborately organized, efficiently managed, consumer-oriented corporations of the Prosperity Decade.

THE EVOLUTION OF GENERAL MOTORS: DURANT AND SLOAN

General Motors has ranked as the largest industrial corporation in the United States for much of the twentieth century. Two very different personalities created and perfected this diversified business combine. William C. Durant initiated the process just after the turn of the century when he began acquiring many of the elements of the future automaking giant. While his bold style benefited the corporation during good years, he lacked the managerial talent to make it function effectively in the long run. In 1920 he lost control of the combine to Pierre du Pont who then placed sober, intellectual Alfred P. Sloan in charge. Sloan restructured and redirected the monumental enterprise and, in the process, established management and marketing techniques that would be widely copied by all sorts of industries and businesses, many with no relationship to automaking.

Durant's acquisitiveness had drawn together many of the properties that made up General Motors. He had previously demonstrated his entrepreneurial genius by creating the largest cart-making establishment in the United States. To supply and support his main assembly plant in Flint, Michigan, Durant bought controlling interests in a number of subsidiary manufacturing concerns and established a nationwide network of dealers. Convinced that automobiles would eventually make his products obsolete, he set out to build a similar integrated combine to produce cars. He began by buying the Buick Motor Co. which had sold a few cars before running into financial difficulties. Durant also tied in some component manufacturing plants and used their parts in his car assembly lines. In 1908 more Buicks were sold than any other American model.

At that point, of course, Henry Ford sprinted ahead by introducing his inexpensive Model T and using his profits to build huge new production facilities. Durant remained committed to creating a competing automaking empire through acquisition. He managed to pursue this objective with relatively little cash. Having incorporated General Motors as a holding company in New Jersey, he exchanged its stock for shares in the operating concerns he wished to control. This transfer enabled him to acquire the Cadillac and Oldsmobile companies along with literally dozens of parts and component firms. He even convinced Albert Champion, the

French sparkplug manufacturing genius, to work for him, turning out the AC sparkplug line incorporated as original equipment in all General Motors vehicles.

Despite Durant's brilliance at arranging takeovers, he failed to anticipate damaging marketing and economic trends. A temporary slump in auto purchases in 1910 threatened to bankrupt his whole operation. To obtain vital capital for GM, Durant agreed to surrender his voting rights in the holding company to a management trust consisting of a group of conservative bankers. General Motors temporarily operated without the leadership of its founder, and Durant threw his backing behind automaker Louis Chevrolet, a former member of the Buick racing team. The Chevrolet Company sold sporty, modestly priced cars that generated enough profit for Durant to buy General Motors shares on the sly. GM stock remained relatively cheap because the trustees chose not to declare dividends on it despite the company's profitability. When the voting trust expired in 1915, Durant offered to trade five shares of Chevrolet for every one of General Motors. He found enough takers to give him the GM shares he needed to reclaim control of his original company.

At that point, the smaller Chevrolet firm technically controlled the much larger General Motors holding company. To rectify that anomaly, Durant dissolved the New Jersey holding company and established a Delaware-based General Motors Corporation. This new organization was designed to be an operating as opposed to a strictly holding company, and many of the elements within it were transformed into semi-autonomous divisions. Most of these divisions continued func-

William C. Durant. (Courtey of General Motors Corporation)

tioning pretty much as they had when they were independent entities, however, since the parent company exerted little central guidance or regulation. The combine prospered anyway, allowing Durant to absorb a farm tractor firm and a refrigerator manufacturing plant when the war seemed likely to slow auto sales. In addition to diversifying the corporation's output and expanding its market reach, GM's Frigidaire line helped transform the nature of the consumer food industry.

At the end of the war, the du Ponts were looking for a promising investment opportunity for their war profits. They eventually sank millions of dollars into GM and gained about one-fourth of the corporation's ownership and considerable influence over its operations. Although Pierre du Pont placed his own financial expert, John J. Raskob, in charge of GM's finances, Raskob gave Durant a free hand in pursuing further acquisitions. The flamboyant entrepreneur continued expanding his corporation's holdings without developing any rational internal structure for them. He had obtained pledges of nearly $100 million from external sources to finance his next buying spree when the postwar recession struck. That crisis dealt Durant such serious personal reverses that he had to give up control of General Motors to its leading stockholder, Pierre du Pont. The company then used the funds Durant had amassed to weather the recession rather than to expand. Durant was permanently excluded from the corporation's leadership. His chief drawback as a corporation chief had been his failure to forge the many elements he had collected into a resilient industrial concern.

Fortunately the firm already had on its staff an ideal manager in Alfred P. Sloan, a man who presented a sharp contrast to the gregarious, outgoing Durant. Sloan had grown up in comfortable circumstances in New York and earned an engineering degree from the Massachusetts Institute of Technology. When he graduated in 1895, the country lay in the depths of depression and jobs even for highly trained engineers were scarce. He ended up working at the small New Jersey plant that inventor John Wesley Hyatt had built to manufacture his patented roller bearings. The company remained shaky until Sloan's father invested $5000 in it, a move that also placed his son in command. A stickler for quality control and precision workmanship, Sloan turned the company into the country's leading supplier of bearings to the auto industry. It inevitably attracted Durant's attention as a desirable acquisition for GM. In 1916 Sloan sold the company to Durant for $13.5 million, mostly in General Motors stock, and a vice presidency in the larger corporation. For four years he headed a subsidiary holding company within GM called United Motors which controlled several accessory producers.

His own operations ran efficiently and generated profits, but Sloan recognized that serious management problems existed up the line. He drew up a reorganization scheme and showed it to a disinterested Durant just before the great entrepreneur had to step down in 1920. When Pierre du Pont took over as president, he encouraged Sloan to implement his plan. Although it has undergone innumerable revisions, Sloan's basic formulation has guided the corporation ever since. His plan allowed division executives considerable autonomy in the management of their manufacturing operations. An elaborate central administrative organization meanwhile handled capitalization, marketing, planning, procurement, and many

Alfred P. Sloan, Jr. (Courtesy of General Motors Corporation)

other functions for the entire corporation. A core staff of experts in fields like law and finance examined and monitored the performance of the operating divisions and made suggestions beneficial to the corporation as a whole. An executive committee made up of central administrators met frequently to develop policies and approve proposals for the various operating units.

Sloan's chief objective was to make the whole concern profitable, an obvious goal but one Durant had signally failed to accomplish. Sloan assigned the General Office at GM responsibility for issuing directives such as those requiring divisional inventories to be streamlined and division heads to buy internally whenever possible. These policies significantly reduced overhead costs. He had detailed marketing surveys from the corporation's dealers all over the country collected in the General Office as well where they could be analyzed to produce realistic and rational production and marketing plans. If demand appeared to be slumping for particular product lines, manufacture of them could be slowed or closed down and the plants and workers reassigned to different activities. No such planning could anticipate every contingency, but Sloan's system brought his corporation much closer than any other major firm to manufacturing and delivering just as many units to its dealers as they could reasonably expect to sell. The marketing staff's sophisticated surveys and directives kept General Motors making profits and declaring dividends even in the devastating depression of the 1930s. Sloan had thus created a successful prototype of a modern industrial supercorporation. Literally hundreds of other diversified business combinations copied or adapted the management pattern he pioneered.

But Sloan was only half done. When he took over from du Pont as president of the corporation in 1923, he was ideally situated to implement a marketing strategy that would establish General Motors as the auto industry's unassailable leader.

SLOAN'S ORGANIZING STRATEGY FOR GM

In his autobiography, Sloan described his original proposals for organizing General Motors. Here he comments on some of the objectives he outlined for Pierre du Pont in 1920.

1. To definitely determine the functioning of the various divisions consti-
   tuting the Corporation's activities, not only in relation to one another, but
   in relation to the central organization.

   (That was a big chew, but it is correct. If you can describe the functions
   of the parts and the whole, you have laid out a complete working
   organization, for by implication the apportionment of responsibility for
   decisions at various levels is contained in the description.)

2. To determine the status of the central organization and to co-ordinate the
   operation of that central organization with the Corporation as a whole to
   the end that it will perform its necessary and logical place.

   (That is a restatement of the first point, but in reverse—that is looking
   from the top down.)

3. To centralize the control of all the executive functions of the Corporation
   in the President as its chief executive officer.

   (Decentralization or not, an industrial corporation is not the mildest form
   of organization in society. I never minimized the administrative power of
   the chief executive officer in principle when I occupied that position. I
   simply exercised that power with discretion; I got better results by selling
   my ideas than by telling people what to do. Yet the power to act must be
   located in the chief executive officer.)

(Alfred P. Sloan, Jr., *My Years With General Motors* [Garden City, NY: Doubleday, 1964], pp. 53-54.)

Henry Ford had operated on the premise that there was an almost infinite supply of customers for standard automobiles. To reach them, all an automaker had to do was continually lower his prices. By the mid-1920s, however, buyers interested solely in cheap transportation could find it on the used car market. A customer looking for a new automobile wanted just that: a car distinctly different from what he currently owned or could pick up second hand. Automobiles had become status symbols. Buyers were willing to pay larger amounts for cars that matched their images of themselves and their social positions.

General Motors had long been offering different models at various prices, but many of them were competing for customers with cars built in other GM divisions. Only the Cadillac and Buick Divisions had made money in 1920, and the giant corporation produced no car that seriously challenged the Model T. Sloan decided, therefore, to "bracket" the market by selling cars in every price range. Luxury Cadillacs topped the GM line, costing a minimum of $3000 dollars in 1926, and Buick aimed its sales pitch at the middle class with prices ranging from $1125 to $2000. Below them in descending price order were Oaklands, Oldsmobiles, Pontiacs, and, finally, Chevrolets with base prices at $525. The least expensive new Model T cost just half that, but many new car buyers were willing to pay a little more for a car with a few refinements.

Having defined the starting point for his marketing strategy, Sloan then moved to make his own cars obsolete as quickly as possible. Most customers were replacing older cars at that point, so he catered to their desire for the new and different by advertising changes in his models each year. Each General Motors division introduced a completely redesigned car every three years, with annual "facelifts" in between to make the same vehicle manufactured the year before appear attractive enough to encourage buyers to trade up. This policy of deliberately creating largely irrelevant product differentiation not only with respect to the competitors but also to one's own previous output worked very well for GM during the prosperity of the late twenties. Hundreds of thousands of customers cashed their savings accounts or took advantage of the General Motors Acceptance Corporation's attractive installment payment terms to buy the latest models.

Sloan's strategy succeeded so well, in fact, that it threatened to destroy Henry Ford. He was producing only two basic cars: a $4000 Lincoln and the Model T he had designed in 1908. Ford decided to shut down his plants for many months so he could retool to produce Model A Fords—well-designed, four-cylinder cars. Chevrolet retaliated by offering a six-cylinder engine, so Ford brought out his famous V-8 engine in 1932.

The third major American automaker, the Chrysler Motor Co., adopted Sloan's marketing strategy much more quickly. In the early days, Walter P. Chrysler had produced Buicks at GM so successfully that Durant had placed him in charge of all production. Chrysler quit in 1919 to build an automaking empire of his own. He began by transforming the failing firm that manufactured Maxwell cars into a successful company he renamed after himself. This organization engulfed the Dodge Brothers' operation in 1928 and introduced its Plymouth line in the following year. With Plymouths at the bottom, Dodges in the middle, and Chryslers on top, the company offered a worthy if imitative product line to compete with General Motors.

While some of this competition in the auto industry was quite beneficial, enormous amounts of production and design energy as well as millions of consumer dollars were frittered away on meaningless distinctions between today's cars and yesterday's perfectly adequate machines. Even so, the General Motors marketing strategy would eventually shape not only the auto industry but the manufacture and distribution of consumer goods of all types. Household appliances large and small, furniture, carpeting, and hundreds of other products are constantly redesigned or repackaged and then advertised as new or revolutionary. Appliance manufacturers bracket their markets by placing identical works inside a variety of housings with "special" features or trim to justify charging different prices. Bracketing the market with varying priced goods and deliberately designed or "built-in" obsolescence has become the standard way of influencing consumer behavior.

THE MASS CONSUMPTION SOCIETY

One of Durant's major assets when he switched to the automobile business was the extensive dealer network that sold his carts. He converted existing dealers and recruited hundreds more to handle GM products. Other automakers also franchised dealers all over the country to distribute and service their cars. In one sense, these dealers were actually the manufacturers' primary customers, buying not only the automobiles but the thousands of replacement parts needed to maintain them. Automakers therefore directed much of their marketing energy toward dealers, holding conventions, participating in auto shows, and offering training programs. They also backed their distributors with elaborate national advertising campaigns aimed at the ultimate buying public.

The dealers supplying standardized products to local customers all over the United States bore many similarities to the retail store chains that experienced enormous growth in the 1920s. As noted earlier, F. W. Woolworth and J. C. Penney had started their enterprises well before the war, but the twenties provided fertile ground for expansion in the number and types of store chains. Some 160,000 stores accounting for about 30 percent of all retail outlets operated as elements in 7000 chains in 1929. The A & P grocery store chain was the most extensive with 15,700 locations in 1930. Grocery, shoe, furniture, drug, and variety stores were the most common, but department stores as well as specialized mercantile operations also operated as chains. As private automobile ownership increased customer mobility, the chain stores threatened to put the major mail-order houses out of business. Sears, Roebuck & Co. fought back by opening its first retail outlet in Chicago in 1926, and Montgomery Ward did the same in the following year. In just four years, Sears added 337 more links to its retail chain, and Wards seriously overextended itself by establishing nearly twice as many outlets. California banking mogul A. P. Gianini extended the chain concept into finance with his Bank of America organization that was operating 453 branches sprinkled throughout the Golden State by 1929.

Chain stores had many advantages over independent retailers. In some instances they controlled suppliers by placing huge bulk orders, although a few wholesalers refused to give discounts to the chains, preferring to maintain good relations with their many independent customers. Even without a break on wholesale prices, the chains could cut costs by developing efficient distribution networks to supply their outlets and by maintaining centralized inventories. On the other hand, customers sometimes found the chain stores less friendly than locally owned shops. A & P, for example, opened "economy" grocery stores that operated on a strictly "cash and carry" basis. They could mark their prices down because they did not have to maintain the equipment necessary to provide home delivery or bear the costs of carrying credit accounts for their customers.

A cash-only policy worked well enough in the grocery business, but credit was essential in the selling of durable goods. The Singer Co. had been advertising installment contracts for its sewing machines as early as the 1850s, and time-payment plans had been helping customers purchase appliances and automobiles for some time. The General Motors Acceptance Company, a William Durant innovation organized in 1919, extended this concept to the corporate level. Individuals no longer had to arrange personal bank loans; they could place down payments on automobiles and then pay the balance over time to the G.M.A.C. Many department stores and neighborhood shops maintained revolving credit accounts for their customers.

Long-term mortgages had traditionally financed home buying and other real estate transactions. The construction industry boomed after the war and continued thriving into the mid-twenties. Some of its activity involved renovating downtown districts with new or remodeled office and commercial buildings; the rest of the industry's energy poured into building of houses of all types. As urban populations expanded, residential areas spread out around cities and towns all across the country. Speculation in suburban properties netted many a real estate investor handsome profits.

Land speculation, that hardy perennial of American enterprise, was particularly prevalent in warmer climates. As tourism and leisure activities became accessible to large numbers of increasingly prosperous Americans, they jumped into their Model T's and flocked to the coasts. Florida was particularly attractive to those seeking an escape from the cold winters and congestion of the Northeast. Property owners in the Sunshine State stood to make huge profits whether they developed their land or sold it to others. With coastal lots bringing as much as $25,000, speculators from all parts of the country rushed to buy Florida real estate. Of course most of these prospective land barons never saw the land they purchased, and many of the lots platted and sold were twenty or thirty miles from the ocean or in swampy, uninhabitable locations. As with the previous land speculation crazes in the United States, the number of actual residents never matched the optimistic expectations of the traders. The enthusiasm and capital flowing into the state peaked in late 1925. The Florida "land bubble" deflated completely in the following year, ruining thousands of overextended speculators large and small and destroying the prosperity of the entire state.

Many of these plungers had fallen victim to exaggerated advertising claims, a common feature of the Roaring Twenties. To reach and influence the national market, producers devoted more of their budgets to advertising than ever before. Expenditures on advertising during the decade more than doubled, reaching a total of $3.4 billion in 1929. Brand name identification was the chief method advertisers used to differentiate their wares from the similar or identical products of their competitors. Advertising agencies developed coordinated campaigns for their clients using color and rhetoric in innovative ways. Newspapers, magazines, billboards, and flyers assaulted the eyes of potential buyers with their insistent sales pitches. By the end of the decade, radios were assailing consumers' ears as well. The personalities who broadcast advertising jingles often became more widely known than anyone else connected with the radio industry.

Radio grew from a specialists' hobby to a commercial success almost overnight. Pioneers like Guliermo Marconi of Italy and American Lee De Forest had developed primitive wireless transmission and receiving equipment before the war. The largely British-owned American Marconi Company dominated the United States market at that point. When this country entered the conflict, however, the Navy Department commandeered all the major radio installations for ship-to-shore and ship-to-ship transmissions. For some time after the armistice, the major focus remained on interoceanic communication rather than on public broadcasting.

Owen D. Young, a vice president of the General Electric Company, ushered in a new era when he superintended the formation of the Radio Corporation of America. RCA had the support of President Wilson and others who were interested in freeing radio communication in the United States from foreign control. Young's company was well placed to assume the lead since GE had developed the Alexanderson alternator, an advanced piece of hardware essential to broadcasting. RCA took over the American Marconi operations and also entered into cross-licensing agreements with Westinghouse, A T & T, and other American patent-holders so it could operate freely in the new medium. These other companies thereby became major shareholders in the fledgling radio monopoly.

The entrepreneurial genius behind RCA was David Sarnoff, a Russian emigre with a forceful personality and a remarkable understanding of both the equipment and the commercial potential for radio. He became general manager of RCA while still in his early thirties and quickly moved up to complete control, a position he would hold for decades. Sarnoff's conception of a "radio music box" to bring live and varied entertainment into individual homes did not initially interest Young and other company executives. Consequently, it was a Westinghouse engineer named Frank Conrad who first broadcast on a commercial basis from station KDKA in Pittsburgh, reporting presidential election returns in November 1920. His audience consisted of tinkerers who had built their own receivers out of kits or component parts. Not to be outdone, Sarnoff erected an antenna in New Jersey in the following year and drew a much larger group of listeners with a blow-by-blow account of a heavyweight boxing championship fight. By 1922 A T & T had built WEAF, a very powerful transmitting station in New York City. The competition grew so quickly that the Commerce Department had issued licenses and assigned frequencies to 500 stations by 1929. RCA, Zenith, Philco, and other companies manufactured receiving sets to sell to the general public. The early equipment could be quite expensive: while a primitive crystal set might sell for $25, customers could chose from a variety of more costly instruments including an eight-tube model priced above $400. More than 7.5 million sets had been sold by the end of the decade.

RCA remained the most active member of the new industry, setting up broadcasting stations all over the country. Sarnoff personally organized the first network by linking several stations together with telephone lines so they could broadcast programs simultaneously. RCA's National Broadcasting Company began service in 1926 and encountered little serious rivalry until William Paley took control of the fledgling Columbia Broadcasting System in 1928. Both networks produced a mix of programming including news, sports, music, and drama. The audience for these networks grew rapidly and, in conjunction with the brisk sales of receivers, made radio one of the glamour industries of the 1920s. For most of the decade, therefore, the share prices of companies involved with radio rose even faster than the amazing performance of stocks in general.

THE GREAT BULL MARKET

Never before or since have American business leaders enjoyed as favorable reputations as they did in the 1920s. A go-getter attitude infused all aspects of American life. Under President Calvin Coolidge and his Republican successor, Herbert Hoover, the federal government was decidedly pro-business. A few novelists and critics found American society sterile, but many other writers and journalists praised the free enterprise system and the entrepreneurs who exploited it to become wealthy. Widespread confidence in the strength of the consumer-oriented industrial economy encouraged Americans to share in its prosperity through the mechanism of the stock exchange.

There, the price of a particular stock might rise or fall on any given day, but the trend was ever upward. Investors and most speculators tend to be optimistic anyway, but faith in the future reached unprecedented heights as the Roaring Twenties drew to a close. People seemed convinced that the value of common and preferred stocks could continue escalating forever. Those who anticipate such an upward movement are known as bulls, and America was definitely bullish in the Prosperity Decade.

Just when the Great Bull Market began is a matter of debate. Some see its roots as far back as 1915 when war orders ignited a period of dramatic growth in American industry. The postwar recession and a minor downturn in 1924 did, of course, exercise some restraint on all but the most enthusiastic plungers. The bulls had definitely taken charge by 1927 when, despite several signs of weakness in the economy, stock prices began a sustained climb. Few seemed to notice or care when the paper value of the outstanding stock certificates a particular company had issued exceeded its total tangible assets. The bull market was self-stimulating, and it often seemed to operate on a plane completely divorced from reality.

Although an amazing diversity of people took part, stock speculation in the 1920s was not as common as one might suppose. Out of the United States population of 120 million, only about three million names appeared on the lists of all of the shareholders in the United States and many of those were duplicates or long-term investors rather than active traders. Around 600,000 Americans maintained margin accounts, the most popular type for speculators. Millions more poured over the daily stock listings either because of their fascination with this exciting, high-stakes financial game or in anticipation of the moment when they would have enough money to invest themselves. Brokerage houses encouraged this interest by opening offices throughout the United States to allow investors to place their orders personally and obtain advice on likely winners. Telephones allowed regional brokers to communicate their buy and sell orders to New York while telegraphic tickers supplied instantaneous stock quotations to the hinterlands.

The brokerage houses also encouraged investment by extending credit to their customers. Brokers' loans had totaled $4.4 billion at the end of 1927, and they rose to a peak of $8.5 billion in October 1929. A prospective investor with $100 might be able negotiate a loan for as much as $900 from his broker in order to buy $1000 worth of stock. This process is called buying on a margin, with the margin in this case being 10 percent. Margin loans were considered safe investments because the stock certificates themselves provided the collateral to back them.

A margin purchase was extraordinarily attractive when stock prices rose. Suppose that in the above example the stock's market value doubled—a quite common phenomenon in the late 1920s. The speculator could then sell his shares for $2000, pay back the broker's $900 plus interest, and still take home $1000, or a 1000 percent return on his initial $100. This fortunate speculator was benefiting from "leveraging," the broker's loan helping to leverage his own small investment into a massive return. Those who believed the bull market would persist ignored the fact that a decline in market prices would place the hapless investor on the short end of the lever. Indeed, a relatively minor drop of just 10 percent in the share price would eliminate his entire initial nest egg. If such a decline appeared likely and the customer could not supply more margin, the broker had to sell out to recover the principle of his loan. As long as the market was rising, however, leveraging was attractive not only to small-time speculators but to financiers and brokers who could use it to their own advantage.

By the middle of the decade, leveraging was being exploited by investment trusts as well as individuals. Investment trusts had existed for decades to spread the risks of investment and obtain the advantages of large-scale purchases. A typical trust would incorporate and then sell bonds or stock to investors. Using the capital thus generated, it could buy blocks of stock in a diversified group of firms. The profits from owning and selling these securities could be distributed as dividends to the holders of the trust's own shares.

The United States & Foreign Securities Co., formed in 1924, represented a further stage of development: the leveraged investment trust. The company financed its operations by selling both stocks and bonds, the latter carrying a fixed interest. When the company's profits rose, it distributed supplemental dividends only to the holders of its stocks. Even a one-to-one ratio of stocks to bonds produced a leveraged effect that gave stockholders the equivalent of twice their usual dividend. Just like industrial or banking corporations, investment trusts sold their stocks on the exchanges where, because of their high dividends, they were very popular with speculators. Sometimes one leveraged company bought the shares of other investment trusts and thus multiplied the leveraging effect. Like the margin buyers, everyone came out a winner as long as stock prices continued to climb. Optimism ran so high that 265 new investment trusts were established in 1929 alone.

With individuals pouring their savings into the market and investment trusts and other large purchasers constantly trading up, the stock market absorbed much of the nation's money supply and a good deal of its credit. Interest rates remained quite reasonable at first, ranging around 5 percent, due partly to the New York Federal Reserve Bank's low discount rate designed to encourage overseas investment. Even when the bank's president, Benjamin Strong, tardily decided to raise his rate and sell federal bonds on the open market to make money scarcer, credit continued to flow to Wall Street. Because leveraging might bring them even greater returns, individual speculators were willing to pay 10 or even 20 percent interest on the money they borrowed to invest. These rates were so attractive that some industrial corporations turned their surplus capital over to speculators. After all, they could earn larger returns on those loans than on bonds drawing a fixed 5 percent interest or even on capital investments that might eventually pay a 10 percent dividend. The continuing influx of capital into the stock market virtually guaranteed that share prices would continue rising and that bulls would continue stampeding to buy.

Some Wall Street operators did even better by manipulating information. Popular journalists and exchange "experts" had great influence over speculators. They could make predictions that a particular stock would rise. When speculators acting on this tip rushed out to buy, the price inevitably went up, just as the pundits had predicted. Insider deals were also common. A group would agree to purchase low-priced stocks and then spread rumors about actual or fanciful takeover bids or corporate developments. Unwary outsiders would then bid up the prices, allowing the insiders to sell their holdings at huge profits. Virtually any type of price-inflating scheme could be successful as long as the winners in the stock speculation game greatly outnumbered the losers. And there were legions of winners—at least on paper—in 1928 and early 1929. Very few realized that their wealth could disappear with sickening speed.

THE CRASH

Plenty of indicators in the late 1920s suggested that the American economy was far from robust, but the sustained rise of stock prices, the most widely consulted barometer of prosperity, masked the country's underlying economic weaknesses. Why should the people be concerned as long as money kept pouring into Wall Street and creating speculative fortunes? Some might have been disturbed that the prices of many corporations' shares were out of line with the value of their assets. On the other hand, stock prices were hardly exaggerated in comparison with corporate earnings which continued to accelerate right through 1929. Even those who followed the relatively conservative investment strategy of comparing outstanding stock value to earnings could find good buys among the companies listed on the Big Board in New York.

By September 1929 the flow of money from outside sources had begun to slow. One cause was the autumnal stringency, an annual event associated with the shipping of large quantities of agricultural commodities to market. In those days, most farmers operated on either a cash or short-term credit basis, so they wanted payment for their produce immediately after it had been harvested. The rural demand for cash diverted it from Wall Street and thereby reduced the amount available to feed the insistent hunger for more investment funds. The bull market could only sustain itself as long as more money was constantly becoming available for investment; any blockage or restriction of that flow would be noticed immediately.

The 1929 autumnal stringency seemed even more significant because its effects were combined with a much more pervasive slowing of the pace of investment. The speculators' reckless splurge in recent months had quite literally tapped every available source of funds. While the United States as a whole did not run out of money, the surplus available for stock investment had essentially been exhausted. As soon as the indexes stopped rising, sell orders flooded the exchanges. Speculators wanted to cash in at the top of the price arc rather than wait a month, a day−or even an hour−and get less when the peak had passed.

Market yardsticks illustrated this leveling-off phenomenon. The New York Times index basically stopped climbing in August and continued to perform disappointingly in September. Brief panics rippled through the investment community, but no serious break occurred until early in the following month. On October 3, many brokers had to call upon their clients to supply more margin because prices had dipped to the danger point where shares would have to be sold to protect the brokers' loans. To everyone's relief, the crisis passed quickly and relative calm prevailed for the next two weeks.

The anxiety level rose again in response to two more major price breaks, one on October 18 and the other four days later. Thousands of margin calls went out as investors confronted the harsh reality of reverse leverage. The market had suffered psychosomatic maladies even in the best of times, but they had nothing like the exaggerated impact of the dire rumors now making the rounds. Stories circulated that "bear pools" made up of big-time speculators were deliberately undermining the market to make killings when the prices really broke. Although there is no evidence of such organized manipulation on a large scale, canny speculators did rearrange their portfolios in anticipation of major declines.

The preliminary shocks seemed trivial indeed after a massive sell-out swept the stock exchanges on "Black Thursday," October 24. When the downward pressure destroyed several of the leveraged investment trusts, it sent their own stocks tumbling and dragged others down with them. Thousands of speculators who ran out of margin saw their stocks dumped on the market, to be sold at any price they could get by the brokers and bankers who were desperate to salvage at least some of their loan principal.

Financier Thomas Lamont convened representatives of the major banking concerns at his J. P. Morgan & Co. headquarters. Reporters and rumormongers

THE BUSINESS OUTLOOK IN 1929

In the 1920s, the New York Times Co. published The Annalist, *a weekly paper devoted to finance and business. Each week editor Benjamin Baker wrote a front-page column entitled "The Business Outlook." The following statements from the column's opening summaries reveal few premonitions of the shocking readjustment that was to occur in late October and, equally surprising, a rather mild reaction to that collapse in the succeeding weeks.*

July 19: Business for the rest of the third quarter seems likely to maintain itself at a high level, though with some recession from the extremely high pitch of the second quarter.

July 26: No indications of a business recession other than slight seasonal slackening appear in the week's records.

August 30: Conditions seem to make it safe for the country—and the Stock Exchange—to take a three-day holiday. Call money has been getting more costly, and the behavior of stocks is somewhat irregular; but there are as yet no large holes in the net.

September 6: With brokers' loans at a new high level, there are evidences of some strain in the money market ... with no broad relief definitely in sight.

September 20: The stock market has righted itself, thus eliminating for the time being one source of business uncertainty.

October 4: With brokers' loans rising to the enormous aggregate of over $8^{1}/_{2}$ billions, retiring President Hazekwood's remarks before the bankers' convention on present dangers constitutes the most important analysis yet made of the credit situation.

October 25: Yesterday's collapse of the stock market may be expected to react to some extent on the business outlook, both by lessening general over-confidence, and by opening the public and the business mind to the reasonable scope of realities.

November 1: Yesterday's broad rally in the stock market tends to limit somewhat the immediately unfavorable reactions of the crash upon business at large. The week's statistical signs, however, suggest a developing decline, perhaps not serious by itself, which is likely to be emphasized by market disillusionment.

November 8: A rather decided recession in business activity appears to be under way, indicated by a heavy decline in steel production.

December 6: The business recession continues moderately and without any spectacular features on the production side.

waited breathlessly to see what these giants of the financial world would do. A few minutes after the meeting broke up, Richard Whitney, a Morgan associate and a New York Stock Exchange official, strode on to the floor to place orders for large blocks of carefully selected shares in an effort to halt their decline. News of this institutional rescue mission spread quickly and helped ease the panic. Trading was far less hectic on Friday and Saturday.

It was only a pause. Selling began again on Monday, and the bottom dropped out completely on "Black Tuesday," October 29. No group of bankers could dam the tide of sell orders as panicked speculators tried to save themselves. As the price levels declined, they squeezed out more and more margin loans and leveraged

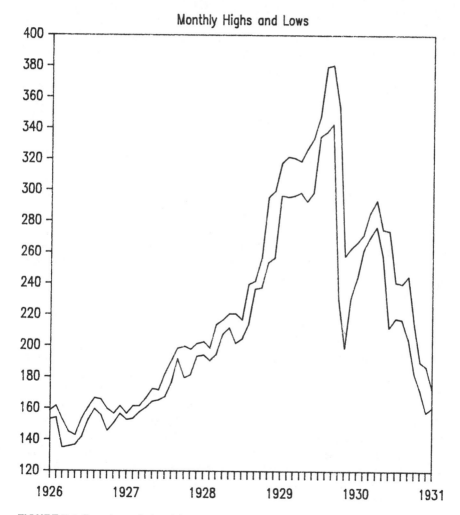

FIGURE 7-1 Dow Jones Industrials

investments, and they further increased the selling pressures. Thousands of investors lost everything and thousands more were driven to the wall. The orgy of selling swept the quoted prices of many shares well below their real worth. Wise speculators like Joseph P. Kennedy, father of the future president, recognized how undervalued some stocks had become and moved in to buy blocks at the low ebb. They collected immediate profits by selling them when prices rose to more sensible levels.

Although Black Tuesday's sharp decline was not repeated and many stock prices did recover somewhat in ensuing days, the general trend on the securities markets continued downward. By the end of the third week in November, the New York Times Index had settled at just about where it had been in July 1927, before the bulls had run wild. As Figure 7-1 illustrates, this level was around half of the index's high point in October. A modest rise in prices took place through the month of December signaling the end of the great crash.

The consequences of the dramatic death of the Great Bull Market have been debated ever since. Many contemporary Americans felt that it not only destroyed the prosperity of the 1920s but also caused the depression of the 1930s. Others view the crash as merely a symptom, though obviously an acute one, of the many weaknesses that were already undermining the economic health of the United States. Historian Robert Sobel goes a step further by insisting that the crash and the depression may have had little direct connection. The realignment of stock prices in late 1929, he argues, represented a readjustment that simply had to occur given the overvaluation of the stocks that the bull market had produced. The crash has been overinterpreted simply because it preceded the worst depression in American history. Had no depression developed—and the stock market crash certainly was not the only or perhaps even a major causative factor for it—Sobel claims that the 1929 readjustment would be seen in its proper perspective as just another in a series of cyclical financial panics, indistinguishable from the ones in, say, 1893 or 1907.

Sobel's analysis may be correct in strictly economic terms, but one should never underestimate the force of emotions in history. Most Americans who lived through the subsequent depression believed that the stock market crash had somehow triggered the devastating economic collapse. It certainly shattered the hopes for an increasingly prosperous nation in which any bold investor could pile up a huge personal fortune. In this as in so many other cases, popular opinion was more important than reality. Whatever historical facts may be marshaled to prove that the depression began in the early 1930s, most Americans considered the stock market crash to have been the first long step toward hard times. The mood of bleak disillusionment that infected the nation as it waded into the depths of the worst depression in its history had first appeared in the wild October days when the dream of permanent prosperity had been ripped up and tossed on the exchange floor like so many superseded sell orders.

READING SUGGESTIONS

Three recent general surveys of the twenties are: J. Joseph Huthmacher, *Trial By War and Depression : 1917-1941* (1973); William E. Leuchtenburg, *The Perils of Prosperity 1914-1932* (1958); and Ellis W. Hawley, *The Great War and the Search for a Modern Order* (1979). John D. Hicks, in *Republican Ascendency 1921-1933* (1960), relates political developments to economic and social occurrences. Economics is the focus of George Soule's *Prosperity Decade, From War to Depression: 1917-1929* (1947). The most entertaining review of the period is Frederick Lewis Allen's irreverent *Only Yesterday* (1931). Two other books that describe life in the Prosperity Decade are *America and the Jazz Age* (1968) by Fon W. Boardman, Jr.; and *Another Part of the Twenties* (1977) by Paul A. Carter.

Two readable narratives on how and why the United States decided to enter the Great War are: Walter Millis, *Road to War, America 1914-1917* (1935); and Ross M. Gregory, *The Origins of American Intervention in the First World War* (1971). A comprehensive look at the war's impact at home is John Maurice Clark's *The Costs of the World War to the American People* (1931). Details of the government mobilization and regulation during the conflict appear in Daniel R. Beaver's *Newton D. Baker and the American War Effort 1917-1919* (1966) and Robert D. Cuff's *The War Industries Board: Business-Government Relations During World War I* (1973). Jordan Schwarz sketches a portrait of Bernard Baruch in *The Speculator* (1981).

Schwarz's book spills over into the 1920s, as does Frederick Lewis Allen's *The Lords of Creation* (1935), a critique of leading American entrepreneurs in the early twentieth century. The complexities of the auto industry are detailed in *Giant Enterprise: Ford, General Motors, and the Automobile Industry* (1964) by Alfred D. Chandler, Jr., and *Pierre du Pont and the Making of the Modern Corporation* (1971) by Chandler and Stephen Salsbury. William Durant is the subject of Bernard Weisberger's *The Dream Maker* (1979) and Alfred P. Sloan tells his own story in *My Years with General Motors* (1965). The radio pioneers are profiled by Erik Barnow in *A Tower in Babel: A History of Broadcasting in the United States, Vol. 1 to 1933* (1966).

Many writers have tackled the question of why the stock market crashed in 1929. *In The Great Boom and Panic, 1921-1929* (1965), Robert T. Robertson places that event in the context of the entrepreneurial and speculative developments of the decade. Robert Sobel provides a similar view of *The Great Bull Market: Wall Street in the 1920s* (1968). In *Panic on Wall Street* (1968) Sobel emphasizes the similarities the 1929 fiasco exhibited to other historical financial panics. In *The Great Crash, 1929* (1961), John Kenneth Galbraith provides the reader with a convincing analysis of the crash and its relationship to the subsequent depression.

Chapter **8**

THROUGH DEPRESSION AND WAR 1929-1945

History relishes statements that make prominent people look foolish. Respected Yale economics professor Irving Fisher made one such memorable pronouncement in September 1929 when he confidently proclaimed that, "Stock prices have reached what looks like a permanently high plateau." As the country toppled into a devastating depression, President Herbert Hoover repeatedly insisted that the economy of the United States was basically sound. Both men honestly believed they were speaking the truth and, to be perfectly fair, most Americans held similar views at the time. Majority opinion, however, does not rule economic reality.

What these gentlemen and their countrymen failed to anticipate was the most severe economic crisis in American history. No one could avoid the impact of the "Great Depression" of the 1930s. Millions of careers were sidetracked, millions of plans permanently shelved, millions of dreams shattered. Banks and businesses, farms and factories by the thousands closed down. Yet only a decade later, American enterprise was experiencing a dramatic recovery. That prosperity carried a high price tag, though: participation in the most destructive war in world history. The Americans who survived the profound depression and fought the global conflict emerged with permanent scars.

American enterprise obviously suffered from many constraints in this decade and a half. Massive unemployment, huge inventories, deflated farm prices, and other factors discouraged the people at the beginning of the period. Although many considered these forces immune to human manipulation, the federal government under the leadership of President Franklin Delano Roosevelt proposed and implemented a broad range of experimental initiatives to relieve suffering and stimulate recovery. Known collectively as "The New Deal," some of these mechanisms became permanent fixtures of the United States economic and political landscape while others quickly proved to be either inadequate or misguided.

The government became even more intrusive in the early forties. Having served their apprenticeships in the First World War, federal authorities now refined their techniques for controlling productive activities at all levels. The government's deficit spending more than replaced the limited private investment and feeble consumer spending that had hindered enterprise in the 1930s, and it transformed the lethargic nation into an economic superpower. The war offered businesses broad opportunities as the country fully utilized its productive capabilities and strained to do even more. The enlistment of 12 million Americans in the armed services left the civilian labor force with plenty of employment options, a welcome change from the doldrums of the 1930s.

The years of depression and war were intensely stressful for the American people, and a half-century's perspective has failed to clarify all that occurred. A lack of consensus still clouds our understanding of the causes of the Great Depression. We can hardly criticize the generation of the 1930s for failing to engineer a recovery from an economic decline that no one yet fully understands.

THE ONSET OF THE GREAT DEPRESSION

The economists and historians who have studied the causes of the depression have identified many contributing factors. Obviously, no single failing could set off such a crippling decline in every major area of enterprise. As noted earlier, the 1929 stock market crash was a severe psychological shock that made investors far more cautious than they had been. But a slowing of investment alone hardly explains the subsequent bankruptcy and closure of so many apparently prosperous businesses.

Perhaps that is as good a place to start as any: maybe this business prosperity was only illusory. A closer look reveals that several sectors of the economy were already depressed long before the debacle on Wall Street. The agricultural problems described in the previous chapter acted as a drag on the whole country's prosperity right through the 1920s, and the farmers were hardly alone in suffering from declining demand for their output. Competition from oil and hydroelectric power as well as reduced demand due to more efficient utilization of energy resources hit the bituminous coal industry hard. Fashion changes and artificial fibers left the conventional textile manufacturers burdened with excess capacity. Even the automakers could not attract as many buyers as they needed to continue expanding at the rates they had previously enjoyed. Henry Ford's reluctant abandonment of the Model T in 1927 was symptomatic of the troubles brewing in the nation's durable consumer goods industries.

The pace of building construction had also slowed in the late 1920s. The homes constructed in the real estate boom following the First World War eventually exceeded the number of customers who could afford them in much the same way that land speculation in earlier days had outreached the capabilities of settlers to use the land. A recurring growth and decline cycle in construction was a predictable aspect of the free enterprise system. Economists in the 1920s had also mapped other, supposedly inevitable business cycles. Some historians therefore blame the Great Depression on a combination of several business cycles that peaked simultaneously and then started down in harmony. The sympathetic resonance of these combined cycles caused much greater damage than any one alone could have inflicted. If cyclical factors alone had the force these analysts claimed, though, one might expect them to generate equally strong pressure for recovery once they hit bottom. But no "natural" revival developed; most indicators continued to decline.

Why did the United States economy fail to overcome the drag of weak sectors? Although he set out to test the monetarist theory outlined below, Peter Temin concluded instead that the key change was a dramatic decline in consumption expenditures. This indicator dropped a full 40 percent between 1929 and the trough of the depression in 1933. That meant that the American people were noticeably less willing or able to spend than they had been earlier. Some of this inability obviously stemmed from the fact that nearly one-quarter of the workforce was idle in 1933, but the beginning of the decline in consumer spending predated the rise of unemployment.

Another explanation for the drop in consumption was the increasingly skewed distribution of wealth that had developed in the 1920s. The rich had grown richer much faster than the poor had become less poor. At the beginning of the decade, the wealthiest 5 percent of the population controlled 24 percent of the nation's disposable income; at the time of the crash their share had risen to 35 percent. The prosperity of the twenties had scarcely touched the majority of American families who were trapped below the poverty line. One cause for this disproportionate distribution of wealth was that labor had received only partial compensation for the increases in its productivity. Industrial workers' real wages had climbed only 11 percent in the 1920s while their productivity had risen nearly 40 percent. The value of that extra output flowed into the hands of employers and investors as profits and dividends.

The inequitable distribution of wealth was particularly harmful to an economy that was so focused upon consumer spending. The relative shortage of disposable income in the hands of salaried and wage workers caused the country to suffer from the malady of "underconsumption." Too few buyers had the money to purchase all the goods that the bountiful farms and scientifically managed factories could produce. A wealthy American who collected the profits from labor's increasing productivity could hardly be expected to buy thousands of toothbrushes, hundreds of radios, or dozens of cars. Consumer spending could never keep pace with production as long as the distribution of wealth remained so inequitable.

Few contemporary Americans recognized the significance of underconsumption in causing and then prolonging the depression. Instead, those who observed the disparity between supply and demand blamed it on overproduction. In the 1930s dozens of public and private initiatives were mounted to reduce production artificially to match existing demand. Unfortunately, those programs often caused workers to be laid off and thereby reduced still further their ability to consume. Idling factories and farms definitely reduced output, but overproduction per se was not the core of the problem. Impoverished middle and working class individuals were eager to buy products of all sorts, they simply lacked the money to do so. Hence they underconsumed, creating a false impression that too much was being produced.

Because underconsumption is difficult to trace and evaluate, many analysts have investigated more tangible explanations for the depression. Milton Friedman is the most famous spokesman for the monetarists who stress the shortcomings of the Federal Reserve System above other factors. Friedman criticizes the Fed for failing to use its power constructively as the extent of the crisis became evident. Interestingly enough, the stock market crash had caused no serious banking insolvency despite the links between many banks and brokerage houses and the billions of dollars they had invested in margin loans. A major round of bank failures did develop almost a year later, though, to be followed by a second round in March 1931 highlighted by the dramatic collapse of the *Kreditanstalt*, the central bank of Austria. The Fed took no rational steps to prevent these failures, and it insisted instead upon reducing the money supply, a course that actually put further pressure on the banks. The organization did temporarily reverse course by purchasing federal bonds on the open market in 1932, but it stopped abruptly in July. By the winter of 1932-1933, runs and panic withdrawals had forced the entire banking system in the United States to its knees. The monetarists argue that the crisis might have been averted if the Fed had tried to rescue endangered banks and increase the money supply in the face of a downward spiral of deflation.

Critics of this analysis deny that monetary manipulation alone could have offset the depressing influences of the other weaknesses in the economy. Furthermore, the Fed's tools might well have been too weak to repair what was, in fact, a very poorly structured banking industry. Ties between banks and brokerage houses represented only one type of interconnection that complicated any attempt at regulation. And the banks were hardly unique in this respect: the nation's corporate structure as a whole had grown up haphazardly. The consolidation that had occurred in the 1920s had followed no system or set of rules. Investors and managers often manipulated top-echelon holding companies with little concern for the welfare of operating companies far down in a pyramidal structure. The depression definitely speeded the deterioration of poorly managed business combinations and intensified the secondary destruction that occurred when they toppled.

Some of the haphazard features of domestic business were reproduced in the international arena. Both the winners and the losers had suffered severe economic depressions after the Great War. Informal consultations had produced the Dawes Plan (1924) and the Young Plan (1928). The heart of both arrangements was a commitment from private American financiers to make substantial investments in Germany. These helped the German government make its war reparations payments to England and France. They, in turn, used some of the money to repay their war debts to the United States. The Wall Street collapse and the shrinkage of the domestic money supply after 1929 eliminated both the American desire and ability to invest abroad. Without United States overseas investment to prop it up, the international financial house of cards disintegrated. Depression once again plagued Europe, and its negative effects mingled with and intensified the American decline.

How did all these factors combine to cause the Great Depression? The weak sectors that had begun to decline in the 1920s went down hill with increasing speed in the 1930s. Shortages of consumer buying power resulting in part from an unequal distribution of wealth led to underconsumption that discouraged factory and farm production. The jerry-built corporate and banking structures were no match for the depression's gale-force winds, and the businesses that managed to survive were slow to resume normal operations. Finally, the postwar global depression that had never really ended hit home when the international financial structure crumbled. These causative factors should be remembered during the following examination of the character of the Great Depression and particularly of the schemes developed to stimulate recovery.

THE DOWNWARD SPIRAL

The descent into the Great Depression was a gentle slide rather than an abrupt plunge. After the debris from the stock market crash had been cleared away, the economy lurched through major periods of decline alternating with minor moments of relief. At any given point, optimists could cite a few recent developments that suggested recovery might really be just around the corner, but the general trend was ever downward. Yearly figures clearly show how much more dismal each succeeding reading of the nation's economic health appeared.

The indicator used to evaluate a country's economic activity is its gross national product, a combination of consumer spending, capital investment, and government expenditures. Table 8-1 shows substantial declines in the first two variables. The drop in GNP from $103.1 billion in 1929 to $55.6 billion in 1933 looks more devastating than it was because prices deflated during the same period. A 1933 dollar could buy much more than a 1929 dollar. The table therefore also shows the GNP in constant dollars. But even taking deflation into account, the real gross national product dropped about 30 percent. As noted earlier, consumer spending, one of the elements in the GNP, fell 40 percent. The plunge in investment was even more startling, going from $16.2 billion in 1929 to only one billion in 1932, a reduction of almost 94 percent.

TABLE 8-1 Gross National Product in Billions of Dollars

Year	Consumption Expenditures	Investment	Government Spending	Total GNP
1929	77.2	16.2	8.5	103.1
1930	69.9	10.3	9.2	90.4
1931	60.5	5.6	9.2	75.8
1932	48.6	1.0	8.1	58.0
1933	45.8	1.4	8.0	55.6
1934	51.3	3.3	9.8	65.1
1935	55.7	6.4	10.0	72.2
1936	61.9	8.5	12.0	82.5
1937	66.5	11.8	11.9	90.4
1938	63.9	6.5	13.0	84.7
1939	66.8	9.3	13.3	90.5
1940	70.8	13.1	14.0	99.7

Economic Report of the President, Washington, DC: Government Printing Office, 1969, p. 227.

Banks seemed particularly vulnerable. President Hoover insisted that if the banks could regain confidence, they could stimulate industrial recovery and job formation. Dedicated to a voluntarist approach, the president urged the bankers to form a privately financed National Credit Corporation to make loans to banks tottering toward insolvency. But this voluntary approach worked poorly because each banker favored salvaging his own institution rather than weakening it by lending to others in worse condition.

As the financial picture continued to darken, the government decided to step in directly. Early in 1932 Congress created the Reconstruction Finance Corporation and appropriated half a billion dollars as its initial funding. Envisioned as a temporary expedient, the RFC made loans to various corporations, always insisting on sound collateral and short terms. So much of the government money flowed directly to the banking community that it was ridiculed as a "rich man's dole." Its loans did carry individual institutions through tight spots, but federal money spent that way failed to generate the secondary investment and jobs President Hoover had anticipated. The RFC also disappointed those who expected it to be short-lived; it operated for twenty years and ultimately loaned more than $50 billion.

With banks absorbing most of the RFC funds, other sectors had to scrounge on their own. Share prices continued to slide, pulling the Dow Jones industrial average down to an anemic 41 in July 1932, just one-fifth of its October 1929 reading. Some major stocks did even worse: Montgomery Ward dropped from 138 to 4 and United States Steel from 262 to 22. At that point the American steel industry was operating at just 11 percent of its capacity. Automobile production was well down. Almost 2.8 million units had rolled off the assembly lines in 1929, but only 626,513 cars were built in 1932. Overall industrial production declined over 40 percent between 1929 and 1934 in conjunction with a 15 percent decline in prices. Agriculture was even worse off, because prices for farm products dropped 40 percent below the already depressed levels of the late 1920s.

HARD TIMES AT COLLEGE

The Great Depression profoundly affected the lives of those Americans who lived through it. These commentators recall its impact on their experiences at college. Pauline Kael is currently a movie critic for New Yorker *magazine and Robert Gard is a drama professor at the University of Wisconsin.*

Kael: When I attended Berkeley in 1936, so many of the kids had actually lost their fathers. They had wandered off in disgrace because they couldn't support their families. Other fathers had killed themselves, so the family could have the insurance. Families had totally broken down. Each father took it as a personal failure. These middle-class men apparently had no social sense of what was going on, so they killed themselves.

It was still the Depression. There were kids who didn't have a place to sleep, huddling under bridges on the campus. I had a scholarship, but there were times when I didn't have food. The meals were often three candy bars. We lived communally and I remember feeding other kids by cooking up more spaghetti than I can ever consider again.

Gard: I set out for the University of Kansas on a September morning with $30 that I'd borrowed from my local bank. I had one suit and one necktie and one pair of shoes. My mother had spent several days putting together a couple of wooden cases of canned fruits and vegetables. My father, a country lawyer, had taken as a legal fee a 1915 Buick touring car. It was not in particularly good condition, but it was good enough to get me there. It fell to pieces and it never got back home anymore.

I had no idea how long the $30 would last, but it sure would have to go a long way because I had nothing else. The semester fee was $22, so that left me $8 to go. Fortunately, I got a job driving a car for the dean of the law school. That's how I got through the first year. . . .

The weak ones, I don't suppose, really survived. There were many breakdowns. From malnutrition very likely. I know there were students actually starving.

Some of them engaged in strange occupations. There was a biological company that would pay a penny apiece for cockroaches. They needed these in research, I guess. Some students went cockroach hunting every night. They'd box 'em and sell them to this firm.

(Studs Terkel, *Hard Times: An Oral History of the Great Depression* [New York: Pantheon Books, 1970], pp. 346-48, ©1970 by Pantheon Books.)

The industrial and agricultural declines hurt millions of individuals. Even prudent and responsible farmers went through foreclosures and became tenants while sharecroppers were pushed off the land altogether. So many blue and white collar jobs were deemed redundant that workers of all types became unemployed. The Labor Department's estimate of a 25 percent unemployment figure for 1933 is the highest in American history. Meanwhile, workers fortunate enough to keep their jobs suffered pay cuts and shortened work weeks, and others fought for positions well below their capabilities.

By 1932 almost everyone had found someone else to blame for the pervasive misery, and President Hoover headed a good many lists. He seemed to personify the expressionless, unsympathetic, selfish forces that had undermined the economy and impoverished the people. They reacted by turning him out of the White House and installing Franklin Roosevelt. During his campaign this charismatic Democratic governor of New York had promised everyone a New Deal. By Inauguration Day, 1933, very few Americans still favored leaving recovery to natural market forces. No one knew what effects an aggressive, intrusive set of federal initiatives would have, but most were eager to see the government attempt corrective measures.

MONEY AND BANKING

As in previous depressions, many Americans blamed the monetary system for causing their economic troubles. All the familiar cure-alls like coining silver or issuing greenbacks were suggested, and Congress authorized the president to use any or all of them in the spring of 1933. But the Roosevelt administration moved quite conservatively, avoiding a doctrinaire approach. Because the price deflation seemed to be intertwined with the malfunctioning banks and stock exchanges, the government decided to take action on several fronts simultaneously.

Of all the ailing sectors, banking seemed most in need of attention. The banks had actually been suffering even before the depression hit. Almost 7000 banks closed their doors between 1921 and 1930 and, as Table 8-2 illustrates, the failure rate rose dramatically after that. In the winter of 1932-1933, rumors caused panicky depositors to rush to withdraw their savings. Such a "run" could force even a carefully managed, sound bank to the wall if it depleted the firm's cash reserves. Local authorities attempted to calm depositors' jitters by decreeing "bank holidays" that allowed financial institutions to reallocate their assets and increase their cash reserves. Thirty-eight states had done so by the time Roosevelt was inaugurated on March 4, 1933. One of the new president's first official acts was to proclaim a federal bank holiday that temporarily suspended all deposits and withdrawals in the United States.

During the holiday, each bank's condition was reviewed. About three-fourths were found to be sound, and they reopened a few days later after Roosevelt had reassured the public in the first of his many fireside chats. On opening day, a relieved public deposited more money than it withdrew. Many of the remaining, weaker banks were restructured or merged with healthier institutions. Some, of

TABLE 8-2 Bank Suspensions

1920	168
1921	505
1922	367
1923	646
1924	775
1925	618
1926	976
1927	669
1928	499
1929	659
1930	1352
1931	2294
1932	1456
1933	4004

U.S. Bureau of the Census, *Historical Statistics of the United States.* Washington, DC: Government Printing Office, 1960, X165.

course, remained permanently closed. In all, about half of the banks that had existed in the peak year of 1921 had disappeared by 1934 through bankruptcy or consolidation. Meanwhile, Congress approved some key banking legislation. First, it ordered a complete separation between banks and brokerage houses to prevent depositors' funds from mingling with speculators' accounts. It also created an insurance scheme to protect individual depositors. Banks were required to pay modest premiums to a government corporation which would make good on customers' funds jeopardized by a bank failure. The Banking Act of 1935 made the Federal Deposit Insurance Corporation a permanent agency that has functioned both as a psychological and an actual protection for depositors ever since.

The Federal Reserve System had come under increasing fire for its failure to stem the tide of depression. Among its major flaws were a lack of strong centralized direction and an overresponsiveness to local political pressures. In 1935 Congress approved a major reorganization in which the central board, renamed the Board of Governors, exercised much greater authority over the twelve regional banks. The Treasury officials who had been on the board were removed and the seven governors were given overlapping fourteen-year terms. The board also centralized decisions relating to open market operations. This new, presumably apolitical system was supposed to pursue wise monetary policies beyond the influence of presidential or congressional attitudes. The Fed's independence has appeared beneficial, allowing it to perform some central banking functions for the first time since Andrew Jackson vetoed the charter renewal for the Bank of the United States in 1832.

Federal reserve notes became the central element in the nation's monetary system once the United States abandoned the gold standard. First, all circulating gold was called into the Federal Reserve banks to be transferred to government vaults, and gold clauses in contracts were declared inoperative. In the fall of 1933,

President Roosevelt experimented with a "commodity dollar," setting a daily valuation for the dollar based on his assessment of what it should be worth compared to various commodities. The final divorce occurred in early 1934 when the Treasury raised its official price for gold from $20 to $35 an ounce, where it was to remain until 1972. That essentially devalued the dollar to fifty-nine cents compared to gold, a move the administration hoped would raise commodity prices.

Among the other devaluation techniques Congress had authorized, Roosevelt selected Treasury purchases of silver to be coined or to serve as backing for silver certificates. He ruled out printing more greenbacks. While these policies somewhat offset the effects of deflation, they did free the dollar from arbitrary restraints. The government and the Fed could now adjust the money supply to match specific policy objectives. The nation's monetary policy has sometimes been foolish or caused unexpected consequences since then, but it remains a powerful instrument for economic manipulation.

The strengthening of the government's regulatory power over money might be seen as inconsistent with a free-enterprise philosophy, but few Americans complained in the 1930s. Business leaders and bankers in particular had toppled from their positions as popular heroes. The Senate Committee on Banking and Currency conducted an intensive investigation that brought to light numerous instances of illegal, dishonest, or unsavory actions on the part of brokers, bankers, and speculators. The committee's relentless counsel, Ferdinand Pecora, uncovered evidence of "preferred lists" of investors given or sold shares at prices well below their quotations on the exchanges, pretended sales of securities to relatives to avoid taxation, stock price manipulation, insider selling, corporate lending to margin speculators lacking adequate collateral, fraudulent or mismanaged investment trusts, and much more. The public could hardly be blamed for concluding that the free enterprise system's supposed self-regulation mechanisms had failed and that government intervention alone could prevent future abuses.

To accomplish that objective, Congress established the Securities and Exchange Commission in 1934, and Ferdinand Pecora became one of its first commissioners. The SEC required all stock-issuing firms to provide full and accurate information to their potential buyers through prospectuses and annual reports. Had such reports been published in the late 1920s, few would have bought into many of the investment trusts. The commission also established stiff margin requirements to prevent reckless speculation with borrowed funds. It also monitored the operations of stock exchanges to guarantee that customers were honestly served. Although brokers and exchange officials criticized this intrusion into their realm, the Securities and Exchange Commission has been an effective Progressive-style reform organization.

Congress also assigned the SEC other chores like enforcing the Public Utilities Holding Company Act of 1934. Consolidated control of utilities companies dated back to the 1870s, but the elaborate holding companies of the 1920s were anything but sound. At one point, five companies including Sam Insull's empire controlled half of the electricity-generating equipment in the United States. The 1934 legislation outlawed holding-company pyramids above the second level to force stockholders and directors to be directly involved with and responsible for the utility services they provided. The SEC began an intensive campaign to dismantle and reorganize the utilities.

THE PEOPLE AND THE DEPRESSION

While the Roosevelt programs in finance, banking, and corporation control did little to ease the depression's impact on individual Americans, the New Dealers showed concern for the people in many other ways. Some relief programs like the Works Progress Administration (WPA) and the Civilian Works Administration (CWA) were thinly disguised federal doles. Others represented deliberate attempts at social engineering. Among them, the 1935 Social Security Act has had the most persistent longterm consequences. It provided minimal financial support to Americans who, because of age or other factors, could no longer hold regular jobs. Although critics called Social Security radical or even revolutionary, the United States had lagged well behind other industrialized nations in adopting such a program.

Despite charges that it had swung to the left and been excessively sympathetic to the poor and out-of-work, the federal government clearly hoped that labor and management would work out their relationships independently. To that end, the government took steps toward bringing about some degree of balance in labor negotiations. The 1932 Norris-LaGuardia Act set a major precedent by outlawing the use of blacklists and yellow-dog contracts that anti-union employers had forced prospective workers to sign. Organized labor had reached a very low ebb at that point. The American Federation of Labor's traditionally conservative philosophy and tactics had contributed to its decline. Furthermore, the fact that the whole nation was suffering from a severe economic crunch assured employers that they could reduce wages and increase work loads without fear of worker rebellion.

The overwhelming Democratic majorities in Congress attempted to reverse this trend by including Section 7(a) in the omnibus National Industrial Recovery Act. This act, to be described in more detail below, was aimed at restructuring all of American industry along more efficient lines. It legalized collective bargaining to give the workers a voice in the restructuring process. The impact of the NIRA was disappointing to labor leaders, though, because industrialists were so good at ignoring or subverting its labor provisions. Workers in some of the exploitative industries struck for better treatment, but the principle of union recognition made little progress.

Even these modest gains appeared in jeopardy when the Supreme Court ruled the NIRA unconstitutional in early 1935. Congress immediately rescued its labor program, though, by reconfirming the right to collective bargaining in the National Labor Relations Act of 1935. Familiarly known as the Wagner Act because New York Senator Robert Wagner was its strongest proponent, the act created a Na-

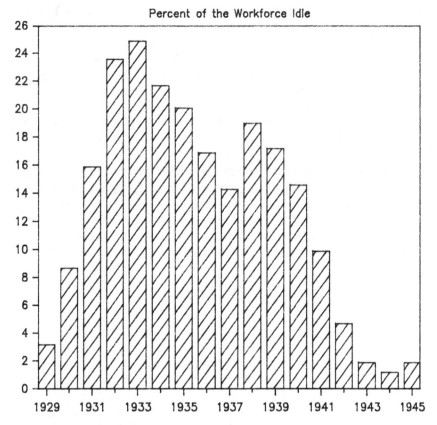

FIGURE 8-1 Unemployment. (From U.S. Bureau of the Census, *Historical Statistics of the United States* [Washington, DC: Government Printing Office, D-47, 1960].)

tional Labor Relations Board to supervise organizing activities and certify elections for the selection of bargaining agents. But, while the federal government was now committed on paper to supporting unionization, it would not instigate any action. The workers themselves had to take the initiative.

Some organizers were eager to do so. John L. Lewis, head of the powerful United Mine Workers, along with garment workers David Dubinsky and Sidney Hillman, urged William Green, president of the American Federation of Labor, to sponsor industrial organization drives. The AFL's craft-union approach had failed to organize workers in the major manufacturing industries like steel, rubber, and autos. When the craft unionists dragged their feet, Lewis and his associates defiantly created a Committee for Industrial Organization within the AFL to pursue their strategy. The Federation refused to sanction its activities, though, and eventually forced the rebels out. The exiles quickly established their own central body named the Congress of Industrial Organization (CIO).

Many industrialists believed the Supreme Court would rule the Wagner Act unconstitutional so they refused to recognize the pugnacious union workers. Indeed, both sides made warlike preparations. In stockpiling a huge arsenal of weapons, for example, Republic Steel became the nation's leading buyer of tear gas. Many corporations retained the services of private "detective" agencies like Pinkerton's, but the Ford Motor Co. had its militant Service Department to spy on and intimidate workers considering union membership.

With CIO sponsorship and funding, the Steel Workers Organizing Committee began an all-out drive in 1936. To nearly everyone's surprise, the United States Steel Corporation quickly recognized it as the workers' bargaining agent and negotiated a new contract authorizing eight-hour days, forty-hour work weeks, a 10 percent wage hike, and other benefits. The company's quick capitulation proved wise since unionization was inevitable. A group known as "Little Steel" consisting of Republic, Bethlehem, Inland, and Youngstown Sheet and Tube meanwhile broke a bloody strike and held out against the organizers. But that same year the Supreme Court ruled in the *NLRB* vs. *Jones & Laughlin Steel Corp.* case that the Wagner Act was indeed constitutional. Thus reassured, the National Labor Relations Board became an increasingly important element in labor disputes, and it helped impose a collective bargaining settlement on Little Steel in 1941.

The auto industry had been as resolutely anti-union as steel. The CIO organized the United Auto Workers in August 1935, and its membership ballooned to 400,000 by January 1937. The UAW pioneered in the use of the sit-down strike in its assault on General Motors. Much of the violence and injury in earlier strikes had occurred in the streets, but when the workers occupied factories, their owners could neither send in strike-breakers nor risk damaging their machinery by setting detectives, policemen, or troops loose inside. GM was the first to surrender to the union and Chrysler followed close behind. Henry Ford reacted like Little Steel, though, stubbornly holding out until 1941.

By the end of the decade, organized labor had undergone a remarkable rejuvenation. Competition from the CIO had forced the stodgy AFL to take advantage of governmental support, so that its membership also grew steadily. It was twice as large as its industrial rival in 1940, and organized labor as a whole claimed a total of 8.5 million members, a sharp increase over the 3 million paying dues in 1932. The Supreme Court did rule sit-down strikes illegal, but otherwise the government was far more sympathetic to the workers than it had ever been before. In 1938 Congress passed the Fair Labor Standards Act mandating a minimum wage of twenty-five cents an hour and a maximum workweek of forty hours for many types of employment. This act also reinstated several features of the Progressives' unsuccessful child and woman labor legislation. Industrial workers and their unions thus developed high levels of confidence, influence, and resilience.

To that extent industrial workers fared better than the nation's farmers. Suicidal dives in income and prices in the early thirties convinced the farming community, long a bastion of stubborn individualism, that group action was essential. Many farmers therefore joined in collective protests like the farm strike of 1932, organized by the Farm Holiday Association. When the deliberate destruction or withholding of commodities from the market place failed to raise price levels, the farmers looked to Washington for help.

The leading personality there was Agriculture Secretary Henry A. Wallace. A prominent Iowa farmer, businessman, and agricultural journalist, Wallace imposed his own philosophy on the Roosevelt administration. He began with a call for a domestic allotment program in which cooperating farmers would voluntarily agree to reduce their output in return for government compensation. Wallace hoped this production-limitation program would reduce surpluses and raise prices. It was hardly a revolutionary concept; rational industrialists always tried to tailor their output to market demand to maintain attractive price levels. Unlike a manufacturer, though, a farmer was too small an operator to have any impact on either production or prices. Only if the farmers cooperated and permitted the government to orchestrate their efforts might they be able to restrict output.

Production limitation emerged as the central goal of the hastily drafted Agricultural Adjustment Act of 1933. Seven basic commodities were initially subject to regulation, with local and regional committees working through county extension agents to assign each farmer a share of the national quota for a given commodity. Proceeds from a special tax on processors of agricultural commodities would be distributed to those farmers who agreed to limit their production. Overall agricultural production did drop significantly in the next couple of years, but adverse weather conditions rather than government planning accounted for most of the decline.

The AAA's goal was to bring the value of agricultural commodities in relation to other goods up to the same level as had existed between 1909 and 1914. This concept of "parity" became an integral part of all future agricultural planning. Agricultural prices did rise in the 1930s but never reached parity because the prices of many non-farm commodities climbed even more rapidly. A second Agricultural Adjustment Act was passed in 1938 after the Supreme Court outlawed the processing tax. The new legislation revised the limitations program and set the goal at a modest 75 percent of parity. The government meanwhile tried to stabilize prices by encouraging cooperative marketing agreements, disposing of surpluses overseas, and operating the Commodity Credit Corporation. The CCC loaned farmers money with their produce serving as collateral, enabling them to keep their harvests off the market until prices improved. Medium and large-scale farmers benefited most because they had a disproportionate say in allotment decisions and could avoid selling their commodities when prices were low.

The problems in rural America were so vexing that the New Dealers developed a number of other farm-related programs with often contradictory objectives. The Farm Security Administration worked to keep individuals from abandoning their farms, and the Rural Electrification Administration and the Soil Conservation Service helped improve farm efficiency. Simultaneously, the crop-limitation programs were encouraging a reduction in farm output while the Commodity Credit Corporation offered price supports for items consistently being overproduced. Per-

ELIZABETH ARDEN

Even in the depths of the depression, there was a steady market for health and beauty products which allowed Elizabeth Arden to continue prospering. Like so many other successful entrepreneurs, Florence Nightingale Graham had immigrated to the United States from her native Canada. After gaining generalized business skills working as a secretary for a number of small firms, she moved to New York City while still a teenager in 1909 to join a brother already living there. While working as a secretary for Eleanor Adair, a London-based cosmetics firm, she learned many chemical secrets and practiced the art of cosmetic massage. After a brief partnership with another woman, she decided to strike out on her own.

In 1910 she borrowed $6000 from a relative and opened her own salon named Elizabeth Arden. Reversing the common practice of naming the business after its proprietor, she adopted that name as her own. Her program involved massage, diet, and exercise as well as cosmetics. The full Elizabeth Arden treatment was expensive, but plenty of wealthy patrons lived in New York, so the business thrived. In 1914, she opened salons in Boston and Washington; after the war her realm expanded overseas with a branch in Paris in 1922. Eventually Elizabeth Arden salons were serving chic clients in major cities all around the world. In the 1930s, she took her total health care concept a step further by opening a health resort in Maine, to be followed later by an even more elaborate one in Arizona.

From the very beginning, Elizabeth Arden had been manufacturing and selling cleansing creams, lotions, and cosmetics. She hired chemists to develop new products which she sold at her salons and other retail outlets. In the thirties she introduced a line of clothing to fulfill her objective of catering to all of a woman's health and beauty desires.

Although she was already rich and world famous by 1930, she never lost interest in the business. Indeed, she applied similar principles to her hobbies. She bought her first race horse in the early thirties and eventually owned a stable of more than 150 animals, including a Kentucky Derby winner and many other champions. She was also prominent in charity work and as a supporter of the arts in New York City and elsewhere. Her company chalked up annual sales of $60 million in the 1950s, and her name is still used as a major trademark by Eli Lilly & Co., the firm that bought her assets when she died in 1966.

haps the only consistency here was the fading of the traditional concept of farmers as independent entrepreneurs.

INDUSTRY AND GOVERNMENT

The Great Depression hit American industry just as hard as it did agriculture. Corporate profits for the manufacturing industries had totaled $5.2 billion in 1929; three years later the same group ended up half a billion dollars in the red. Profits failed to surpass the 1929 level until 1940. The depression's impact was uneven, though, with the production of paper, food, and chemicals declining by less than half, while metals, construction materials, and furniture tumbled more than 70 percent. The drop in consumer spending was the major culprit because it caused purchases of durable goods to fall much more sharply than did the buying of other products. Complementing the underconsumption problem, industry also suffered from a poor business structure.

Like all other Americans in their darkest hours, industrialists looked to Washington for help, but confusion reigned there over which philosophy and mechanisms to use. Some planners favored enlarging the trade association approach Hoover's Commerce Department had advocated to relieve some of the competitive pressures. Progressive thinkers around Roosevelt proposed two other policies. One group saw national economic planning as the ideal means for the government to salvage American industry and set the nation on the road to recovery. Other, more cynical advisors urged strict enforcement of the antitrust concept to reestablish "free competition."

The omnibus National Industrial Recovery Act of June 16, 1933, ruled out none of these proposals. Rather than select a particular approach, Congress authorized the President to move in a number of directions. One of these was the federally funded Public Works Administration that was to develop construction projects that would hire the unemployed. The act's recovery mission depended upon what Roosevelt lauded as a partnership involving the government, industry, and labor. The next few months showed it to be an unequal partnership, with industry definitely calling the tune.

The National Recovery Administration was the central element of the act, and it used a trade association or cartel approach. General Hugh Johnson had cut his industrial-regulation teeth while working for the War Industries Board. Now he superintended the NRA's efforts to establish rules and guidelines in the form of codes for each industrial sector. As noted above, Section 7(a) of the law stated that those drafting NRA codes must include representatives of labor and assure the workforce the right to bargain collectively. In practice, it was the industrialists, with minor assistance from government officials, who dictated the collective policies developed for each sector. The goal was recovery and, as with the AAA, driving up prices was the major strategy proposed. The codes therefore included production limitations, quotas for participating manufacturers, price-fixing, standardization of products, and limitations on the use of labor and plant capacities. The government, in turn, promised immunity from antitrust litigation to the plants or companies that participated.

HAWKING THE BLUE EAGLE

As head of the National Recovery Administration, ex-cavalry General Hugh Johnson served as its chief publicist. These excerpts from a radio address illustrate his awareness of how important consumption was in helping his NRA programs stimulate economic recovery.

There is one reason to expect success. This is a move to bring happiness back to homes, and homes are the peculiar province of wives and mothers. It is they who have borne the brunt of the four years' blight on decency in living. They are the purchasing agents of America. Women do 80% of our buying. It is they who can put the Blue Eagle on everything that moves in trade or commerce. This cause could not be in surer hands. . . . a woman in support of her home is about as safe for triflers as a Royal Bengal Tigress at the door of a den full of cubs. When every American housewife understands that the Blue Eagle on everything that she permits to come into her home is a symbol of its restoration to security, may God have mercy on the man or group of men who attempt to trifle with this bird. . . .

To preserve a hostage to future fortunes, people who have a little left have adopted a non-buying policy that is fatal to recovery. It is an unemployment psychology that sends us shabby to our work. Unpainted houses−cracked shoes, many times half-soled−shiny pants−rattling automobiles−dyed dresses−refurbished wardrobes−all these badges of unselfish husbandry must now be replaced if this plan is to have a fair chance to do what we hope for it. We must shake ourselves out of this four-year-old idea of doing without against a rainy day and we must do that overnight. . . . Buy! Buy now! Buy within prudence everything you need and have so long denied yourselves. It is the key to the whole situation.

(Hugh S. Johnson, *The Blue Eagle from Egg to Earth* [Garden City, NY: Doubleday, 1935], pp. 263-65. Copyright ©1935 by Doubleday & Co., Inc. Reprinted by permission of the publisher.)

Within a matter of months, each industrial sector had drafted its code and allocated resources and quotas to constituent companies. The NRA set off a tremendous publicity campaign, employing as its symbol a blue eagle and "We do our part" as its motto. Millions of workers in thousands of plants joined consumers all across the United States in pledging to make the NRA a success. But enthusiasm faded quickly. Workers and smaller producers complained that the codes favored the bigger firms which had largely written them. Early in 1934 the famous criminal lawyer Clarence Darrow was appointed to head the National Recovery Review Board charged with investigating such criticisms. Some of the larger operators who found the code provisions limiting simply ignored them, relying on their attorneys' advice that the whole arrangement was unconstitutional anyway. The Supreme Court agreed in the 1935 Schecter decision, and the entire system collapsed.

The NRA had become so unpopular at all levels that few mourned its disappearance. The Roosevelt administration had become estranged from big business in any case, and the White House appeared increasingly sympathetic to the many voices protesting the past and present performance of the business community. Besides, there was no clear proof that the NRA codes had stimulated any industrial recovery, and the program's failure discredited the whole concept of industrial collectivism. Congress did, of course, rescue its labor provisions and restate them in the Wagner Act. And a few hard-hit industries solicited federal assistance like that involved in the Guffey Coal Act of 1935 to help them rationalize, reorganize, and manage their affairs for the common good.

The government's anti-business bias continued to grow. Congress created the Temporary National Economic Committee to examine the conduct and misconduct of American businesses so it could develop legislative remedies for any wrongdoing discovered. At the same time, the Justice Department's Antitrust Division began to enforce existing laws like the Clayton Act. This drive led to several highly publicized but ultimately rather unimportant suits. When the TNEC completed its multi-volume report in 1941, the United States was distracted by the Second World War. A healthy, cooperative industrial community was vital to the American war effort so the reports were shelved, for the most part unread and soon forgotten.

Except for the rapid growth of labor unionism under federal protection, industry neither gained nor lost much from the New Deal. The government's policies certainly did nothing to restore prosperity. To a large degree, then, exclusive of the the financial community, business was responsible for its own revitalization. The depression obviously left many marks on American industry, and a couple of examples will illustrate some of the challenges they faced during this unusual period.

HOLLYWOOD'S GOLDEN ERA

American motion pictures enjoyed worldwide popularity in the 1920s and 1930s. Although the actors, writers, and directors who made these films preferred to think of themselves as artists, they were functioning within a thriving industry. Like any other consumer-oriented industry, the movie business involved labor, financing, distribution, advertising, management, and organizational aspects. It also became the subject of antitrust litigation even though it had begun on a very small scale.

Many people in the United States and abroad helped develop motion pictures into a popular entertainment medium. One familiar figure was Thomas Edison whose major contribution was the idea of punching regularly spaced holes along the sides of celluloid film so it would move smoothly over sprocketed wheels and pathways. Edison also produced short films for individual viewing in a "peep show" mechanism. Meanwhile others developed equipment for displaying moving pictures on a screen for larger audiences. In the early 1900s, tiny screening rooms were offering brief shows at minimal prices, and a number of firms were producing and distributing films for these "Nickelodeons." As profits from the business grew, Edison and other inventors decided to form the Motion Picture Patents Company in 1908. This organization demanded royalty payments from anyone who used processes its members had patented. Several fiercely competitive independent producers like William Fox and Adolph Zukor objected to this attempt at monopoly, and the Supreme Court ruled in their favor in an antitrust suit in 1917.

Many independent movie makers had already migrated to Hollywood, in part to establish distance between themselves and the patents combine. There they experimented with the medium and worked on feature-length films and packaged programs. The industry involved three distinct elements: production, distribution, and exhibition. An aggressive distribution company went through several name changes before becoming Paramount Pictures. It then expanded backward into production by hiring talented directors like Cecil B. DeMille. When Paramount then attempted to monopolize the distribution business, though, some exhibitors fought back. Marcus Loew, for example, owned a chain of theaters and, to guarantee an independent source of films, he hired the best talent money could buy and merged it into a subsidiary production company called Metro-Goldwyn-Mayer. Louis B. Mayer ran this highly successful entertainment business for many years. Paramount retaliated by purchasing its own theaters. These two vertically integrated organizations which combined production, distribution, and exhibition had definite competitive advantages over their rivals. They hired teams of writers, directors, and actors on contracts to grind out films in a matter of weeks for distribution to their own theaters for first-run showings.

To merchandise their wares, the independent producers had earlier created the star system based on a correct presumption that audiences would pay to see popular actors and actresses in any films they made. Soon, however, some of Hollywood's most creative individuals came to resent having their talents and personalities exploited, so they cut loose from the big companies. Established stars could set up their own production companies in pursuit of artistic freedom and, not incidentally, a larger share of the profits. Four of the most famous movie celebrities decided to pool their resources in 1919. Director D. W. Griffith, whose *The Birth of a Nation* had set the pattern for all subsequent feature films, joined movie stars Mary Pickford, Douglas Fairbanks, and Charlie Chaplin in a company called United Artists. It remained strictly a production company through the 1930s and relied on others to distribute and exhibit its films.

Although the four Warner brothers had become deeply involved in the industry by the mid-twenties, they were looking for a gimmick to set them apart from and, they hoped, ahead of the others. Western Electric, the American Telephone & Telegraph Co.'s research group, had developed a movie sound system using discs,

The Golden Age of Hollywood. (National Archives)

so the Warners set up the Vitaphone Corp. to market this process. They retained 70 percent of the corporation's shares for themselves and therefore profited enormously from the phenomenally successful "talking" movie *The Jazz Singer* in 1927. Its popularity insured that sound would replace silent films. Warner Brothers Pictures moved energetically to cash in on its success, and the entrepreneurs had accumulated assets of $160 million by 1929, compared to the $5 million they controlled in 1925.

Meanwhile, the Radio Corporation of America, with its close ties to industrial giant General Electric, had perfected an optical sound reproduction process. To establish itself in the movie industry, RCA entered a combination with the Kieth-Orpheum theater circuit which became known as RKO. Even so, the future looked bleak for RCA when the major studios decided to standardize on the Western Electric process under a licensing agreement with Electrical Research Products, Inc. This company had been created to undermine Vitaphone and, consequently, Warner Brothers' influence. Eventually, E.R.P.I. worked out an agreement with RCA that allowed both companies to produce movie sound equipment.

The industry had begun attracting the attention of major financial houses by the late 1920s, but the advent of sound greatly increased the capital required not only to produce the films but also to equip theaters with sound projection equipment. Unfortunately, this change-over coincided with the onset of the depression. Hard times strengthened the influence of the major studios at the expense of independents. MGM was the least concerned because it possessed able management, popular products, and an efficient vertical structure. Warner Brothers also weathered the thirties, primarily by developing a Hollywood equivalent of an assembly-line in which its large stable of contract players put out a standardized product line consisting primarily of crime and musical films. RKO had always been well connected with the Morgan and Rockefeller banking organizations, so it, too, avoided some of the financial uncertainty that plagued its rivals.

THE MAKING OF A CLASSIC

It Happened One Night *won the five major Academy Awards in 1935. Here director Frank Capra describes how haphazardly the project came together.*

But we couldn't cast *It Happened One Night*. No girl wanted to play the part. Five girls turned it down, five girls. And finally we got Claudette Colbert to agree to play the part if we doubled her salary and could get through with her in four weeks' time. She had a vacation [she wanted to take]. But then we couldn't get a leading man. We wanted Bob Montgomery. He turned it down. Well, the perils of *It Happened One Night* just grew and I finally got pretty sick of it and said, "Let's call it off, Harry, everybody says that bus pictures won't go, so the heck with it." And Cohn says, "No, no, we have to make it. Louis B. Mayer wants to punish an actor and he's told me I could have Clark Gable." That was an order from Louis Mayer. Every time Mayer got a cold, Cohn did the sneezing. And so we had to make the picture because Louis Mayer had to punish Clark Gable. This is not a pretty way to start a film, so I asked Clark Gable to come over. He was absolutely roaring drunk when he came over to see me. I won't tell you about the whole *maquilla*, but we made the picture really quickly—four weeks. We stumbled through it, we laughed our way through it. And this goes to show you how much luck and timing and being in the right place at the right time means in show business: how sometimes no preparation at all is better than all the preparation in the world; and sometimes you need great preparation, but you can never outguess this thing called creativity. It happens in the strangest places and under the strangest of circumstances. I didn't much care for the picture, [yet] it turned out to be *It Happened One Night*.

(From Richard Schickel, *The Men Who Made the Movies* [New York: Atheneum, 1975], pp. 72-73. Copyright 1975 Educational Broadcasting Corporation. Reprinted with the permission of Atheneum Publishers, Inc.)

The other two major studios barely survived. Despite its earlier prominence, Paramount failed to keep its theaters filled even after developing double feature programming. The company went bankrupt in 1933, but its valuable assets attracted new investment from outside. Revived in 1935, it ended the decade in reasonably good shape. William Fox had meanwhile pioneered his own Movietone sound system and his newsreels achieved lasting fame, but he became overextended and had to declare personal bankruptcy. The Chase Manhattan Bank reassembled the pieces of his empire and merged them with Twentieth Century Films in 1935. While Twentieth Century-Fox specialized in inexpensive, lower quality films, it did promote the career of one of the period's most popular stars, Shirley Temple. Independent producers like Walt Disney and Howard Hughes preferred to work in the less-confining atmosphere of United Artists. Two smaller studios, Columbia and Universal, rounded out the Hollywood scene in the 1930s.

As the movie industry developed into an oligopoly, it generated criticism. One of the lures the Los Angeles area had exerted on movie producers was its open-shop reputation. The industry avoided collective labor problems for some time, in part by creating the Motion Picture Academy of Arts and Sciences in 1927 as a sort of company union. But when the movie moguls drafted an NRA code in 1933 highly favorable to the studios, their employees protested. The Screen Actors Guild and the Screen Writers Guild became increasingly militant union organizations which took advantage of New Deal legislation in arranging contracts for their members. Film technicians and craftsmen had already begun their own organizational drives, and eventually even the directors formed a guild of their own.

The studios also came under fire from private theater owners who objected to one-sided distribution contracts. They organized a major antitrust action in 1938, and two years later the defendants accepted a consent decree that terminated many of their monopolistic practices. Even so, the powerful studio system that had developed during the depression continued to dominate the entertainment business for many years. Its oligopolistic character made sense in an industry that required elaborate machinery and sizable budgets for each of its products. Despite protests over the business practices of the studio system, the 1930s have come to be regarded as the golden era of American filmmaking. The industry produced extraordinarily popular mass entertainment that helped millions of Americans forget their own troubles, if only for a couple of hours at a time.

THE AVIATION INDUSTRY

Federal government spending rose significantly in the 1930s, and some of that money kept certain industrial sectors and specialized firms afloat. Even as the United States was erecting walls of neutrality legislation to insulate it from overseas involvements, some aircraft companies were building almost exclusively for the army and navy. At the same time, primitive domestic airlines earned much more revenue from their mail-carrying contracts than from passenger fares. Recognizing that federal funding of one sort or another offered air pioneers the only certain return on their expensive experimentation, aviation business leaders naturally worked hard both to exploit and to satisfy their prime customer.

After the European armistice in 1918, aviation fell into the status of an avocation or hobby. The aircraft industry, such as it was, consisted of a few larger concerns among dozens of shoestring fabricators and operators. Barnstorming biplane pilots thrilled crowds at country carnivals with death-defying aerial maneuvers. Short airmail routes were established, but most were quickly abandoned. Even after General Billy Mitchell graphically demonstrated the military potential of airplanes by bombing and sinking several surplus ships in a matter of minutes, most Americans treated aviation as entertainment rather than a cause for military concern. While Mitchell's zeal earned him a court-martial conviction, he had managed to influence key minds in the War and Navy Departments. Planners began discussing air strategies ranging from the use of light observation planes to carrier-based bomber squadrons. Then Charles Lindbergh galvanized public opinion in 1927 with his solo flight across the Atlantic. Lindbergh's achievement was far more effective at dramatizing aviation than any previous daredevil stunt.

Flying became a national fad overnight. Wall Street had shown little interest in the industry earlier, but now it poured $400 million into aviation investments. Most of this money flowed into the treasuries of the four major business combinations which dominated all aspects of aviation. William E. Boeing, heir to a timber fortune in Seattle, had only toyed with postal contracts and other aviation interests earlier. In 1928 he organized a Delaware holding company named United Aircraft and Transport Corp. and installed F. B. Rentscher as its president. Because Rentscher's brother headed the National City Bank, the new firm had ready access to the capital it needed to buy controlling interests in other aviation companies like Pratt & Whitney, Chance Vought, Northrop, and Sikorsky. Another well-funded holding company, North American Aviation, Inc., took over Curtiss-Wright, the only rival to Pratt & Whitney in the manufacture of aircraft engines. In 1929 General Motors teamed with Fokker and drew upon its substantial financial resources to create a manufacturing and operating combine. The final member of the Big Four was Aviation Corporation or AVCO. Its key asset was its close tie to the Republican administration in Washington, the source of government funding.

The major combinations won most of the government contracts stemming from a couple of ambitious five-year military-purchasing programs and the establishment of national airmail service in the late twenties. Democratic President Roosevelt's postmaster general shattered the Big Four's complacency in 1934, however, when he canceled all of the mail contracts his Republican predecessor had assigned to them. Although no evidence of collusion or influence-peddling ever surfaced, the Roosevelt administration's move was certainly in line with the anti-business mood of the times. After several Army Air Corps pilots had been killed while attempting to carry mail, negotiations for a new set of private contracts began. The government did insist, though, that the air carriers must divorce themselves from the manufacturing end of the industry. The United Air and Transport

DC-3 by Douglas. (Courtesy of McDonnell Douglas Corporation)

Corp. split into United Airlines, a separate Boeing manufacturing operation, and a third major entity centered around Pratt & Whitney. North American collected its manufacturing activities into a new company under the same name and set up as a distinct unit Transcontinental and Western Airlines, the precursor to Trans-World Airlines. American Airlines emerged from the breakup of AVCO. From then on, aviation involved two separate lines of endeavor, one in transportation and the other in manufacturing.

Dramatic technological advances were occurring throughout this period of business combination and dissolution. In the mid-1920s both Curtiss-Wright and Pratt & Whitney began building higher horsepower air-cooled radial engines. The aircraft these engines powered meanwhile were changing from wood and fabric bi-planes into sleek aluminum-skinned, internally braced monoplanes. Variable-pitch propellers, retractable landing gear, and wing flaps improved their airworthiness.

The most versatile new aircraft designed in this exciting developmental period was built by the Douglas Aircraft Corporation which had remained primarily a manufacturing unit all along. In 1935 it introduced the third model in its Douglas Commercial line, the DC-3. This twin-engine, twenty-one-passenger airplane set the standard for all aircraft built into the 1950s, and it quickly became the workhorse for all the world's commercial airlines. Later, designated the C-47 Skytrain in the United States Air Force and the Dakota in England, it was a highly reliable cargo carrier. A combination of civilian and military uses for the same aircraft was common at this stage.

JUAN TERRY TRIPPE

Few Americans have been as successful as Juan T. Trippe at translating their visions into reality. His ancestors had been intimately associated with the sea and the U.S. Navy, so it was only natural for Juan to leave his studies at Yale to volunteer for service in the navy's flying corps when the United States entered the war in 1917. Rejected because of a slight vision problem, he took flying lessons on his own and enlisted anyway. Assistant Secretary of the Navy Franklin D. Roosevelt helped the earnest young man obtain a reserve commission that qualified him for combat training in Florida, but the war ended before he could be assigned overseas.

He returned to Yale, graduated, and worked for a year in his father's bank, before resuming his aviation career. He virtually singlehandly founded and ran Long Island Airways which flew socialites to their summer homes in a couple of decommissioned military aircraft. He then teamed with a Baltimore banker and war ace named John A. Hambleton and another Yale graduate, Cornelius Vanderbilt Whitney, to form New York Airways. It established a regular New York-Boston run and obtained an airmail contract in 1926.

But the restless Trippe nursed broader ambitions. He moved to Florida where he won a contract to carry mail from Key West to Havana. In the process he negotiated exclusive landing rights in Cuba that enabled him to establish a route that was the foundation of the Pan American Airways System. He quickly opened up routes to other Caribbean and Latin American destinations. In the early thirties, he pioneered in the use of Clippers to link the United States with China. He even opened up a route to Africa in the early 1940s, which was a major asset when the United States began its land operations in the Second World War with an invasion of North Africa. No one in the organization knew as much as Trippe not only about the business but also the aircraft themselves. He was constantly consulting with mechanics, pilots, financial officers, and government officials as he superintended the most broad ranging of all the American-based air carriers.

Until the mid-thirties the air carriers viewed passenger service as a sideline to their mail deliveries, but a comfortable, dependable aircraft like the DC-3 made passenger travel much more profitable. To accommodate the rapidly growing passenger demand, manufacturers like Sikorsky, Martin, and Boeing constructed huge "flying boats." These roomy, four-engine aircraft were often called clippers as a tribute to the speedy, globe-girdling sailing ships of the previous century. Any patch of calm water was suitable for landing, so they could inaugurate air service to many parts of the world long before expensive land runways had been constructed.

Like their maritime predecessors, however, the flying clippers' heyday was relatively brief.

Both the transport and manufacturing arms of the aviation business had become highly competitive by the late 1930s. Although the expensive clippers had eaten into profits, they did spur the development of four-engine land planes. Large passenger transports like Boeing's Stratocruiser, the DC-4, and Lockheed's Constellation shared many design and engineering features with the military aircraft under construction. Military and naval purchases continued to account for the majority of all aircraft manufacturers' sales. The army bought fighters, transports, and bombers while the navy contracted for carrier-based craft and seaplanes. The industry remained rather small, though, employing fewer than 50,000 skilled or semiskilled workers in plants that resembled eighteenth-century artisans' shops in many ways. The relatively small number of sophisticated and costly units built meant that mass production was simply not feasible.

The outbreak of the Second World War in Europe in 1939 triggered phenomenal growth in the American aircraft industry. In that year, it had ranked forty-fourth among all United States industries in the dollar value of its output; five years later it would be first. British and French orders poured in and the United States government also stepped up its military purchases. Production of fighters and bombers had been running years behind the design stage, but now advanced prototypes were hastily assembled and flight tested. The aviation industry's capacity and output grew exponentially once the United States itself entered the war in late 1941.

Managing this unprecedented expansion strained both public and private capabilities. Few new firms entered the business; the growth occurred within the framework of the existing manufacturing companies both large and small. Prewar light aircraft makers Piper and Cessna, for example, built training and observation planes, while Boeing won contracts for the largest bomber, the B-29. The government's Aircraft War Production Council allocated and distributed raw materials, parts, engineering reports, and designs among the many manufacturing plants. Competition took a back seat to patriotism as corporations shared their expertise and designs with one another. Because the manufacturers quite reasonably feared being saddled with a serious overcapacity problem once the conflict ended, they insisted that the federal government provide much of the funding for the construction of new facilities. Prewar contracts had included maximum-profit clauses, but that system had to be abandoned because no one knew what a reasonable profit should be in the noncompetitive emergency situation. Cost-plus contracts became the favored substitute.

Production techniques had to change as well. Although the traditional pattern of unit-by-unit assembly involved many inefficiencies, it could not be completely revamped, especially for larger aircraft. Subcontractors and licensees could mass produce many of the component parts, though, freeing skilled craftsmen and engineers for final assembly work. This change is apparent in the percentage of aircraft manufacturing that was subcontracted. Only one-tenth had been farmed out before the war, but that figure rose to 40 percent during the conflict. Many new assembly plants were located in the Midwest and the South, well away from the coastal locations the aircraft industry had previously preferred. This geographic shift was partly a response to fears of enemy attack, but it also allowed the manufacturers to tap different labor pools.

When the federal government ordered a cancellation of private automobile production, many Americans thought the automakers could easily switch to aircraft manufacture. The carmakers did a lot of the subcontracting like Packard, Buick, Chevrolet, Studebaker, and Dodge who assembled liquid-cooled engines. Mass-production techniques transferred far less effectively to airframe construction. Henry Ford and his chief subordinate Charles Sorensen toured several airframe plants and roundly criticized what they saw as unconscionable waste and inefficiency. Using $200 million from the Army Air Force, the Ford Motor Co. constructed the world's largest factory at Willow Run near Detroit. So many problems plagued the eighty-acre plant that it earned the nickname "Will It Run?" It finally did, manufacturing B-24 bombers using Consolidated Aircraft Corporation blueprints. Unfortunately, most of the 8685 bombers it built in 1944 were completed after the design had become outmoded. General Motors was the only other auto maker to produce whole airplanes, building Grumman-designed fighters and torpedo bombers at its Eastern Aircraft Division.

The aircraft industry's performance exceeded even the most optimistic estimates. President Roosevelt had appeared highly visionary in the summer of 1940 when he called for the development of an industry capable of producing 50,000 planes a year. After all, fewer than 6000 had been turned out in 1939. But by the war's end, 300,000 airplanes had been manufactured along with 800,000 engines and 700,000 propellers. About half were built in preexisting facilities, the rest in new plants. In addition to bombers and fighters, the air arsenal included 23,000 transports and 15,700 gliders. The $45 billion the government spent on aviation revitalized an industry that had barely maintained itself through the 1930s. The war effort had thus strengthened this fundamental element in the developing military-industrial complex. No other industry had been so well positioned to exploit the commercial opportunities of the Second World War. The transition from peace to war production seemed quite logical for the aircraft industry, but most Americans in the 1930s had hoped never again to be drawn into a global conflict. They were slow to acknowledge and accept its inevitability.

FROM ISOLATION TO INVOLVEMENT

Except for the Roosevelt administration's unilateral decision to abandon the gold standard in the early 1930s, the federal government had pursued a rational approach to foreign economic affairs. Enlightened internationalists drafted the Reciprocal Trade Agreements Act of 1934 which gave the president authority to negotiate mutually beneficial reductions in tariff rates with other countries. It was a permanent change because reciprocal trade agreements have been the principal method of setting customs duties ever since. The lower rates did revive international trade somewhat in the late 1930s, but each nation was primarily concerned with combatting the internal effects of the global depression.

Americans considered the expansionistic regimes that arose in Italy, Germany, and elsewhere in the 1930s to be highly disturbing. And because many agreed with President Hoover's claim that the Great War had caused the Great Depression, they brooded over how and why the United States had been drawn into that conflict. In 1934 Senator Gerald P. Nye headed a congressional committee that blamed certain businesses. Several prominent historians also reached similar conclusions. The villains were "merchants of death," arms and ammunition manufacturers who supposedly prolonged the European war to increase their sales at the same time they were working to get the United States directly involved. International bankers came in for criticism as well. They had loaned money to England and France and then insisted that the United States rescue their struggling debtors in 1917. The business community was, of course, the favorite scapegoat for all of the nation's problems in the 1930s, so this blanket criticism of business influences in drawing the United States into war was both predictable and popular.

To prevent such evil from occurring in the future, Congress passed a series of neutrality laws. So that merchants of death could not profit from external calamities, the first neutrality act prohibited the sale or shipment of arms from the United States to belligerent nations. Later revisions modified the arms embargo to allow the sale of American goods but only if the buyers paid cash and transported them on their own vessels. No American loans were permitted; all sales must be strictly cash and carry.

These laws seemed naive indeed when Hitler's armies invaded Poland in the fall of 1939 and plunged all of Europe into war. While the German military rolled from one victory to another, two rival philosophies developed in the United States. America First wanted to keep the nation's energies and material resources for its own defense. Opponents of such isolationism joined the Committee to Defend America by Aiding the Allies. It advocated sending as much material and financial support as possible to England and her allies so they could defeat Hitler without directly involving American armed forces. Both groups did agree on one point: the United States must begin a massive military and naval buildup.

The jump in federal budget outlays from $9.6 billion in 1940 to $14 billion in 1941 reflects the rearmament commitment. A peacetime draft began in September 1940, and both the army and the navy expanded their construction, training, and supply programs. The economy began to shake off its depression lethargy as thousands of unemployed workers joined the armed forces and orders for military goods streamed out of Washington. In anticipation of future scarcities, manufacturers stepped up production and wholesalers and retailers piled up inventories of both civilian and military goods. As factories and farms found markets for their output at last, the workforce earned ample money to spend. Wage levels climbed twice as fast as price increases, whittling away at the underconsumption problem that had defied all previous remedies.

Foreign governments naturally increased their orders for American goods. As they had in 1914, Great Britain and her allies ran short of funds, so President Roosevelt seized upon the expedient of lending them equipment rather than money. After considerable debate, Congress wrote the concept into the Lend-Lease Act of March 1941. Under its provisions, $49 billion worth of supplies, including food and equipment, were distributed to dozens of nations including the Soviet Union after it entered the war against Germany in 1941.

By the fall of that year, the United States had stopped just short of declaring war on the European Axis powers, but it was an incident halfway around the world that precipitated that fateful step. The seeds of the Far Eastern crisis had been planted four years earlier when a right-wing government in Japan mounted an invasion of China. Hoping to avoid driving Japan into an alliance with Germany and Italy, the United States delayed limiting Japanese purchases of strategic materials like iron and aviation fuel until the summer of 1940. When their resources neared exhaustion in the fall of 1941, the Japanese decided to capture Indochina, Indonesia, and the Philippines to obtain needed supplies. The surprise bombing of the American fleet at Pearl Harbor was supposed to destroy the power of the United States to prevent Japanese expansion in Southeast Asia. The attack dramatically ended America's isolation. American participation in the Second World War lasted nearly four years and completely altered the domestic economy at the same time it permanently reshaped the international situation.

MOBILIZATION AND COORDINATION OF THE WAR EFFORT

Never before or since has the United States government imposed its will as pervasively as it did between 1941 and 1945. Comprehensive national planning overshadowed whatever free-enterprise characteristics the American economy had retained. Constraints and restrictions interfered with private decision-making at every turn. The American people accepted this broad-gauged control because of their previous experience with government intervention in the economic and business realms. The Progressives had developed an appropriate philosophy and laid the legislative groundwork; the earlier war had stimulated a broad application of their proposals; and the recent cornucopia of New Deal programs had accustomed the people to expansive federal initiatives. Furthermore, a high degree of patriotism helped make any sacrifices associated with the war effort more tolerable.

None of this insulated the Roosevelt administration from criticism, nor was the transition from a peace to a war footing accomplished smoothly. Prior to 1939 isolationism combined with concern over the domestic depression had discouraged military planning. Not until the German armies went on the offensive did the president appoint an Advisory Commission to the existing Council of National Defense and make it responsible for monitoring military production and sales. The commission lacked authority to coordinate the flow of orders to American factories, though, so serious bottlenecks and shortages developed. In January 1941 the Office for Emergency Management was established as an adjunct to the White

House. Operating under the OEM umbrella, the Office of Production Management tried to rationalize purchases and production of military and strategic goods for both the United States and its overseas customers. In the late summer another OEM offshoot, the Supplies, Priorities, and Allocations Board, began grappling with the continuing chaos. Only after the United States entered the war was a new agency, the War Production Board, given sufficient authority to sort out the competing civilian and military demands on the American economy.

The War Production Board was a stronger version of the War Industries Board of 1917-1918. Headed by Donald M. Nelson, it contained several cabinet officers and other experts. The board sent directives to producers, manufacturers, and distributors to coordinate the nation's productive capabilities so that all priorities would be met. It also allocated raw materials and parts as well as locating manufacturers and suppliers. The board could halt production of nonessential items as it did automobiles and many other consumer durable goods. The factories and workers were encouraged to redirect their efforts to more essential areas. Where no facilities existed to be converted, the board built new ones. It also sorted out purchasing requests from the army, the navy, and the allies to make sure each got what it most needed.

Dozens of other agencies worked in tandem with the War Production Board. The Reconstruction Finance Corporation, Hoover's emergency depression fighter, provided much of the government's funding for new plants and conversions. The Office of Defense Transportation established schedules and dictated operating procedures for all means of transportation including oil pipelines, busses, and even taxis. The Office of Lend-lease Administration located and distributed a bewildering array of supplies and weapons to client nations. The Board of Economic Warfare tried to manipulate international trade to the advantage of the allied war effort. Keenly aware of the public outcry over war profiteering that had developed in the early 1930s, Congress took steps to curtail it. Missouri's Harry S Truman won respect for heading the Senate's Special Committee to Investigate the National Defense Program that examined all aspects of the government's contracting system.

Basic raw materials were crucial. The United States already produced one-third of the world's iron ore, one-fourth of its coal, and about two-thirds of its oil. For once, the American steel industry ran at full capacity. It was estimated that the army deployed more than ten tons of steel in support of every soldier at the front. Despite the demand from the booming aircraft industry, the United States had a surplus of aluminum on hand by 1944. Copper was harder to come by, forcing the United States to import heavily from Chile and the Congo. Other metals were carefully allocated by the Metals Reserve Company, an arm of the RFC that had begun stockpiling tin and manganese in 1940.

The rubber shortage was acute. When the Japanese drew Indochina and Indonesia into their Greater East Asia Co-prosperity Sphere, they cut the United States off from the prewar sources of 90 percent of its natural rubber. Conservation and reuse of rubber became major concerns. Civilian purchases of tires were virtually eliminated, and gasoline rationing coupled with a nationwide speed limit of 35 miles per hour helped reduce tire wear. Meanwhile, the War Production Board built a synthetic rubber industry from scratch. The technology was so new and the need so great, however, that the industry was unable to match the prewar usage level until 1944.

Converted consumer-products plants filled many military orders. The switch of automakers to aircraft production has already been noted. Other conversions showed considerable imagination. A vacuum cleaner factory produced gas masks, a tombstone maker used his grinding equipment to smooth steel plates for welding, a toaster manufacturer turned out gun mounts, and carpet weavers made canvas for tents. The lucrative contract to build the army's jeeps went to the relatively small Willys rather than Ford because government planners thought the giant automaker's resources could more easily be converted to other product lines.

The jeep award was unusual; major corporations captured most of the big contracts. General Motors alone handled $14 billion worth of war orders. Chrysler streamlined production of thousands of M-3 tanks for the army. At the same time, several smaller firms worked on design modifications that led to the advanced M-4 model. Chrysler incorporated these changes when it switched over its assembly line to produce M-4 tanks.

As it had in the First World War, the fighting crippled European agriculture and forced the allies to rely on American farmers. Total farm output in the United States expanded by one-third over its prewar level despite a net decline of almost 15 percent in the agrarian workforce. Female workers replaced many of the men who enlisted and some of the 300,000 prisoners of war brought to the United States worked in the fields as well. Increased use of farm machinery also boosted labor productivity at the same time it freed pasture acreage for the planting of food and

M-3 Tank assembly line at Chrysler. (Courtesy of Chrysler Corporation)

HENRY J. KAISER

The American war effort demonstrated the flexibility of many industries and individuals, but few transformations matched the one in which paving contractor Henry J. Kaiser became the world's most efficient ship builder. But then again, Kaiser had made a number of remarkable transitions in his busy life. Born into a poor family in 1882 in upper New York State, he had quit school at eleven to become a photographer's assistant and later ran his own studio. Seeking more stable employment, Kaiser moved to Spokane, Washington, to work as a salesman for a paving contractor. As with his brief career in photography, he was an apt student and went into business for himself in 1913.

The country was in desperate need of paved roads for its expanding automobile population, and California in particular was well on its way to becoming the most auto-conscious state in the Union. Kaiser moved to Oakland in 1921 and consistently underbid his competitors. His efficiency stemmed from his willingness to buy or build ever larger implements. In addition to highway building, he applied his expertise to dams, heading a consortium of six major contractors who completed Boulder Dam in 1935, well ahead of schedule. Kaiser also made major contributions to the Grand Coulee and Bonneville Dams, as well as the Oakland-Bay Bridge.

Disappointed when he lost the bid for the Shasta Dam in 1939, he determined to subcontract most of the work. He tendered a very low bid for concrete for the project even though he had no facilities for producing it. When he won the award, he built the monster Permanente Concrete plant in Los Gatos and made his deliveries on time and at cost. To move the cement, sand, and gravel, he bought a couple of cargo ships and, as in his other endeavors, became thoroughly familiar with their operation.

That experience led to his decision to submit bids to the government so low that they stunned the staid shipbuilding establishment. He built shipyards along the San Francisco Bay that exploited all of the proven techniques for mass production. He divided projects into individual tasks and set teams of specialists to work on each part of the ships. He used hollow concrete dry docks that could be floated into the bay and then sunk to launch the ships constructed on them. His yards eventually turned out over 1500 vessels, and his workforce broke all records by completing a 10,800-ton Liberty Ship in just eight days from start to finish. A classic American entrepreneur, Kaiser would continue to be active in all sorts of ventures after the war ranging from automobile manufacturing to health-care programs.

fiber crops. Total farm income rose from $10 billion in 1940 to $24 billion in 1945. Prices were soon running ahead of the government's 90 percent parity support levels and threatening to overwhelm its price-control system. Responsibility for coordinating the use of agricultural products and limiting price inflation after 1943 fell to the War Food Administration which operated like the War Production Board in industry.

The federal government had to tax and borrow at unprecedented levels to pay for all the raw materials, factory output, and farm commodities it required. Taxes provided about 43 percent of the $281.5 billion spent on the war. Both income and excise tax rates went up sharply, and a much broader range of items was subjected to excise levies. Higher corporate and estate taxes boosted revenues as well. To speed up collection of income taxes, the federal government introduced a withholding system in 1943 that effectively gave it the equivalent of an extra year's income at the height of the war. The government also obtained revenue from the sale of $185.7 billion in bonds. Individuals bought just under 30 percent of these bonds, with the rest going to corporations and banks. The national debt ballooned from $40 billion to nearly $260 billion in four years. Fortunately, interest rates averaged less than 2 percent, so the government had relatively little trouble funding this debt.

THE DOMESTIC IMPACT OF THE WAR

The war affected all aspects of American enterprise from the largest industrial firms to individual workers and soldiers. The exhilarating climb from the depths of the Great Depression to the heights of the wartime boom dramatically reversed collective and personal fortunes. National income had doubled by 1943, and the distribution of this income was in no way confined to wealthier Americans. Despite federal controls, industrial wages rose nearly 40 percent between 1941 and 1945 and farm wages posted even higher gains. But so much civilian production capacity was converted to military purposes that a scarcity of consumer products was inevitable. Whether they liked it or not, the American people had to save much of their income. The personal savings accumulated by 1945 coupled with higher real wage levels canceled the underconsumption problem.

Inflationary pressures from this growing volume of disposable income became a matter of great concern. Reversing the strategies the AAA and NRA had employed, government officials now tried to prevent price increases mainly through the Office of Price Administration established in late August 1941. It relied initially on informal agreements with producers and distributors to stabilize prices at the levels reached in early October. Inflationary momentum quickly overwhelmed these well-meaning intentions, so Congress passed the Emergency Price Control Act of January 1942 to give the OPA enforcement authority.

Its most unpopular policies related to rationing. The rubber shortage dictated a halt to tire purchases just after the Pearl Harbor bombing, and the subsequent months saw controls placed on cars, typewriters, sugar, gasoline, fuel oil, coffee, meat, processed foods, and even shoes. Coupon books distributed at neighborhood elementary schools gave each family unit a quota of "points." To buy a rationed item, a consumer needed both cash and the required number of coupon points. Retailers had to post lists of the OPA's authorized maximum prices for the items they carried. A black market developed for those willing to pay premiums for price-controlled or rationed goods. Gasoline was in great demand, and inventive methods for delivering it illegally tested the OPA's vigilance.

The OPA also controlled some rents. That program initially applied only to designated defense-area locations, but these ultimately expanded to include more than half of the dwellings in the United States. Greedy landlords and homeless or crowded renters sometimes winked at OPA restrictions, but most Americans patriotically accepted them as emergency measures. The OPA's activities protected the United States from what could have been very debilitating inflation.

Price and rent controls also helped justify wage controls. The Labor Department's Bureau of Labor Statistics had begun computing a cost-of-living index in the First World War, and it became the benchmark for adjusting wage levels. The National War Labor Board reviewed wage demands and approved appropriate increases. Many workers supplemented their controlled wages by working overtime or moonlighting. The full-employment economy offered plenty of opportunities for extra income.

Like underconsumption, unemployment evaporated in the early 1940s. Figure 8-1 (p. 257) showed that the unemployment estimates for some of the war years actually fell below the theoretical 3 percent minimum level. The enlistment of 12 million people in the armed forces, including more than 200,000 women, absorbed the cream of the nation's labor supply. The number of civilian employees working for the federal government meanwhile doubled to 2 million. Expanding and newly constructed war plants had to hire anyone and everyone they could. The number of women working outside their homes rose from about 13 million in 1940 to almost 17 million four years later. The workforces at some aircraft plants were 40 percent female. These employees were particularly adept at intricate mechanical tasks, but women also handled every type of job from riveting to engineering and management. Retired workers returned to their old jobs or found new ones, and some high school students worked half-time at defense plants. Handicapped individuals whom personnel officers previously considered unemployable were hired and performed a variety of tasks.

The war affected working conditions as well. The federal government tacked an extra eight hours onto its traditional forty-hour work week, and many defense plants never shut down at all, rotating through three fifty-six-hour shifts of workers. Labor pirating forced the government to establish the War Manpower Commission to allocate human resources to positions that would contribute most to the war effort. The commission also developed categories of essential occupations which were coordinated with Selective Service boards' decisions about whom to draft into the armed forces.

The growth of labor unions that had begun in the late 1930s persisted through the war years. The unions continued to demand wage increases and other benefits for their members, and the National War Labor Board, established in January 1942, coordinated the government's policies and exercised the unpopular responsibility

---

THE WARTIME LABOR FORCE AT LOCKHEED

Here the Lockheed Aircraft Corp. reports on its wartime labor policies.

It took at least two untrained persons to replace each one who left for service. Despite every effort to keep skilled workers at their posts as long as possible, men still donned uniforms faster than substitutes could be found and trained.

Recruiting sources included the visually handicapped, the elderly, and disabled veterans. Lockheed pioneered in hiring them. And it found their employment stability high, accident frequency rate low, and morale and efficiency surprisingly good. One man with no hands was a tool dispatcher—and a capable one—although he had to keep track of things in his head. Numerous "seeing eye" dogs guided their masters through the maze of corridors to their work benches.

At the height of the manpower shortage employment interviewers used a somewhat grim jest. "If the applicants are warm," they said, "we'll hire them. We've even come close to hiring a few that were cold."

. . . by far the greatest source was women.

"Big airplanes are made up of small parts," Courtland Gross declared when Vega was achieving its record production of B-17s. "And women build small parts to perfection."

They did much more than build small parts. Lockheed hired them by the thousands—when employment reached its 94,000 maximum in June, 1943, nearly 35,000 were women, about 40 percent of the total. It was the era of "Rosie the Riveter."

But handling riveting guns was only one of the hundreds of jobs the "weaker" sex did—and did well. Housewives, war widows, grandmothers became stress analysts, expediters, production engineers, tool planners, inspectors, turret lathe operators, and office workers.

(Lockheed Aircraft Corp., *Of Men and Stars*, Ch. 6, pp. 15-16.)

---

of holding the line on wages. Top labor leaders issued no-strike pledges. Despite the best of intentions, however, thousands of short-lived walkouts and disputes erupted during the conflict.

The United Mine Workers under John L. Lewis were harder to please. They struck repeatedly despite the War Labor Board's attempts to deal with their demands. Incensed at what it viewed as subversive behavior, Congress passed the Smith-Connally Act over President Roosevelt's veto in the summer of 1943. It authorized the president to seize control of any strike-threatened plants engaged in war work and outlined methods for forcefully resolving such disputes. The government did take over the railroads late in 1943 but managed to placate the workers and restore private control in a matter of weeks.

Military successes in Europe and Asia were already convincing the people that the war would end fairly soon. Conventional wisdom held that the huge war expenditures had only temporarily alleviated the depression and had failed to correct its underlying causes. Most Americans expected a return to hard times once the fighting ended. As it turned out, the succeeding decade and a half defied these gloomy predictions. Indeed, the postwar years seemed reassuringly calm and comfortable when compared to the economic extremes the American people had suffered from 1929 to 1945.

READING SUGGESTIONS

Several well-written general surveys of the Great Depression and World War II are available including: Richard S. Kirkendall, *The United States, 1929-45 Years of Crisis and Change* (1974); Dexter Perkins, *The New Age of Franklin Roosevelt, 1932-1945* (1957); Gerald D. Nash, *The Great Depression and World War II* (1979); and Robert Goldston, *The Great Depression: The United States in the Thirties* (1968). Jim Potter's *The American Economy between the World Wars* (1974) starts in the 1920s and is particularly insightful. Broadus Mitchell provides a thorough survey of economic conditions in *Depression Decade: From New Era though New Deal, 1929-1941* (1947). John A. Garraty recently turned his seasoned analytical skills on the era in *The Great Depression* (1986).

Most New Deal programs were enthusiastically praised or thoroughly criticized in books written in the 1930s and early 1940s which seem very dated today. A sympathetic political history is presented by Arthur M. Schlesinger, Jr., in *The Age of Roosevelt* (3 vols., 1957-1960). Two balanced and readable accounts are: Frank Freidel, *The New Deal and the American People* (1964); and William E. Leuchtenburg, *Franklin Delano Roosevelt and the New Deal, 1932-1940* (1963). In *The New Deal and the Problem of Monopoly* (1966), Ellis W. Hawley provides a thorough analysis of the conflicting philosophies which underlay the NIRA and the antitrust programs. Michael E. Parrish's *Securities Regulation and the New Deal* (1970) examines the impact of the SEC as does the more readable volume by Ralph F. De Bedts, *The New Deals' SEC, The Formative Years* (1964). Labor in the 1930s gets ample coverage in Irving Bernstein's *Turbulent Years 1933-1941, A History of the American Worker* (1969) and Harry A. Millis and Emily Clark Brown's *From the Wagner Act to Taft-Hartley* (1950). The farmer's plight is the subject of C. M. Hardin in *The Politics of Agriculture* (1952) and of Theodore Saloutos and John D. Hicks, in *Agricultural Discontent in the Midwest, 1900-1939* (1951).

Hundreds of publications are concerned with the films and the personalities who made them, but it is the commercial end of the industry that stars in Robert H. Stanley's *The Celluloid Empire* (1978) and *The American Movie Industry: The Business of Motion Pictures* (1982), edited by Gorham Kindem. The business aspects of the aviation industry are best described by John B. Rae in *Climb to Greatness* (1968). Of more limited scope is Elsbeth E. Freudenthal's *The Aviation Busi-*

ness (1940), a polemical essay, some of which is excerpted in *The History of the American Aircraft Industry* (1968), edited by G. R. Simmonsen.

Government mobilization and management in the Second World War are praised by Francis Walton in *Miracle of World War II: How American Industry Made Victory Possible* (1956) but given more objective treatment by Eliot Janeway in *The Struggle for Survival* (1951). John R. Craf's *A Survey of the American Economy, 1940-1946* (1947) is a dispassionate, fact-filled compendium of information about every aspect of the domestic war effort. Donald M. Nelson's *Arsenal of Democracy, The Story of American War Production* (1946) was written by the War Production Board's director and may be contrasted with the highly critical work by Bruce Catton, *The War Lords of Washington* (1948). A more balanced analysis appears in David Novick, Melvin Anshen, and W. C. Truppner's *Wartime Production Controls* (1949).

Chapter *9*

AN ERA
OF
EQUILIBRIUM
1945-1960

Many Americans recall the 1950s as a comforting, undemanding period. With a popular, amiable Republican in the White House, it was as though the country had returned to the 1920s or even the late 1890s. Bulls once again roamed on Wall Street, living conditions improved, and the United States was at peace. These pleasant memories overlook the conflicts and doubts that coexisted with the equilibrium of the Eisenhower years.

The postwar decade and a half saw revived growth and expanded opportunity for American enterprise. The consuming population grew briskly as a "baby boom" more than compensated for the low birthrates of the depressed 1930s. The 1940 census had counted 132 million Americans, but twenty years later the United States boasted almost 180 million citizens. Furthermore, these individuals were financially much better off as a group than their parents and grandparents had been. Americans had spent an impressive $120 billion on personal consumption in 1945, but that same measure had nearly tripled to $325 billion fifteen years later. During the same period, per capita disposable income had almost doubled.

New products and marketing techniques were constantly being introduced to cater to the whims of this larger and richer population. Growth industries like electronics, aviation, and communication showed the most impressive gains, but many of the older, less technical sectors also made progress. Freed from the constraints the government had imposed during the depression and the war, business and financial leaders plunged into a new round of corporate consolidation. Huge conglomerates emerged, buffered against economic downturns and adaptable to changing marketing conditions.

Although far less intrusive than what had gone before, economic and political factors did temper the expansion of American enterprise. The federal government's continuing international commitments had important ramifications, beginning with the Marshall Plan's crash program to reconstruct Europe and followed by the persistently high defense expenditures of the Korean and Cold Wars. Despite the best efforts of a government now dedicated to fine tuning the economy, periods of recession interrupted the general prosperity. Some of the most distressing uncertainty about the future had involved the demobilization and reconversion just after the war. The United States readjusted to peace with a certain clumsiness.

THE POSTWAR SHAKE-OUT

Hoping to avoid a repeat of 1919, the federal government began postwar planning as early as 1943. The Office of War Mobilization and Reconversion had just begun reviewing various proposals in the fall of 1944 when the human and material losses associated with the Battle of the Bulge sidetracked plans for a measured reduction in military procurement and production. Suddenly no one knew when and at what cost a final armistice could be achieved. In fact, resistance collapsed rather quickly in Europe in May 1945, and the atomic bombing of two Japanese cities three months later brought an abrupt end to the Pacific war before the government planners had mapped out a comprehensive reconversion plan.

The first major relaxation of control came on August 15, 1945, the day after Japan sued for peace, when the War Manpower Commission freed all individuals to pursue their own interests. The War Production Board quickly curtailed its operations as well, closing down permanently in November. By early 1946 the War Assets Administration was busy disposing of the hundreds of plants the government had constructed, often selling them cheaply to the private companies that had operated them during the war. The armed services also dumped enormous amounts of "war surplus" goods on the market, and stores all over the country sold them at bargain prices. Meanwhile, the federal government was canceling billions of dollars worth of contracts and trimming its bloated wartime bureaucracy.

The Office of Price Administration was a prominent exception. Pent-up consumer demand and bursting personal savings accounts coupled with severe shortages of consumer goods threatened to trigger massive inflation. Manufacturers, wholesalers, and retailers were annoyed with the OPA's price controls, and many customers would gladly pay extra for items in high demand. Many did just that on the black market. A car buyer, for example, might agree to pay an exorbitant price for an irrelevant accessory just to obtain title to the scarce but price-controlled automobile to which it was attached. Bribery of salespersons was not uncommon.

Some Americans treated OPA dictates with the same contempt they accorded to prohibition in the 1920s.

The OPA's authorization was slated to lapse in the summer of 1946, so Congress had to reconsider the whole issue of price controls. President Harry Truman vetoed the watered-down reauthorization bill it finally approved. In just over two weeks, prices jumped 25 percent, more than three times as much as they

---

THE POSTWAR BOOM

Historian Eric Goldman vividly describes the consuming public's frustration with inflation and shortages after the war.

The inflation jabbed people wherever they turned. Trolleys and subways went up two cents, then a nickel. The ten-cent Sunday newspaper was disappearing in America. For years the insurance company, Bankers Life, had run a magazine ad which began: "You can become financially independent. Mary and I did. . . we're living on a life income of $150 a month." In June, 1946 the ad changed. Now Mary and I were "happy as kids on a life income of $200 a month."

Still more irritating were the things that were hard to buy at any price. . . . . But there were ways and ways of getting things. Housewives kept an eye on the front street, alerting each other that a supply truck was on its way to the chain store. Tipping became more and more correct—perhaps a half-dollar to the butcher for the backbreaking labor of handing the chops over the counter. The tie-in sale was commonplace; you could get Scotch if you were ready to load up on wine and rum. Here and there barter came back. A car would get you an apartment; football tickets, good liquor, soap, auto batteries, and sugar were all part of the day's currency.

And there were the under-the-table deals, on a scale far beyond the wartime activity. The black market was most extensive in the new-car field (an estimated 75 percent), and the techniques took on rococo variety. Customers would drop four or five hundred-dollar bills on the desk and quickly look the other way. You could get a new automobile by trading in your old car for a reasonable price—say ten dollars. In other salesrooms, the customer would look toward a wall a hundred feet away and say: "Bet you five hundred dollars I can hit that wall with my hat." In Oklahoma City, a dealer sold you the car and, for four hundred dollars more, a hound dog. The dog, decidedly a postwar model, would then shuffle back to its master.

(Eric Goldman, *The Crucial Decade: America, 1945-1955* [New York: Alfred A. Knopf, 1956], pp. 25-27, ©1956 by Alfred A. Knopf, Inc.)

had in the whole previous year. Congress hastily passed a slightly stronger bill acceptable to Truman, but the price-control program had suffered a mortal wound. Most controls were canceled in the fall of 1946. Fortunately, reconversion had essentially been accomplished by 1947, so American industry could gratify consumer wishes. Even so, inflation persisted until supplies of consumer goods finally caught up with demand and relieved market pressures on prices.

Demobilization went even faster than reconversion. Many returning veterans took advantage of the Servicemen's Readjustment Act of 1944, popularly known as the G.I. Bill, and went to school. At the same time millions of women who had taken outside jobs during the war gave them up to become housewives and mothers. Older and younger workers retired or went back to school. These voluntary withdrawals from the labor force coupled with intensive consumer demand left plenty of jobs open for veterans seeking employment.

Labor unions' activities ended up costing their members far more than did unemployment. As the wartime no-strike pledge lapsed, millions of workers walked off their jobs. Most strikes centered on wage demands. The return of shorter work weeks and reduced opportunities for overtime substantially reduced take-home pay. The unions felt that about a 30 percent increase in pay scales was needed to assure their members adequate weekly wages.

When United Auto Workers President Walter Reuther called for a strike against General Motors, he claimed the company could easily afford to pay higher wages without raising the prices of the cars it sold. President Truman appointed a fact-finding body to examine the matter, but GM refused to open its books to prove or disprove the union's claims. The government commission therefore arranged a deal involving a 17.5 percent wage hike and a corresponding relaxation of price controls. Having depleted their strike funds and their personal savings in the 113-day walkout, the workers reluctantly accepted it. The GM agreement became the prototype for settlements in other industries. The companies often came out way ahead. The 18.5-cent wage increase the steel producers accepted cost them $185 million, but the $5-a-ton price increase the industry imposed brought in $435 million. The workers were quick to notice the gains their employers were making as a result of the agreements, so they struck for still higher wages. A spiral of wage and price hikes continued through the end of the decade.

As usual, John L. Lewis and his United Mine Workers became involved in the most controversial labor squabble. In 1945 coal generated 60 percent of the nation's electricity, 55 percent of its mechanical power, and 90 percent of the railroads' locomotion. Thus the UMW walkout in April 1946 threatened the whole country's well-being. President Truman moved decisively by ordering his interior secretary to seize control of the mines. The UMW then won a favorable wage agreement from the government. When the union staged another strike six months later, though, the government refused to buckle under. The union leaders were eventually cited for contempt of court and assessed stiff fines, but the UMW won its demands after the government restored control of the mines to their owners in the following summer.

These events caused many to question the extent and nature of federal intervention, and the Republican party was in a position to make changes after elections in 1946 gave them control of both houses of Congress for the first time since 1930. President Truman's "Fair Deal," a call for an extension of the New Deal philosophy, found little support on Capitol Hill. Instead, Congress drafted the Taft-Hartley Bill and passed it over Truman's veto. The new legislation specifically outlawed union tactics like an insistence on a closed shop and secondary boycotts. It also authorized the President to call for a cooling-off period of up to eighty days if a strike threatened to close down a vital industry. The act restricted some of the liberties the unions had taken in the wake of the Wagner Act and put them on the defensive. Furthermore, they had to do some house-cleaning in response to the Taft-Harley Act's rule that labor leaders must take anticommunist oaths.

Leadership of the AFL passed to George Meany at almost the same moment Walter Reuther assumed command of the CIO in 1952. Both immediately headed their groups toward a reunification that took place three years later and left Meany presiding over the combined AFL-CIO and Reuther serving as second in command. This enormous labor combine's reputation suffered, however, when Arkansas Senator John L. McClellan's investigating committee publicized evidence that some of its member organizations were engaged in racketeering. The AFL had already expelled the International Longshoreman's Association for criminal behavior; now the AFL-CIO threw out the 1.5 million member Brotherhood of Teamsters. Combative Teamster boss James R. Hoffa attempted to duplicate John L. Lewis's 1930s strategy of using his maverick position as a base for building an independent union empire, but his conviction on a charge of jury-tampering undermined his reputation.

While struggling to put their own house in order, the workers faced a major external threat from automation in which machine operations replaced human labor. The scientific management techniques of the early twentieth century had tried to integrate workers into the manufacturing process as efficient cogs in the larger mechanism. But the simpler and more streamlined these tasks became, the more susceptible they were to automation, especially given the advances in electronics and related fields. Machines had been replacing men for centuries, but now the ultimate blue-collar nightmare loomed; a factory running without a single worker seemed technologically feasible. Unions that protested automation were frequently charged with "featherbedding," an insistence that a company pay workers to do nothing at all if their jobs had been automated out of existence.

Labor militancy faded somewhat in the 1950s because the industrial workforce found itself much better off than earlier generations. Longer-term union contracts created a measure of job security. In recognition of the effects of inflation, these contracts often promised cost-of-living adjustments, or COLAs, to keep wage rates current with price levels. Negotiators also bargained for a host of fringe benefits such as employer-financed pension plans, accident and health insurance, longer vacations, and profit sharing. The unions' recruitment zeal also waned as the organizations themselves became bureaucratized.

THE BUSINESS CLIMATE

The business community basked in a comparatively stable atmosphere. Spurts of relatively modest inflation just after the war and in the early fifties helped buoy sales and profits. Just when the economy seemed on the verge of overheating, a minor recession developed to cool it down again. The unemployment rate during these downturns never reached 7 percent, so it was far lower than for any year during the decade of the 1930s. The switch to longer-term labor contracts helped managers make better projections of future costs and earnings. A bullish mentality reminiscent of the 1920s prevailed on Wall Street so that even companies lacking imaginative or innovative leadership saw the prices of their shares rise.

Like the 1920s, the 1950s stand out as a decade of wide-ranging business consolidation. Although the total number of mergers in manufacturing and mining amounted to just over 4000 in the 1950s compared to the nearly 7000 consolidations recorded in the 1920s, they had far-reaching consequences. The friendly Republican administration in the White House allowed consolidation to take place without much threat of antitrust action. Sometimes it was healthy firms seeking economies of scale that came together in mutually beneficial combinations. Other mergers were more one-sided, with a prosperous company deliberately seeking a feeble target for takeover. The resulting combination could reduce its tax obligations considerably when the losses from the weaker acquisition were deducted from the profits of the stronger partner. Other mergers were desperate efforts to salvage failing firms, as when automakers Studebaker and Packard joined forces in a futile attempt to remain solvent.

A desire to diversify also lay behind many merger decisions in this decade. Some of the resulting firms were "conglomerates" rather than vertically integrated operations engaged in a single line of endeavor. A conglomerate structure had certain advantages over undiversified corporations. It was less susceptible to antitrust action since its share of the business in any single area was usually limited. A well-managed conglomerate could weather unfavorable economic conditions better than a single-purpose firm because it could cancel failing product lines and reallocate resources to more profitable ones. It could eliminate some middleman expenses by acquiring parts or raw materials from wholly owned subsidiaries.

Diversification could be accomplished in several ways. Some companies diversified when their primary activity left them with marketable byproducts. Meatpackers, for example, generated all sorts of inedible materials that could be processed and sold for fertilizer and other uses. Chemical and oil companies frequently expanded their product lines and developed a variety of customers for both producer and consumer goods. In some instances, corporate diversification was carefully planned in advance, and the resulting combinations exhibited considerable flexibility.

Regardless of how it had come into being, the diversified corporation of the 1950s required skilled and imaginative management. Stockholders continued to recede into the background as professional managers assumed total control of enormous firms. Company-wide planning would occur in centralized finance, marketing, accounting, legal, and engineering offices, while operations were generally left to autonomous division heads or general managers. Executives in the central planning offices needed expertise in law, accounting, finance, and the like, and they might have little or no direct experience with the manufacturing, processing, or services the company's operating divisions performed. Business and management skills therefore had wide applicability, so corporate experts of all types could move freely from one company to another.

The success of many firms in the postwar years stemmed from their research and development (R&D) activities. While experimentation and innovation had been characteristic of American enterprise all along, the commitment of extensive resources specifically for these purposes represented a growing trend. The federal government itself provided much of the R&D funding in defense-related areas, and it also financed the bulk of the basic scientific research conducted in private laboratories or on university campuses. Companies were much more willing to fund applied as opposed to "pure" research, and a still larger share of corporate funds paid for the development of marketable products and processes. A firm's R&D commitment depended upon the size of the company itself, its degree of diversification, its ability to attract government contracts, and its major product lines. This last consideration was the most important. Aircraft, electronics, and chemical companies devoted far more of their resources to research and development than did the food processing or basic metals companies.

Funding for research and expansion came from a variety of sources in addition to government contracts. Corporation managers could and did deliberately limit stock dividends in order to retain the company's income for research and other internal uses. Substantial sums were, of course, plowed back into plant and equipment expenditures to increase capacity or replace obsolete machinery and methods. Favorable conditions on Wall Street in the fifties encouraged companies to issue more stock to raise money, and the bond market was often even more attractive to both borrowers and lenders. Because the interest paid on mortgages and federal securities remained low, corporate bonds could offer returns of as little as 5 percent.

The stock and bond buyers had plenty of capital to invest. Insurance companies, for example, doubled their holdings in the 1950s to almost $100 billion, primarily in land, buildings, industrial ventures, and public utilities. In the real estate field, they had to compete with banks and savings and loan institutions which together had poured more than $80 billion into home mortgages alone by 1960. Private pension funds in that year totaled $44 billion, up from just $11 billion in 1950, and most of that money was invested in corporate stocks and bonds. Investment companies created mutual funds of various types to buy into businesses of all types.

Money alone did not guarantee success. Inflation ate into some firms' profits far more than it did others. The companies that tried to offset its effects by boosting their own prices and wages contributed to more inflation down the road. Wage increases in particular were hard to justify given the relatively modest rise in American workers' productivity during the 1950s. It was especially disappointing in comparison to the substantial increases in labor productivity in Europe and the Far East during the same period. Several basic American industries found themselves facing serious foreign competition for the first time. In the United States, although the business climate was generally favorable, some firms and industrial sectors did much better than others.

THE PROGRESS OF POSTWAR ENTERPRISE

The 1920s was the most recent decade that could be considered "normal" in that it encompassed neither a profound depression nor a major war. It therefore provides a compelling point of reference for the 1950s. One similarity involved the structure of American enterprise. Some industries definitely qualified as growth sectors, defined as those expanding at a rate faster than that of the GNP. Aircraft, electronics, energy, advertising, and television posted such gains in the fifties. The growth rates of other sectors like steel and autos paralleled that of the economy as a whole. Some, of course, fell behind. Significantly, many of these floundering sectors like railroads, textiles, coal mining, and agriculture had also been poor performers in the 1920s.

The true irony of the continuing decline in agriculture was that it coincided with and, to a large degree, stemmed from the farmers' phenomenal efficiency. Agricultural production in the 1950s climbed far more rapidly than did manufacturing output, posting on average a 6 percent gain each year. Furthermore, individual productivity nearly doubled in the decade, more than offsetting the dwindling of the agricultural labor force from 7.5 million in 1950 to 5.2 million in 1960. Mechanization, advanced management techniques, and chemicals helped produce these impressive gains. Improved plant hybrids and animal breeds maximized the use of land and feed resources. Extension services and land-grant colleges distributed information freely, encouraging ambitious farmers to innovate and improve their operations.

The depression and war years had accustomed the farmers to expect government assistance and planning. Despite their many flaws, the familiar panaceas of price supports and production limitations were prescribed for postwar agricultural ills. Congress pegged support levels at 90 percent of parity, although it did shift the baseline for determining parity from the 1910-1914 levels to a composite of commodity prices for the preceding ten years. To reduce the flow of produce from increasingly efficient farm operations, variations of the 1930s-style acreage-allotments were introduced. The "soil bank" arrangement of 1956, for example, encouraged farmers to withdraw some of their land from production and devote it to conservation. Predictably, farmers "deposited" their poorest plots in the soil bank and harvested bumper crops from the remainder by concentrating fertilization and cultivation on it.

Surpluses were just one feature in the disheartening agricultural picture. Despite federal price supports, farm income lagged behind inflation in the late 1950s. Virtually all of the government funds went to the commercial operations that constituted about half of the farm units in the country but produced 90 percent of the output. Chronic poverty persisted in rural America and encouraged migration to urban areas.

Overproduction also plagued other weak sectors. Coal had generated more than half of the nation's energy in 1945, but its contribution had declined to one-fourth by 1960. Energy usage did, of course, grow during that period, so the actual as opposed to the comparative consumption of coal dropped less precipitously. Even so, the industry had considerable excess capacity. Mechanization of many operations reduced the need for miners and the ranks of the United Mine Workers thinned dramatically. Workers in other mature industries like textiles and logging also lost out to automation and competition from alternative products like plastics, artificial fibers, and synthetic building materials.

The steel industry did only marginally better. It remained a major industrial employer, ranking fourth in number of workers after the chemical, aircraft, and automotive industries. Concern about aging equipment caused the steelmakers to divert much of their revenue to modernizing plants and processes. This revitalization drive boosted the industry's productivity by a remarkable 50 percent by 1960. Unfortunately, that turned out to be much more than the market could bear. Research and development in other areas had increased the appeal of competing products like aluminum, fiberglass, plastics, and prestressed concrete. The demand for steel also suffered when some of the industry's most important customers, the automakers, encountered problems of their own in the late 1950s.

Immediately after the war, the demand for new cars and trucks was so great that manufacturers could literally sell anything and everything they could produce. Long waiting lists accumulated for 1946 models even though they were identical in most cases to the 1941 or the few 1942 cars built. Independent makers like Nash, Packard, Studebaker, and Hudson prospered despite their limited shares of the market. Henry J. Kaiser teamed with Joseph Frazer in purchasing the Willow Run factory complex to produce autos. As the pent-up postwar demand eased, technological advances like power steering and brakes and automatic transmissions made new models attractive to buyers, so sales remained brisk for several years.

American automobile production peaked in the mid-1950s when the new models had little to offer except higher horsepower and fancy frills, fenders, and fins. Critics meanwhile assailed the industry's strategy of planned obsolescence in design. Worse yet, rumors circulated that parts had been deliberately engineered to wear out or break relatively quickly to coerce owners into paying expensive repair bills or, better yet, buying new cars. The recession of the late fifties hit the automakers hard and squeezed out the independents at last. Only the merger of Nash and Hudson, renamed American Motors, survived as an alternative to the big three: General Motors, Ford, and Chrysler.

The industry giants were hardly secure themselves in the face of an insidious invasion from abroad. At first, American automakers paid little attention to the small, ugly, underpowered car from Germany, the utilitarian Volkswagen Beetle, built from plans developed in the 1930s. But buying and operating this economical little car made good sense to the many Americans disenchanted with the bulky, highly inefficient domestic models. American Motors, under the leadership of

George Romney, was the first to respond in kind by developing the Rambler. The half million compact Ramblers sold pulled the company back from the brink of oblivion. The Big Three grudgingly began to design and build compact models of their own late in the decade. They also expanded their overseas operations. Their European affiliates manufactured smaller cars for sale locally and as imports in the United States. But the problems facing the nation's premier consumer industry were only beginning: as of 1960 Japan had not yet exported a single four-wheeled vehicle to the United States.

Wise investors in the fifties transferred their capital from lagging or slow-growth sectors to the growth industries. Among the glamor stocks were those of the many companies working to meet the country's rapidly expanding demand for power. Energy consumption rose 6 percent a year in the postwar decade and a half, and its character changed as well. As noted earlier, coal declined in relative terms to oil and natural gas. The convenience, high energy yield, and low price of gas made it the most attractive fuel for home heating. Drilling for and distributing this natural resource grew exponentially in conjunction with the postwar housing boom.

Because its continental oil fields could no longer fulfill the U.S. demand, foreign exploration and pumping expanded after the war. Equipped with technological expertise and ample capital, American oil companies moved aggressively in tapping the huge reserves in the countries ringing the Persian Gulf and the Caribbean. They also cooperated with European companies like Royal Dutch Shell and British Petroleum in joint ventures in the former European colonies. Exports of refined petroleum derivatives paid for some of the U.S. imports of crude oil, but a growing reliance on foreign supplies of this vital resource for energy and the manufacture of plastics and other synthetics would have serious diplomatic and international trade consequences in the years ahead.

The prospects for peaceful exploitation of atomic energy looked very promising at that point. Tapping the tremendous energy released during atomic fission appeared to be an ideal solution to the incessant American demand for more power. The federal government set up the Atomic Energy Commission to superintend its research and development programs, and the AEC carried on extensive experimentation at Oak Ridge, Tennessee, and Los Alamos, New Mexico. Despite the considerable expense involved, the few electricity-generating reactors that had gone on-line by 1960 seemed to justify the optimism about atomic energy. Few were aware at that point of the problems associated with the disposal of radioactive wastes or the inherent inefficiencies in atomic energy production. Furthermore, the AEC's activities were closely coordinated with the development of nuclear weapons systems, so they received ample government funding. Concern over national security also fostered rapid growth in the aircraft and aerospace industries.

THE MILITARY-INDUSTRIAL COMPLEX

The reconversion of American industry from a war to a peacetime footing had been completed by 1947 just when mounting paranoia about communism caused a revival of extensive defense contracting. The Cold War that persisted through the 1950s turned hot during the Korean Conflict from 1950-1953. Defense expenditures therefore accounted for an average of 62.3 percent of all federal outlays in the 1950s, nearly double the percentage for that purpose in the late 1940s.

Faith in air power was the centerpiece of the postwar defense strategy. Both the air force and the navy were eager to incorporate advanced fighters and bombers into their squadrons, so plenty of government money poured into research, development, and procurement. Air, sea, and land based missiles began entering the nation's arsenals in the 1950s. The aircraft industry quickly slid into the missile-building business at the same time it improved its manned equipment. The industry thus maintained its dominant position at the core of the defense complex.

All this activity gave a second wind to an industry that had faced an uncertain future as the Second World War drew to a close. Manufacturers and subcontractors had attempted to anticipate and plan for peacetime conversion, but their success depended upon management skill, luck, and the unpredictable character of the postwar economy. Some mistakenly anticipated a boom in private flying; other, more perceptive analysts thought commercial airlines would offer the most lucrative market for their products. Therefore each of the major aircraft companies set out on a slightly different path.

Supplying the airlines with commercial air transports was highly profitable for some, particularly Douglas which maintained its traditional leading position for some time. It stretched its four-engine DC-4 into a roomier DC-6 and eventually a DC-7 capable of flying nonstop across the continent and across some oceans as well. Douglas had built half of all the passenger aircraft in use around the world by the late fifties. The other popular four-engine, long-range transports were Lockheed's Constellation and Boeing's Stratocruiser. The Consolidated-Vultee Aircraft Corp. hoped to capture the shorter-hop market with its twin-engine Convair 110 through 440 line. When Lockheed tried to compete in that area, it encountered serious design problems with its gas-turbine, prop-driven Electra and decided to concentrate on filling military orders.

Although the Federal Aviation Administration set rigid standards and monitored the performance of the commercial carriers, the government here was far less important than overseas where state-supported airlines were common. Airline passenger service in the United States remained a strictly private enterprise. Pan-American and American Airlines kept a step or two ahead of United and Trans-World Airlines. TWA suffered serious management and financial problems after it fell under the control of eccentric billionaire Howard Hughes.

In general, however, the airlines enjoyed robust growth in routings and passenger-miles flown, and they ended the decade with over a million employees. Ample revenues and a keen sense of competition induced them to purchase complicated and costly aircraft. The opening of commercial air service to every significant city in the United States further undermined the railroads already reeling from private automobiles and expanding trucking service. The rapid spread of reliable scheduled air service was also responsible for the cooling of interest in light aircraft ownership. The anticipated boom in private flying simply never developed.

Jet engines did not appear on passenger planes until they had been thoroughly tested on military aircraft. Jet propulsion had reached the prototype stage by the end of the war, allowing Lockheed to produce its successful Shooting Star fighters. Although North American Aviation underwent a rather rocky transition from war to peace, it created a winner in the F-86 Sabrejet. Design and production problems were ironed out soon enough to make it the basic air force fighter during the Korean War. When Hughes Aircraft then developed a highly sophisticated electronic guidance system, several companies attempted to design fighters that would maximize its potential. Convair won this competition with the F-102 fighter that sold well in the 1950s.

Like the first ocean-going steam engines, the early jet engines consumed so much fuel they were impractical for long-range flying. The propeller-driven B-29s' atomic-bomb carrying capability kept them in production after 1945 and helped Boeing bridge the gap from war to peace. Convair built the next generation bomber, the gigantic B-36 pushed along by six reverse-mounted propeller engines. A raucous political and strategic debate which had nothing to do with its airworthiness gave the behemoth aircraft an undeserved bad name. Convair equipped the last B-36s delivered to the air force with four supplemental jet power plants that brought the aircraft's engine count to ten. Boeing had meanwhile designed its fully jet-propelled B-47 and B-52 models, the latter destined to become the workhorse of the United States Air Force for the succeeding quarter century.

Boeing 707. (Courtesy of the Boeing Company)

Boeing then took the short technological step necessary to create its 707 passenger airliner, the first of which began flying commercially in 1958. The competition shook Douglas out of its complacency and into a development program of its own in 1955. It began delivering jet-propelled DC-8s four years later to its commercial airline customers. British and Russian manufacturers had successfully flown commercial jet-liners before the first American airplanes reached the market, but both domestic and foreign buyers favored the Boeing and Douglas models. Although American dominance had slipped a bit by 1960, the United States still produced 80 percent of all the airplanes in commercial service worldwide.

Commercial sales actually represented a minor portion of the aircraft and the burgeoning aerospace business. By the end of the decade many smaller firms were relying almost exclusively on defense contracts. Even industry leaders like Lockheed, Douglas, and North American were drawing almost half of their earnings from missiles and related defense development and production. Guidance systems were often far more complex than the missiles themselves, so companies like Hughes Aircraft assembled teams of talented electronics engineers to keep them ahead of their competitors. Two Hughes researchers, Simon Ramo and Dean Woolridge, left the company in 1953, however, to join forces with the Thompson Products Corp. and create TRW. It quickly established itself as a leader in the aerospace field.

Aircraft and aerospace definitely qualified as growth industries in the 1950s. They employed over a million workers, far more than in any other manufacturing sector. Firms bidding for defense contracts often hired retired high-ranking military officers to help them negotiate with the Pentagon. Such arrangements provoked criticism of the whole defense establishment and were part of the problem President Dwight D. Eisenhower referred to in his 1960 warning to the American people to be wary of the growing influence of the military-industrial complex. This massive industry had become almost wholly dependent upon a single customer, the U.S. government. Entrepreneurial decisions and development proposals obviously reflected this marketing situation. Competition could hardly be said to exist where complex and sophisticated components had to meet exacting performance standards. Often only one firm had the necessary expertise in a given area. In other instances lobbyists and company officers worked hard to insure that government contract specifications matched their firm's capabilities. And, because so much of the work was classified as secret, accountability was almost impossible to assess or enforce. Despite these concerns, the military-industrial complex continued to occupy a prominent position in American enterprise in succeeding years.

ORGANIZATION MAN: THOMAS J. WATSON

The stereotypic businessman in the 1950s was a white, clean-shaven, middle-level executive wearing a conservative grey flannel suit, white shirt, and tie. He worked in a large, dehumanizing corporation rather than for himself. He mainly did paper work and therefore relied on secretaries and business machines for assistance. His goal was to generate profits for his company and to earn personal rewards like bonuses, promotions, and, ultimately, a seat on the board of directors. A number of popular books and films reinforced this image of the modern American business-man, and he was also subjected to extensive sociological and psychological study and analysis.

The International Business Machines Corporation supplied the machinery the man in the grey flannel suit used, and IBM itself seemed to epitomize the ideal American corporation at mid-century. The company's nonunionized sales, mainte-nance, and research personnel wore neat, conservative clothing and exuded quiet confidence. IBM paid high salaries to its employees, half of whom were college graduates, and they reciprocated with intense loyalty and pride in their company. In 1960 it was supplying 90 percent of the complex machinery modern businesses used, and it had achieved a solid position as one of the leading corporations in the United States.

Thomas J. Watson had presided over the growth of this remarkably success-ful organization, running it singlehandedly until the early 1950s when he installed his son and namesake, Tom Watson, Jr., as his successor. The senior Watson had begun his business career in the 1890s as a traveling organ and piano salesman in upstate New York. He was good at it, so good, in fact, that he soon landed a job with much greater potential for advancement at the National Cash Register Com-pany. There he became a disciple of John Henry Patterson, the driving, charismatic head of the company. This master promoter used all sorts of techniques to inspire and reward his sales force including revival-like conventions to exhort them to greater achievements. Watson was an apt pupil, and he used similar tactics to build a team spirit when he assumed command of his own company.

National Cash Register also gave Watson practical lessons in competition. Aspiring to monopolize the cash register business, Patterson established a "competition department" that included a research arm to improve the company's machines. But superior products were only part of the strategy; the department also set out to undermine its opposition directly. Watson became the company's chief clandestine operative, moving from city to city to open competing retail out-lets which undersold or sabotaged the machines rival companies were marketing. The campaign was so successful it caused angry competitors to sue NCR. Both Patterson and Watson, among others, were convicted in 1913 of conspiring to re-strain trade. Appeals and judicial rulings saved Watson from serving a prison sen-tence, and he insisted all along that he personally had done nothing wrong. Ten-sions at the company grew so severe, though, that Patterson fired Watson in 1914.

Many other firms were eager to hire this talented, clever businessman, now approaching his fortieth birthday. He finally accepted an offer from Charles R. Flint to serve as general manager and later president of the Control-Tabulating-Recording Company. Flint's holding company controlled a jumble of small firms that manufactured scales, calculators, and other business machines and technical instruments. Watson immediately created a centralized research department to im-prove the quality and competitiveness of the company's many products. He also

THINK

Thomas J. Watson, Sr. (Courtesy of International Business Machines Corporation)

personally directed an elaborate training and motivational program for his sales-force. The company prospered under his leadership and expanded its operations overseas in the early 1920s. These foreign linkages justified Watson's decision to rename the enterprise the International Business Machines Corp. in 1924. Chairman of the board Flint died late that same year, leaving Watson in sole control.

Central to the company's growth was its expertise in data processing. One of the original elements of the C-T-R combine had been the Tabulating Machines Co. that Herman Hollerith had founded in the 1890s to market mechanical counters. His equipment could read and tabulate data punched onto paper tape or cards, and it had earned high marks in analyzing the data collected in the 1890 census. By the 1930s punched IBM cards had become the world's standard for machine recording and sorting of statistical information. The company's equipment was invaluable in keeping track of social security data during the depression. Though not a scientist himself, Watson was very supportive of researchers and willing to fund experiments that might later lead to practical and profitable applications. In the 1930s, for example, he supplied at no cost machinery and support for a Columbia University professor who needed to process thousands of examination scores. His experiences led to the development of the machine-readable answer sheets all too familiar to present-day college students.

Versatile IBM equipment found plenty of new applications during the 1940s. Military personnel and financial records were punched onto millions of IBM cards. Some of the company's largest calculating machines churned through the complex computations needed to publish navigational manuals and ballistics tables as well as to analyze weather information. The company's sales had risen from $40 million in 1939 to $140 million by 1945, and that was just the dawn of its most expansive period. No modern office was complete without an IBM electric typewriter, and thousands of firms large and small owned or leased the company's data-processing units consisting of a keypunch machine, a sorter, and a tabulator. The only serious challenge to the company's dominance in the field of business machinery came from rivals developing true computers.

A number of individuals have been credited with inventing the modern digital computer because, as with motion picture equipment, several key stages of development took place. Watson became involved in the early 1940s when Harvard University mathematics professor Howard H. Aiken proposed linking several of IBM's huge mechanical calculators together to carry out elaborate mathematical computations. Watson donated half a million dollars worth of equipment and lent some of his research staff to the project which produced the Mark I computer in 1944. Aiken then alienated the egotistical corporation president by slighting his contribution to the project, so Watson exhorted his own research staff to surpass the Harvard experiment.

In fact, two University of Pennsylvania professors with army funding had already made the Mark I obsolete by substituting vacuum tubes for slower-moving electric switches. They called their machine ENIAC, an acronym for Electronic Numerical Integrator and Calculator, and its successors included a UNIVAC and a MANIAC. Meanwhile, IBM's researchers developed its first SSEC (Selective Sequence Electronic Calculator) in 1948. In a couple of years, the SSEC evolved into a much more advanced 701 model, which in turn was quickly superseded by the popular 704s and 705s. By the end of the decade, these room-sized IBM computers, using data stored on magnetic tapes and capable of being accessed randomly, were performing computational feats undreamed of even a few years earlier. Use of the company's equipment far outdistanced that of its many rivals in the computer business like Sperry-Rand, Honeywell, NCR, Burroughs, and Control Data.

IBM's success rested on a number of pillars. Watson effectively used his drive and authoritarian personality, which his son inherited, to manage and inspire his employees. Though his company often failed to be first with innovations, it made up for that deficiency with its remarkable skill at incorporating such advances into reliable, attractive packages. The company distributed much of its equipment under leasing contracts which allowed the customer to benefit from the fast, efficient service of the IBM army of technicians. Internally, the company elicited extra effort through profit-sharing plans and a continuing reliance on psychological motivation techniques. The large and small signs displayed throughout IBM's offices and laboratories admonishing the employees to "THINK!" were symbolic of the company's zeal in the realm of human engineering.

IBM 701 Computer. (Courtesy of International Business Machines Corporation)

THOMAS J. WATSON ON THINKING

In addition to serving as the driving force behind IBM, Watson wrote speeches, editorials, and inspirational pieces. These 1947 comments illustrate his rationale for the motto he designed for his company: "THINK!

During the past century such great improvements have been made in machinery and methods for getting raw materials from the earth, forests and farms, processing them into finished products, and delivering them to the consumers, that we frequently hear it said that it is no longer necessary for people to think.

The facts are that as a result of these developments it is more necessary today for people to think than ever before, because it was sound thinking that brought these machines and methods into being and it requires real thought to put them to constructive use.

When we realize the importance of further developments in all that has been started, we understand how important constructive thought is.

The real contribution of improved machines and methods is to relieve thinkers from routine operations, giving them more time to think.

(Thomas J. Watson, *"As A Man Thinks..."* [New York, International Business Machines Corporation, 1954], p. 123.)

Watson's years at NCR had profoundly shaped his attitudes. Interestingly enough, his own company also ran afoul of the antitrust laws. Shortly before Tom Watson, Sr.'s death in 1956, his son signed a consent agreement terminating a lengthy court battle over the company's alleged monopoly practices. The chief point of contention was IBM's dominant position in the production of data cards that other companies' machines also used. IBM cards actually represented only a minor aspect of the company's operations at that point, as it was the unquestioned leader in producing and distributing all types of business equipment. Company officials argued that IBM's predominant position had resulted from the superiority of its products rather than illegal or unethical practices. To the extent that IBM seemed the very model of the modern high-technology business organization, this claim had the ring of truth. Despite its prominent position, IBM could never relax given the number and variety of technological advances constantly appearing in the postwar electronics bonanza.

HIGH TECHNOLOGY FOR THE MASSES

Along with the businessman in the grey flannel suit, the public had a stereotype of a scientist: a man wearing thick glasses and a knee-length white lab coat hunched over a microscope or watching colored liquids bubbling in glass retorts. The researchers who had redefined the art of war with radar, advanced avionics, and atomic weapons were now expected to alter civilian life just as profoundly. University professors shared their expertise with corporate investigators and theorists, producing a flood of technical publications. Research spending of all types rose from just under a billion dollars a year in 1940 to over $10 billion in the late fifties. Public faith in the ability of science and engineering to improve, ease, and extend life remained strong throughout this period.

Many startling advances involved electronics, and whole new industrial sectors grew out of research findings. The transistor was clearly the most important single invention. It not only replaced bulky, fragile electron tubes, but its success stimulated exploration of other practical applications of solid-state physics. Three physicists, John Bardeen, Walter Brittain, and William Schockley, working at Bell Laboratories, AT&T's huge New Jersey research facility, had originally hoped to develop reliable, solid-state electronic switches. Late in 1947 they found that the germanium crystals they were using could, if properly bonded, amplify electric signals just as vacuum tubes did. They deliberately kept their discovery a secret until the following June, and it provoked little fanfare when it was finally announced. The research team pressed ahead with its invention, though, extending its properties and developing improved fabrication techniques.

In 1952 Bell Labs staged an elaborate symposium to inform potential manufacturers of the attributes and advantages of transistors and of the techniques they had developed to produce them. AT&T offered the outsiders licenses in return for royalty payments if they wished to go into production. One company that paid the $25,000 license fee was a small firm that had begun as the research arm of a geophysics company in Texas. It had subsequently developed expertise in electronics while working on instrumentation projects during the war. As Texas Instruments, the company now plowed most of its profits into further research that led to the invention of silicon transistors which were far cheaper to produce and capable of operating at higher frequencies than Bell's germanium ones. TI cranked them out by the millions. Even though the company had become the world's largest manufacturer of transistors of all types by 1960, it had only begun to capitalize on the potential market for solid-state devices that would develop in the coming decades.

Television manufacturers were prime customers for electronic devices and components. The chief proponent of what was to become the leading entertainment industry in the United States was David Sarnoff, still piloting the Radio Corporation of America. Sarnoff's commitment to television had begun in the 1920s when Vladimir K. Zworykin, a brilliant Russian emigré like Sarnoff, suggested to the corporation president that he could develop a working television system if given a grant of $100,000. That estimate proved to be highly optimistic: Sarnoff eventually spent $10 million to perfect the basic components and an additional $40 million to turn television into a profit-maker. RCA demonstrated its prototype to the public at the New York World's Fair in 1939, but the war slowed its development.

Having used commercially sponsored, nationwide network broadcasts to make radio a paying enterprise, Sarnoff envisioned a similar mass market for television. He also recognized that RCA could never run such a vast enterprise on its own. He therefore ordered his researchers to share their findings with other television pioneers like Alfred Du Mont as well as the established radio manufacturers like General Electric, Philco, and Zenith. This group petitioned the Federal Communications Commission in 1941 to establish standards for the embryonic industry, and the FCC authorized eighteen transmission channels, specified FM sound carriers, and adopted a 525-line screen scanning arrangement. In 1946 RCA set up a small broadcasting network on the east coast and began selling receivers with ten-inch screens for $375 each. Other manufacturers quickly jumped on the bandwagon, and the number of sets sold skyrocketed from 175,000 in 1947 to 7 million in 1950. A decade later, 87 percent of the nation's households had at least one television set and nearly 10 percent had more than one.

Television's rapid spread did not please all Americans. Those in the motion picture industry feared, and with good reason, that home television broadcasts would cut theater attendance. They tried to attract more ticket buyers with widescreen and three-dimensional projection systems. Gradually, however, Hollywood realized that its dramatic talents and technical skills could be sold to the broadcasters on a regular basis either in the form of older films or as first-run productions. Radio networks and manufacturers were also leary of new medium, but it affected them less in the short run than it did the filmmakers. Sarnoff's traditional business

EDWIN LAND

Although huge combines with bureaucratic management seemed to dominate the business community after the Second World War, opportunities still remained open for ambitious entrepreneurs. Edwin Land was one of the most successful of these. In developing his products, he accumulated more than 500 patents, second only to Thomas Edison's record. Land's approach began with a fully formed ideal vision of a product. He then created, in some cases from the ground up, the scientific and technical methods he needed to fulfill his vision.

A visit to New York's brightly lit Times Square gave him his first goal: to develop a method for reducing glare. He interrupted his undergraduate studies at Harvard to pursue research that ultimately produced glass and plastic sheets that transmitted polarized light. At the age of twenty-eight, he established the Polaroid Corporation in 1937 at the depth of the Great Depression. Its investors were so impressed with Land's capabilities that he had a free hand in both research and business decisions. His lenses and filters were vital parts of the sophisticated optical instruments the armed forces used during the war. Looking for a mass consumer use after the war, Land became involved in three-dimensional movie projection. He manufactured millions of cardboard frames with plastic lenses to sort out the polarized images on the screen, but the business soon collapsed, a victim of television and poor screenplays.

Fortunately for Land, he was already selling his most famous product, the instant-developing camera. He conceived of it while vacationing in 1943 and claims to have solved the technical details within six months. Turning the concept into a consumer product took considerably longer, so it was not until 1948 that the first Polaroid Land Camera went on sale. Never complacent, Land and his research team constantly improved their system. The basic marketing strategy was to make better film and cheaper cameras. Sales boomed as they made earlier products obsolete and thereby encouraged customers to scrap older equipment and pay for improved versions.

The Polaroid Corporation quickly moved into second place behind the personal photography industry's leader Eastman Kodak. At a cost of half a billion dollars, Land developed the ultimate instant camera, at first called the SX-70, that would instantly develop full color snapshots. Kodak meanwhile introduced its own instant cameras and films, but Polaroid continued to dominate the market for these specialized products. With that challenge met, the restless Edwin Land moved on to other visionary concepts like instant-developing movies.

adversary was William Paley, head of the rival Columbia Broadcasting System radio network that had succeeded in outdrawing Sarnoff's NBC radio audiences. At first Paley opposed the whole concept of television, but then he established a powerful CBS TV network when the new medium's popularity became obvious.

To outflank RCA, CBS engineers worked on a color TV transmission system that segregated the colors with spinning disks inside both transmitters and receivers. Sarnoff's research staff simultaneously experimented with an all-electronic system they hoped could be made compatible with the current black and white sets already in millions of homes. In early demonstrations RCA's color reception was clearly inferior to that of CBS, so the FCC announced guidelines making the CBS system the industry standard. An outraged Sarnoff exhorted his researchers to perfect their system and sued the FCC for ignoring the compatibility issue. The Supreme Court refused to void the FCC guidelines, but common sense prevailed anyway, and the agency reversed its decision to favor compatible color in 1953.

It caught on rather slowly. Manufacturers knew that expensive color sets would not sell until a lot of programming was available, but no one wanted to pay the much higher costs of color broadcasting for the limited number of receivers in use—no one, that is, except Sarnoff. RCA continued to pour money into both color broadcasting and receivers, eventually spending an estimated $130 million on these activities before enough consumer demand arose to make the venture profitable. At that point, having long since abandoned their clumsy mechanical system, Paley and CBS jumped in just in time to ride the crest of popularity and profitability that developed in the late 1950s.

Other forms of media also experienced technological change and improvement in the postwar years. While the superior RCA television equipment had easily overwhelmed its CBS competition, the company's 45-rpm phonograph records quickly lost most of their market to Columbia's popular 33-1/3 rpm system. These long-playing discs were sold to owners of equipment advertised as "high fidelity." The audio quality of radio reception improved as well through the use of frequency modulation. FM revolutionized the nature of radio broadcasting because it allowed a number of smaller stations to direct their transmissions to specialized audiences. Home photography became an almost universal hobby, spurring sales of still and movie cameras and film.

Somewhat less dramatic changes occurred in other products for the home. Electronic research improved electric stoves and encouraged the manufacture of "automatic" washing and drying machines. Du Pont scientists created a versatile coolant they named "freon" for use in refrigerators and food freezers, and freon also stimulated sales of building and home airconditioning systems. Plastics of all sorts worked their way into widespread domestic usage. "Labor-saving" devices like vacuum cleaners and dishwashers were particularly appealing to American housewives burdened with child-rearing duties during the baby boom.

THE PEOPLE OF THE AFFLUENT SOCIETY

Many commentators in the 1950s discussed the impact prosperity and material well-being were exerting on society in the United States. Economist John Kenneth Galbraith's study of *The Affluent Society* criticized what he considered an overemphasis on individual materialism at the expense of concern over broader social ills. In *The Lonely Crowd*, sociologist David Riesman painted a bleak portrait of a society becoming increasingly conformist in its attitudes. Having examined a suburban, middle-class, white-collar community, William H. Whyte, Jr., described the signs of conformity and mediocrity he discovered in his widely read *The Organization Man*. Novels, plays, films, and an occasional television program addressed similar themes, portraying Americans as narrow-minded, thoughtless, politically apathetic, and self-satisfied. A few critics "dropped out" of society, refusing to condone the materialism others appeared to value.

Implicit in many of these critical comments was the fact that the United States was moving into a postindustrial phase. At some point in the 1950s the number of workers in the service fields surpassed those engaged in production. White-collar jobs definitely outnumbered blue-collar ones by 1960, but class distinctions had become blurred as the labor unions obtained for their members many middle-class trappings like long-term employment contracts, pension plans, and extensive fringe benefits. At the same time, the number of self-employed individuals had declined dramatically. About 85 percent of all Americans worked for someone else in the late 1950s. A couple of hundred supercorporations employed more than half of these workers and imposed conformist pressures of their own. Simultaneously, television broadcasting created a common national cultural experience that worked against individuality and regional distinctiveness.

With the whole United States population as potential customers, billions of dollars were spent on advertising campaigns to influence consumer preferences. Some social scientists devoted their energies to market research, seeking to determine what the public really wanted; others used their persuasive skills to manipulate and influence potential buyers. The airwaves and the print media bombarded people with a constant stream of ballyhoo. These messages were deliberately designed to encourage the buying of more products, and Americans responded in a materialistic fashion. Middle-class goals advanced far beyond the simpler ambitions of earlier times. Now a family might feel deprived unless it owned two cars, a color television set, two bathrooms, and a full complement of household appliances. "New and improved" products were touted every day so no one could ever be complacent. The service sector also expanded in size and in the types of support offered. Specialists who performed a whole range of personal and product services absorbed substantial amounts of consumer money.

Market research was one service sector that developed many clients among the manufacturing industries. As noted earlier, they had been able to sell every thing they made to the product-starved consuming public right after the war. When that demand eased in the early fifties, though, many companies adopted the

THE "WELL-ROUNDED" ORGANIZATION MAN

William H. Whyte, Jr.'s book, The Organization Man *described the educational and societal influences that created a class of consensus-seeking corporation employees and executives. Here he describes the typical attitude of the "well-rounded" mediocrity he claims was all too common in the 1950s.*

On the fundamental premise of the new model executive, however, the young men who hope to be that vary little, and from company to company, region to region, you hear a litany increasingly standard. It goes something like this: Be loyal to the company and the company will be loyal to you. After all, if you do a good job for the organization, it is only good sense for the organization to be good to you, because that will be best for everybody. There are a bunch of real people around here. Tell them what you think and they will respect you for it. They don't want a man to fret and stew about his work. It won't happen to me. A man who gets ulcers probably shouldn't be in business anyway.

This is more than the wishful thinking normal of youth. Wishful it may be, but it is founded on a well-articulated premise—and one that not so many years ago would have been regarded by the then young men with considerable skepticism. The premise is, simply, that the goals of the individual and the goals of the organization will work out to be one and the same. The young men have no cynicism about the "system," and very little skepticism—they don't see it as something to be bucked, but as something to be co-operated with.

"marketing concept" that General Electric had pioneered. They sought to determine what their consumers really wanted so they could tailor their research, development, and production to match those preferences. They hired economists and other social scientists to investigate through interviews, questionnaires, and other methods just what the buying public desired. Processing the information gathered in marketing surveys was a tedious process before the introduction of computers, but the results were so promising that the marketing concept became a firmly entrenched aspect of the modern mass consumption society.

Even though real per capita personal income rose throughout the fifties, there never seemed to be enough money to pay for everything one felt motivated, for whatever reasons, to purchase. The personal savings rate fell far below its wartime level and much of the earlier backlog was cashed in to pay for goods and services. Lenders stepped forward eagerly to extend credit to customers short on cash. Gasoline credit cards were distributed by the millions to induce customer loyalty to a particular oil company's products. Department stores issued credit cards with revolving payment plans to encourage repeat patronage. And, of course, appliance and car dealers continued to arrange loans to allow customers to buy their expensive products immediately. "Buy now, pay later," became the watchword. The outstanding balance of consumer credit grew from $73 billion in 1950 to $196 billion a decade later.

Inflationary pressures arising from monetary factors and perhaps even more from rising expectations influenced the employment picture. Through the 1950s most employees in government, education, and personal services remained non-unionized. They depended on their employers to make periodic adjustments in their salaries either because of increasing seniority or because the workers had obtained additional training and experience. They also expected to improve their positions through promotion. The ladder from bank teller to vice president seemed easier to climb than the one from lathe operator to shop foreman. If one's current position or prospects seemed unsatisfactory, one could always transfer to other jobs across town or across the continent. The population was in a constant state of flux, with a typical family moving from house to house or town to town every two or three years.

All Americans aspired to own homes of their own, and the large number of children born in the postwar years increased the demand for individual family dwellings. The GI Bill and Federal Housing Administration mortgage loan guarantees encouraged the building of millions of new homes and apartments. To meet the demand some builders streamlined their production methods with standardized plans that allowed for few modifications. William Levitt's company carried the process to an extreme. Using assembly-line techniques, it constructed whole "Levittowns" of inexpensive, virtually identical houses.

To find space for all these houses, contractors developed huge tracts of land in the suburbs. Critics of suburbia saw the building of thousands of similar houses in treeless, featureless rows as evidence of the homogeneity and conformity of modern American society. The suburban migrants tended to be upwardly mobile whites who left the congestion of the cities in search of more private residences. The contingents of non-whites simultaneously moving into the central cities further goaded the whites to leave. Suburbs soon ringed the older industrial cities of the Northeast and the Middle West. The millions of Americans who migrated to the coastal regions of California, Texas, and Florida often created similar sprawling residential areas unrelated to any core city.

The universal ownership of private cars encouraged moves to the suburbs and the Sun Belt. Public transit systems lost riders, and parking lots engulfed thousands of city blocks. California pioneered the development of an urban freeway system, building limited-access, multilane highways to allow traffic to flow quickly from one section of urban sprawl to another. Many superhighways built elsewhere were financed by the collection of tolls. The Pennsylvania Turnpike was the most famous of these trunk highways. The high cost of building and maintaining these massive internal improvements naturally argued for a resort to federal financing just as the railroads had done earlier. In 1956 the Eisenhower administration sponsored a plan to improve highways all across the country with the revenues from special gasoline and use taxes. The proposal to construct 41,000 miles of high-speed thruways seemed visionary at the time, but three decades later the interstate highway system seems barely capable of handling the traffic flow.

Businesses followed the population migration to the outskirts of the cities and the edges of the continent. Huge grocery supermarkets, often units of national chains, served as "anchors" for suburban shopping centers. Hoping to capitalize on the commuter traffic that passed by daily, thousands of small businesses sprang up along the highways linking the cities to the suburbs. While suburban shops might lack the variety and scope of downtown stores, free parking and accessibility offset such disadvantages. Branches of central businesses were also established in the suburbs. Banks and other service firms joined the retailers in expanding their market reach to newly populated areas. By the late fifties huge discount department stores were altering American buying habits. The pioneering discount-store mogul was Eugene Ferkauf who developed his Korvette store chain into a major retailing enterprise, undercutting competitors and stimulating imitators.

As both the people and the businesses moved out, many industries did the same. The well-developed transportation system and the nationwide character of marketing weighed heavily in such decisions. So-called footloose industries no longer needed to build plants near sources of raw materials or power. Finding a capable workforce could be the key consideration in selecting locations for "clean" industries like electronics and small appliances. This phenomenon was obvious even in the older industrial regions. Circling Boston on a ten-mile radius, State Route 128 became nationally known as the address for dozens of high-technology research and manufacturing industries. Air conditioning made year-round work more comfortable in southern California, Texas, and Florida. Some corporate headquarters and business offices also abandoned the cities for pleasantly landscaped, roomy buildings in the country. The suburbanization of America would continue in succeeding decades.

As the white population left the central cities, blacks moved in seeking economic opportunities. The manpower demands of the Second World War had pulled hundreds of thousands of blacks out of their rural homes in the South. After the war many decided to take their chances in the cities rather than return to the certain poverty of southern sharecropping. The black migration to the Northeast and Sun Belt cities triggered societal upheavals. Some urban districts switched from being white to predominantly black residences in a matter of months. The blacks increasingly expressed impatience with their second-class treatment, and articulate leaders like Martin Luther King, Jr. insisted upon fair treatment.

By the mid-1950s the federal government began taking steps to reverse a half-century of neglect and discrimination. Buttressed by favorable court deci-

JOHN H. JOHNSON

In the 1950s black Americans were asserting their rights and self-reliance through legal, political, and economic means, and some individuals took advantage of opportunities that had previously offered little promise. One successful business strategy involved catering to "special markets" by producing, advertising, and selling to a targeted audience. *Ebony*, the magazine with the widest readership in the black community, was both an example of a product aimed at a special market and a means for others to advertise their products to that same group of consumers.

The flagship of the Johnson Publishing Co., *Ebony* was only one of several publications that an energetic entrepreneur developed for his fellow blacks. John H. Johnson was the son of an Arkansas mill worker, and he began his education in segregated schools. After she had been widowed, his mother moved to Chicago where the youth could benefit from a much more challenging high school curriculum and win a scholarship to the University of Chicago. Although he dropped out after two years, Johnson continued his formal education as a writer and publicist after being hired in 1938 to edit a house organ for the Supreme Liberty Life Insurance Co.

Convinced there was a market for a specialty magazine, he began publishing the *Negro Digest* in 1942, a compendium of original or reprinted articles. He then used the popular *Life* magazine as a model for *Ebony*, which he introduced three years later. Filled with photographs and breezy writing, the first issue was an immediate sell-out, encouraging Johnson to continue editing and distributing the magazine. Responding to activists in the fifties who criticized the publication for middle-class complacency and values, Johnson gradually introduced more substantive editorial material, and *Ebony* remains to this day the best selling magazine in the black community.

Over the years, the Johnson Publishing Co. has introduced other magazines and moved into book production, making it the largest publisher in the United States of materials for blacks. While continuing to run his journalistic enterprises, John Johnson has also served as CEO of an insurance company and he owns a radio station and a cosmetics firm. And, like other successful business leaders, he is very active in promoting educational and artistic charities.

sions, blacks used sit-ins and other tactics to achieve recognition of their civil rights. But the reintegration drive did not necessarily lead to economic improvement. The urban areas where many blacks now lived were costly to maintain and manage, and better-paying employment in the suburbs left the urban population the dregs of the job market. Urban and black unemployment figures consistently ran higher than the national averages and, when recession set in, the jobless rates in some cities reached levels reminiscent of the Great Depression. While some advocated the development of "black capitalism," the reluctance of the white community to invest in such enterprises limited many blacks to dependence on their own meager resources.

Despite the urban decay and racism that disturbed the complacency of the American people in the Eisenhower Era, the decade would be remembered as a time of national well being. The equilibrium of those years hardly prepared the American people for the economic and social upheavals that were to erupt in the succeeding twenty years. These, in turn, would cause some Americans to question the course of enterprise in the United States.

READING SUGGESTIONS

Several historians have taken up the difficult task of writing objective histories of their own lifetimes. Among the most successful are Dewey W. Grantham in *The United States Since 1945: The Ordeal of Power* (1976), Robert D. Marcus in *A Brief History of the United States Since 1945* (1975), and James T. Patterson in *America in the Twentieth Century, Part Two: A History Since 1939* (1976). A book with more emphasis on social factors is William E. Leuchtenburg's entertaining *A Troubled Feast: American Society since 1945* (1973). Charles C. Alexander provides fuller coverage of the latter period in *Holding the Line: The Eisenhower Era, 1952-1961* (1976).

An insightful analysis of the elements interacting during this period is Bert G. Hickman's *Growth and Stability of the Postwar Economy*, published by the Brookings Institution in 1960. Ralph E. Freeman collected relevant papers from a number of experts in *Postwar Economic Trends in the United States* (1960). Harold G. Vatter produced a thorough but objective review of a single decade in *The U.S. Economy in the 1950s* (1963). Three other books on specific aspects are: Wilfred Lewis, Jr., *Federal Fiscal Policy in the Postwar Recessions* (1962); A. E. Holmans, *United States Fiscal Policy 1945-1959* (1961); and William H. Peterson, *The Great Farm Problem* (1959). Those interested in a less formal survey of postwar conditions should consult John Davenport's *The U.S. Economy* (1964).

In *Climb to Greatness* (1968), John B. Rae describes the aircraft industry up to 1960. Thomas J. Watson is the subject of Thomas Belden and Marva Robins Belden in *The Lengthening Shadow* (1962), an informal, highly laudatory work written with the encouragement of IBM. William Rodgers was excluded from company assistance so his book *THINK: A Biography of the Watsons and IBM* (1969) is, in many ways, more interesting. Two major biographies of David Sarnoff have appeared: Carl Dreher, *Sarnoff: An American Success* (1977); and Eugene Lyons, *David Sarnoff: A Biography* (1966). Both are fact-filled and sympathetic portraits of the "Father of Television." The focus of Ernest Braun and Stuart MacDonald in *Revolution in Miniature* (2nd. ed., 1982) is less on people than on the development of semiconductor electronics.

Chapter **10**

CONGLOMERATES, CONSUMERISM, AND SOCIAL CONSCIOUSNESS 1960-1980

Democratic presidential candidate John F. Kennedy told the American people in 1960 that they had reached a New Frontier and urged them to move beyond the complacency of the 1950s. The American people did enthusiastically attack or attempt to evade the problems they encountered in the sixties. Much of their optimism and drive seemed to ebb, however, when inflation and recession dogged the economy in the seventies.

Perhaps the early challenges really had been easier to meet. President Kennedy insisted, for example, that the United States must overtake the Soviet Union in space exploration and, in less than a decade, American astronauts were walking on the moon. The costs were high, of course, and the related arms race demanded continuing intensive efforts on the part of a military-industrial complex which loomed as an ever larger force in the American economy. The escalation of American involvement in the Vietnam War also contributed to an upward spiral of government expenditures that contributed to the domestic prosperity of the 1960s.

Toward the end of that decade, though, the economy passed beyond prosperity into an unhealthy, over-driven state. A prime symptom of this malaise was a nagging peacetime inflation. Unexpected and arbitrary increases in energy prices in the early seventies pushed prices even higher. Because the United States had developed a dependency on foreign supplies of oil, it had to export billions of dollars just to keep the country running. This financial drain, in turn, was a major factor in the increasingly severe international trade imbalance. American consumers' desires to buy more and higher priced products from foreign manufacturers undermined several basic domestic industries like steel and autos and all but eliminated the manufacture of radios and television sets in the United States.

The American people were meanwhile becoming aware of just how fragile the environment was. Individually and in groups, they expressed concern over air and water pollution, the dangers of nuclear energy, and the importance of conserving natural lands and resources. They armed the government with new regulatory tools and besieged corporations to reduce pollution and waste. The crusade to preserve the quality of life for future generations imposed obstacles to business initiatives and added costs to industrial production. At the same time, advances in technology were fundamentally altering not only the processes of that production but also the nature of the products that both private and public consumers desired.

THE HIGH-TECHNOLOGY BONANZA

Concern over national security in the sixties and seventies kept Defense Department expenditures high. A horde of military suppliers benefited. Some 20,000 companies obtained Pentagon contracts in this period, and 100,000 more won subcontracts from those dealing directly with the military. A relatively small group of contractors held a disproportionate share of these contracts: the top one hundred companies consistently performed about two-thirds of all defense work. Many of these firms reciprocated by directing almost all of their marketing and research efforts toward the Pentagon. In 1978, for example, Lockheed, McDonnell-Douglas, Hughes Aircraft, and Grumman ranked among the Pentagon's top ten suppliers, and each sold more than two-thirds of its output to the government. General Dynamics was the most prominent contractor outside the airframe category, building the navy's nuclear-powered submarine fleet and selling virtually all the rest of its many products directly to the armed forces.

Congress and the Pentagon often had conflicting priorities, so the type of equipment ordered in any year reflected differences of opinion over the nature of the external threats and appropriate strategic responses. Enormous sums of money continued to be spent on manned aircraft despite Defense Secretary Robert McNamara's effort to cut procurement and maintenance costs by insisting that all the services purchase a single type of fighter. Simultaneously, the nation's commitment to unmanned weapons increased dramatically as it deployed intercontinental ballistics missiles (ICBMs) in underground silos and on board submarines. Shorter range missiles festooned surface ships and fighter aircraft, and the moon race encouraged the design, construction, and testing of massive booster rockets and space vehicles.

Spending for all types of weapons and military equipment escalated along with American participation in the Vietnam War between 1965 and 1968. Manufacturers of mines, explosives, small arms, and military vehicles worked overtime to supply American troops and their allies. Chemical companies experienced a predictable wartime boost due to the use of products like Agent Orange, a defoliant with yet to be determined longterm human and ecological aftereffects. While the air force relied on its aging B-52s to conduct bombing runs, the army and the marines used helicopters for transport, supply, and combat missions. The Pentagon therefore stepped up its purchases of these specialized aircraft, not only to expand the number in commission but also to replace the 600 or so lost every year.

Many commercial aircraft were sold during this period as well due to the airlines' decision to switch almost exclusively to jet aircraft. To meet the combined civilian and military demand, the airframe industry employed over 850,000 workers, all working long hours. Boeing 707 and 727 models headed most airline shopping lists, but DC-8's were popular as well. Douglas became so overextended trying to fill its orders that it had to merge with the McDonnell Corp., primarily a military contractor.

Other companies ran into financial difficulty when the bottom dropped out of both the civilian and military markets almost simultaneously. American participation in the Vietnam War was winding down by 1970, and the commercial aircraft market had become surfeited as well. Even Boeing, the industry leader, had to conduct a major retrenchment due to its troubles with the controversial supersonic transport (SST). That project had originally taken shape because both the Soviet Union and a British-French consortium were rushing to complete high-speed passenger airplanes. President Kennedy had urged Congress to fund the development of an American SST, and Boeing and Lockheed spent millions of dollars vying for the government contract that Boeing won in 1967. But searching financial and environmental questions continued to surface. Because the proposed aircraft would burn enormous amounts of fuel per passenger mile, it would be an extraordinarily inefficient means of transportation. Furthermore, it would operate in the stratosphere where engine exhausts could have serious environmental consequences. In a stunning departure from the traditional American attitude that if something could be done it should be done, Congress cancelled all funding for the SST in 1971.

Boeing survived that shock by marketing its 747, a jumbo jet that eventually captured almost half the market for "wide-bodied" commercial aircraft. The McDonnell-Douglas DC-10 accounted for another third of those sales, leaving Lockheed's L-1011 well behind with only 18 percent of the market. Beleaguered Lockheed appeared on the verge of total insolvency in 1971. Arguing that the country could not afford to lose one of its leading defense contractors, Congress wrote off a $200 million loss on an air force contract for the Lockheed C-5A transports it had purchased. It also approved a $250 million federal loan guarantee to help the company recapitalize, a move that further blurred the line between private and public enterprise.

Western European governments were meanwhile much more forthright in their underwriting of major industries. One example was a multinational European consortium called Airbus which began to threaten the long-standing American dominance of the commercial aircraft market. Foreign competitors also invaded another major market for American industry by offering to sell offensive and defensive weapons of all sorts to third parties. Even as they scrambled to fulfill their own country's needs, American businesses had been peddling billions of dollars worth of military equipment to overseas customers. The United States government financed some of its allies' purchases, but even so arms made up a hefty percentage of all American exports. These purchases were not always wise or effective for one or both parties. The Shah of Iran, for example, bought all sorts of naval and air weapons to turn his country into the leading military power in the Middle East, but they were useless when religious zealots overthrew his regime from the inside.

American weapons and equipment were particularly attractive to foreign buyers because they often included advanced electronic components. The U.S. electronics industry's research and development programs outshone all others in the 1960s and 1970s and led to the production of a bewildering variety of products as well as astounding reductions in prices. To suggest just how dramatic these changes had been, one commentator noted that if the auto industry had advanced at the same rate as the computer industry, a new Rolls Royce would sell for less than three dollars, get three million miles to the gallon, and have an engine powerful enough to drive an ocean liner.

The central advance in computer design was the microchip, a descendent of the transistors first produced in the 1950s. Military funds financed much of the experimentation in the early sixties with the objective of developing rugged, lightweight, reliable switching and communication equipment for aircraft and missiles. A lot of effort therefore went into reducing the size of various components. Engineering improvements meanwhile enabled manufacturers to turn out millions of solid-state devices at very low cost. The combination of reduced size and price made electronics equipment attractive to private consumers and thus vastly extended the potential market for them. Consequently, the percentage purchased for military purposes declined sharply through the late sixties and seventies until it amounted to less than 20 percent of all sales.

By the mid-sixties, sophisticated manufacturing techniques made tiny integrated circuits possible. These could include several transistors linked to one another by a printed circuit on a single silicon chip. Chips with integrated circuits could be very small, and they usually were very reliable and durable. They also consumed so little energy that minute batteries could power them. By the early seventies, tiny circuits were being incorporated into millions of digital devices including watches and clocks that indicated the time with recently invented light-emitting diodes (LEDs) or liquid crystal displays (LCDs).

A new company named Intel announced the next major breakthrough in 1971: it had crowded the entire circuitry for a computer onto a single chip. The company called the world's first microprocessor the 4004 because it used 4-bit processing. Intel surpassed its own remarkable achievement the very next year when it introduced the 8008, a much more versatile 8-bit microprocessor. Dozens of different 8-bit microprocessing chips had reached the market by the mid-seventies, soon to be followed by 16-bit and 32-bit chips. The latter could duplicate the processing capabilities of the largest mainframe computer systems then in existence. The bulky room- or building-sized computers were on the road to obsolescence, but they had provided vital guidelines for the designers of the microprocessors to follow.

One remaining capability of the larger systems was their virtually unlimited memory storage, but the chips quickly ate away at that advantage, too. They could be designed either for preprogrammed read-only memory (ROM) or more versatile random-access memory (RAM). The first memory chips could accommodate one kilobyte or a thousand discrete pieces of data, but technological advances soon produced 4, 16, and even 64K memory chips. Meanwhile, magnetic storage devices were expanding the capabilities of mini and micro computers. Standard audio tape cassettes and specialized floppy and hard magnetic disks enabled desk-top units to store programs and data even more conveniently than the larger systems could.

There seemed to be no limit to the potential uses for microchips and electronic memory devices. Relatively simple ROM computers linked to television sets were packaged as video games, spawning a revival of arcades full of coin-operated amusement machines. The Atari company competed against its own arcade games with an inexpensive portable version that held interchangeable ROM game cartridges and could be wired into the family's television set. Apple began producing thousands of versatile RAM computers in the late seventies for both home and office use.

Microprocessors also figured in the construction of interactive computers that stored and retrieved information from centralized data banks. Instantaneous processing of airline reservations and schedules through central computer networks

The IBM PC sets the industry standard. (IBM Personal Computer)

STEVEN JOBS

Seldom has a young man been so ideally positioned as Steven Paul Jobs to take advantage of a unique opportunity. An orphan, he was adopted by a couple who lived in what was to become California's Silicon Valley. While attending high school, the young man met William Hewlitt, president of Hewlitt-Packard, a pioneering company in semi-conductor and solid-state research and development. Impressed with the young man's drive and technical skills, Hewlitt gave him a summer job where he met Stephen Wozniak, a college drop-out but a brilliant engineer. Jobs went off to Reed College in Oregon in 1972, but dropped out himself to become a member of the counter culture. He returned to Silicon Valley in 1974 to work briefly for Atari, Inc. as a video game designer. There he renewed his friendship with Wozniak who was already assembling a primitive microcomputer.

It was Jobs who recognized the huge market potential this device could have under proper management. Reminiscent of Henry Ford, the two young men assembled the prototype of their first marketable computer in the Jobses' garage. They called it an Apple because of Steven Jobs's pleasant memories of a parttime job he had held in an Oregon orchard. They demonstrated their device to an electronics company official who ordered twenty-five of them. The two Steves then sold everything they owned to create the $1300 fund they needed to begin producing the Apple I, a ROM computer that sold for $666. The profits from its sales allowed them to introduce in 1977 their equivalent of the Model T Ford: the Apple II, a RAM computer that could be hooked to a home television set and sold for $1350. Steven Jobs made a brilliant marketing decision at that point when he invited independent programmers to develop software for the Apple II. Some 16,000 programs had appeared by 1983, virtually all of which could be used on the company's subsequent models like the Apple IIe and the Apple III.

A third similarity to Ford stemmed from the enormous demand that the abundance of software and low prices created for Apple IIs. The company had to expand very rapidly. Wozniak preferred to remain as the resident engineering guru, leaving Jobs in charge of the business aspects. In 1980 the company went public, a move that established a market value of $1.2 billion for an organization that was barely four years old. Apple suffered a setback, though, when its Apple III failed to dent the growing market for IBM's popular PC. Jobs fought back by making his new MacIntosh line very "user friendly," but the company continued to suffer from intense competition in the computer industry. Still, no one could feel too badly about an enterprise that had turned 300 people into millionaires and given Steve Jobs a personal fortune of over $200 million before he reached the age of thirty.

had become commonplace around the world by the late seventies. Electronic transfers of funds through interlocking financial systems transformed banking. Electronic cash registers appeared at check-out counters everywhere, many of them connected to accounting and stocking databases that provided store managers and head offices with constant updating of sales and inventory records.

The versatile microchips found their way into consumer products of all kinds. Automakers substituted solid-state devices for mechanical sparkplug timing and ignition mechanisms. Printed circuits and electronic switches operated home appliances and heating and cooling systems. Desk-top, hand-held, and finally credit-card calculators made slide-rules obsolete and threatened to do the same for primary mathematics education as well. The media, too, became fascinated with miniaturization. Bulky, suitcase-sized tape recorders gave way to compact portable cassette or cartridge tape players that produced high fidelity stereophonic sound. Record companies simultaneously had to market cassettes and cartridges or lose a large share of their potential market. By the late 1970s, dramatic cost reductions had brought magnetic tape recording devices for storing and rebroadcasting television shows into an affordable price range for home use.

The industries producing this cornucopia of electronic products were highly volatile. Rapidly improving production and design methods constantly drove the cost of chips and components downward while brilliant engineers formed brand-new companies to manufacture devices that instantly outmoded those already on the market. No manufacturer could come close to monopolizing the business or even maintaining for any length of time the prices for his own products. Slim profit margins, intense engineering and marketing competition, and recessions in the 1970s destroyed many high-tech companies.

Some corporations resorted to vertical integration to improve their relative positions. IBM initially bought microprocessors from outside suppliers, but the company gradually integrated backward and began manufacturing many of its own chips. Texas Instruments moved the other way. As the leading manufacturer of transistors in the late fifties and a major supplier of integrated circuits in the seventies, its position would seem to have been quite secure. But the prices others were willing to pay for its components declined and undermined their profit potential so TI integrated forward and began selling calculators and microcomputers under its own brand name.

Price competition also influenced where and how production would take place. Because many of the manufacturing steps required delicate hand crafting, some electronics companies opened factories overseas to exploit the cheaper labor available there. At the same time, many retained their corporate headquarters and processing facilities in California's vibrant industrial community nicknamed Silicon Valley which lay between San Francisco and San Jose. Most of these were "clean" industries utilizing electric power and modest supplies of raw materials. The area had become so overbuilt by the late 1970s, though, that extraordinarily high real estate prices made living and working there difficult even for highly paid engineers.

FAST TIMES ON WALL STREET

Investors tended to view the shares of any Silicon Valley company as glamour stocks. The founders of some of the smaller engineering and electronics firms preferred to retain full control of their companies, but those that "went public" by selling shares to outsiders usually did very well indeed. Almost any corporation with a name ending in "tek" or "onics" could expect a dramatic rise in its stock prices. Except for a minor hesitation in 1966, the stock market coasted along on an eight-year wave of prosperity.

Most of the thirty million Americans who owned stocks and bonds knew next to nothing about the companies that listed their stocks on the various exchanges. Many investors who lacked the information or expertise to make wise selections put their savings into mutual funds. These had been around for decades offering small investors the opportunity to share in the combined returns from a diversified portfolio of stocks. A fund's manager would select suitable stocks, buy and sell blocks of shares to enhance the portfolio, and provide the investors with periodic statements. The manager's compensation might have little relation to the fund's overall performance, though, since it came from the fees charged for opening customer accounts as well as regular deductions for management services.

Mutual funds were generally regarded as conservative, stabilizing forces on the exchanges until a new style of fund management appeared that emphasized fast buy-ins and sell-outs. Gerald Tsai, Jr., working through the Boston-based Fidelity Fund, led the way with a dazzling series of moves as he continuously reassessed the relative strengths of the companies in and outside his fund's portfolio. One profitable tactic was to buy glamour stocks just as they hit the market and then sell them when other bidders had pushed their prices sky high. Other managers copied this strategy, and the action came so fast that many funds experienced more than a 100 percent turnover in their holdings in a year. The payoff was that some of these funds appeared to be outperforming composite indicators like the Dow Jones Industrial Average by a factor of two or three times.

Funds had become so popular in 1965 that they were conducting one-fourth of all the transactions on the New York Stock Exchange. Other institutional buyers like pension funds and insurance companies expanded their operations so that by the end of the decade more than half of all securities transactions involved large block sales. The mutual funds had meanwhile lost much of their luster. The market had failed to move upward consistently after 1966, preventing even the most adventuresome managers from squeezing positive performances out of their funds. Cynics claimed, in fact, that a hypothetical investment several years earlier in a portfolio of stocks chosen at random would have netted a larger return than most of the mutual funds had achieved by 1970. The weakening performance of the funds and their penchant for leveraging and buying into other leveraged funds contributed to a growing unsoundness in the securities system.

The haphazard creation of conglomerates had a somewhat destabilizing effect as well. In theory a highly diversified business combine would be so broadly based that it should be able to survive any economic crisis. If one or more of a conglomerate's operating arms ran into trouble, the central administration should be able to shift resources to more profitable activities. Because it would seldom aspire to control more than a minor share of the market for a single industrial or service sector, it would be exempt from antitrust actions. In fact, many of the new diversified corporate giants resembled General Motors as it had existed under Durant and before Sloan had imposed his brilliant management strategy. And like Durant some of the high-rollers in the sixties seemed to glory in acquisition alone, lacking the interest or expertise to overcome longterm debilities. They pulled together bizarre combinations that encompassed producing and marketing activities that bore no visible—or invisible—relationships to one another aside from their centralized control.

The creators of the new corporate juggernauts like James Ling of LTV, Charles Bludhorn of Gulf and Western, Eugene Klein of National General Corporation, and Tex Thornton of Litton Industries, assumed the mantles and the mystique of the business greats of the past. Like the nineteenth-century moguls, many built mansions and flaunted their wealth in a manner "old money" families considered undignified. Indeed, ostentation often seemed to be a prerequisite for the corporate predators as they pursued courses others would have considered irrational or unfeasible.

One of the most notorious conglomerates was International Telephone and Telegraph. By 1970, ITT had engineered a hundred mergers and quadrupled its assets to four billion dollars. Its aggressive chief executive officer, Harold S. Geneen, engendered both respect and fear around the world. His company eventually roused a storm of unfavorable publicity for its unsubtle efforts to prevent the election of a Marxist as president of Chile.

Real or imagined threats from conglomerate buccaneers preoccupied the directors of thousands of companies and distracted them from normal managerial duties. The activities of Saul Steinberg and the Leasco Data Processing Equipment Corporation are a case in point. Established to buy and then rent IBM equipment to third parties, Leasco served as the base from which Steinberg mounted his raids on other companies. One of his early conquests was the staid Reliance Insurance Company of Philadelphia. With Reliance tucked in his fold along with other acquisitions, Steinberg controlled about $400 million in assets and decided to go after really big game: the Chemical Bank New York Trust Company. It was one of the nation's leading financial institutions with over $9 billion in assets. Despite their apparent invulnerability, the Chemical's directors had to orchestrate a complex and costly defensive campaign that included lobbying to get legislation introduced in both Albany and Washington to prevent Steinberg's takeover.

Although the assembling of diversified business combines continued into the following decade, a collapse in stock prices in 1970 brought a number of conglomerate founders to their knees. Many of the sixties glamour stocks suffered disastrous declines, far greater than the 36 percent drop the Dow Jones Industrial Aver-

JAMES LING

One of the most widely diversified conglomerates, Ling-Temco-Vought (LTV) won praise as the fastest growing company in the United States between 1955 and 1965. In many ways its founder and chief executive, James Joseph Ling, seemed a throwback to the Gilded Age with his rags-to-riches rise. Born into a working-class family in Oklahoma in 1922, Ling had a rough childhood and he dropped out of high school when he was fourteen. After holding a series of odd jobs, he completed a correspondence course and obtained additional training in the navy that qualified him as an electrician.

Living in Dallas after his discharge in 1946, Ling sold his house to obtain the $2000 he needed to set up his own independent contracting firm, Ling Electric Co. He quickly expanded from routine residential wiring into industrial contracting which brought his company so much business that he decided to incorporate it in 1955. Unable to attract commercial or bank capital, Ling distributed prospectuses for his company at the Texas State Fair and used other unorthodox but quite successful methods to attract investors. With the proceeds from his stock sales, he bought control of a California firm that manufactured testing equipment vital to the aerospace industries. The attractiveness of defense contracting encouraging Ling to pick up two other firms—Temco Electronics and Missiles Co. and Chance Vought, Inc., an old-line airframe manufacturer. He incorporated these properties into Ling-Temco-Vought in 1963.

In the following year, Ling "redeployed" his diverse holdings into three autonomous subsidiaries, each of which issued its own shares. Public purchases of these stocks gave Ling more working capital but did not interfere with LTV's control. He subsequently bought into the Okonite Co., a cable manufacturer and, in 1967, the Wilson Co., a meatpacking firm that had itself already diversified into sporting equipment and chemicals. These moves saddled LTV with $80 million in debts, so Ling redeployed again to create new stock-selling subsidiaries. Two more major purchases completed his conglomerate: Greatamerica, which controlled banking and insurance operations as well as National Car Rental and Braniff Airways, and Jones & Laughlin, the sixth largest steel producer in the United States when it joined LTV in 1968. Ling's conglomerate had held a respectable ranking at 204 among the top 500 industrial corporations in 1965, but it rose all the way to fourteenth place in 1968.

The good times were coming to an end, though. Most experts had presumed that a diversified conglomerate would be antitrust proof, but the Justice Department took LTV to court in 1969 and demanded that it dispose of its steel subsidiary or make some other divestiture that would lessen its market control. The negative publicity from this suit combined with a nationwide economic downturn in 1970 caused LTV's share price to plummet from 170 to 16 and forced Ling out as its CEO. Although James Ling continued to be a major stockholder and to pursue many other business activities, his glory days as a conglomerate-builder were over. LTV, the ungainly combine he had created, had deteriorated so much by 1985 that it had to file for bankruptcy.

age registered. One of the most disturbing events was the collapse of the Penn Central. A merger of two of the nation's leading railroads, its bankruptcy in the spring sent shockwaves through the entire financial community.

Despite the accumulated experience of forty years and the installation of all sorts of supposed safeguards, the stock market decline bore many similarities to the 1919 crash. In both instances, there had been excessive speculation in stocks of dubious value. A good many mutual funds had encountered difficulty and their desperate efforts to regroup added to the general panic. Even though the Federal Reserve had imposed an 80 percent margin requirement for brokers' loans through the late 1960s, stock prices declined so much in 1970 that thousands of margin calls went out to investors just as they had in 1929, and forced sales drove prices ever lower.

The brokerage houses themselves were in deep financial trouble. The volume of shares bought and sold had skyrocketed in the previous couple of years, so the brokers had hired additional staff and installed expensive record-keeping machinery, both of which greatly increased their fixed overhead expenses. In 1969, though, the trading volume dramatically dropped thereby reducing the commissions brokers collected far below their operating costs. Some investment firms had no choice but bankruptcy; others negotiated costly mergers to avoid insolvency. These untoward developments heightened the alarm sweeping Wall Street.

Just as in 1929, the trouble extended far beyond the financial district. The country had fallen into a post-Vietnam War recession, and the economy floundered helplessly for over a year before President Richard Nixon announced his "New Economic Policy." It was new only in the sense that neither he nor his conservative Republican advisors would previously have even considered taking such steps. The policy had three major elements: devaluing the dollar in relation to foreign currencies to spur exports; boosting government expenditures to stimulate the economy; and imposing wage and price controls to slow inflation. Nixon's decision to institute peacetime wage and price controls for the first time in American history was quite a surprise coming from a president who had consistently criticized any proposal that would increase the government's influence on the economy. Although Phase I of the controls lasted just ninety days, it seemed to break the back of an unhealthy inflationary wage-price spiral. Phases II through IV were less intensive and correspondingly less effective.

Nixon's emergency program failed to prevent a much deeper recession from developing in 1973. In this downturn, consumer spending declined for the first time since World War II, an indication of just how pervasive public concern over the nation's economic ills had become. An international oil shortage and a worldwide scarcity of food added to the inflation that was eroding incomes. Meanwhile President Nixon spent many agonizing months before admitting that he would have to resign due to the Watergate revelations. This political crisis left the country essentially rudderless and contributed to its sense of insecurity and instability.

The stock market naturally reflected these broader economic problems. Indeed, stocks continued to do poorly through the rest of the decade. Only twice, and then briefly, did the Dow Jones Industrial Average manage to creep above 1000. Even when inflation and other factors swelled the gross national product, stock prices drifted along at levels reminiscent of the previous decade. Of all the forces pressing down on the market, in fact, inflation was clearly the most discouraging.

INFLATION

The previous bouts of inflation the United States had suffered had been associated with other unusual circumstances. Shortages and high demand, for example, had combined to cause price rises in each of the nation's previous wars. The inflation that first developed in the late 1960s therefore seemed to be a consequence of the Vietnam conflict. But it persisted into the 1970s, causing politicians and businessmen to begin to take drastic, often counterproductive steps to combat the relentless rise in prices.

The behavior of the Consumer Price Index illustrated the seriousness of this inflationary onslaught. After the postwar reconversion ended in 1948, the CPI rose quite slowly at an average annual rate of 1.7 percent from 1949 to 1965. The inflationary impulse from the Vietnam War first appeared in 1966, and the average annual increase in the index amounted to 6.9 percent through the succeeding decade and a half. But average figures tell only part of the story. In three of those years, double-digit inflation had buffeted the U.S. economy. The first peak came in 1974 when the CPI rose 12.2 percent, and the decade closed with two bad years in a row: a 13.3 percent rise in 1979 and 12.4 percent in 1980.

Two types of factors appear to have caused most of this inflation. One was a series of unpredictable events like the Arab oil embargo in 1973 to 1974 and a temporary global food shortage. These had relatively short-lived impacts and, to a large extent, are responsible for the peaks illustrated in Figure 10-1. The second set of factors driving prices upward were longterm institutional conditions or policies which, taken together, generated a relatively consistent 4 to 6 percent increase in the CPI each year. Three seemed especially important: the federal government's fiscal and monetary policies; an upward wage-price spiral; and the influence of worldwide inflation which was often much more severe than that in the United States.

The persistent inflation affected many aspects of American enterprise, with particular impact on consumer behavior. Those who anticipated that prices would continue to rise often stocked up on goods at what would later seem to be bargain

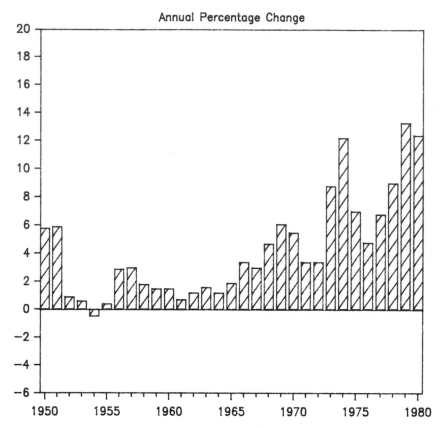

FIGURE 10-1 Consumer Price Index. (From *Economic Report of the President*, Washington, DC: Government Printing Office, 1983, p. 225.)

prices. Their buying sprees had two important consequences. Because they added extra demand to a market already short on supply, they themselves triggered further inflation. And the buy-now mentality reduced the American people's desire and ability to save for an uncertain future. The per capita personal savings rate in the United States remained far below the levels in other industrialized countries in the 1970s, reducing the amount of domestic capital available for investment and contributing to soaring interest rates.

In addition to changing when Americans spent their money, inflation also affected what they chose to buy. As the price for gasoline rose from less than forty cents a gallon to more than a dollar, fuel-efficient cars gained great popularity. Rising housing costs convinced millions of Americans they could never afford to purchase their own homes. At the same time, many of those already paying off mortgages decided to cash in their equity and trade up to larger houses, hoping to profit from the remarkable rise in real estate prices that inflation had created. Assessed property values in some areas increased 20 percent or more every year. For similar reasons, many people invested in "collectables" including art works, jewelry, coins, and any other item whose value appeared likely to rise more quickly than the inflation rate. For those who could afford them, classic automobiles and wine cellars looked like good investments.

The desire to purchase precious metals as a hedge against inflation generated a lively market for Krugerrands, the gold coins minted by the South African government. The United States Treasury Department entered the competition by striking off medallions containing one troy ounce of gold and selling them at the prevailing world market price. The mania for gold was a global phenomenon, and it forced the price of bullion to the unprecedented heights illustrated in Figure 10-2. Speculators disillusioned with the stock market's failure to keep pace with inflation crowded into the business of trading futures contracts in gold, silver, copper, and other scarce or intrinsically valuable commodities.

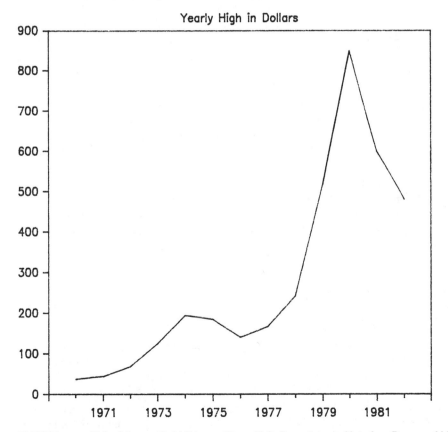

Yearly High in Dollars

FIGURE 10-2 United States Gold Prices. (From U.S. Department of Interior, *Bureau of Mines, Minerals Yearbook* [Washington, DC: Government Printing Office, 1970-1982].)

Inflation boosted interest rates as well. Home mortgages rose from the 5-percent range common after the war to 8 percent in the late sixties and all the way to 12 percent or even higher by 1980. Banks and savings and loan associations reeled under the burden of maintaining millions of older mortgages that earned for them far less each year than inflation. These institutions were hard put to pay depositors the high returns they expected in an inflationary era. Variable-rate or limited-term mortgages began replacing the traditional fixed-rate contracts. High interest rates also forced many states to cancel or amend their rate-ceiling or usury laws passed to protect individuals in less inflationary times. Higher interest rates naturally filtered down to auto loans, credit cards purchases, and revolving charge accounts.

Americans fortunate enough to have money set aside could earn unprecedented returns at their local banks, savings and loan associations, and credit unions. Federal restrictions on financial institutions were lifted to allow them to compete with one another in offering short and long term certificates of deposit bearing attractive interest rates. In the long run, of course, these savings instruments offered customers little protection from inflation. In an idealized inflation-free economy, the basic cost of borrowing money was presumed to run about 3 percent, so a lender could expect to earn interest equivalent to the inflation rate plus 3 percent. When the overall inflation rate had climbed above 10 percent in the late seventies and early eighties, however, the best average depositors could hope for was a return of 11 or 12 percent—scarcely sufficient to preserve the value of their principal.

Thus almost nobody benefited from the inflation. It killed the incentive to save, discouraged home ownership, put capital out of the reach of many who would otherwise have used it, altered normal buying habits, depressed initiative, and fed political discontent. Americans living through this troubled period felt a sense of drift and insecurity. Consumer confidence eroded, gnawing at the very roots of American enterprise. To make matters worse, aggressive manufacturers and exporters were laying siege to the United States from the outside, most obviously in the automobile industry.

DETROIT ON THE DEFENSIVE

Eighty percent of all the cars built in the world in the 1950s came from Detroit, and Japanese factories produced just under half a million four-wheeled vehicles in 1960, two-thirds of which were trucks. The relative positions had undergone a stunning reversal by 1980: Japan turned out 11,042,884 units that year, or almost twice as many as the 6,377,667 manufactured in the United States. Furthermore, the high quality and reliability of the Japanese vehicles insured that every one of the 1.68 million exported to the United States could be sold without the rebates or other inducements American manufacturers had to offer to clear their inventories. Indeed, the only factor preventing the sale of many more Japanese automobiles in the United States was a voluntary export limitation Tokyo had imposed to prevent the United States from boosting its tariffs or establishing import quotas. It was hardly surprising, therefore, that 1980 ranked as the worst year in the history of American automaking, with the Big Three suffering combined losses totaling over $4 billion.

That disastrous performance represented the culmination of the American automobile industry's awkward response to twenty years of increasingly stiff foreign competition. A first round victory in the marketing contest had lulled Detroit into complacency. After Volkswagens and other German and British imports had engulfed 10 percent of the American market in the late fifties, General Motors had counterattacked with its Corvair, Ford with its compact Falcon, and Chrysler with its scaled-down Plymouth Valiant. Next, Lee Iococca, head of the Ford Division, captured the imagination of youthful America with the Mustang, a small, sporty car that oozed charm next to the dumpy VW, a sort of Teutonic Model T. American manufacturers continued their traditional reliance on image as a competitive tool, a strategy that in the late 1960s led to the production of "muscle cars," powerful sports models that sold well to a generation indifferent to fuel efficiency. The utilitarian Japanese Toyotas and Datsuns that trickled into the United States attracted few buyers in a market bedazzled with horsepower, length, and ostentatious style.

The American automakers' complacency began to erode when several blows struck at the heart of their traditional marketing strategy. Ralph Nader, an articulate critic of American consumerism, took perverse delight in blasting the auto industry's poor safety record. His critique of the Chevrolet Corvair, *Unsafe at Any Speed* (1965), proved so damaging that General Motors had to abandon production of the car entirely. Congress acted by creating the National Highway Traffic Safety Agency in 1966 to prod manufacturers into building safer vehicles. Amendments to the 1963 Clean Air Act meanwhile forced the automakers to reduce auto exhaust emissions as well. But the most disconcerting external shock to the industry came in 1973 when oil prices began their spectacular rise. With customers suddenly demanding fuel efficiency and Congress imposing a nationwide speed limit of 55 miles per hour, the high-performance engines the American automakers produced fell into disfavor. Detroit business leaders despaired. How could they turn the lumbering, overpowered models they had long insisted the American people preferred into safe, non-polluting, fuel-efficient vehicles?

One answer, of course, was to ignore the past and approach the task with a fresh outlook. Preconceptions had never clouded Soichiro Honda's vision. He began by revolutionizing the world's attitude toward motorcycles. His lightweight, efficient machines were so attractive that they destroyed the previously dominant British industry. The Japanese entrepreneur then began designing cars, and his company built its first model in 1963. Ten years later, it introduced the Honda Civic, an inexpensive, comfortable, relatively roomy, highly efficient, and essentially nonpolluting vehicle. It sold very well in competition with the American "subcompacts" then on the market, the Fort Pinto, Chevrolet Vega, and American Motors Gremlin. Honda topped his own performance in 1976 with the Accord, universally acclaimed as the best inexpensive car built anywhere. Meanwhile, Volkswagen had replaced its "Beetle" with the stylish Rabbit which became the prototype for most of the smaller American cars in the years to come. Their mod-

---

RALPH NADER ON THE CHEVROLET CORVAIR

Nader's book Unsafe At Any Speed *was a general indictment of the lack of regulation and safety standards in the American auto industry, but his comments about the Corvair were the most memorable muckracking.*

At a critical point of lateral acceleration (or centrifugal force), there is a sudden rear-wheel tuck-under. Technically, the positive camber increases radically 40o to 10o or 11o camber—a horrifying shift causing violent skidding, rear-end breakaway or vehicle roll-over. The change occurs without any warning and in an instant. A variety of disturbing forces may cause this sudden tuck-under—tire side skidding, gust of crosswind, the second leg of an S-shaped curve or a comparable cornering maneuver. All these are conditions that the engineer should take into account during his advance analysis of vehicles for potential design faults. Near the critical point, it takes an expert driver to provide the correct steering action—assuming highway conditions permit and there are no obstructions, such as another vehicle or a tree.

But the Corvair was not built to be sold only to champion racing drivers. And when the critical point is reached, even Dan Gurney would be unable to control the Corvair. The car was built and sold as "easy handling," "as a family sedan," as a car that "purrs for the girls," according to some of the General Motors advertisements. Understanding the way it was built during the first four years of the model provides in turn a better understanding of General Motors' great emphasis on "defensive driving" when it exhorts the drivers of this country to be more careful.

In ways wholly unique, the Corvair can become a single-minded, aggressive machine.

(Ralph Nader, *Unsafe At Any Speed* [New York: Grossman Publishers, 1965], pp. 32-33.)

---

els sold so well that both Honda and Volkswagen built assembly plants in the United States.

For some time, the Americans simply ignored the foreign invasion and continued building cars that matched the traditional Detroit image. Whether compacts or mid-sized, the cars produced in the seventies resembled earlier models in the variety of accessories and color choices available. Ads stressed the comfort of American cars, which were often no roomier inside than smaller foreign models, or choices of engines and trim packages that automated (and therefore very efficient) foreign factories could not match. This avoidance strategy did nothing to prevent the steady encroachment of imports.

Aging plants and a hidebound labor force in the United States hampered the American automakers when they finally decided to meet the competition directly. Worse yet, Detroit's design system proved itself inferior as well. Only twenty individuals were specifically assigned to designing tasks at Honda compared to the 1700 employees working in the General Motors design department. This army of technicians and engineers finally created the "J-car" to compete with the imports, but it was a dud—underpowered and marred by poor handling and sloppy finish. Ford meanwhile incorporated design concepts from its European affiliates into the Escort which it proudly proclaimed to be a "world car" capable of attracting customers in all countries. International collaboration in design and production became common as Americans tried to exploit foreign technology and assembly methods through cooperative marketing agreements. Chrysler, for example, agreed in 1971 to sell cars under its Dodge and Plymouth trade marks that Mitsubishi Motors manufactured in Japan. French automaking giant Renault purchased 48 percent of the ailing American Motors Corporation's stock for $350 million and began distributing its compact Le Car model through American Motors dealerships. Renault then took the logical step of designing a car in Europe called the Alliance which it assembled in Kenosha, Wisconsin, for sale throughout the United States.

COMPETING WITH THE WORLD

The massive inroads foreign competition made in the American automobile business, traditionally one of this country's great industrial success stories, was just one example of the broad dependence the United States was developing upon imported goods of all types. Its proud image as the world's leading industrial nation tarnished considerably in the sixties and seventies. Goods that required intensive hand labor in their manufacture had, of course, begun flowing into the United States immediately after the Second World War from factories in Hong Kong and Japan. After being forced off the mainland in 1949, the Nationalist Chinese turned their stronghold on Taiwan into a hive of labor-intensive industrialism as well. Americans came to expect that toys, plastic products, simple machinery, and other inexpensive items would bear the inscription "Made in Hong Kong" or Taiwan or Japan or even Malaysia, Singapore, or Pakistan as the years passed.

Americans saw no reason for concern about this influx of goods. After all, they benefited from the use of cheap labor in other countries that turned out low-status items while American workers continued to earn decent wages. By the 1970s, though, Asian factories were clearly doing much more than exploiting workers. The quality of the items they produced had improved so much that American shoppers deliberately chose Japanese-built cameras, television sets, tape recorders, and other high-technology items whose finish, reliability, and durability seemed superior to those of comparable American products. Even after the 1971 dollar devaluation had significantly boosted the prices of imports, Americans continued to buy them in increasing volume. Quality, performance, engineering, and efficiency—not low prices—made Japanese cars popular.

Imports of all sorts climbed, reflecting the growing dependence of the United States upon external sources, not only for manufactured products, but also raw materials including the most fundamental of all—oil. Although the country had never deliberately sought economic self-sufficiency, its dependence began to arouse alarm, especially when the costs of imported goods and materials rose even as their volume increased. Severe trade imbalances began to develop as the value of the merchandise exported from the United States fell far below that of the goods imported. Figure 10-3 illustrates the magnitude of these imbalances. Fortunately, American corporate stock, real estate, and other investments remained so attractive to foreigners that many pumped their surplus funds right back into this country or held their excess dollars to exchange on the international financial market.

American business leaders and politicians who recognized the dangers of dependency tried to determine its causes and debated strategies for reversing the trend. A key contributor to the trade imbalance was the United States consumption of foreign oil. Conservation and further exploration of continental and offshore oil

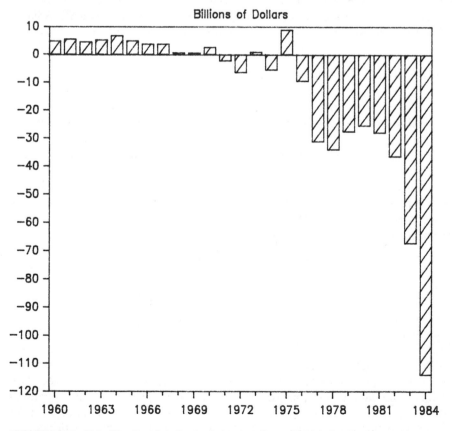

FIGURE 10-3 U.S. Merchandise Trade Balance. (From *Economics Report of the President* [Washington, DC: Government Printing Office, 1986], p. 366.)

reserves helped ameliorate this dependence to some extent when the unprecedented rise in world energy prices made deep wells, recycling, and reclamation economically feasible. Another cause for the merchandise trade imbalance was the fact that the United States had become a postindustrial society in which only about one-quarter of its GNP derived from industry. The country was therefore bound to rely to some extent on overseas manufacturers and processors to fulfill its demands. Japan and several other countries still in the throes of expanding industrialism were eager to exploit the apparently insatiable desire Americans had for material goods.

Imports even began to outsell domestic products in consumer industries that American invention and innovation had created. Whereas twenty-five firms had made television equipment for the American market in the 1950s, only fourteen were doing so by 1980—and eleven of those were foreign owned. Zenith mounted a major advertising campaign in the 1970s to stress the quality of the products it manufactured in the United States. Unfortunately, quality control was often far more rigorous in the newer automated factories abroad. Familiar American brand names began appearing on the outside of equipment actually manufactured overseas. Where the final assembly process still took place in the United States, it often incorporated components produced "off shore." Whole new product lines were developed abroad, a notable example being the home video cassette recorders (VCRs) that Sony and Mitsushita began marketing in the United States in 1976.

American firms occasionally beat down foreign competition. When inexpensive conventional tires began arriving in the United States from Japan in the 1960s, American manufacturers countered by copying the radial tires Europeans had been using for years. An effective advertising blitz convinced domestic buyers of the superiority of the American products, and the Japanese competition withered away. Domestic steelmakers, on the other hand, had little success in discouraging the importation of Japanese and European specialty steel. Claiming that foreign governments were subsidizing industrial exports, American manufacturers demanded that Congress and federal agencies like the International Trade Commission (ITC) protect them with higher tariffs or import quotas. Labor leaders meanwhile asked the ITC to authorize federal compensation and retraining programs for workers at steel plants that had closed or curtailed production due to import competition.

Hoping to discover the sources of their rivals' efficiency, American business experts examined the Japanese industrial system from top to bottom, analyzed the country's society seeking psychological clues to its entrepreneurial success, and then tried to adopt the technological and management strategies that had worked for them. The capabilities and motivations of the workforce were of particular interest. Productivity increased overseas much more rapidly than it did in the United States in part because of foreign workers' acceptance of automated production lines. Japanese investors also seemed satisfied with lower returns on their capital than Americans considered reasonable. Furthermore, Japanese companies paid their executives on a much less lavish scale than did U.S. corporations. But despite intensive study and comparison of the two systems, Americans failed to approach Japan's efficiencies of production.

To pay for the manufactured products it imported, the United States continued to rely, as it had since colonial days, on agricultural exports. Almost 40 percent of the country's cultivated land in 1980 grew crops destined for sale overseas, and the value of farm exports that year was three times greater than it had been fifteen years earlier. American corn and soybean production rose a remarkable 60 percent in the 1970s, most of the increase being shipped abroad to feed a hungry world.

These impressive gains in agricultural output and productivity carried a high price tag. Farmers became increasingly dependent on pesticides, fertilizers, and mechanization, all of which required large capital expenditures even as farm income failed to keep pace with inflation. This financial bind undermined thousands of family farming operations. In the early sixties, just 3 percent of the nation's farms accounted for one-third of all commercial sales, and less than half produced 95 percent of the commodities reaching the marketplace. Farmers often found their raw produce selling at relatively fixed prices compared to rapidly inflating ones paid for processed foods. As it had in the nineteenth century, the agricultural community complained that middlemen were siphoning off profits that rightfully belonged to farmers.

To soften the impact of high processing costs as well as to obtain capital to fund their operations, many farmers signed contracts with processors. Vertical integration therefore became quite common in American agriculture with some firms controlling every level from company-owned or contracted farms, through processing and distribution operations, and finally to marketing itself. Oligopolies of major distributors dominated the sales of canned foods, sugar, dairy products, soup, and cereal, and they were able to set prices that assured themselves adequate profits. Their effective market control attracted outside investment into agribusiness and stimulated corporate takeovers from unexpected quarters. Standard Oil of California, Aetna Life and Casualty, Ling-Temco-Vought, and RCA ranked among the leading organizations engaged in agricultural production in the 1970s. To a degree, then, commercial farming had evolved into just one more element in the highly integrated industrial and financial community that controlled American enterprise.

GROWTH AND THE QUALITY OF LIFE

The concern over exhaust pollution and fuel efficiency that gave the automobile industry such trouble was part of a broader interest in preventing the deterioration of the environment. Several reform strands came together as Americans acknowledged the impact industrial and population growth had on the world around them. Some individuals and interest groups focused on specific issues like water quality or the preservation of wilderness areas; others advocated broad review of the consequences of human activities on the global ecology. Many environmentalists openly stated their willingness to forego economic growth to achieve their objectives. Demographers warned that exponential population growth rates could crowd every other species off the planet in just a few human generations. Other experts claimed that the supply of recoverable fossil fuels could be exhausted as early as the middle of the twenty-first century. The energy crisis of the mid-1970s and the inflationary spiral that closed out the decade seemed to confirm these ominous predictions.

Despite the fact that environmentalists tended to be opponents of the "establishment," they were quite effective in convincing the federal government to further their objectives. An early success was the Clean Air Act of 1963 and its subsequent amendments that set goals and outlined procedures for reducing auto exhaust pollution. A switch to lead-free gasoline and the installation of catalytic converters helped reduce harmful pollutants. Federal oversight also extended to factories and businesses with particular attention to the chemical industry. Government authorities called upon industrialists to alter their processes so they could meet reduced emission standards in the future. The clean-air campaign had a measurable impact. Harmful auto emissions declined by 90 percent in a decade, and the number of days in which twenty-three monitored metropolitan areas experienced unhealthful air quality declined from ninety-seven in 1974 to fifty-nine in 1980.

The passage of the Environmental Policy Act in 1969 represented another response to reform sentiments. It required the preparation of an Environmental Impact Statement (EIS) for any proposed development project. The Council on Environmental Quality would review these statements and block implementation of any project with potentially harmful ecological effects. Occasionally the evidence in a statement alerted the public and generated enough outcry to kill a proposal, but only the most blatant and thoughtless assaults on the natural environment were

Urban pollution in the seventies. (Laimute Druskis)

likely to be impeded. Developers became quite skilled at complying with the letter of the law in filing an EIS that allowed them to carry on much as they had before.

Rachel Carson's poignant critique of chemical pollution, *The Silent Spring* (1962), set off one of the most successful environmental crusades in American history. Her chief concern was DDT, a pesticide that had entered general use after the Second World War. No one had realized that the workings of the natural food chain over time could concentrate DDT sufficiently to cripple or kill birds and other wildlife. Within a decade, this potent chemical had been banned. Unfortunately, it was just one of thousands of chemicals indiscriminately being distributed around the world.

The dangers inherent in the use and disposal of toxic chemicals became increasingly evident in the 1970s. For decades industrial plants had dumped waste products wherever they chose with no thought about the possible environmental consequences of their actions. In many instances toxic wastes were buried under shallow land fills. Later these dumping grounds were identified as sources of harmful chemicals and bacteria seeping into underground water supplies, streams, and lakes. Some lakes in the industrial Northeast "died" in the sense that neither plant nor animal life could survive in their polluted waters, and occasionally an oil-incrusted river caught fire. To reverse these trends, Congress passed the Clean Water Act in 1972 and followed it up two years later with the Safe Drinking Water Act. These programs helped slow the spread of pollution but did little to clean up older hazardous waste sites. In 1980, therefore, Congress created the so-called Superfund financed by special taxes on polluting industries to enable the Environmental Protection Agency to tackle the worst of the existing toxic waste dumps.

The business community responded to the popularity of environmental concerns in a variety of ways. Some entrepreneurs exploited them in the marketplace. New companies, mostly operating on a small scale, sprang up all over the country to manufacture wind or solar powered devices. Other firms designed clothing and equipment for customers interested in exploring wilderness areas. Still others attracted environmentalists' dollars by manufacturing products exclusively from recycled raw materials. *The Whole Earth Catalog* (1968) which described thousands of "ecological" products became a national bestseller.

The larger and more established a company was, the less enthusiastic it was likely to be. Industrialists ordered to upgrade their pollution control systems complained of the high costs involved and, in some cases, insisted that the government's standards were impossible to meet. Lobbyists and agents in Washington obtained exemptions or delays in the enforcement of federal controls, and some of those who failed to obtain relief filed suits anyway hoping to delay or escape penalties. The automakers were particularly noisy in protesting stiffer pollution and safety regulations which they claimed would force car prices even higher just when inflation threatened to drive them beyond the reach of many potential buyers. The fact that many relatively inexpensive imported models met or exceeded all federal standards—often without the cumbersome smog control devices bolted onto Detroit's products—definitely weakened the American industry's case.

Oddly enough, the energy suppliers emerged from a gauntlet of criticism more powerful than ever. Both the production and consumption of energy in the United States rose each year until 1970. At that point domestic production began to decline so that, because consumption continued to climb, imports were necessary. That unhealthy situation made the United States vulnerable to the Arab boycott and subsequent OPEC price increases that triggered the "energy crisis" of 1973 to 1974. It marked the end of the era of cheap energy that had powered American industry and transportation from its earliest days. Large domestic reserves of oil remained in the ground, of course, but to the extent federal regulations permitted, distributors boosted their prices for gasoline and home heating oil. Meanwhile the major oil companies' costs rose much more slowly and allowed them to reap enormous profits. In 1975 Exxon, the successor to ESSO, the New Jersey-based Standard Oil Company offshoot, moved ahead of General Motors to become the nation's largest corporation. Four other oil companies ranked among the top seven.

The perceived energy scarcity had a number of other consequences. It led to hasty approval of a plan to construct an enormous pipeline to carry oil from Alaska's North Slope to ice-free ports in the south. Many industries switched from increasingly expensive fuel oil to price-regulated natural gas or abundant coal. But the rising demand for coal threatened to produce an environmentalist's nightmare: unregulated strip mining. Public and private capital poured into ambitious projects to liquify or gasify coal and to convert oil shale into a readily usable form. Nuclear power had earlier enjoyed considerable popularity, so many plants were already operating or being constructed. Public opposition to this energy alternative grew strident, however, in the face of unanswered questions concerning plant safety and the disposition of radioactive wastes. To make matters worse, some critics pointed out that the building and operation of a typical nuclear power plant actually absorbed more energy than it could ever generate.

Spiraling energy costs forced consumers to take conservation steps of their own. Home insulation sales boomed. Thermostats were set lower in winter and higher in summer. Smaller, lighter cars sold well. The results of these moves invalidated the revered belief that increasing energy consumption was necessary to ensure economic growth. The nation's Gross National Product continued to climb through the late seventies even though its overall use of energy declined. Indeed, the United States became far less dependent on foreign energy resources. Nearly half of the petroleum consumed in 1977 was imported; just three years later that figure had dropped to slightly over one-third. The emotional rhetoric of the environmentalists had played a major role in encouraging the move toward an efficient, leaner United States economy. Their crusades in the 1960s had thus helped prepare the American people for the sacrifices needed in the 1970s.

CATERING TO THE CUSTOMERS

Retailers modified their selling practices in the 1960s and 1970s to match changing attitudes and behavior patterns among their potential customers. People continued to flock to homes in the suburbs, for example, so businesses established themselves there as well. Suburban shopping centers were soon attracting more shoppers and dollars than many downtown districts. And as they assumed central rather peripheral retailing positions, they naturally absorbed larger amounts of capital.

Food supermarkets had "anchored" the typical fifties shopping center which served a largely neighborhood clientele. In the next two decades, shopping centers expanded both their physical dimensions and their customer reach. Sprawling air-conditioned malls insulated from hot or cold weather sprang up all over the country and resembled, in many ways, the diversified commercial districts in older city centers. With ample free parking, these malls could attract shoppers from considerable distances. Planners therefore studied traffic flows and highway access before settling on sites for building new centers. Beltway roads either connected to or parts of the interstate highway system surrounded major cities and drew shoppers not only from the suburbs but out from downtown as well.

Mall developers recognized that landing popular, established stores with assured clientele would encourage other retailers to rent space nearby to take advantage of the customer traffic. Major national chains like Sears, Montgomery Ward, and Penney's were especially welcome. New, clean, architecturally pleasing malls also attracted urban department stores to establish branches in them. Carson, Pirie, Scott, and Marshall Fields stores were always welcome near Chicago; Hudson's opened outlets around Detroit; Macy's and The Emporium built or leased huge buildings all over California.

Upscale department stores usually avoided locating in shopping centers that included discount stores. The Korvette chain continued to grow, but K-mart quickly surpassed the early leader. Subsidiaries of the giant Kresge Corporation, a variety store chain, the barnlike K-marts sold a broad range of consumer goods from clothing through hardware to auto parts and service. Florescent lighting and

The modern American shopping environment. (Courtesy of Citibank)

featureless rows and aisles of products made these discount stores seem more like grocery supermarkets than conventional department stores, but their popularity stemmed from low prices. Volume buying and advertising reduced their operating costs, as did their expectation that customers would serve themselves and bring purchases to centralized check-out counters. With computers handling inventory control and finances, store managers could hire relatively few clerks, pay them low wages, and put them to work with minimal training.

Although it operated the most prominent department store chain in Minnesota, Dayton's decided to move into discount retailing by opening a chain of Target stores in the Midwest. Its strategy for competing with the other discount houses was to sell nationally advertised products at 10 to 20 percent below their list prices. Target also published newspaper advertising inserts as attractive as those the major department stores distributed, and it avoided merchandising gimmickry like the "blue light specials" K-mart employed. Consequently, these stores appealed to middle-class shoppers interested in purchasing better-quality goods at reasonable prices. Because Target stores offered no postpurchase service on any of the countless items they stocked, they maintained a no-questions-asked exchange or refund policy.

While some discount houses occupied whole blocks by themselves, most retailers preferred to cluster with other establishments to reduce overhead costs and share customers. Along with a department store or two, a typical mall leased space to dozens of smaller firms many of which were members of national chains. Drug and variety stores, shoe and clothing retailers with familiar names stocked popular brands in malls all over the country. The chain stores spread so quickly, in fact, that few independent proprietorships could be found in most malls by 1980.

An ambitious local entrepreneur could still succeed in the retail business by taking up a franchise. Authorized distributors for particular product lines had existed for decades, of course, with auto dealerships and service stations being common examples. Those who agreed to handle the products of a particular manufacturer benefited from its national advertising, its recognized signs and trademarks, and its reputation for quality. Thousands of auto mechanics became independent proprietors of service stations that sold the products of major oil companies. Service stations and automobile dealerships suffered when gasoline prices began rising in the 1970s, and many had to consolidate or diversify by the end of the decade.

Many other franchising opportunities existed, though, and new ones cropped up every day. Fast-food franchises are the most familiar examples of this business format, but motels, real estate offices, equipment rental firms, tax preparation, and other personal services all operated along similar lines. The trend had become so pervasive that franchised establishments were ringing up almost one-third of all retail sales by 1980.

The growth pattern had been somewhat uneven. About one hundred different fast-food franchisors were operating in 1950, and that number had doubled by 1960. It doubled again in the next five years in what was dubbed a "franchise boom." The recession of the mid-seventies forced a good many individual proprietors out of business and bankrupted some of the central franchising organizations as well. Expansion resumed through 1980, when just under half a million franchised proprietorships were operating with well over four million employees.

Signing a franchise contract had several advantages over going into business independently. An aggressively advertised product like McDonald's hamburgers obviously had an excellent chance of attracting customers. Furthermore, franchisors often provided advice on location, construction design, operations, quality control, and marketing. Some central organizations conducted management training programs and extended financial assistance to those wishing to open new outlets. Ultimately, of course, the major appeal of a franchise lay in the confidence it gave an operator that many of the basic business risks had already been eliminated.

Certain costs associated with franchise operations somewhat offset their advantages, though. Substantial fees might be charged to someone who signed a franchise agreement, and royalties were often collected out of an operator's profits. If these payments were set too high, they could reduce or even eliminate the proprietor's personal income. Some franchisors insisted that their agents buy supplies from their own warehouses at higher costs than they would have paid on the open market. Or a contract could demand that an outlet meet performance standards based on national or regional trends that had little relevance to its immediate market situation. There was always the chance that a central organization would be mismanaged into bankruptcy or that its products or format would lose their customer appeal and leave franchisees trapped in a doomed enterprise. Generally, however, proprietors of franchised operations enjoyed a significantly lower failure rate than did operators of independent enterprises, and a good many bobbed along on the crest of rising waves of popularity.

Although not by any means the first of the fast-food franchisors, the McDonald's Corporation certainly became the most famous. When a small independently owned hamburger stand in California attracted Ray Kroc's attention in 1954, he bought its brand name. Kroc then developed the equivalent of a food assembly line incorporating a machine that precut 1.6-ounce patties of beef and a cybernetic deep-fryer that brought French fries to the peak of crispness. His first outlets were drive-ins where customers bought precooked hamburgers and fries rather than putting in orders and waiting for them to be prepared. The chain thus became famous precisely because it offered "fast food."

The McDonald's system was hardly novel in one sense: it simply duplicated the shift in consumer marketing that had already occurred in other industries in which a craftsmen's made-to-order items gave way to a factory's prefabricated inventory of consumer products. Like any factory owner interested in speed and efficiency, Kroc limited his output to a few standardized sandwiches and related items. With the process thus simplified, the chain could hire unskilled workers, many of them teenagers young enough to fall outside federally mandated minimum wage guidelines. At first glance a McDonald's outlet may appear to be labor intensive with its workers bustling about behind the counter, but that labor expenditure is concentrated on production rather than service. There are no waiters or waitresses, and the counter staff handles the duties that conventional cafes assign to cashiers and bus boys. Streamlined production and minimal labor costs allow Mc-Donald's to sell food at comparatively low cost for the same reasons that Henry Ford could market his Model T so cheaply.

THE ORIGINAL McDONALD'S

In 1954, Ray Kroc was a 52-year old salesman of Multimixers, machines that made six milk shakes at a time. When he learned that an establishment in San Bernardino, California, owned eight of these machines, he determined to investigate personally. Here he describes what he found.

I cruised past the McDonald's location about 10 a.m., and I was not terrifically impressed. There was a smallish octagonal building, a very humble sort of structure situated on a corner lot about 200 feet square. It was a typical, ordinary-looking drive-in. . . . Then the cars began to arrive, and the lines started to form. Soon the parking lot was full and people were marching up to the windows and back to their cars with bags full of hamburgers. Eight Multimixers churning away at one time began to seem a lot less farfetched in light of this steady procession of customers lockstepping up to the windows. . . .

I don't remember whether I ate a hamburger for lunch that day or not. I went back to my car and waited around until about 2:30 in the afternoon, when the crowd dwindled down to just an occasional customer. Then I went over to the building and introduced myself to Mac and Dick McDonald. They were delighted to see me ("Mr. Multimixer," they called me), and I warmed up to them immediately. We made a date to get together for dinner that evening so they could tell me all about their operation.

I was fascinated by the simplicity and effectiveness of the system they described that night. Each step in producing the limited menu was stripped down to its essence and accomplished with a minimum of effort. They sold hamburgers and cheeseburgers only. The burgers were a tenth of a pound of meat, all fried the same way, for fifteen cents. You got a slice of cheese on it for four cents more. Soft drinks were ten cents, sixteen-ounce milk shakes were twenty cents, and coffee was a nickel. . . .

That night in my motel room I did a lot of heavy thinking about what I'd seen during the day. Visions of McDonald's restaurants dotting crossroads all over the country paraded through my brain. In each store, of course, were eight Multimixers whirring away and paddling a steady flow of cash into my pockets.

With its success spawning a host of imitators, the McDonald's chain expanded the size of its outlets to include tables for eating and playgrounds for children, and it added larger sandwiches and breakfast dishes to its menu. Fundamental to the chain's continuing success was its enormous national advertising budget that exceeded $200 million in 1979 alone. McDonald's did differ somewhat from most other franchisors in that the central organization owned three-fourths of its land and buildings and leased these properties to local operators. This huge stockpile of real estate assets supported its corporate operations and gave it control over where its outlets would be located. Ray Kroc's corporation also studied the urban market and decided to open hundreds of branches in downtown districts where clerks, secretaries, shoppers, and quite a few business executives could buy quick, inexpensive lunches. And, like many other expansionist American franchisors, McDonald's moved aggressively into overseas markets.

The fast-food outlets that established beachheads in the suburbs, fanned out along the highways, and finally invaded city centers were elements in a general process that has encouraged a homogenization of retailing in the United States. By offering predictable levels of quality and service, franchise operations and chain stores undermined independent proprietorships. At the same time, national advertising was making all consumers aware of new, standardized products, and an efficient distribution network was making those items available nationwide with a minimum of delay.

Americans lacking the capital to qualify for a franchise or wishing to work only parttime could take advantage of an expanding number of personal selling programs. At one extreme were firms like the Fuller Brush Co. which had been selling products door-to-door for many years with salespeople on commissions assigned to specific territories. At the opposite end of the personal sales spectrum were the housewives who invited their neighbors to parties where they demonstrated and took orders for plastic containers and other products supplied by Tupperware. The more successful or ambitious participants in this scheme could become regional distributors who kept local salespeople supplied and constantly sought likely prospects to add to their sales networks.

The housebound market that Tupperware and Avon Cosmetics had been exploiting for years encouraged Mary Kay Ash to introduce her own line of personal care products in 1963. She formed a company that, while specializing in only a limited number of items, grew into a nationwide marketing organization providing income to 70,000 self-employed sales people, virtually all of whom were women. As a means to spur competition and expansion, Mary Kay Cosmetics held inspirational meetings and conventions where it awarded its most energetic workers prizes of various types ranging all the way up to cars painted in the company's distinctive pink color.

An even more dynamic and pervasive direct-sales organization was the Amway Corporation founded in 1959 to market house-cleaning and maintenance products. Like many others Amway was a multilevel marketing mechanism. Several layers of management existed, each supporting and paying a percentage of its receipts to those up the line. Local Amway distributors were constantly urged to climb the organizational ladder by recruiting teams of distributors who would buy products directly from them for resale to consumers. And, like Mary Kay and Tupperware, the central organization devoted much of its energy to inspirational and motivational rallies and conventions as well as to selling books and cassettes to keep its affiliates in a selling frame of mind. Amway distributors and recruiters were predominently white, middle-class individuals attracted not only by the prospects of profits but also by the organization's strident dedication to free enterprise, conservative politics, and evangelical Christianity.

LIFESTYLES IN TRANSITION

Wherever they shopped in the 1960s and 1970s, Americans bought goods that reflected popular taste. The anti-establishment mood of civil rights, environmental, and antiwar movements encouraged a reassessment of lifestyles in general. Protesters' beards and blue jeans were a deliberate challenge to the complacency of dutiful white collar workers in their three-piece suits and trimmed hair. But even as the members of the counterculture were ridiculing or disavowing materialism, they constituted a sizable market in their own right. As emotionalism ebbed in the seventies, the demarcation between societal extremes blurred, permitting many Americans to cross back and forth at will. Thus a rising junior executive could exchange his button-down collar and tie for a comfortable T-shirt on the weekends.

Some were quick to recognize the marketing opportunities that changing lifestyles created. The universal popularity of the look Levi Strauss had invented during the Gold Rush encouraged manufacturers and retailers to market jeans of several types. The leading fashion houses sold slightly modified versions as "designer jeans" for twice or three times the price of the workhorse levis. Denim fashions were popular with both sexes. A majority of women now worked outside their homes, so sensible pants, jackets, tailored suits, and blouses replaced the print housedresses of the thirties and forties.

Footwear underwent a similar transformation. The cost of leather shoes climbed, making inexpensive rubber-soled sneakers much more popular. Many children grew up without ever owning a pair of leather shoes, and casual footwear became acceptable for adults at home or out shopping or doing other leisure activities. Just as designer jeans had upgraded levis, dramatically styled running shoes edged out the old utilitarian sneakers. Speciality manufacturers like Nike and Etonic grew from tiny firms into monster enterprises with factories all over the world. Indeed, most of the shoes bearing American brand names were assembled in Taiwan and other countries where labor costs remained low.

Some people actually ran in their running shoes. A personal fitness craze fostered whole new industries; special clothing and shoes were just the beginning. Health centers opened everywhere, many as elements in national chains, to provide customers with access to expensive training equipment and instructional classes. Aerobic exercise programs sold by the millions in a variety of forms: individual instruction, records, books, and videotapes. Diet consciousness ran up sales in health food stores. Major food processing companies and supermarkets joined the fad as well, advertising and selling nutritional foods like granola.

Americans could devote so much of their energy to fitness because they had increasing amounts of leisure time. Thousands of products appeared to help them while away their off-work hours. Public and private swimming pools were installed, and tennis clubs and golf courses were no longer confined exclusively to the wealthy. Skiing enthusiasts spent billions on equipment, travel, lift fees, and accommodations. Recreational boating boomed as well, even in the Midwest where boats sometimes had to be hauled hundreds of miles to water. So many families convinced themselves that they could save money by camping out that chains of campgrounds opened to serve them. To avoid the discomforts of actually roughing it, of course, many of these same families then purchased recreational vehicles, some of them large enough to qualify as land yachts. A tiny firm in Forest City, Iowa, exploited the enormous market potential by growing into a major distributor of RVs sporting the Winnebago brand name. Enthusiasm for these gas-guzzling vehicles faded considerably when energy prices began to rise, but the American people continued to take expensive and extended vacations.

Spectator sports offered an alternative for those either too lazy or too poor to participate in other leisure activities. Professional athletics became a big business as television dramatically increased the size of viewing audiences. Advertisers who paid huge sums for commercial spots during major sports events provided the networks with the money they needed to offer the leagues lucrative contracts for the right to broadcast their games. The resulting income encouraged team owners to bid against each other for players whose salaries therefore skyrocketed. The athletes then completed the circle by endorsing products on television commercials. The leagues expanded the number of team franchises to accommodate the individuals and syndicates offering to pay millions of dollars for them. Team logos were pasted on all sorts of products with no other relationship to athletics. Similar merchandising schemes spread to the nonprofessional college teams which also received hefty monetary compensation whenever they appeared on television. Despite the surfeit of electronic coverage, ticket sales and live attendance at sports events continued to rise throughout this period.

Americans spent a lot of their leisure time dealing personally with their homes. They had always enjoyed tinkering, and now inflating labor and construction costs made personal home repairs financially attractive as well. Do-it-yourself projects ranged from routine maintenance to full-scale remodeling and redecoration. The demand for professional painters and paper hangers shrank after easy-to-use latex paints and glue came on the market. Hardware and discount stores stocked plans and materials for home handicrafts of all sorts. Hobbyists assembled everything from simple radio sets to replicas of classic cars out of parts or kits.

Shopping itself became a popular leisure activity. So much of the population of both sexes held regular jobs that the old nine-to-five hours for stores were no longer adequate. Shopping centers had to stay open in the evenings and on weekends to serve working Americans. Access to banking services had traditionally been even more restricted than shopping, but now banks, too, had to offer greater flexibility with longer hours, branch offices, and credit cards.

The use of credit cards became endemic. Earlier, oil companies and department stores had issued cards to funnel repeat purchases through their outlets. The Mastercard and BankAmericard (later Visa) systems introduced in the 1960s, however, placed few restrictions on where one could shop. The banks that issued these internationally acceptable cards profited from the interest and service charges they collected on their customers' outstanding balances as well as the fees they assessed to the retailers who accepted the cards in payment. While offering broad access to goods and services, the cards also expanded customer buying power. Many Americans routinely ran their charges up to the bank's dictated limit and then maintained this indebtedness through each succeeding billing period by paying only a percentage of the total due each month. In this way, the cards added substantially to the growing total of consumer credit that also included the car and appliance loans and home mortgages nearly everyone had contracted.

Credit cards became so universal, in fact, that some forecasters predicted that cash transactions and paper currency itself would disappear within a matter of a few years. Although that prophecy has yet to be fulfilled, most Americans were certainly using less currency in the seventies than they had earlier. Checking accounts handled most financial transactions, especially those for larger sums. Consequently, even though inflation made hundred-dollar purchases all too common, the only time an average American saw one-hundred-dollar bills was on television where they were neatly bundled and carried around in attache cases by spies or criminals.

Unfortunately, cash payoffs were not strictly figments of scriptwriters' imaginations. The sixties counterculture had encouraged many people to experiment with various drugs. Despite the enforcement of stiff criminal laws for drug-dealing and the enactment of harsh penalties for possessing even a few grams of marijuana, the illicit drug trade flourished. The prospect of earning enormous profits led to the development of elaborate international networks for importing controlled substances just as prohibition had done during the 1920s. Florida was particularly attractive to drug smugglers operating out of Latin America, and some banks in that state handled huge transfers in untraceable hundred-dollar bills. Profits from this underground enterprise were estimated to range into the tens of billions of dollars, and some insisted that marijuana was the nation's third largest cash crop after corn and wheat.

Tobacco, the cash crop with the longest history, was meanwhile losing much of its appeal. Because evidence linked smoking to fatal diseases, the federal government banned all radio and television advertising of cigarettes. Even though the tobacco processors continued to spend lavishly for advertisements in other forms of media, the industry lost much of its robustness. Southern congressmen lobbied and logrolled to keep federal support payments for tobacco farmers in line with those for other agricultural commodities, but high excise taxes and nonsmokers' rebellions made undeniable inroads. The percentage of adults who smoked habitually declined each year.

Economic and societal factors cooled the enthusiasm for the counterculture as a whole as the 1980s approached. Inflation, worry about scarcities, recurring recessions, and a lack of attractive job opportunities for the post-Second World War baby boom generation helped steer the United States onto a more conservative path. President Lyndon Johnson's Great Society's liberalism appeared in retrospect to have promised too much; transfer payments—tax revenue spent directly on welfare and other personal support programs—ended up swallowing monumental shares of both federal and state government budgets. When the 1980 elections swept a conservative Republican into the White House and gave his supporters majority control of the Senate, it seemed as though the American people were ready for major changes. Although all the changes were not necessarily welcome, the 1980s would turn out to be quite different from the decades that had preceded them.

READING SUGGESTIONS

An intensive analysis of the aircraft and aerospace business is Barry Bluestone, Peter Jordan, and Mark Sullivan's *Aircraft Industry Dynamics* (1981). Two less formal studies are: Charles D. Bright, *The Jet Makers: The Aerospace Industry from 1945 to 1972* (1978); and John Newhouse, *The Sporty Game* (1982), which focuses on the commercial airliner market. Edwin P. Hoyt, in *The Space Dealers* (1971), details the business aspects of the space exploration program. J. Ronald Fox's *Arming America: How the U.S. Buys Weapons* (1974) covers funding, contracting, and production. Russell Warren Howe provides a more comprehensive view in *Weapons, the International Game of Arms, Money and Diplomacy* (1980). *Transnational Corporations, Armaments and Development* (1980), by Helena Tuomi and Raimo Vayrynen, also takes an international perspective and includes information on electronics. The most useful book on that topic, however, is the previously cited work by Ernest Braun and Stuart MacDonald, *Revolution in Miniature* (2nd ed., 1982).

Three informative and very readable books on Wall Street in the 1960s are: John Brooks, *The Go-Go Years* (1973); John F. Lawrence and Paul E. Steiger, *The '70s Crash and How to Survive It* (1970); and Robert Sobel, *The Last Bull Market, Wall Street in the 1960s* (1980). A rather different perspective on these events comes from the head of the Merrill, Lynch brokerage firm and later Reagan administration official Donald T. Regan in *A View from the Street* (1972). Two quite technical works on the causes of recent economic problems are Alan S. Blinder's *Economic Policy and the Great Stagflation* (1979) and Otto Eckstein's *The Great Recession with a Postscript on Stagflation* (1978). Both these economists are highly critical of the federal government's actions. Jules Backman has collected several interesting essays in his *Business Problems of the Seventies* (1973).

A persuasive effort to explain the troubles of the American automobile industry is Brock Yates's *The Decline and Fall of the American Automobile Industry* (1983). Emma Rothschild takes a somewhat longer view in *Paradise Lost, The*

Decline of the Auto-Industrial Age (1973). Two more specialized studies are C. S. Chang's *The Japanese Auto Industry and the U.S. Market* (1981) and John B. Rae's *Nissan/Datsun* (1982), a corporate history of the American marketing activities of a major Japanese manufacturer. William H. Davidson looks beyond the auto industry in his thoughtful book *The Amazing Race: Winning the Technorivalry with Japan* (1984).

Literally hundreds of books have been published on environmental issues, many of them quite polemical. A balanced survey, however, is Joseph M. Petulla's *American Environmental History* (1977). In *The Logarithmic Century* (1973), Ralph E. Lapp projects historical trends into a none-too-promising future. Although the Conservation Foundation's *State of the Environment 1982* (1982) was published as a call to arms, it judiciously reports the progress of the environmental programs to date. Two other well-written books on this topic are Gerald Garvey's *Energy, Ecology, Economy* (1972) and Allan Schnaiberg's *The Environment: From Surplus to Scarcity* (1980).

Chapter 11

AMERICAN ENTERPRISE IN THE MODERN WORLD

Inflation, federal budget deficits, foreign competition, and a no-growth economy had generated stress and concern in the American business community in the late 1970s, but much of that anxiety eased in the next decade. In many ways, though, the emotional change was just that: a psychological readjustment or reevaluation that ignored a continuation of marginal economic performance. Overall growth was disappointing and both the federal budget and the international trade balance piled up monthly deficits in the $10 to $20 billion range. The inflation rate, however, did fall dramatically. Perhaps because the stabilization of prices was readily apparent to consumers as well as producers, it was quite comforting. It seemed proof that the American people's faith in their capitalistic system was justified after all.

A prime beneficiary of this national contentment was Ronald Reagan, the conservative Republican who had easily triumphed over beleaguered Democrat Jimmy Carter in the 1980 presidential race. Economics had emerged as the key issue in that contest. The central premise of Reagan's "supply-side" economic philosophy was that the federal government had become so intrusive it was stifling business initiative and encouraging nonproductive investment. He proposed a huge tax cut and a comprehensive deregulation campaign. Supply-siders claimed such policies would unleash the free enterprise system and cause productivity to soar. The revenues a healthier economy would generate should offset the impact of the tax cut and allow the Reagan administration to balance the federal budget even as it dramatically increased defense spending.

Responding to Reagan's persuasiveness, Congress implemented much of his economic program. Federal taxes dropped 25 percent, the Pentagon's budget grew much faster than inflation, and regulatory programs were canceled or weakened. At first the economy failed to meet Reagan's rosy projections, stumbling instead into the worst recession the United States had suffered since the 1930s. Unemployment topped 10 percent and the bankruptcy rate rose correspondingly. The hard times eased after two years, though, and the United States entered a phase of relatively modest growth. The stock market responded to this recovery with a remarkable bullishness, and certain regions and economic sectors basked in prosperity.

While President Reagan naturally claimed credit for the upturn, the curbing of inflation was probably its most important single cause. The sharp recession of 1980-1981 had bled off much of the upward pressure on prices, and the Federal Reserve Board's unusually tight control of money and credit further discouraged price increases. Simultaneously, the easing of the food and fuel shortages that had been plaguing the whole world also reduced inflation. The supply of oil mounted daily, driving energy prices far below the levels OPEC and other producers wished to maintain.

Except for a few doctrinaire politicians, no one was certain just how long the feeling of complacency would last. Growing concern over the budget and trade deficits had led to extreme measures by the mid-1980s. Congress adopted the Graham-Rudman-Hollings proposal that required substantial and progressive reductions in the federal deficit and then struggled to meet these optimistic quidelines. Protectionists revived the nineteenth-century call for high tariffs to ward off foreign competition. Contradictory economic signals in the United States and around the world thus generated concern even as they created opportunities for workers, farmers, and consumers.

TRADING OLD ANXIETIES FOR NEW

Few Americans understood the causes of the recession that struck in the early eighties. Both consumer confidence and spending fell rapidly as employers laid off millions of people or, as they had in earlier downturns, imposed pay cuts and shorter hours. Both salaried and wage workers found themselves losing ground despite the curbing of inflation.

The surprising outcome of an air traffic controllers' strike dispelled any hope of assistance from the federal government. The members of the Professional Air Traffic Controller's Organization (PATCO) had previously bargained successfully for higher salaries and less stressful working conditions. In June 1981, the union membership rejected a new contract that fell short of its demand for $10,000 across-the-board raises and a four-day work week, and the controllers staged a nationwide strike against the Federal Aviation Administration. A government agency, the FAA ultimately answered to anti-labor President Reagan. Supervisory personnel struggled to sort out the hundreds of planes stacked up over airports, but the president refused to rehire anyone who persisted in striking. The government eventually trained a whole new generation of nonunion controllers, leaving the PATCO irretrievably broken.

Similar pressures eroded the strength of other unions. Lacking inflation to justify raises and facing a recession that threatened massive lay-offs, many workers realistically lowered their expectations. In one collective bargaining session after another, labor spokesmen traded reduced wage levels for guarantees of job security. The cost of living adjustments (COLAs) that had automatically raised wages to match inflation in the 1970s disappeared from many contracts. Even the feisty United Auto Workers moderated its demands. The unions' realism contributed significantly to the revival of the American automobile industry in the 1980s, even though it remained burdened with much higher wage levels than its foreign competitors.

Labor negotiators continued to make concessions long after the recession had faded because the demand for industrial workers remained so soft that few unions dared even think about striking. Each succeeding year saw fewer and fewer confrontations. In 1985 the Labor Department recorded only fifty-four major strikes or other work stoppages, the lowest annual figure ever noted. The unions' failure to preserve earlier gains or to obtain new benefits naturally had adverse effects on membership.

Any prospect that traditional unionization would revive appeared doubtful as the United States became increasingly service oriented and less than one-third of the labor force worked in industry. As noted earlier, the declining number of blue-collar jobs had encouraged the AFL-CIO and the Teamsters to expand their organizing efforts among white-collar employees. But disillusion with a confrontational approach in the 1980s and the persistence of unemployment at around 7 percent definitely hampered efforts to broaden the base of unionization. Employers held the upper hand in determining the nature of the American work environment, and they appeared likely to do so for some time to come.

The simultaneous easing of both inflation and scarcities hit the farmers even harder than organized labor. Just as they had in the land booms and busts of earlier years, Americans had become victims of excessive speculation. The global shortages that had tripled prices for many commodities in the 1970s had set off this round of buying. Farmers and other investors bid up land prices all across the country even though inflation was driving mortgage interest rates to extraordinary heights. Land speculators did not hesitate to take out high-interest loans to pay the premium prices their own greed had generated. After all, American farm land had an excellent record as a longterm investment.

Collapsing food prices in the 1980s quickly undermined that faith. Unable to meet mortgage payments predicated on ever-increasing commodity prices, landowners had to sell for whatever they could get, reversing the price escalation of the previous decade. The average price for an acre of Iowa farmland fell from

$2147 in 1981 to just $746 in 1986—virtually the same figure that had prevailed in 1974 when the speculative frenzy had begun. The only farm owners who could survive such a catastrophic devaluation were those who had bought or inherited their land earlier and had avoided assuming high-interest mortgages. Some embattled speculators grimly held on, hoping that mortgage rates would decline enough for them to refinance their land contracts at more sensible interest rates.

The effects of the "farm crisis" spread far beyond rural America. Tax benefits associated with productive agricultural land had lured many city-dwellers and financial institutions into the latter-day land rush. These investors were exceedingly naive about agricultural production costs and prices in an interdependent global market place. The farmers could derive cold comfort from the fact that a great many urban speculators had accompanied them in their disconcerting financial plunge.

REVIVAL OF THE BULL MARKET

The speculative enthusiasm evident in the farm states in the late 1970s seemed to shift to Wall Street in the 1980s. After wallowing through the recession, the stock market began a recovery that would reach unprecedented heights. The Dow Jones industrial average rose from 700 to over 2400 in just five years, though the climb was far from smooth. Oil company shares did very well until the worldwide petroleum glut materialized. Electronics and computer firms had good and bad years. The domestic automakers engineered a resurrection that attracted new money and some reinvestment. The Reagan administration's emphasis on "rebuilding" the nation's armed forces brightened the prospects for defense contractors.

Investors who concentrated their funds in one or two firms, however, inevitably risked more than those with diversified portfolios. Union Carbide Corporation shareholders, for example, could never have anticipated the damage that would occur to the company's reputation when one of its fertilizer plants released a cloud of poisonous gas that killed more than two thousand people in Bhopal, India, in December 1984. To protect themselves from such risks, many investors bought shares in the growing family of mutual funds. Each major brokerage house offered several different types so that its salespeople could stress product differentiation.

The money the funds drew to Wall Street boosted stock prices, and the resulting bull market attracted additional investment. As long as the dollar remained valuable compared to foreign currencies, overseas speculators were eager to buy American securities. The declining interest rates that accompanied the drop in inflation made stocks more attractive investments than bonds or real estate. Managers of the enormous pension funds that labor unions, corporations, and other groups had established naturally expanded their stock purchases and further stimulated the bull market. These and other "institutional" traders conducted about 80 percent of all the transactions on the New York Stock Exchange in the 1980s.

Their size and influence so overshadowed individual speculators that the funds' decisions on when and where to move millions of dollars had profound impacts on all financial markets.

Institutional investors with huge sums to deploy became major players in futures trading. The Chicago Mercantile Exchange introduced speculation in stock-index futures options for the first time in January 1983. The most popular index was Standard & Poor's 500, a summation of the values of one share of each of 500 major corporations. Speculators could buy or sell contracts for future delivery of "baskets" containing shares of all the companies. Their strategy involved predictions as to the movement of the stock market as a whole rather than the behavior of particular companies listed on the Big Board. Under normal conditions, whenever prices on the New York Stock exchange went up or down, the index would rise or fall correspondingly.

An added nuance in the speculation game was arbitrage—buying in one market for immediate resale in another. One group of arbitragers took advantage of slippage between the S & P Index and NYSE prices. Although variations in the S & P figures usually followed the shares' New York exchange performance quite closely, buying and selling pressures in Chicago or New York occasionally created gaps between them. These could result because those who bought and sold futures contracts were influenced by their reading of longterm trends that had little direct relationship to the pressures that affected a company's stock prices. When a gap opened, arbitragers with investments or contracts in both New York and Chicago could reap an automatic profit by selling whichever package was currently overvalued.

Arbitraging and the mass movement of institutional investors' funds could be quite destabilizing. Computers continuously monitored even tiny shifts in stock index futures and share values and alerted traders to take advantage of these minor divergences. Because so many investors employed virtually identical monitoring and forecasting programs, they tended to lunge for their profits simultaneously and thereby set off a frenzy of buying and selling. On particularly hectic days, this "program" buying and selling caused the Dow Jones Industrial Average to plunge forty, sixty, or even eighty points. Although these were larger numerical drops than those experienced in 1929, they actually represented much smaller percentage declines than the 12.9 percent drop that had given Black Tuesday its name.

Many stock exchange officials and analysts considered this volatility alarming. Program buy and sell decisions based on composite indexes or extra-market forces imposed direct, often unsettling consequences on individual corporations. Stock-index futures trading could set prices without regard to a particular company's earnings to assets ratios, dividends, marketing strategy, or leadership effectiveness—all factors that had traditionally been very influential in determining share prices. Impersonal program trading was thus worlds away from the social gatherings of gentlemen who discussed the intrinsic value of the shares they exchanged personally under that long-forgotten buttonwood tree in old Manhattan.

CORPORATE CANNIBALISM

The financial exchanges also shuddered from a barrage of mergers in the 1980s. Rumors of a potential takeover usually caused the price of the target corporation's shares to skyrocket. One expert estimated that three-fourths of the rise that stock prices experienced in 1985 had stemmed directly or indirectly from takeover bids and mergers.

Large-scale consolidation had, of course, been common among United States businesses since the 1890s, but the magnitude of mergers in the 1980s eclipsed all previous records. Where just twelve deals exceeded the $1 billion level between 1969 and 1980, thirty such monster transactions occurred in 1985 alone, and many of them involved exchanges of more than $5 billion. Oil and other natural resource concerns had conducted most of the larger consolidations in earlier decades, but all types of corporations were sucked into the takeover scramble in recent years. Two old-line tobacco companies, Philip Morris and R. J. Reynolds, for example, engulfed General Foods and Nabisco respectively.

SAVING THE VILLAGE

Carl Icahn stunned the corporate world with his takeover of troubled Trans-World Airlines. He justified his move by claiming that the company had been terribly mismanaged, a situation which he called an "outrage." When he was preparing a buyout bid for USX, the new name for U. S. Steel, in the fall of 1986, he was questioned as to his motives.

I do it to make money. I'm not saying I don't. I'm a competitive guy and I do it with a profit motive. That's how you score in this game and those are the points. I'm not saying I'm an altruist.

I've thought about this. Maybe it sounds a little self-serving but you get a lot of satisfaction from correcting something you think is wrong, in changing what you consider to be an outrage. If you can change the outrage and get the points, that's the best of all worlds. I have to admit that otherwise I might look for a different outrage.

It's almost like a tiger hunter. All right, it might be fun to hunt tigers but after a while, unless you hunt the tigers because you're saving the village it's sort of just bloody and messy. So you want to be saving the village and if the village is paying you very handsomely and it has a lot of poor little babies in it, there is a great deal of satisfaction in taking on the risk of fighting the tigers. And I think that's why I do it.

("Confessions of a Raider," *Newsweek* [October 20, 1986], p. 55.)

Unvarnished acquisitiveness motivated many mergers. Some buyers freely acknowledged their intentions to resell immediately component parts of a takeover target either to retire the huge debt load the buyout created or simply to streamline the resulting combination. Logical planning lay behind other deals. In 1984 General Motors began a coordinated expansion program by acquiring the enormously profitable Electronic Data Systems (EDS) from its billionaire founder, H. Ross Perot. GM wanted EDS to develop sophisticated software for managing the production flow at the assembly plant it then began constructing in Tennessee to manufacture its Saturn car. The auto giant later bought Hughes Aircraft so that company's engineers and workers could design innovative electronics devices for both the Saturn plant and its products.

Billions of dollars had to be collected to pay for such properties. A wealthy acquiring company like General Motors might be able to use its own cash reserves or conventional bond sales for capitalization. In many instances the predator was much smaller than its prey, however, so it had to borrow on a massive scale. Novel financial instruments dubbed "junk bonds" generated some of the needed cash. A company preparing a bid would issue IOUs carrying interest rates about 3 percent higher than those of standard corporate bonds. Although rating services refused even to evaluate junk bonds, plenty of lenders appeared willing to take unknown risks to earn their higher yields. Ideally these expensive bonds would be retired quickly with money from the new combine's enhanced profits or from the sale of some of its unwanted components. The combination of junk bonds and conventional borrowing had inflated the total corporate debt to a staggering $1.4 trillion by 1985.

The takeover process began when a bidder had collected enough capital to offer to buy the target's shares at a premium over their current price. Naturally many stockholders were eager to sell their holdings at these elevated prices. Institutional investors in particular exhibited none of the loyalty that had traditionally influenced smaller investors' behavior. The promise of quick profits caused huge blocks of stock to change hands. Arbitragers who sensed an upcoming deal often bought furiously and thereby bid prices up more rapidly and sometimes far higher than anyone had anticipated. Enormous profits could be collected if the takeover actually occurred, but many individuals and firms suffered devastating losses when a bid failed for one reason or another.

T. BOONE PICKENS

Just a hint that T. Boone Pickens might be on the move caused jitters among Wall Street traders and company executives. Because several of his elaborate takeover bids did fail, though, some complained that he was deliberately engaging in "greenmail." Had he purposely bought large blocks of shares only to sell them at huge markups when the company countered his offers to shareholders? Pickens never apologized for his activities, claiming instead that all shareholders benefited from the increased stock prices his activities induced.

A personable southwestern oil tycoon, Thomas Boone Pickens, Jr., had been born in Oklahoma, the son of an attorney who worked for Phillips Petroleum. After earning a geology degree at Oklahoma State University, young Boone worked briefly for his father's employer before deciding to become an independent oil and gas wildcatter. With just $2500 in cash in 1955, he formed the Petroleum Exploration Co. of Amarillo, Texas. It ran up a remarkable record of locating new energy sources before Pickens transformed it into the Mesa Petroleum Co. in 1964. For the next fifteen years, it emphasized the exploration, drilling, and production end of the oil business while carefully avoiding the riskier distribution and consumer sales aspects.

In the late seventies the company sold some of the overseas properties it had acquired to clear the deck for Pickens's takeover activities. His first major target, Cities Service Co., managed to escape his clutches by selling itself to Occidental Petroleum instead. Pickens and his Mesa shareholders prospered anyway by selling stock they had previously accumulated at lower prices to the new owners for a profit of $31.5 million. A similar assault on the General American Oil Co. ended with a buy-out by Phillips—and a cool $43.6 million profit for Mesa.

These moves were just practice runs for Pickens's assault on the Gulf Oil Co. in the summer of 1983. Although it ranked as the fifth largest oil company in the United States, several recent setbacks had driven the price of Gulf stock below $40 a share. By January 1984, Pickens's group controlled 13.2 percent of the outstanding shares and was offering other stockholders $50 for each one they held. Once again, a "white knight" intervened: Standard Oil of California made a counter offer of $80 a share and then consolidated Gulf into its Chevron operations. Pickens happily sold his shares at that price which was double what he had paid in many instances, and Mesa was $760 million to the good.

Some compared T. Boone Pickens to Jay Gould and Jim Fisk, the financial swashbucklers of the previous century. But the president of Mesa Petroleum insisted throughout that he was only bringing the share prices of the target corporations up to levels that reflected their real worth. To the extent that he saw himself rationalizing corporate finance, Pickens is more like J. P. Morgan who dismissed the millions he accumulated as a secondary consequence of his determination to improve the American business structure.

The spree of mergers had many negative consequences. A company that swallowed another could find itself saddled with appalling debts that neither streamlining nor sell-offs could service. Even if it could manage its debt load, a bloated successor's stock might never recover its earlier resiliency. Takeovers also levied a human toll. The new management shifted executives about or laid them off according to its whims. Employees often had to move from one city to another or from one job to quite a different one within the restructured firm. And, because streamlining was a major objective of consolidation, many jobs disappeared altogether, throwing employees from all levels out of work.

Some questioned whether these consolidations had any societal and economic benefits at all. A takeover bid could artificially boost stock prices far higher than a corporation's assets justified. Worse yet, the funds absorbed in the buying process itself–not to mention the huge fees that lawyers, financiers, and brokers collected– produced few if any improvements in the overall productivity of the business structure. Even as the American people were being urged to save and invest their money in productive enterprises for the good of society, junk bonds were sopping up vast quantities of potentially productive investment capital.

In other eras, the federal government might have stepped in to contain the merger impetus and stem the tide of high-risk bonds. But the Reagan administration claimed to be firmly committed to freer enterprise in every sense, and Congress seemed equally disinterested or incapable of halting the trend to ever larger combines. The Federal Reserve Board finally implemented a policy early in 1986 that could, if not halt the mergers, at least prevent the worst financial abuses. The Fed insisted that no more than half of the funding in a takeover bid could come from junk bonds or other high-risk credit schemes. The remainder of the capital must be assembled through more traditional and presumably sounder financial methods.

Lacking government protection from predators, many potential targets took themselves off the market by "going private" through a leveraged buy-out (LBO). A corporation's officials or other "friendly" investors would round up enough cash or loans to repurchase stock from its public shareholders. Restoring private control of the company often seemed so advisable that its managers might even sell junk bonds themselves to complete the LBO. In many instances the officials planned for the company to go public later after all takeover threats had evaporated. At that point they hoped to sell new shares at far higher prices than the old ones had commanded.

The public would not necessarily be foolish to pay premiums for the stock of a reorganized company. After an LBO, the firm might sell some of its less-productive assets to pay debts and create a more self-sufficient and efficient operation. Members of the founding family executed an LBO in 1985 that restored to them 92 percent ownership of Levi Strauss & Co. The firm's new management then quickly sold five of nine corporate divisions in order to concentrate most of its remaining assets in its highly profitable Jeans Division.

The merger that reunited General Electric and RCA in December 1985 represented another case in which historical ownership and control were restored. The $6 billion GE paid for the electronics and entertainment giant made it the largest acquisition of a non-oil firm in American history. General Electric had, of course, created RCA in 1919, but a 1932 antitrust ruling had forced the parent company to sell its entertainment subsidiary. Both firms had thrived separately, with RCA's success due largely to David Sarnoff's intelligence and drive.

The pioneering television corporation suffered reverses in the late 1970s, though. Audience ratings for its NBC network fell behind those for ABC and CBS. The videodisc fiasco was costly as well. RCA introduced its system for broadcasting from prerecorded discs over home television sets just when relatively inexpensive video cassette recorders (VCRs) came on the market. In addition to playing prerecorded programs like RCA's videodiscs, VCR owners could record and erase shows received on their television sets. Videodisc technology possessed some information and data retrieval capabilities unmatched by other systems, but the specialized market for this function was far too small to offset the huge losses RCA suffered in failing to corral a major share of the home entertainment market.

GE chairman John Welch masterminded the merger. When he had taken command of the appliance manufacturer and defense contractor in 1980, he had concluded it was far too diversified and therefore sold over 150 of its divisions. He retained the units engaged in electronics, defense work, and technical services and disposed of many of GE's small appliance manufacturing facilities and other segments that were competing poorly with foreign imports. Welch outlined a similar strategy for his new, larger combine. Together, GE and RCA constituted the seventh largest industrial firm in the United States. Even so, the merger provoked little comment from a Washington committed to a relaxation of the regulatory philosophy that had prevailed since the 1930s.

TOWARD FREER ENTERPRISE?

The relationship between government and business in the eighties resembled that of the twenties. Just as the Harding and Coolidge administrations had deliberately weakened the Progressive watchdog agencies, the Reagan administration relaxed controls and dismantled parts of the regulatory structure. The goal was to "get the government off the back" of private enterprise and to permit "natural" economic and entrepreneurial forces to determine which businesses would succeed or fail.

Several techniques helped implement this return to Harding-style "normalcy." Attrition dried up federal funding that had previously paid for all sorts of public projects. Tax cuts freed funds for private investment and the Tax Reform Act of 1986 eliminated the sheltering of income in nonproductive investments. Meanwhile deregulation was profoundly affecting certain sectors.

The momentum for deregulation had been building for some time. Indeed, the architect of one of the most sweeping deregulation programs of all was President Carter's advisor on wage and price controls, Alfred Kahn, a former chairman of the Federal Aviation Administration (FAA). He insisted that both FAA and Civilian Aeronautics Board (CAB) rules forced private airline companies to function inefficiently. These federal agencies controlled ticket prices, airport access, allocation of routes, and many other matters in ways that private managers might never have chosen on their own. Some air carriers, for example, were required to maintain unprofitable routes to assure that the whole country had a comprehensive air transport system. At the same time, rate regulations prevented full exploitation of profitable airways. Deregulation began in 1978 with the hope that it would spur constructive competition in the industry.

Although no one expected the transition from regulated to free enterprise to be smooth, even Kahn did not anticipate all of the consequences of deregulation. He did, however, expect new competitors to enter the field. Emulating Freddie Laker, the iconoclastic British businessman who had made millions by setting his ticket prices well below the established fares for trans-Atlantic flights, American companies offered inexpensive service along well-traveled routes. A company named People Express blossomed overnight, attracting passengers with cheap, no-frills flights in the early 1980s. By reducing the number of cabin attendants and squeezing more seats into its jumbo jet aircraft, the company prospered for a time.

Freed from an obligation to serve all potential customers, the major carriers trimmed their flights to intermediate points to concentrate on the profitable coast-to-coast market or the heavily traveled eastern corridor. Soon competition among airlines pursuing identical marketing strategies forced all carriers to make repeated reductions in their ticket prices. As profit margins declined, weaker companies suffered. Braniff International was a prominent casualty. The company had prospered for years serving the southwestern United States and maintaining links to Central and South America. Deregulation encouraged it to compete directly with larger, established companies in the prime markets where it became overextended and lapsed into bankruptcy in the summer of 1982.

As the advocates of deregulation had hoped, it did open new opportunities for some entrepreneurs, although only about one-third of the new airline companies formed after 1978 survived. When major companies abandoned their secondary routes to concentrate on transcontinental service, small, often locally owned companies appeared to fill the gaps. "Commuter" airlines ferried passengers to and from hubs like Chicago's O'Hare or Denver's Stapleton Airports. By the mid-eighties some of these smaller carriers had sounder financial standings than the traditional giants.

Consolidation was inevitable. Some major airlines took over the profitable routes and services of smaller companies, but quite a few mergers went the other way. An aggressive regional company named Texas Air first acquired Continental to extend its reach to the West Coast. In 1986, it became even more voracious, taking over People Express, the all-but-defunct Frontier Airlines, and financially troubled Eastern Airlines. At that point, Texas Air controlled more assets than the industry's perennial leader, United Airlines.

The companies engaged in the competitive scramble often seemed to forget that their revenue came from customers. Passengers suffered abrupt cancellations, endured long delays at overcrowded hub airports, risked being stranded, and faced wildly fluctuating ticket prices. On busy routes, to be sure, average fares dropped about 40 percent below their regulated levels, and occasional bargains were even more attractive. Where they encountered no competition, however, carriers could charge whatever the traffic would bear. The resulting fare structure recalled the long-haul—short-haul abuse for which the railroads had been so criticized a century earlier. A passenger might have to pay far more for a short hop to a hub airport than for a transcontinental flight. Fortunately, one fear of the opponents of deregulation was unfounded: there was no deterioration in the safety record for air travel in the United States.

Deregulation was just one strategy for encouraging more competition in business. A landmark antitrust action in the early 1980s completely altered the communications industry. The American Telephone and Telegraph Co. had been the dominant force in this sector since the late nineteenth century. A monster holding company, "Ma Bell" had evolved from the profitable business structure Theodore N. Vail had created to exploit Alexander Graham Bell's patent. By 1974 the Bell System included twenty-two regional companies providing local phone service for the vast majority of the U.S. population. And, although hundreds of small independent companies controlled restricted local markets, they all utilized the long distance facilities that AT&T's Long Lines Department maintained.

Attorneys in the Justice Department's Antitrust Division concluded at that point that AT&T was exercising monopolistic control over the industry. Their indictment charged that, to maintain its control of long distance service, "AT&T has engaged in predatory pricing, refusals to supply transmission service, preselling and other marketing and operational practices available to it as the monopoly suppliers of long-distance service." The federal lawyers also viewed its twenty-two service companies as a virtual monopoly. The corporation's defense counsel argued, in the case of the *United States* v. *AT&T*, that it did not really monopolize all those markets and that whatever dominance it had achieved was the result of its efficiency in using communications technology to fulfill its obligations as a common carrier.

After six years of pretrial discovery, opening arguments were delivered at the U.S. District Court in Washington in January 1981. A year later, AT&T expressed its willingness to settle with the government, and the presiding judge approved a final agreement in 1983. It dismembered a corporation with $150 billion in assets, the largest in the world at that point. AT&T insisted upon retaining its Long Lines operations and its manufacturing and research arms, Western Electric and Bell Labs, but agreed to divest itself of its local phone companies. These local Bell companies were reorganized into seven regional groupings, each of which became a separate entity. Stockholders began receiving eight separate dividend checks corresponding to their proportional shares of the now independent companies.

Although the streamlined AT&T retained less than two-thirds of the assets of the original combine, it remained a powerful force in the electronics and communications industries. It quickly entered into competition with IBM by producing, among other products, a microcomputer modeled after Big Blue's Personal Computer. At the same time, it remained dominant in the long-distance business even though the regional Bell companies were specifically prohibited from urging their customers to stay with AT&T.

In one way, the divestiture did encourage more competition than the telephone business had ever experienced. Companies like Sprint, MCI, and Teleconnect which used microwave or optical fiber technology to transmit messages over long distances attempted to woo customers away from AT&T's Long Lines Department. They were far less successful than they had hoped to be; Ma Bell continued to handle the vast majority of calls outside local service areas. The competition did, however, force all long-distance companies including AT&T to reduce substantially their charges for this service.

Customers meanwhile saw their rates for local service escalate, doubling or tripling in some markets. AT&T had been subsidizing local service out of its long-distance revenues; now all services were supposedly self-supporting. Customers interested in reducing their telephone costs could take advantage of a related aspect of deregulation. They were now permitted to install instruments they owned rather than being required to rent from Bell. But even though millions of inexpensive telephones manufactured by other suppliers replaced the more costly ones Western Electric produced, AT&T's manufacturing division continued to sell its tough, reliable receivers through retail outlets. The full impact of the breakup of AT&T has yet to be determined, but it did allow other companies working in a free enterprise structure to capture minor segments of the expanding communications market.

MEETING CUSTOMER PREFERENCES

Telephone lines served as the arteries of the nation's communications network, connecting 96 percent of the households in the United States in the 1980s. Radios were even more common. Only 1 percent of the households did not contain a radio, and the average was six per family. Television followed close behind with an average of just under two sets in 98 percent of the nation's homes. Yet sales of these popular devices made up just a fraction of Americans' expenditures on electronics. Consumers took home millions of VCRs, microwave ovens, stereo music systems, and computers every year. Shortly after their introduction, compact discs and players were selling by the millions and threatening to make analog sound recordings like tapes and records obsolete.

Following the same strategy Alfred P. Sloan had devised for General Motors in the 1920s, manufacturers tried to bracket the market. A basic telephone might sell for ten dollars, but "message centers" with call recorders and other accessories cost several hundred. In between were a series of slightly different products, with each "improvement" or addition justifying a higher price. By the 1980s, advertisers had refined their skills at marketing appeals directed at specific groups or classes of customers. Retailers benefited from the higher prices they could charge for minor modifications to otherwise identical products.

A similar trend altered the marketing of entertainment. The three major television networks lost viewers to alternative broadcasting from cable systems and satellite dishes. Just as FM radio stations had in the 1950s, cable systems provided specialized programming for smaller audience segments. The Music Television channel (MTV) created something of a new art form with its elaborate rock video broadcasts. Fundamentalist religion, minor sports, round-the-clock news, and even video sales shows filled out cable schedules. The latter stressed audience participation by urging viewers to phone in bids or orders for goods advertised on na-

TED TURNER

An expert at exploiting the media to advance his career, Ted Turner pursued many activities designed to rivet popular attention. After prepping at a couple of southern military academies and briefly majoring in classics at Brown University, Robert Edward Turner III headed for Atlanta to work for his father's successful billboard company. When the senior Turner committed suicide shortly afterward, his son discovered that the company had been sold out from under him. Young Ted fought off the buyers and reclaimed control of the firm in 1963 when he was just twenty-four.

It provided him with a base for his rapid rise in the advertising business. He made his first foray into television in 1970 by purchasing a struggling UHF station. The enterprise languished until Turner copied the Home Box Office strategy and began distributing his programming via satellite to cable companies all over the country. Overnight Atlanta's WTBS became known as the "SuperStation." An avid sports fan, Turner bought the franchises of the Atlanta Braves baseball team and the Atlanta Hawks basketball team, in part to generate programming for his independent television station. In 1977 he personally captured the sports headlines by piloting his yacht *Courageous* to victory in the America's Cup competition.

Continuing his pioneering role in the rapidly growing cable television business, Turner stunned the industry in 1982 with the introduction of 24-hour programming on his Cable News Network. Going head to head with the news bureaus of the established broadcasting giants proved costly indeed: CNN lost an estimated $50 million in its first few years on the air and survived only because the Turner Broadcasting System's earnings from WTBS more than offset its losses from the news channel.

The Atlanta media mogul staged a typically audacious takeover attempt in 1985 when he announced his intention to buy a controlling interest in the Columbia Broadcasting System without putting up any cash at all, just a bundle of securities. CBS defended itself by paying a hefty price to buy millions of its outstanding shares back from public stockholders. In the fall, Turner salved his bruised ego by purchasing the MGM/UA combine for $1.5 billion. He then immediately resold the United Artists segment of the combine to reduce his debt load. MGM's primary attraction were the 2200 films in its vaults that Turner could use to fill his own television schedules and lease to other cable companies and networks. He then generated further controversy by "colorizing" many black and white classic films with a computerized system. Regardless of the ultimate success or failure of his many ventures, Ted Turner had already carved a prominent if controversial niche in the thriving entertainment industry.

tional hookups. Some promoters insisted that video-buying represented the wave of the future.

Demographic changes created new divisions or brackets in the market. One of the most important caused a decline in the youth orientation of earlier decades. While the youngest of the postwar baby boomers was reaching adulthood in the late seventies, the percentage of Americans fifty and older was rising significantly. Many producers and retailers began tailoring their products to appeal to older consumers. Gray-haired models appeared in advertisements for a broad range of products, not just traditional ones like hair color and patent medicines. Greeting card publishers invented another excuse for their existence—Grandparents' Day—and even the toy manufacturers directed some of their sales pitches to indulgent oldsters likely to buy presents for younger relatives.

The growing population of older Americans created new types of business opportunities. Nursing homes maintained long waiting lists. Retirement communities in areas with mild climates like California, Arizona, and Florida boomed even when recession dogged other parts of the nation. Retirees who combined company pensions with social security payments often did as well or better financially than they had when working full time. They thus became potential customers for high quality housing and furnishings. Inflation-pegged Medicare payments also allowed them to pay for extensive medical treatment.

Those who offered medical services, however, found themselves facing unprecedented competition in the 1980s. Medical charges had traditionally risen much faster than those for other services, but both private and public concern became evident when costs failed to moderate after inflation ebbed. Cutbacks in federal funding for human services and critical ad campaigns by private insurers like Blue Cross definitely put medical professionals on the defensive. Companies and individuals turned to comprehensive health maintenance organizations (HMOs) to contain health care costs. The length of the average hospital stay declined in part because of improved treatment methods, leaving many facilities with empty beds. Hospitals themselves began to advertise to attract customers not only for standard treatments like childbirth and surgery but also for well-patient services like weight-reduction, alcoholism, and smoking clinics.

A persistent interest in personal health fed the demand for such programs. Continuing the upward trend of the previous decade, sales of sporting goods rose from $10 billion in 1980 to $14 billion in 1985. Health clubs, spas, aerobics clinics, and martial arts schools sprang up in shopping malls and downtown storefronts. Some belonged to national chains; others represented local entrepreneurship. The nation's health kick simultaneously hurt some food producers. Rich dairy products like butter and cream steadily lost customer appeal as did red meat. A persistent decline in the popularity of smoking was a major factor in convincing tobacco giants like Philip Morris and R. J. Reynolds to diversify.

Changing fads kept the beverage distributors in turmoil. All the major brewers began marketing "light" beer with fewer calories. Health consciousness also reduced the demand for liquor, but wine sales boomed. White wine emerged as the predominant drink of the eighties lifestyle. Hundreds of new wineries began bottling operations all over the country, and many experts rated American wines equal or superior to Europe's classic vintages. Coolers that combined wine with soft drinks were a stunning market success: sales rose 500 to 600 percent each year and the actors who portrayed Bartles and Jaymes became as familiar as Ronald Mac-Donald to television viewers.

Americans also suffered through the "Cola Wars." The popularity of soft drinks as alternatives to alcoholic beverages continued to grow although health concerns particularly stimulated sales of low- or no-calorie drinks. Cancer scares had removed several artificial sweeteners from distribution, but in July 1981, after an eight-year wait, G. D. Searle & Co. obtained FDA approval to sell aspartame. Marketed under the brand-name "Nutra-sweet," it was added to virtually every kind of food and soft drink. Convinced that public preferences were shifting toward sweeter drinks, Coca Cola mounted a multi-million-dollar campaign to advertise a new recipe for the beverage that had created the soft drink business in the first place. The resulting consumer rebellion was so intense and costly that the company hastily brought back "Classic Coke." Sales of its new recipe remained substantial, though, and their continued growth proved that the company's market researchers had not been completely misguided.

The competition between the two manufacturers of instant photography equipment ended abruptly in the eighties. When Polaroid's SX-70 and One-Step cameras had begun drawing customers away from Eastman Kodak's products, the photography pioneer mounted a frontal assault. Although the instant-developing cameras and film Kodak introduced never achieved the desired sales levels, they reduced Polaroid's profits. Edwin Land fought back with a lawsuit that claimed Kodak's processes had infringed on seven of his company's patents. After a court injunction temporarily prohibited Kodak from selling its equipment, the company terminated all manufacture of both cameras and film. It then agreed to trade one of its conventional cameras or a share of Kodak stock for each instant camera already purchased. Land once again enjoyed a monopoly of the business he had fathered.

In addition to changing what they bought, consumers in the eighties continued to alter how and where they shopped. Women who accepted paying jobs outside their homes simply could not shop during the day. Many customers with more money to spend than time to spend it turned to catalogs. Unlike the bulky, utilitarian volumes Sears and Montgomery Ward still published, many modern catalogs were slick, full-color publications offering upscale and often quite expensive items. Companies like L. L. Bean and Eddie Bauer subsisted primarily on their mail-order sales, even though both also operated retail stores.

These specialty shops inhabited equally specialized malls. While many shopping centers still offered the basics—food supermarkets, department stores, routine services—others with names like "Galleria" or "Bonaventura" set out to attract customers interested in recreational shopping and impulse buying. A third type of mall became common in the eighties, one devoted to specialized discount stores. Famous Footwear, The Burlington Coat Factory, Marshalls, and other chains sold wider assortments of brand-name products at low prices than could be found in discount department stores like K-mart. As a group, shopping malls absorbed more than half of all consumer dollars spent in the eighties. Conventional department stores, downtown businesses, and other historically profitable ventures thus saw both their customers and profits flowing to the malls.

Earlier in the century, the corner gas station had symbolized small-town private enterprise. It offered few frills, simply selling gas at its pumps and servicing cars in its garage. But time and technological progress altered both these activities. Detergent oil, sealed bearings, long-wearing radial tires, "permanent" antifreeze, and other products eliminated the need for frequent auto maintenance while self-service pumping spread nationwide. Some station operators glassed in their service bays and stocked them with sundries. Others simply closed down in the face of competition from "convenience" chain stores.

THE STATE OF AMERICAN BUSINESS

The transformation of the corner gas station in no way signaled an end to the American love affair with cars. True, a great many of them were imported models. Tokyo continued to enforce "voluntary" export controls that limited the number of vehicles shipped to the United States, but Japanese manufacturers continually upgraded their cars' quality, accessories, and prices. European automakers like Sweden's Volvo and Germany's Mercedes-Benz retained loyal followings. To compete in the bottom end of the market, Korea and Yugoslavia began sending automobiles to American priced well below domestic and other imported models.

Despite continuing foreign competition, the fortunes of all three major domestic auto manufacturers rebounded in the early 1980s. While the Chrysler Corporation appeared to have staged the most dramatic resurrection under the Lee Iacocca, Ford may well have done even better under the presidency of Donald Peterson. Peterson had worked his way up in the Ford organization as an engineer rather

Lee Iaccoca. (Courtesy The Chrysler Corp.)

LEE IACOCCA

When Lee Iacocca's autobiography became the bestselling hardcover nonfiction book in the history of American publishing, many people began to consider the talkative, folksy, and energetic president of the Chrysler Corporation as an ideal candidate for the White House. Iacocca dismissed the idea, but it was one of the few promotion tactics he had ever rejected. He had begun starring in Chrysler commercials even as the company was losing $3.5 billion from 1978 to 1981. Bouyed perhaps by the confidence that Iacocca projected, the company had managed to reverse that trend by 1982.

The dramatic turnaround was all the more surprising because it was the accomplishment of a man whom Henry Ford II had fired as president of his company after thirty-two years of loyal service. The son of an Italian immigrant, Lido Anthony Iacocca had grown up in Pennsylvania and obtained an engineering degree from Lehigh University and a masters degree from Princeton. He started at Ford as an engineer but soon switched to truck sales. Vice-president Robert McNamara promoted him to marketing manager for the whole firm in 1956 and, four years later, to chief of the Ford car division.

There Iacocca received credit for two major developments: the introduction of the sporty Mustang in 1964 and, later, of the luxurious Lincoln Continental Mark series. Although designers and engineers had obviously had the most to do with creating these models, the dynamic Iacocca developed immensely successful selling strategies for them. As a reward for his services, the company promoted him to the presidency in 1970, the position he held until the very bitter falling out with Henry Ford II.

Rather than retire on his substantial pension, Iacocca took the helm of the deeply troubled Chrysler Corporation. Saddled with debts, antiquated plants and equipment, uninspiring designs, and intense foreign and domestic competition, the company teetered on the brink of bankruptcy. After exhausting all the standard refinancing possibilities, Iacocca lobbied for a massive federal loan guarantee similar to the one that had bailed out Lockheed a decade earlier. Congress eventually approved a $1.5 billion package that helped Chrysler borrow in a tight market.

Money alone could never have saved the company had it not developed its K-car. Although it was a boxy, rather utilitarian model, its front-wheel drive, passenger comfort, and good gas mileage helped it win awards and attract buyers. Meanwhile, the company was closing sixteen of its fifty-two plants and cutting its workforce in half. These changes in conjunction with the general revival of the American auto industry in the early 1980s helped generate an amazing $2.4 billion profit in 1984. But many Americans assumed, and the feisty executive did little to dissuade them, that Chrysler's revival had been engineered singlehandedly by Lee Iacocca himself.

than a salesman and thus became the first Ford CEO with direct product knowledge since the retirement of Henry Ford himself. Along with many other executives, Peterson had served a tour of duty in Ford's European division where he had observed both the competition and the capabilities of overseas designers. That experience convinced him when he became president in 1980 to scrap the clunky, lumbering models the company had been building for years.

The new Ford line emphasized smaller, aerodynamically shaped cars with solid road handling and construction. The compact Ford Escort became the top selling car in the world while sleek Thunderbirds and Tauruses competed head to head with German and Japanese imports. Peterson's low-key management style was a welcome relief in a corporation notorious for bitter infighting. He brought the workers directly into the decision-making process by asking them to make suggestions for manufacturing improvements on designs long before they went into production. Labor responded enthusiastically, and Ford cars began consistently earning top ratings for production quality and performance.

While its car business was prospering, Ford suffered a major humiliation on a defense project. For years the army had been feeding research and development contracts to the company for a sophisticated antiaircraft gun known by the acronym DIVAD. But field trials of the prototypes were so discouraging that the Pentagon scrapped the $5 billion program in August 1985. The DIVAD fiasco was symptomatic of serious imperfections and inadequacies in the defense contracting system. Congressmen and news services reported one case after another of outrageous costs amounting to thousands of dollars that the armed services had paid for percolators, toilet seats, and even hammers. Some blamed the Reagan administration for generating a tidal wave of increased appropriations that simply could not be adequately monitored.

Despite the widespread cynicism about the Pentagon's competence and in the face of considerable skepticism from the scientific community, the president convinced Congress to approve massive appropriations for the Strategic Defense Initiative (SDI), popularly known as Star Wars. Its goal was to orbit enough sophisticated anti-ballistic missiles, lasers, and other weapons to constitute an impermeable shield against incoming Soviet rockets. At the height of the controversy over the feasibility of SDI, the space shuttle *Challenger* exploded shortly after lift-off. This tragedy not only halted NASA's ambitious space program but it called into question the nation's ability to launch the millions of pounds of payload that SDI would eventually require.

The *Challenger* incident also raised doubts that high technology could solve other problems. As American consumers became well versed in what personal computers could and could not do, the popularity of these devices appeared to reach a plateau. Reminiscent of the emergence of the Big Three automakers out of dozens of early competitors, a shake-out in the computer industry beached hundreds of hardware and software producers and left a few major firms in charge. In 1986 industry leader IBM celebrated the sale of its three millionth personal computer, the product that had set the world's standard for microcomputing. To maintain its sales levels, though, the company had reduced its prices substantially to meet the competition from manufacturers of PC "clones." Meanwhile a series of revamped versions of the Apple II computer kept its manufacturer afloat, helped along by the attractiveness, capabilities, and moderate prices of its MacIntosh line.

Just as the computer makers adjusted to changing demand patterns, so too did the construction industry. Many Americans had concluded during the discouraging economic conditions of the late 1970s that privately owned housing might become a historical artifact. But lower interest rates in the mid-eighties made mortgages accessible to many more potential buyers. Now families found themselves competing for housing with older couples, divorced men and women living apart, and a growing number of individuals who chose to remain single. Together they created an enormous demand for housing units that stimulated a flurry of new construction. At the same time, high construction costs and fear of spiraling interest rates in the future kept the boom within bounds.

The lower energy costs and interest rates that benefited the building trades were quite harmful to the oil companies. The reverses the energy giants suffered seemed particularly intense because Exxon, Shell, Mobil, and others had collected such huge profits when their recovery costs failed to rise as quickly as world oil prices in the late seventies. When OPEC's control over production levels deteriorated in the early eighties, global prices fell swiftly. Many an American oil company found itself in a tight corner. Chevron, the California-based heir of the old Standard Oil trust, had to cut almost 20 percent of its workforce in 1986 to make ends meet.

Earlier predictions of permanently high oil prices had provoked other costly miscalculations. Anticipating a never-ending oil boom in Texas, Houston luxuriated in a phenomenal burst of growth in the late 70s and early 80s. By the middle of the latter decade, though, the forest of steel and glass skyscrapers in the city's center was suffering unprecedented vacancy rates. Several brand new buildings had never had a single renter and no prospect of any tenants in the future. Like those who had rushed to buy parcels in the wilderness of the Old Northwest Territory after 1800, Houston's urban real estate speculators faced monumental losses.

Like the farm crisis, the oil and real estate troubles in the Southwest had nationwide effects. In 1982 the sudden collapse of the Penn Square Bank of Oklahoma City rocked the business world. Poorly managed from the start, the institution had been very lax in investigating the creditworthiness of loan applicants. The bank's officers seemed especially eager to loan huge sums to independent oil-exploration firms hoping to profit from the surge in world oil prices. Penn Square then "sold" most of the high-interest loans it arranged to other banks for a fee ranging from 0.5 to 1 percent. These loans were very high-risk investments even before plummeting oil prices undermined the value of in-ground reserves. In the wake of the bank's collapse, the FDIC decided to limit its compensation to depositors in the defunct institution to its $100,000 legal obligation. Those more heavily tied into the Penn Square were left to cope with their losses any way they could.

The Continental Illinois Bank and Trust Co. had bought over $1 billion worth of high-risk loans from Penn Square, and it had to write off $191 million of them in 1982 alone. These losses and other troubles caused the nation's ninth largest bank holding company to stumble along for the next two years, barely managing to remain solvent. A classic run on the Chicago-based firm materialized in the summer of 1984. As institutional investors and depositors clamored to withdraw millions of dollars at a time, all of the bank's $30 billion in assets seemed threatened. With the Federal Reserve Board's support, the Morgan Guaranty Trust Co. arranged a sixteen-bank agreement that established a $4.5 billion line of credit for the foundering Continental Illinois. It saved the company momentarily, but no one would guarantee that such a support package could be arranged to rescue troubled financial institutions in the future.

The thrashings of these monster banks diverted attention from the many smaller institutions that closed their doors or had to be bought out to avoid bankruptcy. Savings and loan institutions caught in the vice of paying high interest to attract depositors out of the proceeds from older low-rate mortgages were in deep financial trouble. Neither the FDIC nor the FSLIC, the federal insurer of savings and loan associations, had anywhere near enough resources to bail out all the threatened institutions. Fortunately, lower interest rates in the mid-eighties gave everyone breathing space, but the longterm soundness of the nation's financial system remained a matter of major concern.

THE CLOUDED FORECAST

The delicacy of the banking structure in the eighties that recalled financial and monetary problems of earlier years was only one of the familiar patterns that reappeared in recent years. The tidal wave of business mergers in the 1980s resembled the spates of consolidation in the 1920s and around the turn of the century. The Reagan-era bull market seemed a reincarnation of several earlier speculative booms. The concurrent federal budget and foreign trade deficits, though much larger than ever before, were certainly not unprecedented. Concern for the plight of the farmers while agricultural surpluses inundated all available storage facilities had been expressed almost continuously in rural America since the end of World War I. And strident calls for the preservation of "free enterprise" once again came, as so often in the past, from business leaders whose companies derived much of their profits from government contracts.

Throughout this book, it has been obvious that many events and circumstances have followed cyclical patterns. Prosperity collapses into depression, hard times give way to recovery, and the resulting boom sets off a new wave of prosperity. Similar cycles have occurred in reform attitudes, government regulation, consolidation, and stock market behavior. Does knowledge of the history of the key elements in American business and of their cyclical behavior then permit one to forecast the future of American enterprise? Several factors suggest that anyone attempting to make such a prediction do so with extreme care.

One obvious reason for caution is that the recent past has been characterized by a unique juxtaposition of otherwise familiar circumstances. Never before, for example, has the United States experienced such massive federal deficits in peacetime. Also, the recent mergers have taken place during a period of recession or, at best, only moderate growth rather than in the prosperity that stimulated earlier consolidations. The weakness of the banking and financial structure is especially disturbing given the fact that SEC regulations supposedly outlawed outrageous behavior and the FDIC and Federal Reserve Systems appear to be functioning as effectively as they ever have. The simultaneous occurrence of such an unusual combination of circumstances creates a unique economic and social situation. Few reliable historical guideposts therefore exist to assist in predicting future trends.

Other factors that cloud the forecast for American enterprise are the permanent and apparently irreversible changes the United States has undergone. Its economy has, for example, clearly lost its industrial focus. Not only are the nation's consumers buying shiploads of goods from overseas but American businesses themselves are relocating their manufacturing and assembling processes abroad. With the percentage of blue-collar and agricultural jobs destined to continue declining, the country must grope its way forward through uncharted economic and social territory. Simultaneously fundamental demographic changes like the rising percentage of older Americans will inevitably alter the character of the workforce as well as the focus of consumer-oriented businesses.

Yet another reason that longterm predictions are subject to qualification is that the United States alone can not control its destiny. Global interdependence has become the norm in resource utilization, raw material distribution, and consumer demand. The energy situation offers a good example of the uncertainty that international events and decisions can introduce into American planning and behavior. Even though the oil scarcity of the 1970s eased by the mid-1980s, there is undeniably an absolute limit to the amount of recoverable fossil fuel available. The world's demand for energy continues to rise much more quickly than do the methods which are developed to meet it. A lot of that demand, of course, stems from the expanding size of the population around the world. Although population pressures are far more acute outside the United States, they will inevitably increase demands on the many resources Americans may wish to exploit in the future.

The historical record does, however, leave little doubt that the American business community will continue to pursue methods to expand its influence and wealth. Regardless of scarcities, changing demographic patterns, and periodic recessions, the entrepreneurial urge will remain strong. One can therefore safely anticipate a continuing stream of new products and processes, new management and marketing strategies, new government priorities and public policies. If none of these appears likely to generate profits, a Jay Gould, a J. P. Morgan, or a T. Boone Pickens can be counted on to promote a scheme to boost the prices of existing corporation stocks, and hordes of speculators will, as they so often have in the past, rush in hoping to reap the dividends. And thus the history of American enterprise will continue recording the ebb and flow of personal fortunes, of the giddy rise and heartbreaking fall of expectations, and the progress and retrenchment of the nation as a whole.

READING SUGGESTIONS

Already a familiar figure on television and in print, T. Boone Pickens capitalized on his fame by publishing his autobiography, *Boone* (1987). It serves as a companion to the bestseller Lee Iaccoca and William Novak wrote, *Iaccoca: An Autobiography* (1984). *The Warning: The Coming Great Crash in the Stock Market* (1985) is representative of the many writings of financial pundit Joseph Granville. A description of the new wave on consolidation appears in *Merger Mania: Arbitrage-Wall Street's Best-Kept Money-Making Secret* (1985), but readers should exercise caution in taking its advice: the book's author, Ivan Boesky, was the first major figure to be indicted by the SEC in a massive insider-trading scandal.

Lester Thurow's *Dangerous Currents: The State of Economics* (1983) discusses the difficulty governments face in developing sound economic policies. Deregulation is one of these and its effect on several industrial sectors is the subject of Roger G. Noll and Bruce M. Owen's *The Political Economy of Deregulation* (1983). Possible future strategies for American industry appear in Gerard K. O'Neill's *The Technology Edge* (1984). The sound management and solid performance of several major American companies are described in Thomas J. Peters and Robert Waterman's *In Search of Excellence* (1982). Peters subsequently collaborated with Nancy Austin in a more eclectic survey, *A Passion for Excellence* (1984).

Two related topics, trade rivalry with Japan and the fortunes of the domestic auto industry, are discussed in four thoughtful books: William Ouchi, *Theory Z: How American Business Can Meet the Japanese Challenge* (1982); Steven Schlossstein, *Trade War* (1984); Robert Sobel, *Car Wars: The Untold Story* (1983); and Brock W. Yates, *The Decline and Fall of the American Automobile Industry* (1983). The best and most thorough of the comparative studies, however, is David Halberstam's analysis of Nissan and Ford in *The Reckoning* (1986).

INDEX

Lockheed Aircraft Corp., 270-71, 280, 293-95, 311, 312
Loew, Marcus, 264
Lonely Crowd, The, 304
Long Island Airways, 270
Los Angeles, 267
Louis XIV of France, 38
Louisiana, 2, 63, 90, 94, 224
Lowell, Francis Cabot, 78-81, 120, 152
Lumber industry, 39, 41, 66, 134, 136, 291

M

MCI Telecommunications Corp., 355
MGM/UA 357
MacDonald, Forrest, 51
Macy, R. H., 170
Macy's, R.H. & Co., 170, 334
Madison, James, 50, 51, 54, 57, 83, 105
Magnin, I., 170
Mail-order marketing, 194, 359
Maine, 41, 260
Main Line Canal, Pennsylvania, 107, 111, 112
Malcomson, Alex Y., 196
Mann-Elkins Act of 1910, 207-9
Manufacturing:
    early techniques, 49, 72, 130, 134
    household, 65-66
Marconi, Guliermo, 237
Margin loans, 239, 241, 255, 320
Marijuana, 341
Marketing:
    retail, 121, 122-23, 170-71, 193-94, 307, 333-35, 356
    strategy, 118, 190-91, 232-36, 296, 308
Marketing concept, the, 305
Marshall, John, 124
Marshall Fields stores, 194, 334
Marshall Plan, 284
Marshall's stores, 359
Martin Aircraft, 269
Mary Kay Cosmetics Inc., 338-39
Maryland, 9, 13, 14, 27, 28, 31, 41, 89, 107, 110
Mason, John L., 120
Massachusetts:
    colonial, 9, 13-14, 20-21
    commerce, 21-24, 34, 36, 124
    finance, 36, 41, 44, 53
    industry, 78-81, 118, 203
Mass production, 197-201
Mastercard, 341
May, David, 170
Mayer, Louis B., 264, 266
McCallum, Daniel C., 2, 115-16
McClellan, John L., 287
McCormick, Cyrus, 98-100, 194
McDonald, Dick, 337
McDonald, Mac, 337
McDonald's Corp., 2, 336-38

McDonnell Corp., 312
McDonnell-Douglas Corp., 311
McGuire, Peter J., 174
McKay, Gordan, 137-38
McKinley, William, 179
McNamara, Robert, 311, 361
McNary-Haugens Bill, 225
Meany, George, 287
Meat Inspection Act of 1906, 212
Mechanization, farm, 137, 175, 224, 276, 290, 330
Medbury, James, 143
Medicare, 358
Mellon, Andrew, 225
Mercantile Agency, 123
Mercantilism, 27, 30-31
Merchants:
    American, 6, 28-29, 40, 49, 90, 122
    British, 6, 19, 21, 31, 48-49, 82, 90
    Scottish, 15-16, 19, 90
Mergers (*see* Consolidation, business)
Mesa Petroleum Company, 351
Metals Reserve Company, 275
Metro-Goldwyn-Mayer, 264, 266, 357
Mexican War, 96
Mexico, 215
Michigan, 114, 195
Microchips, 313-16
Microcomputers, 355, 356, 362-63
Middle Ages, 3-5
Middle Colonies, 13, 14, 28, 33
Middle East, 292, 313
Middlesex Canal, 109
Middle West, 97, 109, 111, 168, 184, 271, 306, 335
Middle Western Utilities, 228
Military warrants for land, 58, 61, 96-97
Miller, Phineas, 64
Mining industry, 126, 201-3, 333
Minnesota, 164, 176, 335
Missiles, 293, 311-12, 362
Mississippi, 60, 83, 92
Missouri, 97
Mitchell, Billy, 268
Mitchell, John, 202
Mitsushita, 329
Mitsubishi Motors Corp., 327
Mobil Oil Corp., 363
Model A Ford, 234
Model T Ford, 197-201, 203, 229, 234, 236, 248, 315, 337
Monetarist theory, 249
Money, early types of, 27-29, 33, 40, 52
Money supply, 77, 210, 249
Money Trust, the, 188-90
Monroe, James, 85
Montana, 164
Montgomery, Robert, 334
Montgomery Ward, 235, 251, 266, 359
Moody, Paul, 79-80